Just Business

Just Business

NEW INTRODUCTORY ESSAYS
IN BUSINESS ETHICS

‹‹›〉

KURT BAIER

DAVID BRAYBROOKE

ALAN GOLDMAN

KENNETH E. GOODPASTER

TIBOR R. MACHAN

HOLMES ROLSTON III

GEORGE SHER

HENRY SHUE

ADINA SCHWARTZ

PATRICIA WERHANE

Edited by
Tom Regan

North Carolina State University at Raleigh

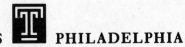

TEMPLE UNIVERSITY PRESS ▪ PHILADELPHIA

Temple University Press, Philadelphia 19122

© 1983 by Random House, Inc. All rights reserved.

Published 1983

Printed in the United States of America

Library of Congress Cataloging in Publication Data
Main entry under title:

Just business.

Includes bibliographies and index.
1. Business ethics — Addresses, essays, lectures.
I. Regan, Tom.
HF5387.J87   1983   174'.4   83-9793
CIP: ISBN 0-87722-335-1 cl.

Manufactured in the United States of America

To Mr. and Mrs. Ralph W. Pannier
for Your Many Past Kindnesses

PREFACE

This anthology consists of original essays on questions in business ethics. Although there is no single order in which the essays must be read, their present arrangement is not arbitrary, and a few words about this arrangement are in order. An individual's incentive to think seriously about a moral question is initially strongest when answers to that question promise to have significant effects on the quality of that individual's life. Whether we should support or oppose a policy of preferential hiring is such a question, especially for those who have yet to occupy a permanent niche in the workplace. The essay devoted to this question is accordingly placed first.

The next three essays also relate to matters that will be of direct personal importance to most readers. The three examine various aspects of the moral ties that bind employer and employee. What duties do we acquire when we assume a job, and how stringent are they? What rights do workers have, and, if they have them, what steps should be taken to insure that employers respect them? And what role, if any, should the government and the courts play in assuring justice in wages and in promoting autonomy in the workplace? "Duties to One's Employer," "Individual Rights in Business," and "Autonomy in the Workplace" explore these and related questions.

The word "justice" was used to describe a central concern of one of the essays. In fact, questions about the justice of economic arrangements, practices, and principles surface in all the essays but especially the next four—"Justice and Injustice in Business," "Should Business Be Regulated?" "Ethical Issues in Advertising," and "Transnational Transgressions."

The final pair of essays is related, one might say, as theory is to practice. How shall we make sense of the idea of corporate responsibility? Indeed, *can* we make sense of it? That is the central concern of "The

Concept of Corporate Responsibility." The final essay, "Just Environmental Business," has a different focus. It assumes that corporations are morally accountable and identifies a series of maxims corporations should use to act responsibly with regard to the environment; and it offers, in addition, a sketch of a non-anthropocentric vision of nature and its values. That vision is one we might better work toward than begin with in a collection of essays on issues in business ethics.

The "Introduction" has two principal aims. First, it attempts to explain some important assumptions shared by all the contributors — for example, some assumptions concerning how not to answer moral questions. Second, by tracing some of the major options in ethical theory, it formulates sets of questions that might help readers work their way through the several contributions. The hope is that people will better understand the discussion of a particular issue in business ethics when it is viewed against the backdrop of ethical theory, and vice versa.

It is a pleasure to thank the contributors for making my job easier than it might have been; Steven Pensinger and Fred H. Burns for their editorial guidance; Steve Darwahl, Mark Pastin, and Nicholas Rongion for helpful comments on the several essays; Ruth Boone and Ann Rives for their help in preparing the manuscript; my wife, Nancy, for her expert typing and unfailing support; and my children, Karen and Bryan, for their cooperation.

Tom Regan

Raleigh, North Carolina
January 27, 1982

CONTENTS

5. Autonomy in the Workplace
ADINA SCHWARTZ   **129**

6. Justice and Injustice in Business
DAVID BRAYBROOKE   **167**

Just Business

I

Introduction

TOM REGAN

§1 JUST BUSINESS

Few things are more important than our jobs to those of us who work. When scientists researching the matter conclude that people who are satisfied with their employment are usually satisfied with their lives, we are surprised not so much by their finding as by the need to reach it scientifically. Our jobs, our work, our careers are so central a focus of our daily lives that a bad fit between worker and work cannot help but redound to the detriment of both. Persons whose employment is dull, monotonous, a grind are not likely to find enough interesting outlets beyond the workplace to overcome the daily tedium and frustration while on the job. Because as adults our sense of self-worth is so intimately tied to our assurance that we are doing important things well, persons who despise their work often do not think well of themselves. A sense of the meaninglessness of one's work can easily turn to a sense of the meaninglessness of one's life. How fortunate, then, are those whose work fits them, whose career is less "a job" than a vocation in the original sense (from the Latin *vocatio*, "a calling"). Challenged and rewarded, confident of the significance of what they do and their skill in doing it well, they are round pegs in round holes, their work not so much a requirement imposed from without as an expression of interests, values, and urges from within. Of course, one's zeal for one's employment, like one's zeal for anything, can be overdone. The proverbial "workaholic" finds meaning in work, but only at the expense of losing it elsewhere, in personal relations, for example, or in squandered recreational and cultural opportunities. Nevertheless, few, if any, would hesitate for a moment if given the choice between a job they judge interesting and challenging or one they judge trivial and dull, even if the latter paid more. It is not for money alone

3

that we choose between jobs. What we seek is a calling that is the shape and size of our self, a workspace we fill and, by filling, are in turn fulfilled.

No doubt few people find the "perfect fit," a marriage of person and job made in the stars. And no doubt, too, people can give meaning to their day-to-day life without being employed. But the ideal symbiosis of worker and work remains intelligible and, judging from the extensive efforts made in career planning and placement in high schools and universities, that ideal remains alive as well. Before us is the example of the architect who, when asked what he would be if he was not an architect, replied, "I wouldn't *be me* if I wasn't an architect."

Because of the vital importance work has for us as individuals, it is understandable that our initial worries about the business world should bear on our individual self-interest. Will this job or that one provide the greater challenge, the more satisfying environment, the better opportunity for advancement, the more desirable fringe benefits? But though we are right to ponder these questions most carefully, no even modestly sensitive person can leave reflection at this level. Precisely because a person's job, *any* person's job, is so important to the quality of that individual's life — not only materially, as measured by how much one is paid, but in less tangible terms, as measured, however crudely, by one's status, power, or sense of self-worth — precisely because of the importance of work to people who work, questions beyond one's own self-interest require our thoughtful attention.

The need to think beyond our own self-interest can be highlighted by imagining that we live in a society that discriminates against blue-eyed people, denying them, because of widespread prejudices against people with blue eyes, educational and other opportunities routinely given to others. Lacking the skills required for better-paying jobs, the blue-eyes get the dregs of the marketplace, vying with one another for the least desirable work — when work is available. The material standard of living of the blue-eyes on average is much lower than that of the brown-eyes, and their sense of self-worth, their status, and their power relative to the political mechanisms within our imaginary society, all are correspondingly diminished. As for their children, their life prospects depend on the fateful roll of their genes: Blue eyes, they lose; other-colored eyes, they win.

Suppose the roll of your genes is fortuitous: Green eyes! Were you so lucky, you would have a clear advantage over your blue-eyed contemporaries and, judged exclusively in terms of your own self-interest, you should have no misgivings about our imaginary society's discriminatory practices. Yet there is something grossly unfair about these practices. There is no reason why people with blue eyes should be assumed to be less deserving of a given social benefit (e.g., an education) than people with green eyes. Put in different words, a difference in eye color, though real enough, is not a *morally relevant* difference — is not, that is, a difference between people that could rationally justify treating them in highly different ways, allowing practices that routinely harm the members of the one group as they benefit the members of others. Since, at the most abstract level, justice is, in the words of the English philosopher Henry Sidgwick (1838–1900), the similar, and injustice the dissimilar, treatment of similar cases, discriminatory practices based on the color of one's eyes are unjust. Though you, as a lucky winner, need have no quarrel with our make-believe society's discrimination when you survey the warp of the social fabric in terms of your own self-interest, the flaws in the woof of the moral weave are readily apparent when viewed in terms of the requirements of justice. Someone who professed not to see this or, conceding the flaws, disowned any interest in correcting them, would take self-interest in the workplace too far. While a concern for one's own welfare in the world of business probably is the begin-all of our informed assessment of the economic scheme of things and our place in it, it cannot be the end-all for those who take justice and other moral concerns seriously.

A society prejudiced against blue-eyed people is a piece of fiction, of course, and a not-very-believable fiction at that. No actual society, and certainly no advanced democratic one like ours, would ever discriminate against people because of the color of their eyes. But regrettable though it is, and difficult as it may be to accept, characteristics no less irrelevant than eye color have figured in social patterns of discrimination, not in fiction but in fact, and not only in barbarian or totalitarian societies but also in enlightened, democratic societies—in our society. Not eye color but skin color has marked some individuals as recipients of harmful differential treatment. And not just skin color: Sex, place of national origin, and religion have played, and in some circumstances continue to play, a similar role. "Kikes," "wops," "coons," "broads," our nation's vocabulary bears the scars of the history of our nation's prejudices, prejudices that, at different times, in different places, and in different degrees, have systematically denied opportunities and advantages to those belonging to the "wrong" race, sex, homeland, or religion, while routinely making them available to others. We, who are as much a product of our society as we are shapers of it, cannot extricate ourselves from past and present prejudice by denying its existence. At least we cannot do this if we accept the importance of living in a just society, including one that values justice in the marketplace, one that insists on *just* business rather than one that writes economic injustices off as "just business."

§2 BUSINESS ETHICS

The view that skin color and eye color are not morally relevant characteristics for determining who shall receive economic harms and benefits does not establish what characteristics are morally relevant. It does bring us face-to-face with the problem of finding a rational basis for deciding this. Were we to offer such a basis, and were we able to defend it rationally and well against all fair criticism, we would likely be as close as humans can be to knowing what justice is. Then could we be as Solomon when, in the press of day-to-day events, we are called upon to separate the just from the unjust, not only in cases involving the claims of particular individuals (recall that Solomon had to decide which of two women was the actual mother of a child) but also at a more general level, when we are asked to decide whether a given policy, affecting many people, is just or unjust.

The systematic inquiry into what justice is illustrates one kind of question examined by moral philosophers. Moral philosophers are persons who take a special interest in thinking carefully about moral right and wrong, good and bad, duty and obligation. When this interest is focused primarily on economic matters, on "business" in the widest sense of that term, it is now customary to say that the questions being examined are questions in business ethics, as distinct from, say, questions in medical or environmental ethics. As is true in the case of internal divisions in other disciplines, the division between business ethics and other areas in moral philosophy is not set in concrete. Questions about justice, for example, arise in medical and environmental ethics, not only in business ethics; so "the wall" separating business ethics from other areas in moral philosophy should be viewed as like a porous membrane through which fundamental ideas, ideas such as individual rights and responsibilities, freedom and the general welfare, integrity and justice, freely pass. It is the perspective in which such ideas are viewed and the real-life settings to which they apply, rather than the presence of the ideas themselves, that mark an essay, a book, a lecture as belonging to business ethics.

Like others who seek to replace opinion with understanding, moral philosophers do not always agree on what is true. The contributors to this volume prove no exception. Some favor government regulation of business, for example; others do not. Some think people have rights where others fail to see them. So we must not expect to find unanimity on all important questions in the pages that lie ahead. But despite the presence of some vital disagreements, the contributors to this volume agree about many essential matters; for example, they think there are some tempting ways to answer moral questions that are mistaken or confused. Agreement at this level is important. Without it, the present collection of essays would have as much organization as Joe, Curley and Moe have, when they try to enter a door at the same time. The remainder of this "Introduction" attempts to highlight some of the shared assumptions the contributors bring to their work, assumptions that, more often than not, go unstated. The hope is that, by understanding what they do not say, we may better understand what they do.

I. META-ETHICS

§3 CONCEPTUAL ANALYSIS

The first idea that requires attention is that of conceptual analysis. Philosophers frequently use the words "conceptual analysis" to refer to the activity of clarifying our concepts or ideas. Since we use words to express our concepts, conceptual analysis' goal is to reach a clearer understanding of the meaning of words. Achieving such clarity is absolutely vital. If we do not have a clear understanding of the meaning of words, we will not have a clear understanding of our questions. And if we do not understand our questions, we will not understand what count as answers to them. This is especially true in the case of questions that ask about the morality of something—for example, whether preferential hiring is morally justified. If we do not understand what preferential hiring is, how can we even begin to consider the question of its morality?

One way to think about conceptual analysis is in terms of necessary and sufficient conditions. If x is a necessary condition of y, then y cannot be the case if x is not the case; in other words, if not x, then not y. Being a plane closed figure, for example, is a necessary condition of something's being a triangle. A sufficient condition is different. If a is a sufficient condition of b, then b will be the case if a is the case; that is, if a, then b. Being a plane closed figure with just three sides or only three interior angles, for example, is a sufficient condition of something's being a triangle.

A necessary condition may not be sufficient, and vice versa. For example, while being a plane closed figure is a necessary condition of something's being a triangle, it is not sufficient: There are many plane closed figures that are not triangles—e.g., rectangles. Again, that something is a Cadillac Seville is a sufficient condition of its being a car, but being a Cadillac Seville is not a necessary condition of being a car: There are many cars that are not Cadillac Sevilles.

The ideas of necessary and sufficient conditions relate to the activity of conceptual analysis in the following way. Conceptual analysis can be understood as the attempt to state the necessary and sufficient conditions of the correct use of a given concept. The aims of conceptual analysis, on this view, are thus (1) to state, so far as possible, those conditions which, if they are *not* satisfied, prevent the concept in question from being correctly applied—the necessary conditions of correct use—and (2) to state those conditions which, if they *are* satisfied, permit the concept to be correctly applied—the sufficient conditions of correct use. In this view of conceptual analysis, an analysis is itself correct to the extent that it states the necessary and sufficient conditions of correct use.

Now, sometimes it is not possible to give a complete set of necessary and sufficient conditions, and sometimes the conditions given cannot be very precise. For example, though a triangle must have neither more nor fewer than three interior angles, how many hairs a person must be missing to be bald is far less precise. We should not expect all concepts to be analyzable in the way concepts in mathematics, say, are. Some "defy analysis" in the sense that it is not possible to give a complete set of quite precise necessary and sufficient conditions. However, even in the case of these concepts, one ought to strive to reach the highest degree of completeness and precision possible. The more complete and exact we can make our understanding of a given concept, the more likely we will understand those questions in which the concept figures.

If we think about the concepts that occupy center stage in the essays in this volume—autonomy, responsibility, individual rights, and government regulation, for example—we can anticipate some problems for conceptual analysis. These concepts are not as precise as "triangle," and it is not unusual to find spirited debates over how they should be understood. Take autonomy. Some people offer an analysis of this concept that implies that persons lack autonomy, understood as the capacity to be self-directed, to the degree that what they believe or want is causally related to their nature (that is, their heredity) or their nurture (that is, their childhood environment). On this analysis, then, people would lack autonomy completely if all their beliefs and wants were causally related to their nature and nurture. But is this a reasonable position to take? Might we not analyze autonomy in a way that makes it possible for people to be more or less autonomous despite the fact that their present beliefs and desires are causally traceable to the joint influence of nature and nurture? This is a question Adina Schwartz considers at length in her essay "Autonomy in the Workplace." To turn this question over carefully, examining it on all sides, is not idle semantic curiosity. Important moral questions are bound up with how we answer this conceptual one. In particular, the question of whether autonomy ought to be promoted in the workplace and, if it should be, whether this requires dissolving the functional distinction between managers (who make decisions) and laborers (who carry them out), cannot be answered intelligently if we lack a firm hold on the concept of autonomy.

The arguments for and against competing analyses of the concept of autonomy must await a reading of Schwartz's essay. And similar remarks apply to alternative analyses of other important concepts that figure prominently in the other essays. In his essay, "The Concept of Corporate Responsibility," for example, Kenneth Goodpaster first distinguishes between several senses of "responsibility" before discussing whether corporations are morally responsible for what is done in their name, and George Sher, in his essay, "Preferential Hiring," displays a similar approach, analyzing the concept "preferential hiring" before considering moral defenses or criticisms of the practices that go by this name. As these examples suggest, philosophers, even when they do not agree on how given concepts should be analyzed, do agree on the need to analyze them. The merits of a variety of analyses certainly will have to be considered in all the essays.

§4 IS THERE A CORRECT METHOD FOR ANSWERING MORAL QUESTIONS?

The conceptual analysis of key moral concepts is one part of what is called meta-ethics. The other major component of meta-ethics is the inquiry into the correct method for answering moral questions. Such a method would function in the case of moral questions in ways that are analogous to how the scientific method functions in the case of scientific questions. This latter method does not itself contain answers to particular scientific questions (for example, about what happens to the pressure of a gas when the temperature is raised). Rather, the scientific method can be understood as specifying how we must approach particular questions *if we are to give scientific answers* to them; it defines, one might say, what it is to think about questions from the scientific point of view. Well, if there is a correct method for answering moral questions, similar things would be true of it: It would not itself contain answers to particular moral questions (for example, whether corporations have a duty to future generations to carry on business in ways that preserve the integrity of the environment, a central question in Holmes Rolston III's essay, "Just Environmental Business"); rather, it would specify how we must approach questions, *if we are to give moral answers* to them — if, that is, we are to give answers from the moral point of view.

Whether there even exists such a method, not surprisingly, is a very controversial question. Some philosophers think there is; others think not. And among those who think there is, some think it is one thing, while others think it is something different.

It will not be possible to examine this controversy in all the detail it deserves. Instead, a rough sketch will be given of some of the central issues. Two ideas in particular are important. First, there is the matter of how *not* to answer moral questions; this idea is explored in §5. Second, there is the idea of an ideal moral judgment; this is discussed in §6. The relevance of these ideas to the essays will be explained as we proceed.

§5 SOME WAYS NOT TO ANSWER MORAL QUESTIONS

Moral Judgments and Personal Preferences Some people like classical music; others do not. Some people think bourbon is just great; others detest its taste. Some people will go to a lot of trouble to spend an afternoon in the hot sun at the beach; others can think of nothing worse. In all these cases disagreement in preference exists. Someone likes something; someone else does not. Are moral disagreements, disagreements over whether something is morally right or wrong, good or bad, just or unjust, the same as disagreements in preference?

It does not appear so. For one thing, when a person (say, Jack) says he likes something, he is not denying what another person (Jill) says, if she says she does not like it. Suppose Jack says "I [Jack] like bourbon," and Jill says "I [Jill] do not like bourbon." Then clearly Jill does not deny what Jack says. To deny what Jack says, Jill would have to say "You [Jack] do not like bourbon," which is not what she says. So, in general, when two persons express conflicting personal preferences, the one does not deny what the other affirms. It is perfectly possible for two conflicting expressions of personal preference to be true at the same time.

When two people express conflicting judgments about the morality of something, however, the disagreement is importantly different. Suppose Jack says, "Government regulation of business is always wrong," while Jill says, "Government regulation is sometimes right." Then Jill *is* denying what Jack affirms; she is *denying* that government regulation is always wrong, so that, if what she said were true, what Jack said would have to be false. Some philosophers have denied this. They have maintained that moral judgments should be understood as expressions of personal preferences. Though this view deserves to be mentioned with respect, it is doubtful that it is correct. When people say that something is morally right or wrong, it is always appropriate to ask them to give reasons *to support* their judgment, reasons for accepting their judgment as *correct*. In the case of personal preferences, however, such requests are inappropriate. If Jack says he likes to go to the beach, it hardly seems appropriate to press him to give reasons to support his judgment; indeed, it hardly seems that he has made a *judgment* at all. If he says government regulation is always wrong, however, a judgment has been expressed, and it is highly relevant to press Jack for his reasons for thinking what he does. If he were to reply that he had no reasons, that he just does not like government interference in business, it would not be out of place to complain that he speaks in a misleading way. By saying that government regulation is always wrong, Jack leads his listeners to believe that he is making a judgment about government regulation, not merely expressing some fact about himself. If all that he means is that he personally does not like government regulation, that is what he should say, not that it is wrong.

This difference between conflicting expressions of personal preference and conflicting moral judgments points to one way not to answer moral questions. Given that moral judgments are not just expressions of personal preference, it follows that moral right and wrong cannot be determined just by finding out about the personal preferences of some particular person — say, Jack. This is true even in the case of our own preferences. Our personal preferences are important, certainly, but we do not answer moral questions just by saying what we like or dislike.

Moral Judgments and Feelings   Closely connected with personal preferences are a person's feelings, and some philosophers have maintained that words like "right" and "wrong" are devices we use merely to express how we feel about something. On this view, when Barbie says that preferential hiring is just, what she conveys is that she has certain positive feelings toward policies that give preferred treatment to members of some groups, whereas when Ken says this practice is unjust, what he conveys is that he has feelings of disapproval. It is as if what Barbie says is, "Preferential hiring — hooray!" while what Ken says is, "Preferential hiring — boo!" This position encounters problems of the same kind as those raised in the previous section. It is not appropriate to ask for support in the case of mere expressions of feeling. True, if Ken is sincere, one can infer that he has strong negative feelings toward preferential hiring. But his saying that preferential hiring is unjust does not appear to be simply a way of his venting his feelings (or eliciting ours). As in the case of a person's preferences, so also in the case of a person's feelings: Neither by itself provides answers to moral questions.

Why Thinking It Is So Does Not Make It So   The same is true about what someone thinks. Quite aside from her feelings, Bonnie, if she is sincere, does think that people have a right to a job if she says that they do. Nevertheless, if her judgment ("People have a right to a job") is a moral judgment, what she means cannot be "I [Bonnie] think people have a right to a job." If it were, then she would not be affirming something that Clyde denies, when he says "People do not have a right to a job." Each would merely be stating that each thinks something, and it is certainly possible for it to be true *both* that Bonnie thinks that people have a right to a job *and*, at the same time, that Clyde thinks that they do not. So if Clyde is denying what Bonnie affirms, then he cannot merely be stating that *he* thinks that people do not have a right to a job. Thus, the fact that Clyde happens to think what he does is just as irrelevant to establishing whether people do or do not have a right to a job as are Ken's feelings about preferential hiring. And the same is true concerning what *we* happen to think. Our thinking something right or wrong is not what makes it so.

The Irrelevance of Statistics   Someone might think that though what one person happens to think or feel about moral issues does not settle matters, what all or most people happen to think or feel does. A single individual is only one voice; what most or all people think or feel is a great deal more. There is strength in numbers. Thus, the correct method for answering questions about right and wrong is to find out what most or all people think or feel; opinion polls should be conducted, statistics compiled. That will reveal the truth.

This approach to moral questions is deficient. All that opinion polls can reveal is what all or most people happen to think or feel about some moral question — for example, "Should we prohibit advertising aimed at impressionable audiences, such as children?" What such polls cannot determine is whether what all or most people happen to think about such an issue is reasonable or true, *or* that what all or most people happen to feel is appropriate. There may be strength in numbers, but not truth, at least not necessarily. This does not mean that "what we think (or feel)" is irrelevant to answering moral questions. Later on, in fact (§6), we will see how, given that certain conditions have been met, "what we think" provides us with a test of the adequacy of competing principles of right and wrong. Nevertheless, *merely* to establish that all (or most) people happen to think that, say, advertising aimed at children is morally objectionable, is not to establish that it is. In times past, most (possibly even all) people thought the world was flat. And possibly most (or all) people felt pleased or relieved to think of the world as having this shape. But what they thought and felt did not make it true that the world is flat. The question of its shape wasn't answered merely by finding out what most people happened to think or feel. There is no reason to believe moral questions differ in this respect. Questions of right and wrong cannot be answered just by counting heads. As Alan Goldman rightly points out in his essay, "Ethical Issues in Advertising," one fails to give a *moral* defense of the programs featured on commercial television if all one does is show that most people happen to think they are good.

The Appeal to a Moral Authority   Suppose it is conceded that we cannot answer moral questions just by finding out what Jack or Jill, or Ken or Barbie happen to think or feel; or by finding out what all or most people happen to think or feel. After all, single individuals like Jack or Jill, or most or all people like them, might think or feel one way when they should think or feel differently. Suppose, then, there is a person who never is mistaken when it comes to moral questions: If this person judges that something is morally right, it *is* morally right; if it is judged wrong, it *is* wrong. No mistakes are made. Let us call such a person a "moral authority." Might appealing to a moral authority be the correct method we seek for answering moral questions?

Most people who think there is a moral authority think this authority is not an ordinary person but a god. This causes problems immediately. Whether there is a god (or gods) is a very controversial question, and to rest questions of right and wrong on what an alleged god says (or the gods say) is already to base morality on an intellectually unsettled foundation. The difficulties go deeper than this, however, since even if there is a god who is a moral authority, very serious questions must arise concerning whether people always understand what this authority says about right and wrong. The difficulties that exist when Jews and Christians consult the Bible can be taken as illustrative. Problems of interpretation abound. Some who think that drinking is wrong think they find evidence in the Bible that God thinks so too; others think they find evidence that He does not. Some who think that capital punishment is declared wrong by God cite what they think are supporting chapters and verses; others cite other chapters and verses they think show that God does not think capital punishment is wrong, or they cite the same passages and argue that they should be interpreted differently. The gravity of these and kindred problems of interpretation should not be underestimated. Even if there is a moral authority, and even if the God Jews and Christians worship should happen to be this authority, that would not make it a simple matter to find out what is right and wrong. The problem of determining what God thinks on these matters would still remain and would be especially acute in areas, such as business ethics, where the Bible offers very little, if any, direct guidance. Where, for example, do we find prescriptions that unambiguously address issues like preferential hiring or a worker's right to privacy in the workplace?

Problems of interpretation aside, it is clear that the correct method for answering moral questions cannot consist merely in discovering what some alleged moral authority says. Even if there is a moral authority, those who are not moral authorities can have no good reason for thinking that there is one unless the judgments of this supposed authority can be checked for their truth or reasonableness by a procedure that does not *assume* that the judgments made by this supposed authority are true or reasonable, and it is not possible to do this unless what is true or reasonable can be determined independently of what this supposed authority says. An example from another quarter might make this point clearer. A plumber proves his "authority as a plumber," not by what he says but by the quality of his work, which can be verified independently of what he says in any particular case. *After* we have come to know, by viewing his work or by relying on the experience of others, that a particular plumber's judgment is reliable, *then* we have reason to rely on his judgment in the future. The same is true of the authority of one's judgment in, say, science, economics, the law, and morality. One's "credentials" can be established in the case of moral judgment only if there are independent ways of testing one's moral judgments against what is known to be true or reasonable. Thus, since in the nature of the case there must be some independent way of knowing what judgments are true or reasonable in order to test for the authority of anyone who makes such judgments, merely to appeal to the judgments of this or that "moral authority" cannot be the method for answering moral questions we seek.

§6 THE IDEAL MORAL JUDGMENT

The ideas discussed in §5 are relevant to the essays in this volume because the authors never argue that something is right or wrong merely on the grounds of their personal preferences, or merely because they personally feel one way or another, or just because they think it right or wrong, or simply because all or most people happen to feel or think a certain way, or because some alleged moral authority has said or revealed that something is right or wrong. It is important to realize the ways that these philosophers do not argue; and it is also important to understand some of the arguments that can be given against arguing in these ways. This is what has been briefly examined in §5. What now needs to be described is an approach to moral questions that is not open to the objections raised against the methods considered so far.

The approach described in what follows turns on how the following question is answered: "What requirements would someone have to meet to make an ideal moral judgment?" Considered ideally, that is, what are the conditions that anyone would have to satisfy to reach a moral judgment as free from fault and error as possible? Now, by its very nature, an *ideal* moral judgment is just that — an ideal. Perhaps no one ever has met or ever will completely meet all the requirements set forth in the ideal. But that does not make it irrational to strive to come as close as possible to fulfilling it. If we can never quite get to the finish, we can still move some distance from the starting line.

There are at least six different ideas that must find a place in our description of the ideal moral judgment. A brief discussion of each follows.

Conceptual Clarity   This idea was mentioned earlier (§3). Its importance is obvious. If someone tells us that employees have an acquired duty to lie in order to protect the interests of their employer, we cannot determine whether that statement is true or reasonable before we understand what is meant by "an acquired duty." Similar remarks apply to other controversies. In the case of the government's role in regulating business, for example, many think the question turns on whether people have moral rights, including a moral right to liberty. But whether people have this right in part depends on what a person is — that is, on how the concept "person" should be analyzed. Clarity by itself may not be enough, but rational thought cannot get far without it.

Information   We cannot answer moral questions in our closets. Moral questions arise in the real world, and a knowledge of the real-world setting in which they arise is essential if we are seriously to seek rational answers to them. For example, in the debate over government regulation of business, some people argue that regulation of the food and drug industries provides the consumer with a degree of protection against fraud and harm that greatly exceeds what would be provided in the absence of regulation. Is this true? Is this a fact? In his essay, "Should Business Be Regulated?" Tibor Machan reminds us that we have to come out of our closets to answer this question (or to find the answer others have tried to reach on the basis of their research); and answer it we must if we are to reach an informed judgment about the morality of government regulation of food and drugs. The importance of getting the facts, of being informed, is not restricted just to this case by any means. It applies all across the broad sweep of moral inquiry.

Rationality   Rationality is a multifaceted concept. The one aspect that concerns us here is when rationality is understood as the ability to recognize the connection between different ideas — the ability to recognize, that is, that if some statements are true, then some other statements must be true while others must be false. Now, it is in logic that rules are set forth that specify when statements follow from others, and it is in part because of this that a person who is rational often is said to be logical. When we speak of the need to be rational, then, we are saying that we need to observe the rules of logic. To reach an ideal moral judgment, therefore, we must not only strive to make our judgment against a background of information and conceptual clarity; we must also take care to explore how our beliefs are logically related to other things that we do or do not believe. For example, imagine that Ozzie thinks there should never be an impartial review of the grounds for dismissing a government employee; and suppose that his wife, Harriet, recently was fired from her government job. Then Ozzie is not being rational or logical if he claims that there should have been an impartial review of the grounds for Harriet's dismissal. Rationally, he *cannot* believe this while believing the other things we assume he believes. Logically, it is *impossible* for both the following statements to be true: (1) There should never be an impartial review of the grounds for firing a government employee, and (2) There should have been such a review in Harriet's case. Whenever someone is committed to two beliefs that cannot both be true at the same time, that person is said to be committed to a *contradiction*. Ozzie, then, is committed to a contradiction. To fall short of the ideal moral judgment by committing oneself to a contradiction is to fall as short as one possibly can. In the course of her essay, "Individual Rights in Business," Patricia Werhane argues in support of workers' rights in this way, claiming, for example, that it is contradictory to affirm that the courts should protect the rights of employers but not those of employees.

Impartiality Partiality involves favoring someone or something above others. For example, if a father is partial to one of his children, then he will be inclined to give the favored child more than he gives his other children. In some cases, partiality is a fine thing; but a partiality that excludes even thinking about or taking notice of others is far from what is needed in an ideal moral judgment. The fact that someone has been harmed, for example, always seems to be a relevant consideration, whether this someone is favored by us or not. In striving to reach the correct answers to moral questions, therefore, we must strive to guard against extreme, unquestioned partiality; otherwise we run the risk of having our judgment clouded by bigotry and prejudice.

The idea of impartiality is at the heart of the abstract principle of justice referred to earlier (§1): Justice is the similar, and injustice the dissimilar, treatment of similar cases. This principle is said to express the *formal* principle of justice because by itself it does not specify what factors are relevant for determining what makes cases similar or dissimilar. To decide this, one must supplement the formal principle of justice with a substantive or normative interpretation of justice. More will be said on this matter (§10). Even at this juncture, however, we can recall the rich potential the formal principle of justice can have in arguments about moral right and wrong. Were we to approve of marketing dangerous products (e.g., highly flammable children's pajamas) in other countries but not in the United States, it would be apposite to ask why the two cases are dissimilar. For they must be dissimilar if, as we are assuming, dissimilar treatment is allowed. If, in reply to our question, we were told that the difference is that people who live in America are Americans while those who are citizens of other countries are not, then it would again be apposite to ask why this difference in nationality *can* make any moral difference to the justice of the treatment in the two cases. To sanction the marketing of dangerous products to some while disapproving it in the case of others because of nationality is a symptom of unquestioned partiality for irrelevant reasons, a point Henry Shue makes in a number of places in his contribution, "Transnational Transgressions." While the formal principle of justice does not by itself tell us what are the relevant factors for determining when treatment is similar or dissimilar, that principle must be observed if we are to make the ideal moral judgment. Not to observe it is a symptom of prejudice or bias, rational defects that must be identified and overcome if we are to make the best moral judgment we can.

Coolness   All of us know what it is like to do something in the heat of anger that we later regret. No doubt we have also had the experience of getting so excited that we do something that later on we wish we had not done. Emotions are powerful forces, and though life would be a dull wasteland without them, we need to appreciate that the more volatile among them can mislead us; strong emotion is not a reliable guide to doing (or judging) what is best. This brings us to the need to be "cool." "Being cool" here means "not being in an emotionally excited state, being in an emotionally calm state of mind." The idea is that the hotter (the more emotionally charged) we are, the more likely we are to reach a mistaken moral conclusion, while the cooler (the calmer) we are, the greater the chances that we will avoid making mistakes.

This position is borne out by common experience. People who are in a terribly excited state may not be able to retain their rationality; because of their deep emotional involvement, they may not be able to attain impartiality; and when they are in an excited emotional state, they may not even care about what happened or why. Like the proverb about shooting first and asking questions later, a lack of coolness can easily lead people to judge first and ask about the facts afterwards. The need to be "cool," then, seems to merit a place on our list.

Valid Moral Principles   The concept of "moral principle" has been analyzed in different ways. At least this much seems clear, however: For a principle to qualify as a *moral* principle (as distinct from, say, a scientific or a legal principle), it must prescribe conduct for all moral agents. Moral agents are those who can bring impartial reasons (i.e., reasons that respect the requirement of impartiality) to bear on deciding how they ought to act. They are thus conceived to be both rational and autonomous. Individuals who lack the ability to understand or act on the basis of impartial reasons (e.g., young children) fail to qualify as moral agents. They cannot meaningfully be said to have obligations or to do, or to refrain from doing, what is morally right or wrong. Only moral agents have this status, and moral principles apply only to the determination of how moral agents should behave. Normal adult human beings are the paradigmatic instance of moral agents.

How does the idea of a valid moral principle relate to the concept of an ideal moral judgment? In an ideal moral judgment, it is not enough that the judgment be based on complete information, complete impartiality, complete conceptual clarity, and so forth. It is also essential that the judgment be based on a *valid* or *correct* moral principle. Ideally, one wants not only to make the correct judgment, but also to make it for the correct reasons. But which among the many possible moral principles we might accept are the correct or most reasonable ones? This is a question we cannot answer merely by saying which principles we individually *happen* to prefer, or which ones all or most people *happen* to accept, or which principles some alleged moral authority issues. These ways of answering moral questions have previously been eliminated from serious consideration (see §5). What is needed are criteria for rationally evaluating and choosing between competing ethical principles.

It is far beyond the modest reach of this "Introduction" to attempt to articulate and defend a complete set of criteria for testing the validity of alternative moral principles. Only a few words about one criterion, one that surfaces in each of this volume's essays, can be offered.

The validity of a moral principle, we have said, cannot be established simply by showing that its implications conform with what all or most people happen to think. The importance of such conformity, however, cannot be so easily dismissed when our *considered beliefs* are at issue. Unlike a belief we just happen to have (and so can have because of the ignorance or prejudice of those from whom we have received it, for example), a considered belief is one we come to have or retain *only after* we have conscientiously thought about the belief's credentials with an eye to some of the previously mentioned elements of an ideal moral judgment. Our considered beliefs, in other words, are those we hold *only after* we have made a conscientious effort (a) to attain maximum conceptual clarity, (b) to acquire all the relevant information, and (c) to think about the belief and its implications rationally, (d) impartially, and with the benefit of reflection, (e) coolly. To show that a given moral principle conflicts with, not one, but a large number of considered beliefs, would seem to constitute a good reason to doubt its validity, while to show that another principle conforms with, not one, but a large number of such beliefs, would seem to constitute a good reason to count its validity as provisionally established. Of course, in saying this one is not claiming that the only test, or even the most fundamental one, is a principle's degree of conformity with our considered beliefs. The place of such conformity in the grand scheme of things, when it comes to testing the validity of moral principles, can be left an open question at this point even while urging, as the authors of these essays imply, that conformity with our considered beliefs must occupy some place, must play some legitimate role, in the reflective assessment of alternative moral principles.

§7 NO DOUBLE STANDARDS ALLOWED

The portrait of the ideal moral judgment sketched in §6, or something very like it, occupies the philosophical background of the several essays in this volume. The authors do not always explicitly say, for example, that rationality and impartiality are ideals worth striving for; but the manner in which they argue makes it clear that these ideals play an important role in their examinations of the views of others. Accordingly, these philosophers imply that it would be fair to apply these same ideals to their own thinking. In the case of each essay, therefore, we can ask:

1. Have important concepts been analyzed, and, if so, have they been analyzed correctly?
2. Does the author argue from a basis of knowledge of the real-life setting(s) in which the moral question arises?
3. Is the author rational? (Do the arguments presented observe the rules of logic?)
4. Is there a lack of impartiality? (Is someone, or some group, arbitrarily favored over others?)
5. Are things argued for in a state of strong emotion? (Are deep feelings rhetorically vented in the place of hard thinking?)
6. Are the moral principles used valid ones? (In particular, do the principles relied upon conform or conflict with a variety of our considered beliefs?)

These six questions, then, though they do not exhaust all possibilities, at least provide a place to begin. It is pertinent to ask how our authors pose these questions of the persons whose views they examine. But fairness requires that these same questions be asked of each author's views too. No double standards are allowed.

II. NORMATIVE ETHICS

Earlier, meta-ethics was characterized as the inquiry into the meaning of key concepts (for example, autonomy and responsibility) as well as the inquiry into whether there is a correct method for answering moral questions. Meta-ethical questions by no means exhaust the philosophical interest in ethics. A second main area of inquiry commonly is referred to as *normative ethics*. Philosophers engaged in normative ethics attempt to go beyond the questions concerning meaning and method that arise in meta-ethics; the goal they set themselves is nothing short of establishing *what are the correct moral principles* — those principles, that is, by which all moral agents ought morally to be guided. There is, then, an important connection between the goal of normative ethics and the concept of an ideal moral judgment. An ideal moral judgment, we have said, must be based on valid moral principles, and it is just the question, "What principles *are* the valid ones?" that is at the heart of normative ethics. Unless the normative ethical philosopher succeeds in establishing what moral principles are valid, therefore, a vital part of the ideal moral judgment will be unfulfillable because unknown.

What then are the valid moral principles? Not surprisingly, a variety of answers have been offered. Not all of them can be considered here, and no one can be considered in much detail. But enough can be said to make some important ideas intelligible.

§8 CONSEQUENTIALIST THEORIES

One way to search for the correct moral principle(s) is to begin with our considered beliefs (that is, those beliefs we hold after we have made a conscientious effort to be conceptually clear, informed, rational, impartial, and cool) and then ask what more general principle(s) unify these beliefs by identifying their plausible common ground. For example, suppose George and Gracie each run used furniture stores. George's business has suffered of late because of the recent competition offered by Gracie's new store, and he decides to eliminate the competition by hiring a professional arsonist with whom he has had dealings in the past. Fire inspectors rule that the fire was caused by faulty wiring, George's business regains its former vitality, and Gracie, who barely had enough money to start her store and had no insurance, is left in a state of abject poverty. Suppose we judge that what George did was wrong, and suppose we make this judgment not only initially but after we have made a conscientious effort to think about the case coolly, impartially, and so forth. What could plausibly illuminate the wrongness of George's acts? Well, Gracie experiences some unhappiness, certainly. When she thinks about her former business, she is distraught and frustrated, and the enjoyment she would have had, if the business had continued to grow, is canceled. Gracie, then, is worse off than she would have been, both in terms of the unhappiness of her present condition and in terms of lost enjoyment. Thinking along these lines has led some philosophers to theorize that what makes George's (and the arsonist's) act wrong is that it is the cause of bad results, in this case the frustration, anger, disappointment, and general unhappiness caused Gracie.

Next imagine this case. Suppose there is a country that makes and enforces a law against giving equal pay to women and men despite the fact that both do equal work. In this country, males are always paid more than females, though both do the same work. Such an arrangement will strike us as unjust. But why? Well, imagine how women are likely to feel in such circumstances. It is not implausible to suppose that they will feel angry, resentful, and envious. These feelings (anger, resentment, envy) are not desirable. As in the earlier example of George and Gracie, then, we again have a situation where (a) we would judge, on reflection, that something is wrong, and where (b) what we judge to be wrong causes bad results.

Many philosophers have not stopped with just these sorts of cases. Roughly speaking, the one common and peculiar characteristic of every wrong action, they have theorized, is that it leads to bad results, whereas the one common and peculiar characteristic of every right action, again roughly speaking, is that it leads to good results. Philosophers who accept this type of view commonly are referred to as *consequentialists*, an appropriate name, given their strong emphasis on results or consequences. Theories of this type also are called *teleological theories*, from the Greek *telos*, meaning "end" or "purpose," another fitting name, since, according to these thinkers, actions are not right or wrong in themselves; they are right or wrong, according to these theories, if they promote or frustrate the purpose or end of morality — namely, to bring about the greatest possible balance of good over evil. Acts are, as it were, arrows we shoot: Right acts hit the target (that is, cause the best results); wrong acts do not.

Now, in normative ethics, when one advances a principle that states what makes all right actions right and all wrong actions wrong, one does so in the course of advancing a *normative ethical theory*. Theoretically, there are at least three different types of teleological normative ethical theories.

1. *Ethical egoism*: According to this theory, roughly speaking, whether any person (A) has done what is morally right or wrong depends solely on how good or bad the consequences of A's action are *for A*. How *others* are affected is irrelevant, unless how they are affected in turn alters the consequences for A.

2. *Ethical altruism*: According to this theory, roughly speaking, whether any person (B) has done what is morally right or wrong depends solely on how good or bad the consequences of B's action are *for everyone except B*. How B is affected is irrelevant, unless how B is affected in turn alters the consequences for anyone else.

3. *Utilitarianism*: According to this theory, roughly speaking, whether any person (C) has done what is morally right or wrong depends solely on how good or bad the consequences of C's action are *for everyone affected*. Thus, how C is affected is relevant; but so is how *others* are affected. How *everyone* concerned is affected by the good or bad consequences is relevant.

These are not very exact statements of these three types of teleological normative ethical theories, but enough has been said about two of them — namely, ethical egoism and ethical altruism — to enable us to understand why most philosophers find them unsatisfactory. Both seem to fall far short of the ideal of impartiality, ethical egoism because it seems to place arbitrary and exclusive importance on the good or welfare of the individual agent, and ethical altruism because it seems to place arbitrary and exclusive importance on the good or welfare of everyone else. Moreover, both theories arguably lead to consequences that clash with a broad range of considered beliefs. This is perhaps clearest in the case of ethical egoism. Provided only that, all considered, torching Gracie's store led to consequences that were as good *for George* as any that would have resulted had he acted otherwise, what he did was not morally wrong, according to ethical egoism. But that is something we would most likely deny, not only in a case involving arson, but in many other sorts of cases (e.g., murder or rape, which also would not be wrong if the consequences *for the agent* were at least as good as those that would have resulted if the agent had acted otherwise). Faced with the choice between accepting ethical egoism or giving up a large class of considered beliefs, most philosophers choose to reject the theory and retain the convictions.

It is utilitarianism, then, that seems to represent the strongest possible type of teleological theory. Certainly it is the one that has attracted the most adherents; not unexpectedly, therefore, it is the one that figures most prominently in the essays in this volume. It will be worth our while, therefore, to examine it at slightly greater length.

§9 UTILITARIANISM

"The Principle of Utility" is the name given to the fundamental principle advocated by those who are called utilitarians. This principle has been formulated in different ways. Here is a common formulation:

> Everyone ought to act so as to bring about the greatest possible balance of intrinsic good over intrinsic evil for everyone concerned.

Already it must be emphasized that utilitarians do not agree on everything. In particular, they do not all agree on what is intrinsically good and evil. Some philosophers (called *value hedonists*) think that pleasure and pleasure alone is intrinsically good (or good in itself), whereas pain, or the absence of pleasure, and this alone, is intrinsically evil (or evil in itself). Others (so-called *preference utilitarians*) believe that the satisfaction of one's desires or preferences is what is good and their frustration bad. The classical utilitarians — Jeremy Bentham (1748–1832) and John Stuart Mill (1806–1873) — favor hedonistic utilitarianism. Most recent utilitarians, especially those who seek to apply utilitarian theory to economic issues, and vice versa, favor preference utilitarianism. Whether either of these views regarding intrinsic value is adequate is a question we can by-pass at this juncture, since the ideas of special importance for our present purposes can be discussed independently of whether value hedonism, for example, is a reasonable position.

Act- and Rule-Utilitarianism   One idea of special importance is the difference between act-utilitarianism and rule-utilitarianism. *Act-utilitarianism* is the view that the Principle of Utility should be applied to individual actions; *rule-utilitarianism* states that the Principle of Utility should be applied mainly to rules of action. The act-utilitarian says that whenever people have to decide what to do, they ought to perform that act which will bring about the greatest possible balance of intrinsic good over intrinsic evil in the situation at hand. The rule-utilitarian says something different: People are to do what is required by justified moral rules. These are rules that would lead to the best possible consequences, all considered, *if* everyone were to abide by them. The rules recognized as valid by rule-utilitarians, in other words, need not be rules that most people *do* accept and act on — what we might call "the rules of conventional morality." If a valid rule, whether or not it is part of conventional morality, unambiguously applies to a situation, and if no other valid moral rule applies, then the person in that situation ought to choose to do what the rule requires, even if, in that particular situation, performing this act will not lead to the best consequences. Thus, act-utilitarians and rule-utilitarians, despite the fact that both profess to be utilitarians, can reach opposing moral judgments. An act that is wrong according to the rule-utilitarian, because it is contrary to a justified moral rule, might not be wrong according to the act-utilitarian's position.

Some Problems for Act-Utilitarianism   Is act-utilitarianism correct? Many philosophers answer no. One reason given against this theory is that act-utilitarianism clashes with a broad range of our considered beliefs. Recall the arson example. According to act-utilitarianism, whether George's hiring of the arsonist was wrong or not depends on this and this alone: Were the net consequences for everyone affected by the outcome at least as good as the net consequences that would have resulted if he had done anything else? It is not *just* the bad results Gracie has to live with (her frustration, anger, and the like) that are relevant. How *others* are affected also is relevant, according to act-utilitarianism, and there is no reason why, just because Gracie is made worse off than she would have been as a result of George's decision, *the sum or total* of the good and bad consequences for everyone involved might not "hit" the utilitarian target. The benefits George derives from eliminating Gracie's competition, the income the arsonist earns, and the possible pleasures and satisfactions others derive (for example, perhaps George's son can now go to college and the arsonist's wife can have her teeth capped) — these pleasures and satisfactions, too, not just Gracie's misery, have to be taken into account. In principle, then, there is no reason why the consequences, all considered, might not add up to the best balance of good over evil, or at least equal a balance that is as good as any other that would have resulted if George had acted otherwise.

Suppose the consequences are at least as good as any that would have been obtained had George acted otherwise. Then act-utilitarianism implies that what he did was right. And yet his involvement in the destruction of Gracie's business must surely continue to strike us as wrong. Thus, we again seem to be faced with a choice between (a) retaining a considered belief or (b) accepting a particular normative ethical theory. And the same choice would recur in a host of other cases involving our considered beliefs (e.g., beliefs about the wrongness of murder and rape, individual cases of which arguably could lead to the best balance of good results over bad, when the good and bad for *all* the involved individuals are totaled). There are, that is, many sorts of cases where the implications of act-utilitarianism are in conflict with our considered beliefs. In the face of such conflicts, many come down on the side of retaining our convictions and rejecting the theory.

Act-utilitarians actively defend their position against this line of criticism. The debate is among the liveliest and most important in normative ethics. The point that bears emphasis here is that *rule*-utilitarians do not believe that *their* version of utilitarianism can be refuted by the preceding argument. This is because they maintain that what George did *was* wrong *because it violated a valid moral rule* — the rule against destroying another's property. Thus, the rule-utilitarian holds that his position not only does not lead to a conclusion that clashes with the conviction that what George did was wrong; this position actually illuminates *why* it was — namely, because it violates a rule whose adoption by everyone can be defended by an appeal to the Principle of Utility.

Some Problems for Rule-Utilitarians   One success does not guarantee that all goes well, however, and many philosophers think that rule-utilitarianism, too, is inadequate. One of the most important objections turns on considerations about justice. The point of the objection is that rule-utilitarianism arguably could justify the adoption of unjust rules. To make this clearer, recall the rule that figured in our earlier example about employment: Men are to receive more pay than women even though both do equal work. The injustice of this rule (R) seems evident. It is unjust to discriminate against people in the workplace in the way R requires. And yet might not this rule be justified by appeal to rule-utilitarianism? Certainly it seems possible that, when the good and bad consequences for each affected individual are taken into account and totaled, we might find that adopting R would bring about the best balance of good over bad results. Granted, the envy, resentment, and anger of the female employees, if it is felt (which in some cases it may not be), must be taken into account. But so, too, must the benefits that males secure. So, *on balance*, the "minuses" for women might be more than offset by the "pluses" for men, especially if most female workers are married to men who earn an income adequate to support both. If, then, rule-utilitarianism could justify rules, not only in employment but across the broad sweep of social policies (for example, in education, voting, and health care, where some might be denied benefits offered to others in the name of "the general welfare") — if this is true, then rule-utilitarianism is not the adequate ethical theory its proponents suppose.

Can rule-utilitarians defend their position against this line of attack? Philosophers are not unanimous in their answer. As was the case with the debate over the correctness of act-utilitarianism, this debate is too extensive to be examined further here. Nevertheless, enough has been said to suggest the importance of utilitarianism, an importance confirmed when we note that this theory makes an appearance in each of the essays. For example, the selection by Kurt Baier, "Duties to One's Employer," includes an examination of attempts to defend laissez-faire capitalism ("the free market") by appeal to the Principle of Utility; Alan Goldman argues, in his "Ethical Issues in Advertising," that utilitarians would have to accept the same moral and legal restrictions on advertising in the free market as those who champion individual rights; and a major concern of Holmes Rolston III's essay, "Just Environmental Business," is whether the Principle of Utility, because it applies directly only to beings who have mental states (e.g., pleasure and pain), is too limited in scope for purposes of developing an informed environmental ethic. In view of the historical and current importance of utilitarian theory, and in light of the frequency with which it is discussed in the present collection, we are forearmed if we take the following set of questions to each of the essays.

1. Is the philosopher being read a utilitarian?
2. If so, of what kind—act or rule?
3. If the philosopher is a utilitarian, are persuasive arguments adduced in support of the utilitarian answers given?
4. Is the possible clash between justice and utility examined?
5. If the philosopher being read is not a utilitarian, then what arguments, if any, are given against the correctness of the Principle of Utility and how rationally compelling are these arguments?
6. Moreover, if the philosopher is not a utilitarian, what other principle (or principles), if any, is (are) subscribed to?
7. How rationally compelling are the arguments, if any, that are given in support of the principle(s)?

§10 NONCONSEQUENTIALISM

Nonconsequentialism is a name frequently given to normative ethical theories that are not forms of consequentialism. In other words, any theory that states that moral right and wrong are *not* determined *solely* by the relative balance of intrinsic good over intrinsic evil commonly is called a nonconsequentialist theory. Theories of this type are also called *deontological* theories, from the Greek *deon*, meaning "duty." Such theories might be either (a) extreme or (b) moderate. An extreme deontological theory holds that the intrinsic good and evil of consequences are totally irrelevant to determining what is morally right or wrong. A moderate nonconsequentialist theory holds that the intrinsic good and evil of consequences are relevant to determining what is morally right and wrong but that they are not the only things that are relevant and that they may not be of the greatest importance in some cases. A great variety of nonconsequentialist theories, both extreme and moderate, have been advanced. Why have some philosophers been attracted to such theories?

The Problem of Injustice   A common argument advanced against all forms of consequentialism is that no consequentialist theory (no form of ethical egoism, ethical altruism, or utilitarianism) can account for basic convictions about justice and injustice—for example, that it is unjust to allow policies that discriminate against people on the basis of race or sex. The point these deontologists make is that such discrimination not only is wrong; it *wrongs the people* who are discriminated against. Fundamentally, according to these thinkers, it is because people are wronged when treated unjustly, quite apart from the value of the consequences this may have for everyone else involved, that all consequentialist theories ultimately prove to be deficient.

Suppose these deontologists are correct. Some deontological theory would then be called for. A number of such theories have been advanced. The one associated with the German philosopher Immanuel Kant (1724–1804) is historically the most influential. In Kant's view, all persons (that is, all rational, autonomous individuals) have a distinctive kind of value — a unique worth or dignity. The value these people have, Kant may be interpreted to believe, is not reducible to the value of their mental states (e.g., their pleasure) and is, in fact, incommensurate with this latter kind of value; one cannot, that is, ask how much pleasure the value of an individual is equal to. That would be like trying to compare apples and oranges. Moreover, the worth of a person is not reducible to that individual's talents (for example, at sports or music), or to that individual's utility or service to others (a surgeon has neither more nor less worth than a dishwasher, a saint neither more nor less than a used-car salesman), or to how others relate to that individual (the loved and admired are neither more nor less valuable than the despised and forsaken). All who have worth or value as individuals, in short, have this value equally. Now, in order to treat such individuals as morality requires, we must never treat them in ways that fail to show proper respect for their unique value. Yet this is precisely what we would be guilty of if, in an effort to justify treating some people in a given way, we claimed that doing so gave rise to the best aggregate balance of pleasure over pain, or preference satisfactions over frustrations, for all affected by the outcome. For Kant, this is tantamount to ignoring the distinctive kind of value people have as individuals because it is to treat them as if their mental states (for example, their pleasures), and not the individuals themselves, have value. Any and all such disrespectful treatment is wrong, for Kant, whatever the consequences.

This Kantian approach to moral questions offers a strikingly different interpretation of equality than the one offered by utilitarians. For Kant, it is *individuals* who are equal in value, whereas, for utilitarians, what is equal in value are similar pleasures or preference satisfactions. Moreover, Kant's position provides a very different way to approach questions of just treatment, something we can illustrate by recalling the rule (*R*): Women are to receive less pay than men though both do equal work. As was suggested earlier (§9), a utilitarian justification of *R* is at hand *if* its adoption would produce the best aggregate balance of good over bad for all those affected by the outcome, assuming that the preferences or pleasures of all have been considered and weighted equitably. The fact that, if this rule were adopted, women would be paid less for doing the same work done by men *by itself* is no objection to adopting it, according to utilitarian theory. What each person is due is equal consideration and weighting of his or her pleasures or preferences, and, as that is what each gets in this case, there should be no cry of injustice.

Kant would be of a different mind. The very approach to *R*'s justification prescribed by utilitarians is morally flawed from the word go. What all people are due is respect for their value *as individuals*, something we fail to show if we attempt to decide the morality of acts or rules by asking which among them causes the best aggregate balance of good over bad (e.g., pleasure over pain) for all affected by the outcome. If, then, the justification of *R* is said to be that its adoption "would promote the general welfare," those who follow Kant would decry its adoption. Conduct prescribed by the rule in question is wrong because it treats women with something less than the respect they are due, treating them *as if their value* is reducible to their mental states or their utility in producing the optimal balance of good mental states over bad for all affected by the outcome.

§11 LEGAL AND MORAL RIGHTS

Philosophers sympathetic with Kant can use his views concerning the unique value of the individual as a foundation on which to rest their positions about the rights of the individual. To make this clearer, it will be useful first to explain some of the differences between the concepts of legal and moral rights.

First, moral rights, if there are any, are *universal*, while legal rights need not be. Legal rights depend upon the law of this or that country, and what is a matter of legal right in one country need not be so in another. For example, in the United States any citizen eighteen years old or older has the legal right to vote in federal elections; but not everyone in every nation has this same legal right. If, however, persons living in the United States have a moral right to, say, life, then *every* person in every nation has this same moral right, whether or not it is also recognized as a legal right.

Second, unlike legal rights, moral rights are *equal* rights. If all persons have a moral right to life, then all have this right equally; it is not a right that some (for example, males) can possess to a greater extent than others (for example, females). Neither, then, could this moral right be possessed to a greater extent by the inhabitants of one country (for example, one's own) than by the inhabitants of some other country (for example, a country to which a company exports and sells its products).

Third, moral rights are *inalienable*, meaning they cannot be transferred to another—for example, they cannot be lent or sold. If Frankie has a moral right to life, then it is hers and it cannot become anyone else's. Frankie may give her life for her country, sacrifice it in the name of science, or destroy it herself in a fit of rage or despair. But she cannot give, sacrifice, or destroy her right to life. Legal rights, on the other hand, are paradigmatically transferable, as when Frankie transfers her legal right to an inheritance to Johnnie or gives him her car.

Fourth, moral rights are "natural" rights, not in the sense that they are discoverable by closely studying Nature from the scientific point of view, but in the sense that they are not conventional—are not, that is, created by human acts. People have those moral rights they have, if they have any, because *they* are the sort of individuals they are, not because other individuals or collections of individuals have decided that they have them.

Kant's view of the unique worth of persons dovetails with these four characteristics of the concept of a moral right. (1) All persons have unique worth (that is, this value is *universal* among persons); (2) no one person has this value *to any greater degree* than any other (that is, all who have this value have it *equally*); (3) those who have this value *cannot transfer* it to anyone else, or buy or sell it (that is, this unique value is *inalienable*); and, finally, (4) the value or dignity persons possess is theirs *independently of the acts or decisions of anyone else* (is, that is, "natural," in the sense explained). Small wonder, then, that those philosophers enamored of the view that individuals have moral rights and ill-disposed toward consequentialist theories should find a strong ally in Kant, with his views about the value of the individual.

§12 LEGAL AND MORAL JUSTICE

Moral and legal rights are connected in important ways with moral and legal justice. Legal justice requires that one respect the legal rights of everyone, while moral justice demands that everyone's moral rights be honored. The two—legal justice and moral justice—do not necessarily coincide. Critics of "the law" frequently claim that certain laws are morally unjust. For example, a country might have a law that unfairly discriminates against some of its inhabitants because of their sex; imagine that it denies women a legal right to privacy in the workplace, but guarantees this legal right to all males. Then *legal* justice is done in this country if this law is enforced. If people have moral rights, however, it would not follow that moral justice is done. That would depend, not on whether there is a particular law in this country, but on whether the law recognizes and protects the moral rights of the country's inhabitants. If it does, then the law is both legally and morally just; if it does not, then, though the law may be legally just, it lacks moral justice. Thus, this law in particular and "the law" in general are appropriate objects of moral assessment, a theme that is especially noteworthy in the essay "Individual Rights in Business," by Patricia Werhane.

§13 SOME PROBLEMS FOR RIGHTS THEORIES

Even were we to agree that people themselves have a unique sort of value and moral rights grounded in this value, we might still disagree on what rights they have. One of the major sources of disagreement in this regard concerns what some call "welfare rights." Though the terminology frequently differs, philosophers who defend the validity of moral rights all seem to agree that some of these rights are *liberty rights*; in many cases, that is, to have a right is simply *to be at liberty* to act as one chooses (for example, to go to a concert, or to stay at home). Other rights are *claim rights*; those who have such rights *have a right not to be treated in certain ways* (for example, not to be injured, or have lies spread about them, or be killed). Both sorts of rights have correlative duties. If Eleanor is at liberty to have the chocolate cake rather than the strawberry yogurt, then Franklin has a duty not to deny her the exercise of her liberty when she makes her choice, something he would be doing if he coerced or forced her to choose as *he* wished. If, in addition, Eleanor has a right to life, then Franklin has a duty not to kill her except in quite exceptional circumstances (e.g., in self-defense).

Now, both those duties correlated with liberty rights and those correlated with claim rights are *negative duties*. They prescribe what people *are not to do*, how they *are not to act*, given that others have such rights. Thus, it seems that we can fulfil these duties by doing nothing. If, that is, Franklin does not personally kill Eleanor, then he seems to do all that is required to respect her right to life, while if he does not personally interfere with the exercise of her liberty, then he seems to do all he is obliged to do to respect her right to do what she decides. The duties correlated with *welfare rights*, however, if there are such rights, differ fundamentally. If people have welfare rights, we have *a duty to help them*, not merely a duty not to harm them or not to interfere with their liberty. And the performance of this duty to help, if this duty is correlated with welfare *rights*, is something that we *owe* to those who need it, is something *they deserve*, and so is their due as a matter of moral justice.

An example might help to make matters clearer. There are at this moment, we know, many people who are chronically unemployed, poor, malnourished, and in need of proper medical care. And this is true even in wealthy nations, such as the United States and Canada, not just in the countries of the Third World. Now, if these people have some moral rights but lack welfare rights, then, it can be argued, we discharge those duties correlated with the rights they have by minding our own business — that is, by doing nothing. We may, of course, do something to help. But if we decide to do so, we give these people more than moral justice requires. Since they have no right to our assistance, we have no duty of justice to give it. Thus, for example, if Pierre does not personally do anything to prevent Margaret from looking for a job, then he does nothing to abridge her liberty right, and if he does not personally do anything that injures her, then he does not do anything that violates her right not to be injured. If, however, people have welfare rights, our duties to them take on an added dimension. For example, if people have a moral right to adequate health care, or a moral right to receive an adequate income, or a moral right to a job, then we cannot discharge the duties correlated with these rights merely by "minding our own business." To do nothing is to do less than justice requires, since those who have these rights *have a right to be helped* (for example, when it comes to securing proper medical attention or financial aid). If people have these rights, we *owe* them our active assistance, and they are due this assistance, not out of "charity" or "because it is nice to help," but because justice requires it. While those who deny that people have welfare rights characteristically hold that we *are* at liberty to help or not to help the poor, the unemployed, and the like, and so have no duty of justice to help, those who affirm that people have welfare rights *deny* that we are liberty in this respect, affirming, instead, that we have a duty of justice to help those who, through no fault of their own, find themselves in situations where they need it. Where the former find "acts of charity," the latter find "the demands of justice."

§14 INDIVIDUAL RIGHTS AND THE FREE MARKET

Of course, merely to claim that people have welfare rights does not establish that they do, and neither does it disclose the moral weight these rights possess. Here, as in other places, we should expect heated controversy. Some argue that the welfare rights of the poor, for example, outweigh the liberty rights of the rich, so that those who have more than is necessary to live comfortably have a duty of justice to help those who have less than is necessary to live a minimally satisfying life. And many of those who argue this far argue further, urging that, since a legitimate role of the government is to insure that citizens have legal rights that protect their moral rights, government should legislate such assistance to those who need it and enforce the terms of the legislation by the use, or the threat of the use, of punitive force for non-compliance (for example, by the use of fines or imprisonment). A system of progressive taxation frequently is defended along these lines. And similar arguments are given to support the legitimacy of a more extensive regulatory role by government in the affairs of business (for example, to insure "truth in advertising" or product safety, because, it may be claimed, consumers have a moral right to be protected against false or misleading information and potentially harmful products). If, then, people have welfare rights, what people are due, as a matter of justice, seems to be considerably more than what they are due if they lack such rights. The case for the legitimacy of an active, extensive regulatory role by government in business seems to turn, at least in part, on whether people have welfare rights and, if they do, what these rights are.

Critics of government regulation of private commerce obviously must think that defenses of such regulation are weak. If the arguments for attributing welfare rights to people are demonstrably inadequate, or if the liberty rights of individuals can be shown to outweigh the welfare rights of others (assuming people have welfare rights), then certain defenses of government regulation will be exposed as inadequate. Or if it can be shown that those who need, and presently lack, health care, a job, an education and the like will have their interests better served by allowing unregulated economic forces (for example, those of supply and demand) to work their will, then the case against government regulation will be to that extent undermined. But if the defenders of the free market fail to expose the weaknesses in their opponents' arguments, or if, for example, it could be shown that the duties correlated with moral rights *are never wholly or purely "negative"* in the sense some defenders of the free market suppose, then the justification of an active regulatory role by government in business will to that degree be made stronger. Clearly, it is no simple matter to decide which side in this dispute—those who condemn, or those who commend, the principle of government regulation of business—is on the side of the angels. Anyone who thinks otherwise obviously hasn't thought much about it.

§15 ANOTHER SET OF QUESTIONS

The preceding discussion of rights provides a set of questions rather than a set of answers. Here are some of the questions that apply to the essays.

1. Does the author affirm or deny that people have moral rights?
2. If moral rights are affirmed, what kind are recognized—liberty rights, *and* claim rights, *and* welfare rights, or one or two but not all three?
3. If all three sorts of rights are affirmed, how are they weighted—for example, are welfare rights said to outweigh or override liberty rights? Or vice versa?
4. Whether moral rights are affirmed or denied, what arguments are given for recognizing the sorts of rights favored by the author? What arguments are given for weighting them in the way they are? And, in both cases, how good are the arguments?
5. What connection, if any, is claimed to hold between respect for the rights of the individual and advancing the general welfare? And how strong are the arguments, if any, given to support the position the author takes in this regard?

Like the other questions mentioned in earlier discussions, the ones just listed go to the center of the essays. Though not all are examined in every essay, some are examined in each. To have them in one's pocket, so to speak, is to have a partial map that one can consult to help one find one's way.

§16 PROPERTY RIGHTS AND THE JUSTICE OF THE FREE MARKET

Though questions about justice have been aired on a number of occasions in the preceding pages, none challenged the justice of one of the central assumptions of the economic philosophy variously known as "the free market," "private enterprise," "laissez faire," or "capitalism." (A concise characterization of this philosophy may be found, for example, at the beginning of Alan Goldman's essay.) The assumption is that people have a moral right to property, including the moral right to own the means of production (for example, a factory). As anyone even slightly familiar with the teachings of Karl Marx (1818–1883) knows, this is an assumption that has not gone unchallenged, and many of the major moral objections to capitalism (for example, that capitalism sanctions the exploitation of the members of the working class by a powerful elite) are, many critics claim, traceable to this assumption.

A complete examination of the philosophy of capitalism would have to include a careful review and assessment of the major arguments for and against recognition of the moral right to own property, including the right to own the means of production. David Braybrooke addresses some of these concerns in his essay, "Justice and Injustice in Business." However, one can ask important moral questions about the workings of the free-market philosophy without asking whether capitalism is morally rotten to the core. The proof that this can be done is that many of the contributors to this volume do it. Thus, for example, one can grant the property rights Marxists challenge and ask, as Patricia Werhane does, whether those who own the means of production have the further right to fire their workers "at will" (that is, for any reason they might have). Or one can concede the property rights in question and inquire, as Adina Schwartz does, about possible defenses of the detailed division of labor historically allied with the implementation of this right (the division, again, between managers, who make decisions, and workers, who carry them out). Or one can concede these rights and examine arguments for and against preferential hiring, which is what George Sher does in his essay on that topic. To pose these and similar questions is not to test the moral mettle of capitalism in the way Marxist critics might prefer. And some may view this as a liability. But first steps, which are what one hopes to take in a beginning course, are not last steps. There are more problems, many of a fundamental nature, than one can hope to do justice to in a semester's outing. By attempting less, we sometimes accomplish more. Though Marxist critics might be of a different opinion, the hope is, we do that here.

2

Preferential Hiring

GEORGE SHER

In 1974, Brian Weber sued his employer, the Kaiser Aluminum and Chemical Corporation, in Louisiana. The occasion of his suit was a program Kaiser had instituted to increase the number of minority employees in its craft jobs. Although Kaiser itself had never been accused of racial discrimination, it voluntarily initiated a plan under which equal numbers of black and white workers were shifted to an on-the-job training program for these jobs. Weber, who is white, was not admitted to the program, while some blacks with less seniority were. Thereafter, Weber brought suit on grounds of racial discrimination, claiming that Kaiser had violated Title VII of the Civil Rights Act of 1964. The case reached the United States Supreme Court, which ultimately ruled against Weber.

Given the Supreme Court's decision, it seems clear that at least some forms of preferential hiring are legally permitted. Moreover, many employers now have affirmative action programs that do appear to involve forms of preferential hiring. Because of this, preferential hiring will directly affect the employment prospects of everyone who reads this essay. But not every practice that is widespread and legally permitted is morally right; and preferential hiring in particular has been both passionately attacked and passionately defended on moral grounds. To those who defend it, the all-important fact is that blacks and members of other discriminated-against groups still suffer from the lingering effects of past injustice. Because they do, and because these effects will not quickly disappear if we merely treat these groups neutrally, it is said to be only fair to grant their members special preference now. But is this really as fair as it looks? From another perspective, it may seem not. Although individuals like Weber are white and male, there is no reason to believe that they themselves have practiced racial or sexual discrimination. Because of this, it seems unfair to make them bear the major burden of its present rectification. To do so, it may appear, is only to shift the injustice from one place to another.

Given these considerations, there are clearly powerful arguments both for and against preferential hiring. Generally speaking, the arguments for it reflect the belief that turn-about is fair play, while those against it reflect the belief that two wrongs don't make a right. Under ordinary circumstances, most of us are inclined to accept both beliefs. However, here they pull us in opposite directions. In which direction should we go?

I. THE PROBLEM CLARIFIED

Before we can evaluate the moral status of preferential hiring, we must address several preliminary matters. In particular, we must get clearer about exactly what preferential hiring is, and what the major arguments for and against it involve. Let us begin by considering these issues.

§1 PREFERENTIAL HIRING DEFINED

As a working definition of preferential hiring, we may accept the following:

> A person is hired preferentially if and only if that person is hired instead of somebody else who better satisfies usual and fair hiring criteria for the job, and is afforded this advantage for reasons dictated by moral principle.

This definition captures the intuitive idea we want to discuss. However, to understand its boundaries, we must look more closely at the crucial notions of "fair hiring criteria" and "reasons dictated by moral principle."

Generally speaking, a hiring criterion is fair when it demands skills or abilities that are reasonably thought necessary for successful job performance. Thus, for a job as a dock worker, it is reasonable to require a degree of physical strength; for a job as a computer programer, some mathematical aptitude and training. But although many criteria are rendered fair by their connection with job performance, some are fair for other reasons. When an employer has several applicants who can do the job equally well, he needs some other way to decide whom to hire. In such a case, he may hire the applicant whose application was received the earliest; or, if this is not feasible, he may simply choose by lot. If he does either of these things, we may also say that his hiring criterion is fair.[1]

The other crucial requirement, that preference must be granted "for reasons dictated by moral principle," is also quite inclusive. The requirement is obviously satisfied when preference is granted to compensate for past discrimination against the applicant or his group. It is also satisfied when preference is granted to achieve an independent moral goal (such as equality) that in fact is jeopardized by the effects of discrimination or other wrongdoing. It is even satisfied when preference is granted to achieve such a goal in the absence of any wrongdoing. It is, however, not satisfied when preference is granted through favoritism, through prejudice, or in the hope of monetary gain. In such cases, no moral principle can plausibly be said to be involved.

§2 SOME USEFUL DISTINCTIONS

This definition brings some initial clarity to our subject. However, more must be said. For one thing, the definition conceals some important differences between types of preferential hiring. In addition, the definition is best understood by contrasting the practices that do fall under it with certain others that do not. For both reasons, we must now make some distinctions.

(a) There are two quite different ways in which an employer may afford preference to job applicants. One way of doing this is to adopt a quota system. Under this procedure, the employer sets aside a certain number or percentage of jobs for members of a targeted group. This was what Kaiser did when it decided to admit one black for every white in its training program; and it is also what a company does when it decides to hire a hundred black or female workers within a specified time. On the other hand, an employer may also give preference on a more individual basis. He may award a certain amount of "extra credit" to the qualifications of certain individuals or members of targeted groups. Done formally, this may involve adding a number of months to a worker's seniority or a number of points to his score on a competitive exam; done informally, it may involve simply taking an applicant's race or sex "into consideration" when assessing his total qualifications. Because any such "extra credit" must be combined with an initial score that varies independently, this second method does not guarantee that any special number or fixed quota of group members will be hired. In general, the first method has the advantage of neatness and administrative convenience, while the second allows greater sensitivity to differences in individual merit and qualification. To keep them distinct, let us call the first the *quota method* and the second the *extra credit method*.

(b) By definition, any employer who hires preferentially must deviate from previously accepted fair hiring criteria. If we define qualifications in terms of such fair and accepted criteria, then anyone hired preferentially is less than best qualified for the job. In programs like Kaiser's, where the usual criteria involve seniority, this does not imply that the chosen applicant will perform less well than others. However, where other criteria are usually used, this implication may indeed be present. If a given job requires considerable intelligence, strength, or skill, then someone who is hired preferentially can be expected to perform less well than those who were by-passed.

It is foolish to deny that such cases exist. However, on closer inspection, they may be both less numerous and less significant than they first appear. Some jobs require only a minimum of a certain skill or ability. Others yield only small improvements in performance for improvements in skill beyond a certain level. Given these and related possibilities, we plainly can distinguish between preference for applicants who are *unqualified* and preference for applicants who are *qualified but not best qualified*. By restricting our attention to the latter, we can avoid the common but irrelevant objection that preferential hiring yields incompetent workers.

(c) In our discussion so far, we have made several allusions to blacks and women. Along with Indians, Hispanics, and members of other discriminated-against groups, these individuals are the ones most often said to have claims to preferential treatment. But we must be careful here. Not all ways of counting an applicant's membership in a discriminated-against group involve preferential hiring. To see this, consider the following proposals:

i. Black students sometimes learn better from black teachers, and female students from female teachers. When they do, and when many of the students to be taught are black or female, being black or female should count in favor of a prospective teacher.

ii. Many black citizens relate better to black policemen than to white policemen. Therefore being black should count in favor of an applicant to a police department in a black area.

Although (i) and (ii) both advocate counting an applicant's race or sex, they do not do so for special moral reasons. Instead, they invoke race and sex to indicate an increased likelihood of successful job performance. Because of this, they involve, not preferential hiring, but rather an expansion of the usual criteria for hiring policemen and teachers. We may wonder whether this is legitimate, since a similar expansion might work to exclude blacks and women when their employment would offend the biases of whites or males.[2] Nevertheless, legitimate or not, the proposals plainly do aim to improve rather than by-pass the usual hiring criteria. To capture this idea, let us distinguish between *preferential hiring* and merely *expanding the criteria* by which applicants are hired.

(d) Because expanding criteria sometimes increases the degree to which blacks and women qualify for jobs, it can be confused with the extra credit method of preferential hiring. But a different confusion is also possible. It is often suggested that in the absence of all discrimination, the proportion of blacks or women in a given profession should be equivalent (or should stand in some other definite numerical relation) to the proportion of blacks or women in the overall population. Thus, as a check on conscious or unconscious discrimination, employers may be asked to monitor the number of blacks or women in their employ, and to take certain steps in response to deviations from the expected proportions. If these steps include the hiring of additional group members, there is no difference between the suggested "goal" and a racial or sexual quota. However, if the steps include only a reassessment of existing hiring criteria, and aim only at insuring genuine equality of opportunity, then no quota or preference is involved. The distinction is sometimes blurred by the fact that employers may be penalized for discrimination, and thus may face pressure to deviate from their standard criteria to meet their goals. However, at least in the abstract, the distinction between *preferential hiring* and *employment goals* is clear enough.[3]

§3 GROUPS AND INDIVIDUALS

With these distinctions in mind, we can proceed to the arguments for preferential hiring. But before examining these arguments in detail, we must get clear about the entities to which they apply. If preferential hiring is to be defended, should it be because it benefits certain individuals, or because it benefits the groups to which these individuals belong?

Consider first the suggestion that preferential hiring aims at benefiting discriminated-against groups.[4] Although this suggestion may take various forms, its most plausible variant asserts that because such groups were wrongfully deprived of their fair share of society's goods in the past, justice now demands that those shares be restored to them. In many ways, this claim seems quite reasonable. Because past racial and sexual discrimination was based on group membership, it does seem natural to say that the conditions to be rectified are its lingering effects on the discriminated-against groups. Moreover, if we do say this, we will be able to answer two very serious objections to preferential hiring. As we have already seen, many people object that preferential hiring places the major burden of rectifying discrimination on innocent white males. In addition, others object that in helping only blacks and women with some qualifications for jobs, it ignores those who were altogether prevented from developing skills, and so were most severely harmed by the lingering effects of past discrimination. But both objections miss the point if the relevant entities are groups and not individuals. If the aim of preferential hiring is to redress imbalances between groups, then its purpose will be served no matter which individual blacks and females are its beneficiaries, and no matter which white males bear the costs. The fact of harm to some innocent persons will remain; but if justice requires a certain balance between groups, then this harm may be dismissed as a regrettable but necessary side effect.

Although many people find these considerations convincing, there are serious difficulties with the claim that the proper aim of preferential hiring is justice for discriminated-against groups. To appreciate these difficulties, we must look more closely at the concept of justice itself. As various philosophers since Aristotle have noted, the three main branches of justice are distributive justice, which involves the distribution of wealth and other goods; retributive justice, which involves punishment for wrongdoing; and compensatory justice, which aims at restoring the distribution of goods that would have been obtained in the absence of wrongdoing. Although they differ in various ways, it seems that all three branches of justice are concerned with the distribution of society's bene-fits and burdens. Thus, a prerequisite for being treated either justly *or* unjustly is a capacity to enjoy benefits and bear burdens. In addition, because what counts as a benefit or burden is so closely bound up with the subject's level of well-being, a further prerequisite is a capacity to enjoy various levels of well-being. If a given entity lacks the latter capac-ity—for example, a rock or a rainbow—then the claim that it has been treated unjustly is defeated at the outset.

With these remarks in mind, it is easy to see what is wrong with the claim that justice requires that the *groups* of blacks and women should be restored their fair shares of society's goods. Because only entities that can enjoy levels of well-being can be treated justly or unjustly, only such entities can have claims to fair shares of goods. But what could it pos-sibly mean to say that racial or sexual groups enjoy levels of well-being? Such groups do not have single organized bodies, and so cannot be healthy or ill. They do not have nervous systems, and so cannot be com-fortable or uncomfortable. They do not have consciousness, and so can-not be amused or bored, happy or unhappy, satisfied or unsatisfied. They do not act, and so cannot be successful or frustrated in their endeavors. But surely to describe an entity as incapable of health, com-fort, happiness, and successful action is just to describe it as being utterly beyond both well- and ill-being. If so, then racial and sexual groups can-not be proper subjects of justice at all.[5]

These objections may seem to miss an obvious point. Even if racial and sexual groups cannot enjoy states of well-being as individuals can, they can indeed enjoy such states in a somewhat different way. In partic-ular, we can easily attach a clear sense to such assertions as that blacks as a group are better off than they were twenty years ago. To do this, we need only take the assertion as saying that the average level of well-being among blacks has risen, that a majority of blacks have improved their position, or something else along these lines. But this contention, though correct, is beside the point. The question to be answered is whether racial and sexual groups are subject to independent claims of justice. To demonstrate that they are, one must establish that these groups can en-joy states of well-being that are distinct from the well-being of their members. But all that has been shown is that such groups can be said to be well off *when and because their members are.* Since this concession does not establish that the groups enjoy independent levels of well-being, it also does not show that they have independent claims of justice.

There is perhaps a further point to be made here. Because race and sex are currently prominent categories of thought in our society, a per-son's membership in a racial or sexual group is apt to connect him in im-portant ways to other members of that group. When a black person is visibly successful, other blacks are apt to identify with his achievements, while whites may have positive reactions that carry over to other blacks. Conversely, when a black person fails, other blacks may feel that this reflects badly on them, while whites may have negative stereotypes reinforced. Because members of racial and sexual groups are bound together in this way, one's membership in such a group is not just another fact about him. To some degree, the success of one black is likely to help other blacks, and the success of one woman to help other women.[6] But while this does imply that membership in racial and sexual groups is psychologically more significant than some other traits, it does not imply that such groups have an independent moral status. Although one's group membership may connect one's fate to that of others, the fact remains that those others are still individuals and individuals only. Because they are, the interconnections among group members will at best support the claim that certain groups of individuals may be benefited or harmed together. They will not support the stronger claim that the groups themselves are independent subjects of justice.

§4 PAST AND FUTURE

Given these considerations, we must deny that preferential hiring is a way of restoring fair shares to discriminated-against groups. If that practice is to be justified at all, it must be through appeal to some moral principle that applies solely to individuals. But what principle could this be, and how would an appeal to it work?

There are, in general, two possibilities. Because blacks and others who would benefit from preferential hiring are often impoverished, powerless, and outside the social mainstream, preferential hiring is sometimes justified simply as a way of mitigating these conditions. It is sometimes defended either as a way of raising the overall level of well-being in society, or as a way of making society more equal. On these accounts, its justification lies entirely in its desirable consequences. On the other hand, one may also stress the fact that the poverty, powerlessness, and exclusion of blacks and others did not develop by accident. Their situation is the result of social patterns produced by unjust discriminatory practices, and so its further perpetuation may itself be unjust. Because of this, a very different justification of preferential hiring is also possible. On this account, the point is to rectify the efforts of past wrongdoing or to compensate its victims. Because the first kind of justification looks entirely to the future while the second refers also to the past, we may call the first kind *forward-looking* and the second *backward-looking*. Of course, an argument need not refer *only* to past events in order to be backward-looking. The conditions to be rectified may be present or even future. However, as long as they are said to require rectification because they were caused by past wrongdoing, the argument is still a backward-looking one.

Because they both invoke the plight of currently disadvantaged individuals, the backward-looking and forward-looking approaches may seem importantly similar. However, on closer inspection, the similarity is deceptive. On the backward-looking account, what is important about disadvantaged individuals is the level of well-being they would have enjoyed in the absence of discrimination. If someone takes this approach, he must first compare the level of well-being that various disadvantaged persons would have enjoyed in a just world against the (lower) level of well-being they have in actuality, and must then show that preferential hiring would narrow the gap. By contrast, if one accepts either one of the forward-looking approaches, a very different comparison is required. If someone believes that the goal of preferential hiring is to make society more equal, then he must first establish the prevailing level of inequality, and then show that preferential hiring would reduce this level. If one believes the goal is to promote overall well-being, he must first establish the prevailing level of well-being, and then establish that preferential hiring would raise this level. In all these cases, the plight of blacks and other disadvantaged individuals plays a crucial role. However, because the required comparisons are so different, it is quite mistaken to say that all the arguments amount to the same thing because they all invoke the plight of disadvantaged individuals.

II. THE FORWARD-LOOKING ARGUMENTS

Of the two basic types of approach to preferential hiring, the forward-looking approach is the simpler and in some ways the more attractive. The past, after all, cannot be changed. Its wrongs, once done, cannot be undone; and so a preoccupation with them can seem morbid and unproductive. Guided by these sentiments, many have felt that the only real justification of preferential hiring is one that appeals to its desirable future consequences. Because these consequences may include either increases in overall well-being or greater social equality, the forward-looking justification may take either of two forms. Let us now consider each in turn.

§5 THE APPEAL TO UTILITY

One very familiar forward-looking argument for preferential hiring is that it promotes overall well-being. The principle that we should promote overall well-being is a version of what is called the Principle of Utility. Thus, we may call this argument the *appeal to utility*. Like all appeals to utility, this one rests squarely on a factual claim. It assumes that preferential hiring will in fact bring more of what we count as good — will in fact yield more overall benefit — than hiring strictly by qualification. Thus, to evaluate the appeal to utility, we must first spell out the basis for this claim.

Why should preferential hiring be thought to maximize overall well-being? A first possible answer is that any individuals hired preferentially will reap the benefits of income and security that flow from the employment they gain. However, this is inconclusive; for even *without* preferential hiring, whoever is hired will receive these benefits. To make the argument work, one must maintain that there are other beneficial effects that accrue *only* when blacks or women are hired. This claim can be defended in a number of ways. For one thing, because many blacks are so impoverished, and because the economic opportunities of both blacks and women are comparatively limited, the economic benefits of employment may well be of greater value to a black or female applicant than to a white male. In addition, the hiring of black or female applicants is often said to yield important psychological benefits that would otherwise be absent. We have already noted the claim that the members of historically excluded groups are apt to identify with other group members, as white males are not. If this is correct, then the employment of blacks and women in visible and prestigious positions may raise the self-esteem of other group members as the employment of white males would not. It may provide "role models" that encourage other blacks and women to seek such jobs. In addition, the presence of blacks and women in such jobs may increase utility by undermining harmful stereotypes, by fostering tolerance, and by promoting an enhanced appreciation of human diversity.[7]

These considerations should not be taken lightly. If correct, they establish that preferential hiring has several real and important advantages. However, even so, the utilitarian case is not necessarily made. A policy with great benefits may have even greater costs; and if so, the Principle of Utility will tell us to reject it. Thus, to see whether preferential hiring is justified by its utility, we must now consider its costs.

Of these costs, perhaps the most often cited is a loss of efficiency. If the best-qualified people are not hired, then jobs will not be done as well as they could be, and productivity will be lost. However, if those who are hired preferentially are qualified, though not best qualified, then the loss in productivity, and thus this cost, will often be small. Of perhaps greater significance are the adverse psychological effects of preferential hiring. If the practice is well publicized, it may generate considerable resentment in those best-qualified candidates who are not hired. Moreover, since even persons who are not best qualified may think they are, the resentment may be quite widespread. In addition, a policy of preferential hiring may well cast doubt on the legitimate achievements of blacks and women. Both in their own eyes and in the eyes of others, it may perpetuate the belief that they cannot compete on their own. Finally, but not least importantly, a policy of preferential hiring, once begun, may become entrenched in our political system. What was introduced as a temporary ameliorative strategy may come to be considered an entitlement. If so, then preferential hiring may end by having the ironic effect of perpetuating the very racial and sexual categories of thought that should be irrelevant to employment.

Given these considerations, the utilitarian defender of preferential hiring cannot simply enumerate its possible advantages. To make his case convincingly, he must provide empirical evidence that *supports* his predictions about benefits and costs. In addition, he must show that alternative policies are unlikely to achieve equivalent benefits at even less cost. Given the speculative nature of the psychological claims involved, these things are not easy to do. But even if they can be done, a more fundamental difficulty will remain. Even if preferential hiring does maximize utility, the propriety of appealing solely to utility is itself highly questionable.

The basic problem is a familiar one. As we have seen, the most compelling objection to preferential hiring is that it ignores the claims of those best-qualified applicants who are not hired. We may express these claims by saying either that such applicants have a *right* to be considered on their merits, that they *deserve* to be hired, or that ignoring their qualifications is *unfair*. Although these formulations differ in important ways, they are all motivated by an idea that has considerable intuitive force. Because they are so powerfully motivated, any genuinely effective defense of preferential hiring must somehow come to terms with them. Such a defense must show that the claims of the best-qualified applicant are either illusory or overridden by other considerations. But taken by itself, the appeal to utility does not do this. By restricting its attention to benefits and costs, it simply *assumes* that considerations of desert, fairness, and rights have no independent weight. However, to assume this is not to resolve the problem, but only to wish it away. Thus, without further supplementation, the appeal to utility is at least crucially incomplete.

§6 THE APPEAL TO EQUALITY

The other main forward-looking argument for preferential hiring is that it will make society more equal. At first glance, this egalitarian argument may appear to avoid the objections to the appeal to utility. For one thing, its factual basis appears unproblematical. Because there are many desirable professions in which few blacks or women are employed, there is little doubt that preferential hiring would equalize overall levels of representation within professions. Thus, the objection that the argument rests on speculative empirical assumptions does not seem to arise. In addition, the concept of equality has important connections with the ideals of fairness and justice. Thus, any problems of unfairness to the best-qualified applicant may also appear to be solved.

In fact, however, the situation is not this simple. It is true that preferential hiring promotes equality in the sense of reducing the "underrepresentation" of blacks and women in various professions. But does any plausible principle of equality *require* such equality of representation? We could answer this question positively if we agreed that goods should be distributed equally among racial and sexual groups. However, this would again assume that such groups are independent subjects of justice. Since we have already found reason to reject this assumption (see §3 above), some other way of defending equality of representation must be found.

A promising alternative may seem to exist. It is widely acknowledged that all persons should in some sense have the same opportunities in life. Moreover, whatever this comes to, the underrepresentation of blacks and women in desirable professions suggests that their opportunities have hitherto *not* been equal. Because equal opportunity is thus importantly linked to equal representation within professions, it may appear that any social policy that promotes the latter is justified by the former. But this appearance is deceptive. Even if equal opportunity always does produce equal representation, it hardly follows that any policy that produces equal representation must produce it *by producing* equal opportunity. In particular, this appears unlikely when the policy in question discounts the qualifications of some job applicants. A policy of this sort appears to enhance the opportunities of some at the expense of others. Of course, it may be replied that many blacks and women were wrongfully deprived of opportunities to *develop* their qualifications, and that simply hiring by qualifications therefore affords only the appearance of equal opportunity. But this suggestion, though important, is out of place in the current context. To accept it would be to expand the notion of equal opportunity to require a history of unimpeded development as well as the absence of present barriers. However, to talk about a history of unimpeded development is necessarily to refer to various past acts. Hence, introducing this idea would only transform the appeal to equality from a forward-looking argument into a backward-looking one.

Confronted with these facts, the proponent of the appeal to equality may change his strategy. Instead of maintaining that preferential hiring promotes equality by equalizing the representation of groups within professions, he may maintain that it promotes equality by equalizing the distribution of goods among individuals. But although this shift does avoid the need to defend equality of group representation, it introduces other problems in its turn. For how, exactly, does preferential hiring equalize the distribution of goods among individuals? Generally speaking, employment is a source of inequality because there are not enough jobs to go around and because some jobs offer greater rewards than others. Hence, the most obvious ways of manipulating employment to reduce inequality are to increase the number of jobs available or to alter the reward structure of existing jobs. But preferential hiring does neither of these things. Whether the recipient of a prestigious and well-paying job is black and female or white and male, the inequality between the recipient and those others who are denied the job remains the same. Hence, preferential hiring does not alter the structure of unequal rewards, but only reshuffles their recipients. It does not abolish the prevailing framework of inequalities, but only redistributes individuals within it. At least directly, preferential hiring does not decrease inequality among individuals.

This may not be the end of the story. Even if preferential hiring does accept a framework of inequality, it may still advance equality through its collateral effects. Because white males generally have other options —

because their job opportunities are usually greater — their economic well-being may be less affected by their failure to be hired for particular jobs than the well-being of blacks and women. In addition, if blacks and women have internalized prevailing stereotypes, then performing well in responsible jobs may raise their self-esteem as it would not for white males. But although these considerations do suggest that preferential hiring increases equality, others suggest precisely the opposite. It may well be, for example, that the self-esteem of some blacks and women is actually lowered when their legitimate achievements are called into question by preferential hiring. In addition, if many women are hired preferentially, then this may promote inequality by bringing some families two incomes while others are left with none. To weigh and integrate these considerations, we must marshal precisely the sort of detailed empirical evidence that we found to be required by the appeal to utility. Thus, the first advantage we attributed to the appeal to equality — that it does not require such evidence — is simply illusory.

The second and more important advantage that we attributed to it is also illusory. It was suggested above that equality has important connections with fairness and justice, and that the appeal to equality therefore automatically avoids the charge that preferential hiring unfairly ignores the claims of best-qualified applicants. But if the relevant principle of equality is that goods should be distributed equally among persons, then this suggestion fails. The connection between equality and fairness is at best a formal one — what is unfair is only to treat people differently without a good reason for doing so. However, what *counts as* a good reason must be established separately. Thus, we cannot automatically assume that fairness requires that goods be distributed equally, and that other considerations have little or no independent weight. This suggestion may ultimately be correct; but it must be defended independently. If it is not, then the appeal to equality will itself ignore the claims of the best qualified. Far from avoiding difficult questions about these claims, the appeal thus only raises them again in altered guise. In this respect, too, there is little to choose between it and the appeal to utility.

§7 THE CLAIMS OF THE BEST QUALIFIED

We have now criticized both forward-looking arguments on the grounds that they ignore the claims of the best qualified. However, this criticism may not be decisive. It would fail if there were independent reason to believe that best-qualified applicants do not *have* serious claims to employment. To assess this possibility, we must look more closely at the claims attributed to them. Although those claims can be articulated in various ways, two of their most plausible versions involve the notions of *desert* and *rights*.

The contention that the best-qualified applicant deserves to be hired is often quite compelling. When someone has worked hard to develop his skills, and when his efforts have required some sacrifice, it is natural to regard his superior qualifications as reflecting his meritorious earlier activity. Hence, it is also natural to say that he and nobody else deserves the job. But as natural as this contention is, not all philosophers accept it. As against it, some have noted that no amount of effort will significantly increase one's skills unless one has some initial talent to develop. In addition, the capacity to persevere may itself stem from an initial effort-making ability over which one has no control. Because one's talents and effort-making ability are both undeserved, it is inferred that the achievements which such talents and abilities make possible are not deserved either. A person who is talented and able to persevere is already lucky; to reward him for his achievements is merely to compound his arbitrary good fortune.[8]

If this argument were correct, it would effectively undercut the claim that best-qualified applicants deserve to be hired. But is the argument correct? Its central inference is that no one deserves to be hired because no one deserves his talents or effort-making abilities; and this in turn seems to presuppose that in order to deserve a thing, one must also deserve whatever enables him to acquire it. But should we really accept the latter principle? Doubts arise when we realize that any action whatever was made possible by innumerable prior events—by the food and care the agent was given as a child, the continued beating of his heart, and so on. Because so many of these enabling conditions are undeserved, the proposed principle will immediately guarantee that the concept of desert has no application at all. For this reason, the principle seems implausibly strong. To salvage the argument, one must somehow weaken it. One must maintain that to deserve something, a person need only deserve *some* of the conditions that were necessary for its acquisition. But which conditions, and why? Although various responses are possible, a plausible answer that supports the argument's conclusion is not easy to find.[9]

Given these considerations, it seems reasonable to suppose that best-qualified applicants sometimes do deserve to be hired. However, even so, the range of cases in which this holds remains open to question. Although the best-qualified applicant clearly deserves the job when he has worked much harder for it than the others, the situation is less clear when his qualifications have come easily to him. If his superior skills stem from natural ability rather than great effort, and if the other applicants have worked harder, then the picture may be clouded. Moreover, it is clouded further when the qualifications in question do not involve skill at all, but rather turn on such facts as personal attractiveness or the time at which one's application was received. Finally, if an applicant's "qualification" is simply that he was selected through a randomizing device, the intuition that he deserves the job may be altogether absent.

These intuitions raise doubts about the contention that best-qualified applicants always have a serious claim to be hired. However, by themselves, they do not refute that contention. For one thing, although the intuitions reflect the plausible view that desert always stems from human activity and effort, another view of desert is also possible. On this other view, giving someone what he deserves is simply to respond in an appropriate way to any fact about him. Desert is a general fittingness between responses and characteristics or actions, "much like that between humor and laughter, or good performance and applause."[10] If one accepts this view, then one may indeed regard desert as stemming from such characteristics as personal attractiveness. In addition, even if one does not accept it, one may still hold that best-qualified candidates have serious claims to be hired that are *not* grounded in desert. In particular, one may still hold that such claims are grounded in a *right* that is connected with superior qualifications.

We often acknowledge that people have rights to things that they do not deserve. A thoroughgoing scoundrel may not deserve the family estate, but if a forgiving father bestows it upon him, he may still acquire a right to it. But what right, exactly, could belong to the best-qualified candidate for a given job? A natural first thought is that when someone is best qualified, he simply acquires a right to be hired. However, this will not do. Such a right, if it existed, would be violated whenever a prospective employer went out of business or decided to hire nobody; and yet some such actions are plainly permissible. Thus, instead of a right to be hired, the best-qualified applicant can at most have a right not to be excluded on certain grounds. Put most strongly, this right will rule out exclusion on the basis of any factor irrelevant to job performance. Put more cautiously, it will rule out exclusion on such grounds as race and sex. On either account, the right will protect (some aspects of) one's ability to compete for jobs on equal terms. Since even the more cautious formulation raises problems for preferential hiring, we may restrict our attention to it.

Do best-qualified job applicants have a right not to be excluded on the basis of their race or sex? Because rights and their grounding are complex and controversial, a full answer to this question cannot be attempted here. But even without such an account, certain facts about our reactions to ordinary racial and sexual discrimination do support such a right. No matter what views we hold about preferential hiring, we can all agree that the straightforward discrimination so often practiced in the past was seriously wrong. Moreover, we can also agree that its wrongness was quite independent of its lack of social utility. Instead of condemning such discrimination because of its lack of utility, most people appear to condemn it precisely because its victims were denied the opportunity to compete on grounds of race or sex. Thus, most people appear to believe that its victims had something like a right not to be excluded on these grounds. However, if the past victims of discrimination had a right not to be denied employment because of their race or sex, then everyone must have such a right. If the right belongs to blacks and women, then it must belong to whites and males as well.

None of this proves that there *must* be a right not to be excluded on grounds of race or sex. We saw above that moral intuitions are not an infallible guide to moral truth. However, when a moral intuition is strongly held and widely shared, it may at least provide important evidence about where the truth lies. In addition, our intuitions about past discrimination are important for another reason. Whatever the truth about such discrimination, the mere fact that we *believe* that blacks and women were wronged when their qualifications were overlooked places important limitations on our further beliefs. In particular, this belief is clearly inconsistent with the further belief that overlooking the qualifications of white males is unproblematical. If someone believes that blacks and women have a right not to be ruled out because of their race or sex, then consistency demands that he believe this of white males as well. Because of this, our beliefs about past discrimination are themselves compelling reasons for us to take seriously the claims of best-qualified white males. If we do otherwise, then we are tacitly adopting a moral double standard.[11]

III.   THE BACKWARD-LOOKING ARGUMENT

Despite their initial promise, the forward-looking arguments for preferential hiring do not appear to succeed. They rest on speculative factual premises, and, more important, do not take seriously the claims of the best qualified, which we acknowledge in other contexts. To disarm those claims, one must somehow demonstrate a morally significant difference between preferential hiring and past discrimination based on race and sex. But the most significant difference between these practices is precisely that the beneficiaries of preferential hiring, but not those of racial or sexual discrimination, are themselves members of previously victimized groups. Thus, anyone who wishes to dismiss the claims of the best qualified is naturally led to consider the backward-looking defense of preferential hiring. Can this argument succeed where its predecessors have failed?

§8 PREFERENTIAL HIRING AS COMPENSATION

To appreciate its prospects, we must first clarify what the backward-looking argument says. The argument defends preferential hiring as restitution or compensation for the victims of past wrongful discrimination. However, many of those who were originally discriminated against are no longer seeking jobs, while many younger blacks and women have not been discriminatorily denied jobs. Thus, the argument's first task is to show how past discrimination has affected the present beneficiaries of preferential hiring.

In a rough way, this is easy to do. People denied desirable employment generally have little money. Because of this, they often lack adequate food, housing, and medical care. They are also apt to suffer various sorts of psychological harm. Moreover, these harms are very often visited not only on the victims, but on their children and more distant descendants as well. In view of this, the lingering effects of past discrimination have undoubtedly harmed many present individuals. Thus, there may appear to be a clear basis for compensating these individuals. Moreover, insofar as the original wrongdoing involved employment discrimination, preferential hiring may seem an especially appropriate form of compensation.

This argument has considerable force. However, as stated, it raises serious problems about both the beneficiaries and the cost-bearers of preferential hiring. We saw above that if preference in hiring is not to yield incompetent workers, it can only be extended to those who are at least minimally qualified for the jobs they seek. But it is extremely unlikely that everyone harmed by the effects of past discrimination is at least minimally qualified for some open job. Hence, if preferential hiring is our way of compensating, then many who were injured by past discrimination will not be eligible for compensation at all. Moreover, because many sorts of injuries can reduce job skills, the individuals who were most harmed by past discrimination are precisely those who are now *least* likely to have even minimal job qualifications. Hence, if we compensate through preferential hiring, we will be systematically unable to award compensation to those with the strongest claims to it. These individuals may realize some indirect gains, but the greatest benefits will go to those who were less harmed.[12]

These considerations suggest that preferential hiring may not be as appropriate a form of compensation as it first seems. This impression is confirmed, moreover, when we turn from the beneficiaries of the practice to those who must bear its costs. We criticized the forward-looking arguments because they ignored the claims of the best qualified. But is the backward-looking defense any better in this regard? Most younger white males have not themselves practiced discrimination. Because they have not, they are plainly no more responsible for its effects than blacks or women. Moreover, we saw that they themselves appear to have a right not to be excluded on the basis of race or sex. In view of this, we may well wonder whether they can justly be asked to bear the main burden of compensating for the harms done by past discrimination. If we make them bear this burden, then aren't we merely substituting one set of innocent victims for another? If this question cannot be answered, then the backward-looking justification of preferential hiring will be just as insensitive to the claims of the best qualified as its forward-looking counterparts.

The objection just advanced presumes that we should never compensate one innocent person at the expense of another. However, although this principle is initially plausible, a closer look suggests an exception to it. Even if compensation at the expense of innocent parties is generally wrong, the situation may be different when one innocent person has unwittingly profited from the wrongdoing of another. If Jones has found a sum of money on the street and has deposited it in the bank without knowing it was stolen from Smith, then it does seem permissible to relieve Jones of the money and return it to Smith. Because this is so — because an innocent party *may* be asked to bear the cost of compensating for wrongdoing from which he has unwittingly benefited — the natural way to answer the objection is to argue that even those white males who have not discriminated themselves have at least benefited from the discrimination of others. Moreover, many defenders of preferential hiring have argued precisely this. Because so many blacks still feel the economic effects of past discrimination, it is sometimes held that most or all whites have been helped economically by that discrimination. In addition, because both blacks and women have been restricted to positions of low prestige, every white male is said to have gained at least an extra measure of free esteem.[13] For both reasons, all white males are said to have benefited from the discrimination of others. If so, then certain rights which they would otherwise have may be qualified or absent. Thus, it may indeed be permissible to make them bear the burden of compensating for past discrimination.

This reply does defeat a crude version of the objection that we should never compensate at the expense of innocent white males. Whatever its other defects, we cannot dismiss preferential hiring merely because it places the burden of compensation on persons who have done no wrong. But there is a further version of the objection which the reply does not defeat. Instead of arguing merely that those who bear the burden of preferential hiring are innocent, the objector may cite other reasons why the practice treats them unjustly. In particular, he may argue, first, that it is far from obvious that every white male *has* benefited from past discrimination. Even if one sector of the population has suffered economic loss, it hardly follows that all members of the other sectors have gained; and it is also unclear that one person's loss of esteem must always be another's gain. Moreover, second, even when someone *has* unintentionally gained from another's wrongdoing, the most that he should have to surrender is what he has gained or its equivalent. Thus, even if every white male has reaped some benefit from past discrimination, it remains to be established that what each has gained is equal in value to a desirable job. If some have gained less, then denying them jobs for which they are best qualified will be asking too much of them. Finally, whatever any particular white male has gained, there is no reason to believe that the greatest gains have gone to those who are best qualified for good jobs. If these individuals have benefited significantly, then so too have many other white males. Hence, at the very least, it seems unfair to place the entire burden of compensation on best-qualified white males alone.

Given all of this, a modified version of the second objection appears to stand. If preferential hiring is advocated as a broad compensatory policy, then it can indeed be criticized on grounds of equity as well as efficiency. Because it can, there is a strong case for rejecting it as a general compensatory instrument. If what we want is to compensate for all the lingering effects of past discrimination, then we will do better to award simple cash settlements to those who were harmed. Because such settlements can be made with the unskilled as well as the skilled, and because they can be made in varying amounts, they can match compensation to harm with far greater precision than can preferential hiring. In addition, because the money to pay for them can be raised from *all* the beneficiaries of past discrimination, such settlements need not impose an unfair burden on any particular individuals. Of course, any general compensatory policy would require far more discussion than has been provided here. However, even if such a policy can be defended, its proper vehicle will not be preferential hiring.

§9 THE ARGUMENT REFINED

These considerations discredit one version of the backward-looking argument for preferential hiring. There is, however, another version, which they do not discredit. By distinguishing carefully between the two versions, we can see that there are some instances in which preferential hiring is indeed justified.

To see how the backward-looking argument must be refined, consider again how past discrimination is likely to have affected present individuals. We saw above that discrimination often results in a lack of adequate food, housing, and medical care for its victims, and that these conditions, together with certain associated psychological effects, often perpetuate themselves through various generations. But why, exactly, should these effects be considered harms? In part, the answer is obvious: A life without decent food and housing is less pleasant and fulfilled than one that contains them. But the degree of nourishment and stimulation that one receives as a child are also important for another reason. These factors play a crucial role in shaping the skills and capacities one will have as an adult; and it is precisely these skills and capacities that will determine one's success in competing for jobs and other goods. Because of this, a person whose childhood lacks adequate food, medical care, education, and stimulation is thereby deprived of the later ability to compete with others on equal terms. Since this competitive ability determines his access to many further goods, its loss is itself a harm to be compensated for if possible.

With this in mind, we can see how the compensatory argument must be altered. Instead of regarding preferential hiring as compensation for all the adverse effects of past discrimination, we must regard it as compensation for a single effect alone. In particular, we must regard it as compensating only for the lost ability to compete for jobs and other goods on equal terms. Once we say this, we can indeed see a deep connection between loss and remedy. If the good whose loss is in question is just the *ability* to compete on equal terms, then the most natural way of compensating for that loss is just to remove the *necessity* for competing on equal terms. But this is exactly what preferential hiring does. Because it is, preferential hiring is an appropriate remedy for the loss of competitive abilities as other forms of compensation are not.[14] With this in mind, we can answer both of the main objections to the earlier compensatory argument.

Of these objections, the first was that preferential hiring does not compensate the right persons. It helps only some of those who were harmed by past discrimination, and it often fails to help those who were harmed most. But if the point is to compensate only for lost competitive abilities, then this objection can largely be met. A reduction in one's competitive abilities is harmful primarily when it causes one to fail in a competition in which one otherwise would have succeeded. In such cases, the harm done is proportional to the desirability of the good competed for. In view of this, the persons who are most seriously harmed by the loss of competitive ability are precisely those who would otherwise have qualified for good jobs. It is just these persons whom it is most important to compensate for their loss. Thus, to the objection that others have suffered reduced competitive abilities as well, we can now reply that those others would not have been best qualified anyhow, and so their losses are far less serious. Because they lacked the potential to acquire the requisite level of skill, the development of that potential was not something they could *lose* in the first place. Of course, this does not resolve the problem of those who would have become best qualified in the absence of discrimination, but who now lack even the minimal qualifications that preferential hiring requires. However, if these persons are compensated in other ways (for example, through intensive remedial training), then this problem need not be decisive.

The second objection, that preferential hiring does not distribute the costs of compensation equitably, can also be met. This objection, we recall, contends that many who are denied jobs for which they are best qualified have not benefited enough from past discrimination to warrant such losses, and that even those who have benefited enough should lose no more than others who have benefited a similar amount. But once we regard preferential hiring as compensation for the wrongful reduction of one's competitive position, we can see that the objection misses the point. Once we focus on competitive positions, we immediately see that a best-qualified candidate's previous gains are irrelevant — that what is important is not the gains he *has* enjoyed, but rather those he *will* enjoy if he obtains the contested position. Because these potential gains are precisely the ones that are denied him by preferential hiring, it can no longer be maintained that he has not benefited enough from past discrimination to warrant his losses. Moreover, neither can it be maintained that he has gained no more from past discrimination than other white males. Even if his *previous* gains have been no greater than those of other white males, the fact remains that he, but not the others, stands to gain a job that he would not have had if his rival's ability were not diminished by the effects of wrongdoing. Because the best-qualified candidate thus stands to gain the most from the lowering of his rival's ability, it is hardly unreasonable that he should lose the most as a result of a policy that compensates for that lowering. For this reason, it does not seem unfair that the best-qualified candidate should bear the major burden of compensation by being denied the contested job.

§10 IMPLICATIONS OF THE ARGUMENT

It has just been argued that preferential hiring can be justified as compensation for losses in competitive position caused by discrimination (and, by extension, by other types of wrongdoing). But not all forms of preferential hiring are justified in this way. To see the limits of what is justified, we must now examine the implications of the argument just advanced.

A first important implication is that preferential hiring along group lines cannot be justified. It is often assumed that if preference is to be given at all, its recipients must always be blacks, women, and members of other minority groups, while those who are by-passed must always be white males. By speaking of the by-passed individuals as white males, we have ourselves implied this. But if preferential hiring is justified as compensation for reductions in competitive ability caused by past wrongdoing, then this assumption must be rejected. There is no reason to believe that past discrimination has reduced the competitive ability of *every* black or *every* member of any other group; and neither is there any reason to believe that other forms of wrongdoing have *not* reduced the competitive abilities of some white males. In view of this, it is quite possible that some blacks might have claims to preference over better-qualified black competitors, and some whites over better-qualified white competitors. It is even possible that some disadvantaged whites might have claims to be hired preferentially over better-qualified black competitors. At best, racial and other group boundaries are rough indicators of reduced ability due to past discriminatory practices. To take them more seriously than this is mistakenly to reintroduce groups as independent moral entities.

A further implication follows. If preference along group lines is unjustified, then so are rigid quotas for blacks and other groups. The quota method of affording preference might be legitimate if our argument for preferential hiring were utilitarian or egalitarian. However, since reductions in competitive ability can be wrongfully inflicted on members of all groups, and since abilities may be diminished to many different degrees, our justification clearly requires a more individualized approach. Because the ideal is to restore to each applicant the competitive position he would have occupied in the absence of discrimination, we need to be able to extend different degrees of preference to different competitors. But the extra credit method of preferential hiring allows precisely such variation. Hence, it is plainly this method that the argument justifies.

A third implication concerns the characteristics that in fact suggest that preferential hiring may be called for. In most discussions, these characteristics are taken to include both race and sex; and here again, we have often followed accepted usage. However, although blacks and women have both suffered widespread discrimination, its effects seem very different in the two cases. Where blacks are concerned, past discrimination often did lead to poverty, malnourishment, inadequate education, and related ills. Thus, in their case, such discrimination is indeed apt to have reduced the ability of many current individuals. But where women are concerned, the situation is different. Although women were often denied employment, such discrimination did not usually affect their husbands' ability to work. In most cases, it did not reduce the nourishment, education, or stimulation received by the victims' children. In addition, where such discrimination did affect the well-being of the victims' children, it affected male and female children alike. Because of this, past discrimination against women did not initiate a cycle of poverty and deprivation that reduced the competitive abilities of current group members. Hence, our argument seems likely to justify preferential hiring for many more blacks than women.

This conclusion might be contested. In response to it, one might contend that even if past discrimination against women did not lead to poverty and deprivation, it still diminished the competitive position of women in other ways. In particular, because discrimination kept women from entering many professions, younger women have lacked exemplars or role models to encourage their own entry into these professions. In addition, many women are said to have adopted society's pervasive assumption that certain sorts of activities are not proper for them. Because of this, women are said to have been prevented from developing the skills and self-confidence that successful competition requires. Hence, they too are said to have claims to be compensated.

This argument is often made; but as it stands, it is far from compelling. The motivational influence of stereotypes and role models, though often mentioned, is hard to document. Moreover, even if we concede it, the injustice of a system that shapes people's preferences and attitudes through shared expectations is far harder to establish than the injustice of actual discrimination.[15] For this reason, the grounds for compensating for the effects of such a system are correspondingly less clear. Of course, the absence of role models is itself partly the result of actual discrimination, and so at least some of its effects may be said to call for compensation on these grounds. However, even if role models do influence one's initial choice of career, the skills and self-confidence that determine competitive success seem more likely to depend on other factors. Hence, the connection between the competitive position of female job applicants and past wrongdoing may well be minimal. Finally, even if some such connection were to exist, female applicants were at least no more harmed by stereotypes and lack of role models than blacks. Since many blacks have also suffered from the effects of poverty, it follows that being black (or American Indian or Hispanic) is a far stronger indication of wrongfully reduced competitive ability than being female.

One further implication remains. Because every job involves some hiring criterion, one may extend preference to an applicant for any job. But although all jobs permit preference, they are not all equally suited to it. Because preferential hiring should aim to restore the competitive positions that would have prevailed in the absence of wrongdoing, it is only called for when the qualifications of some job applicants have been reduced through wrongdoing. But this is not always equally true. When a job requires delicate abilities, which can be disrupted in various ways, many applicants who were not themselves denied access to the job may have been rendered less qualified for it by wrongs done to others. Thus, our account may justify a good deal of preference for persons seeking jobs in education and some areas of industry. However, when a job requires less refined abilities, an applicant's qualifications are less likely to have been reduced by his early environment or education. Being a good carpenter or plumber certainly requires considerable skill, but that skill can be acquired by anyone within a broad range of ability. Because this is so, the applicants for entry-level positions in these trades are not apt to be disadvantaged by the lingering effects of previous discrimination. Thus, although blacks, women, and others were systematically denied well-paying jobs in plumbing, construction, and related trades, the only persons with claims to preference here are apt to be the very ones who were previously excluded. Where others are concerned, the connection between past wrongdoing and the present inability to qualify is simply not likely to be present.

§11 THEORY AND PRACTICE

Thus far, our argument has been that preferential hiring is justified when it restores the competitive position that each applicant would have had in the absence of wrongdoing. However, to restore the rightful competitive place of each applicant, we must first know *how much* each applicant's abilities were affected by past wrongdoing. Unfortunately, such detailed knowledge is hopelessly beyond our grasp. Because it is, affording just enough preference to restore each applicant's competitive position is a practical impossibility. The closest we can come is to extend preference to all individuals with characteristics strongly *associated* or *correlated* with wrongfully reduced abilities. However, even this presumes a significant amount of factual knowledge. Since any claims about such correlations are in as much need of documentation as the factual claims of the utilitarian or egalitarian, the compensatory argument may seem just as questionable as the arguments considered earlier. If we accept it after rejecting them, we may appear to be applying a double standard.

There is clearly something right about this. If we require documentation for the empirical claims of utilitarians and egalitarians, then we must require it here as well. Lacking it, the compensatory argument will justify no actual preferential policy. But whatever problems this may raise, it clearly does *not* show that all the arguments are equally questionable. For one thing, the central objection to the forward-looking arguments was not that they lack an empirical basis, but rather that they ignore the claims of the best qualified. Because the compensatory argument addresses these claims and disarms them, it remains clearly stronger than the others. Unlike them, it sketches a defense of preferential hiring that is at least theoretically adequate. But it is stronger in another way. Although the compensatory argument does require empirical evidence, the evidence it requires is of a comparatively limited statistical sort. What it must show is only that certain backgrounds are strongly correlated with reduced adult abilities. By contrast, what the utilitarian and egalitarian must establish is much more global. They must show that a system of preferential hiring will increase overall utility or equally when *all* of its numerous effects are taken into consideration. This claim requires the integration of much more complex data, and so is far harder to document adequately. Thus, even on purely practical grounds, the compensatory argument seems clearly stronger.

These considerations rebut the charge that we are applying a double standard. However, at the same time, they raise other questions. Which characteristics, if any, *are* so strongly correlated with wrongfully reduced abilities that they warrant preferential treatment? In particular, is this true of membership in previously discriminated-against groups? If it is, then haven't the pressures of practicality forced us to retreat to the very group approach that we rejected earlier?

Despite appearances, I do not believe they have. There is little doubt that membership in discriminated-against groups will often display *some* correlation with reduced competitive ability. It is, however, far less clear that such correlations are strong enough to warrant preferential hiring along group lines. To establish this, one would have to show that (a) affording preference to all group members will move us closer to a situation in which everyone occupies his rightful competitive place, that (b) no other identifiable policy of preference will move us even closer to that situation, and that (c) if preference along group lines *does* bring us as close as possible to a situation in which everyone occupies his rightful competitive place, it should be adopted despite any new injustices it may produce. There are, however, serious questions on all three counts.

For consider, first, the claim that affording preference to all group members will move us closer to a situation in which everyone occupies his rightful competitive place.[16] Given the remarks of the previous section, this claim seems obviously false for women. But what is less obvious is that it may well be false for blacks as well. We have seen that the competitive positions of many blacks probably were reduced by past discrimination. However, we have also seen that if preference is extended equally to all blacks, then the blacks who are hired will generally be those whose abilities were reduced the least (or were not reduced at all). Whenever this happens, a wrong will be done to the best-qualified white applicant who is by-passed. In addition, a further wrong may be done to a different black applicant who would have been best qualified in the absence of wrongdoing. It was partly to avoid such difficulties that we insisted on matching degrees of preference to degrees of reduction in competitive ability. However, if we simply extend preference to all group members, then any such matching is eliminated. Hence, the objection returns in full force.

In view of this, it is far from obvious that a policy of uniform preference for all members of discriminated-against groups would move us closer to a situation in which everyone occupies his rightful competitive place. However, even if such a policy did have this result, it would still not be justified; for policies that move us even further in this direction are easily identified. To arrive at such policies, we need only refine the list of features that we take to indicate wrongfully reduced competitive abilities. Of the possible ways of doing this, one is to reduce or eliminate preference for blacks who have affluent backgrounds and good educations, or who have only recently come to this country. By making this change, we reduce the risk that the wrong persons will receive preference. In addition, we may further extend our policy by affording preference to both blacks *and* whites whose abilities were lowered by crime or other non-discriminatory forms of wrongdoing. We may even afford it to everyone whose upbringing was extremely harsh or impoverished. At first glance, this last suggestion seems to be ruled out by the requirement that the reduction in competitive position be *wrongful*. However, it is not ruled out if every child in an affluent society is entitled to a certain level of comfort, education, and support. On this assumption, any extremely harsh and impoverished childhood can itself be said to be wrongfully inflicted.

Given these and other possible refinements, there are clearly ways of affording preference that are more just than simple preference by race. If any system of preferential hiring is adopted, it should be one of these. But before we accept any such system, we must resolve a final serious difficulty. No matter how strongly a set of traits is correlated with reduced competitive ability, any system that favors all persons displaying those traits will mistakenly afford preference to some persons whose competitive positions were *not* reduced by the effects of wrongdoing. Hence any such system will invariably treat some best-qualified applicants unjustly. Because this is so, we cannot pass final judgment on any preferential system until we have determined the relative moral value of compensating for old wrongs and creating new ones. Shall we say that there is a flat equivalence here—that we should do anything that minimizes the net balance of unrectified wrongs? Shall we entirely reject this balancing approach, and say that no number of rectifications of old wrongs warrants the creation of any new ones? Shall we take a middle position, and say that new wrongs are tolerable only when the gains in rectified old ones are very great? These questions are deep, difficult, and beyond our present scope. However, the problem of preferential hiring cannot be fully resolved until they are answered.

§12 *WEBER* REVISITED

Given these unanswered questions, we cannot yet say that any specific program of preferential hiring is definitely justified. However, what we can say is that some such programs *might* be justified, while others are definitely unjustified. Having come this far, we may now return briefly to the question with which we began. On what moral grounds, if any, can the preferential hiring program of the Kaiser Aluminum Company be defended?

Of the possible answers to this question, one is that the program brings various benefits to an impoverished black community; another is that it rectifies an obvious imbalance in the occupations of local blacks and whites. However, these arguments are obviously variants of the appeals to utility and equality; and such appeals have already been found to raise serious difficulties. Thus, our discussion suggests that if the Kaiser program is to be defended, it must be on some other basis. In particular, what its defender must argue is that it is justified on compensatory grounds.

Interestingly enough, the argument that Kaiser used before the Supreme Court *was* a compensatory one. The company was not itself accused of discrimination, and did not admit to it in legal argument. Nevertheless, it maintained that its preferential hiring plan was needed to rectify the more general effects of past societal discrimination. However, although the Supreme Court found this argument legally persuasive, our preceding discussion suggests a problem with it. We have seen that preferential hiring cannot be justified as compensation for any and all harmful effects of past discrimination. Instead, the effects to be compensated for must take the form of reductions in job qualifications. Hence, to complete the moral argument for the Kaiser program, one must establish that many of its beneficiaries are likely to have had their qualifications for the company's craft training program reduced by previous discrimination.

If admission to the Kaiser program depended on competitive test scores, then the question of whether the qualifications of the program's beneficiaries were wrongfully reduced would not be resolvable in advance. In that case, the question would be a factual one, and its answer would require empirical documentation. But given the actual situation, an easier resolution is possible. Admission to the Kaiser program was based not on skill or ability, but instead on simple seniority. Because it was, past societal discrimination could not have reduced the competitive position of any applicant. Instead, an applicant's competitive position could have been reduced only by the past behavior of Kaiser itself. If in the past that company had discriminatorily resisted hiring black workers, then its present black employees would have been wrongfully prevented from amassing as much seniority as they otherwise would have had.

Given these considerations, the moral justifiability of the Kaiser program depends entirely on the past actions of Kaiser itself. At first glance, this may appear decisive against the program; for we have seen that Kaiser neither acknowledged nor was accused of past racial discrimination. However, there may be a final irony here. It has been suggested that "close scrutiny of its past employment practices would undoubtedly have given the company a reasonable basis for believing it had used some discriminatory practices previously,"[17] and that Kaiser did not admit this because it feared "lawsuits by other individuals and by the government."[18] If so, then the program may in the end be morally justified for reasons quite unrelated to Kaiser's official arguments. But whether or not it is, the justifiability of other preferential programs the reader is likely to encounter remains a separate question. There is no reason to expect the answer to *that* question to be either uniform or easy to ascertain.

NOTES

1. It is surprisingly hard to say *why* these sorts of criteria are fair. For discussion, see George Sher, "What Makes a Lottery Fair?" *Noûs*, 14 (1980), pp. 203–16.

2. For a discussion of these issues, see Alan Wertheimer, "Jobs, Qualifications, and Preferences," *Ethics*, forthcoming.

3. For an exchange on hiring goals, see Alan H. Goldman, "Affirmative Action," *Philosophy and Public Affairs*, 5, 2 (Winter 1976), pp. 178–95; Gertrude Ezorsky, "Hiring Women Faculty," *Philosophy and Public Affairs*, 7, 1 (Fall 1977), pp. 82–91; and Alan H. Goldman, "Correspondence," *Philosophy and Public Affairs*, 7, 4 (Summer 1978), pp. 391–93.

4. This suggestion is defended in Paul W. Taylor, "Reverse Discrimination and Compensatory Justice," *Analysis*, 33, 6 (June 1973), pp. 177–82, and Michael D. Bayles, "Reparations to Wronged Groups," *Analysis*, 33, 6 (June 1973), pp. 182–84.

5. This and related arguments are elaborated in George Sher, "Groups and Justice," *Ethics*, 87, 2 (January 1977), pp. 174–81.

6. For discussion of these facts in a legal context, see Owen M. Fiss, "Groups and the Equal Protection Clause," *Philosophy and Public Affairs*, 5, 2 (Winter 1976), pp. 107–77.

7. For versions of the utilitarian argument, see Thomas Nagel, "Equal Treatment and Compensatory Discrimination," *Philosophy and Public Affairs*, 2, 4 (Summer 1973), pp. 348–63, and Ronald Dworkin, *Taking Rights Seriously* (Cambridge, Mass.: Harvard, 1977), pp. 223–39.

8. This argument is advanced by John Rawls in *A Theory of Justice* (Cambridge, Mass.: Harvard, 1971), p. 104; see also pp. 15, 75–76, 310–15, and *passim*. For another version, see Richard Wasserstrom, "The University and the Case for Preferential Treatment," *American Philosophical Quarterly*, 13, 2 (April 1976), p. 167.

9. For elaboration of the argument of this paragraph, see George Sher, "Effort, Ability, and Personal Desert," *Philosophy and Public Affairs*, 8, 4 (Summer 1979), pp. 361–76.

10. Joel Feinberg, "The Nature and Value of Rights," in Samuel Gorovitz et al., eds., *Moral Problems in Medicine* (Englewood Cliffs, N.J.: Prentice-Hall, 1976), p. 456. For further discussion, see Joel Feinberg, "Justice and Personal Desert," in his *Doing and Deserving: Essays in the Theory of Responsibility* (Princeton: Princeton University Press, 1970), pp. 55–94.

11.   There is a further reason to take seriously the claims of the best qualified. If someone has developed his skills under a system that awards jobs on the basis of qualifications, then it seems unjust to change the rules after he has invested his effort, and so to frustrate his legitimate expectations. But although such expectations do have significant moral force, they do not tell against all forms of preferential hiring. In particular, they do not tell against that practice when the intention to grant preference has been announced well in advance.

12.   See Robert Simon, "Preferential Hiring: A Reply to Judith Jarvis Thomson," *Philosophy and Public Affairs*, 3, 3 (Spring 1974), pp. 312-20.

13.   Nagel, "Equal Treatment and Compensatory Discrimination," p. 360.

14.   For further discussion, see George Sher, "Justifying Reverse Discrimination in Employment," *Philosophy and Public Affairs*, 4, 2 (Winter 1975), pp. 159-90.

15.   Some problems with the idea that such a system is unjust are explored in George Sher, "Our Preferences, Ourselves," *Philosophy and Public Affairs*, 12, 1 (Winter 1983), pp. 34-50.

16.   If compensatory justice demands that we rectify the effects of even the most ancient of wrongs, then rectifying the effects of recent wrongs is unlikely to bring us any closer to a totally just distribution of goods. However, there are good grounds for believing that claims to compensation fade with time, and that ancient wrongs therefore do *not* call for compensation. For details, see George Sher, "Ancient Wrongs and Modern Rights," *Philosophy and Public Affairs*, 10, 1 (Winter 1981), pp. 3-17.

17.   Robert K. Fullinwider, *The Reverse Discrimination Controversy* (Totowa, N.J.: Rowman and Littlefield, 1980), p. 138.

18.   *Ibid.*, p. 137.

SUGGESTIONS FOR FURTHER READING

Two helpful general discussions of preferential treatment are Robert K. Fullinwider, *The Reverse Discrimination Controversy* (Totowa, N.J.: Rowman and Littlefield, 1980), and Alan H. Goldman, *Justice and Reverse Discrimination* (Princeton: Princeton University Press, 1979). A valuable collection of essays, including several of those cited above, can be found in Marshall Cohen, Thomas Nagel, and Thomas Scanlon, eds., *Equality and Preferential Treatment* (Princeton: Princeton University Press, 1977).

In addition, discussion of particular issues raised in the text can be found in the following books and articles.

§5.   A classic statement of the utilitarian position is John Stuart Mill, *Utilitarianism* (Indianapolis: Hackett, 1978). For clear discussion of the theory's virtues and defects, see J.J.C. Smart and Bernard Williams, *Utilitarianism: For and Against* (Cambridge: Cambridge University Press, 1973). Somewhat more difficult, but also very illuminating, is David Lyons, *The Forms and Limits of Utilitarianism* (Oxford: The Clarendon Press, 1965).

§6.   The concept of equality has been much discussed by philosophers. For three excellent treatments, see Gregory Vlastos, "Justice and Equality," in Richard B. Brandt, ed., *Social Justice* (Englewood Cliffs, N.J.: Prentice-Hall, 1962), pp. 31-72; Bernard Williams, "The Idea of Equality," in Peter Laslett and W. G. Runciman, eds., *Philosophy, Politics, and Society*, Second Series (New York: Barnes and Noble, 1962), pp. 110-31; and Michael Walzer, "In Defense of Equality," *Dissent* (Fall 1973), pp. 399-408. A collection that includes discussions of equal opportunity and other pertinent topics (as well as the Williams paper just cited) is Jane English, ed., *Sex Equality* (Englewood Cliffs, N.J.: Prentice-Hall, 1977).

§7.   For illuminating discussion of the concept of desert, see James Rachels, "What People Deserve," in John Arthur and William H. Shaw, eds. *Justice and Economic Distribution* (Englewood Cliffs, N.J.: Prentice-Hall, 1978), pp. 150–64; and all the essays in Joel Feinberg, *Doing and Deserving* (Princeton: Princeton University Press, 1970). For discussion of rights, see David Lyons, ed., *Rights* (Belmont, Calif.: Wadsworth, 1979). Also relevant to the claims of the best qualified is Norman Daniels, "Meritocracy," in Arthur and Shaw, *Justice and Economic Distribution*.

§8.   For a discussion that places compensation within the framework of a wider approach to justice, see Robert Nozick, *Anarchy, State, and Utopia* (New York: Basic Books, 1974), ch. 7, sec. 1. Nozick's views are interestingly criticized by David Lyons in "The New Indian Claims and the Original Right to Land," *Social Theory and Practice*, 4, 3 (1977), pp. 249–72. For discussion of compensation to blacks, see Boris Bittker, *The Case for Black Reparations* (New York: Random House, 1973).

§10.   For additional discussion of the case for affording preference to women, see Mary Ann Warren, "Secondary Sexism and Quota Hiring," *Philosophy and Public Affairs*, 6, 3 (Spring 1977), pp. 240–61, and Anne C. Minas, "How Reverse Discrimination Compensates Women," *Ethics*, 88, 1 (October 1977), pp. 74–79.

§11.   The need to couch discussions of justice in statistical terms, and some of the problems it raises, are interestingly discussed by Lester Thurow in "A Theory of Groups and Economic Redistribution," *Philosophy and Public Affairs*, 9, 1 (Fall 1979), pp. 25–41. The inevitability of weighing different types of injustice when we select our policies is discussed in the context of punishment by Alan Wertheimer in "Punishing the Innocent—Unintentionally," *Inquiry*, 20 (1977), pp. 45–65. The related question of whether it is worse to initiate harm than merely to tolerate it is explored in the essays in Bonnie Steinbock, ed., *Killing and Letting Die* (Englewood Cliffs, N.J.: Prentice-Hall, 1980).

3

Duties to One's Employer

KURT BAIER

=================================== ‹〉› ===================================

§1 THE PROBLEM EXPLAINED

It may seem that there can be no serious controversy about the duties to one's employer: Employees, it may be thought, simply have all the duties everyone has — not to harm, deceive, hurt others, and so on — and in addition all and only those that they have agreed to in their employment contracts. But is this really so? Do not employees have, for instance, the duty to be loyal to the employer, that is, not to divulge business secrets or compete with the employer, to obey all lawful orders and instructions, to exercise reasonable care and skill, to disclose to the employer all relevant information acquired in the course of his work, not to delegate his duties to others where his skill and discretion play a part, fully to document his use of company money and property, and the like? Employees now have these duties by law and so have them independently of whether or not they have agreed to them in their employment contract. And is not this quite right and proper?

Conversely, are all tasks really their duties as long as they have contractually undertaken them? For some time now, the federal government has administered a number of equal opportunity and worker protection laws, federal health and safety regulations, federal protection of workers' pensions, legal protection against sexual harassment by superiors, and the like. This, together with a widespread rise in expectations of many kinds, has spawned demands for greater job satisfaction, for greater attention to employee interests and grievances, and for greater freedom in respect of dress, lifestyle, political ideology, and expression. Against this background, employees have claimed new rights, such as rights of expression and dissent (for instance, dissent concerning the marketing of unsafe products, safety and health hazards on the job, pollution of the environment, payment of bribes and kickbacks, or the greasing of the palms of government officials); rights of employee privacy (such as not being asked about race, religion, or sex, where this is irrelevant to job performance); not using certain forms of job surveillance (e.g., closed-circuit TV, lie detectors, phone taps, and so on); rights of fair procedure and due process (such as instituting grievance and appeal procedures, and supervision and review of such procedures by ombudsmen, employee advocates, or even outside arbitration); rights of participation on the board of directors or at lower levels of decision-making; and rights to information (for instance, about the effect on employees of work with substances and products involving health hazards). Should the legitimate interests of employees in these matters be protected only if they have insisted on them in their employment contract? Can employees be expected to have the courage to insist on them?

Again, what are we to say when the contractually undertaken tasks are immoral or illegal? Does a person who has been specifically hired to kill someone or, less dramatically, has been instructed by his employer to offer some government official a bribe in order to land a government contract, have a duty to do what he contracted, or to carry out the employer's instructions? Suppose it also involves "laundering money," doctoring the firm's accounts, and defrauding internal revenue? Even if bribing foreign government officials is not against the law (in this country it was not, prior to 1977),[1] is it not, nevertheless, *morally wrong* and for this reason alone the employee's duty (at least her moral duty) not to follow this instruction by her employer, even if she has contractually agreed to carry out all his orders?

Some will agree that employees do not have a duty to carry out illegal or immoral contractual provisions. They may even concede that they have a moral duty not to carry them out. Milton Friedman suggests that business discharges its moral duty "so long as it stays within the rules of the game, which is to say, engages in an open and free competition, *without deception or fraud.*"[2] Theodore Levitt suggests that the employee's moral duty is only "to obey the canons of everyday face-to-face civility (honesty, good faith, *and so on*)."[3]

But this raises new difficulties. What exactly are "the rules of the game" and "the canons of civility" Friedman and Levitt refer to? Is loyalty to the employer one of these rules or canons? Is palm-greasing or misleading advertising or selling dangerous products part of face-to-face civility, part of playing the game? And what about business bluffing, dumping dangerous wastes, keeping down costs by saving on safety features? Is that now part of the way the game is played?

A second difficulty is this: Do the moral constraints give rise merely to moral duties? Could it then be someone's *legal* duty to perform the tasks he has undertaken in his employment contract and his *moral* duty not to? And which should one carry out if one cannot do both, the legal or the moral, or sometimes one, sometimes the other? Or does one always have only one duty, either the duty to perform or the duty not to perform a certain act, and never both, even if the two duties are of different kinds, one moral, one legal?

Are we perhaps making a mountain out of a molehill? After all, moral duties in conflict with contractual ones are employee duties not to the employer but to other people, whereas here we are concerned only with duties to one's employer. Well, perhaps so. But we still need an explanation of the distinction between employees' duties *to their employers* and their other duties. We shall want to know, for instance, what difference it makes whether an employee's duty is one to her employer, to someone else, or just a duty to no one in particular; which class of tasks undertaken by the employee in her employment contract are her duties and which are not, and why this is so; whether her duties to her employer always or never outweigh her other duties (for instance, those to her family, her customers, or society); and, if in some cases they outweigh the others and in some they do not, when they do and why. We shall want to know whether having a duty to an employer implies that intentionally not carrying it out would be unwise, illegal, immoral, all of these, or something else. Does one have only those duties one has voluntarily and explicitly taken on? Can one take on *any* duty in this way? Does one acquire duties simply by virtue of coming to play a particular role? Does one have them even if one has come to play that role against one's will? (Suppose one has become a mother because one has been raped. Does one then have all or indeed any of the duties that attach to the role of being a mother?) How stringent are the duties of a given role, say, in relation to the duties of other roles, or to duties acquired in other ways?

Part of the problem is that the question of what the duties of employees to their employers are hinges on the contested nature and function of a very complex institution, namely, business, in which the roles of employer and employee are embedded, and which shapes the roles of employees, whose duties we are trying to determine. It is difficult enough to answer the question when it is permissible or obligatory (if, indeed, it ever is) for one person to kill another. But the difficulties are compounded if the killing occurs in the performance of a certain role: Suppose the killer is a CIA employee charged with the task of "terminating" an enemy agent "with extreme prejudice"; or suppose the killer is a physician asked by the closest relatives to terminate the life of a patient who has been in a coma for some years but who, prior to lapsing into it, had expressed the wish to be kept alive should this happen. The problem of what is morally required of, or permitted to, persons in such circumstances is greatly complicated by the need to determine the relevant role-duties, and to reconcile them with all the other duties they might have. It is uncontroversial that the role-duties of a lifeguard include the duty to save the life of a drowning swimmer, even at great risk to himself, whereas other sunbathers do not have such an onerous or stringent duty. But it is not comparably clear what the role-duties of employees are, as opposed to those of non-employees, because the nature and function of the institution that determines the role-duties of the roles defined by it is not comparably clear.

Ideally, the result of our investigations would be a complete list of the duties to one's employer. However, in view of the complexities already sketched, this is plainly beyond the reach of an introductory treatment such as this. More realistically, we can hope to get clearer about something no less important, namely, *the method* for answering our central question: "What are the duties to one's employer?" My investigation here is organized around what today still is, at any rate to very many people in this country, the intrinsically most attractive and on the face of it highly plausible view, namely, the doctrine of contractual freedom. It says that our title question must be answered by reference to *the principle of contractual freedom*, which allows people complete freedom to enter into mutually binding agreements imposing duties and conferring rights on one another as they see fit, and that people therefore have, in relation to one another, only the rights and duties they have acquired in this way. As far as our title question is concerned, this principle gives support to the Contract Thesis (CT): Employees have *all* and *only* those duties that they have freely undertaken in their employment contract. The *method* for answering questions about employees' duties to their employers, then, given this approach, is always the same, even though the specific duties different employees have to their employers may differ. In each case, the way to find out what these duties are is to determine what tasks they have voluntarily undertaken in their employment contract.

How adequate is this method? More basically, how reasonable are its assumptions and implications? These are the central questions examined in this essay. This examination proceeds in the following way. In Section I, I examine the implications of CT, including the nature of duties, the various ways in which they are acquired, the relative strengths of the various types of duties, and the most telling objections to CT. The upshot of this section is that although some of these objections are based on wrong interpretations of CT, others are firmly anchored in plausible moral convictions widely held in our society and, therefore, need to be met if CT is to be found acceptable. In Section II, I outline one very widely held account of the nature and function of business, of the roles of employer and employee, and of the duties of the latter to the former. I then show how several widely held ethical theories, when applied to the role of business so conceived, appear to meet the difficulties for CT brought to light in Section I. Appearances are deceptive in this case, however, and I argue that these theories fail to rescue CT from the difficulties raised in Section I. The specific conclusions toward which we are working, then, are that widely accepted defenses of CT and its implied method for determining employees' duties to their employers are unsatisfactory. To know this much is not, of course, to know all there is to know about the vexing question of employees' duties to their employers, but it answers the most fundamental question and lays firm foundations for further normative inquiries.

I. PROBLEMS FOR THE CONTRACT THESIS

§2 THE CONTRACT THESIS

The Contract Thesis (CT) assumes that employers and employees should be free to determine in their employment contract what rights they have against and what duties to one another. CT is intrinsically appealing because it results from the application of two very attractive general principles to the domain of voluntary interaction between people. The first is what might be called the Doctrine of Freedom, that within certain limits people should be free to do whatever they see fit to do. In the domain of voluntary interaction this means that they should be free to undertake whatever tasks or services they see fit to shoulder. The second is the plausible *Volenti non fit iniuria*, the principle that what a person voluntarily agrees to cannot be a harm or injury to him.

Nobody accepts the Doctrine of Freedom without qualifications. Many have followed the nineteenth-century English philosopher John Stuart Mill in holding that liberty may be restricted only for the purpose of preventing people from using their liberty to harm others. Other thinkers insist that additional restrictions are necessary, for instance, the offense principle (people should be prevented from causing offense to others); the principle of legal paternalism (people should be prevented from inflicting harm on themselves); or the principle of legislating morals (people should be prevented from violating important moral principles). We have already encountered two formulations of such restrictions, Friedman's prohibition of deception and fraud and Levitt's preservation of the canons of everyday civility. However, we must postpone examination of these constraints on CT until later (§7ff).

Right now, we must look at another problem, namely, how strong a reading it is reasonable to give to CT. In its strongest interpretation, CT means that whatever tasks employees undertake in their employment contracts are their duties, and nothing else is their duty. However, this is implausible. A person also plays other roles, such as parent, teacher, spouse or citizen, and so has additional duties arising out of these other roles. Clearly, CT need not be taken to imply that employees can have only those duties that they have *as* employees; that they can have only their *employee role*-duties. We should, therefore, grant right away that CT should be interpreted to mean, not that employees have no duties other than their role-duties, but rather that employees' *role*-duties to their employer are all and only those that they have freely agreed to in their employment contract.

But what exactly are "employee *role*-duties"? How do they differ from the other duties an employee has? How exactly are they acquired? Only by freely agreeing to them? By coming to play the role of employee? In yet other ways? And what if an employee role-duty conflicts with another of his duties? Let us look at this more closely.

§3 DEFINITION OF "DUTY"

A duty is the required performance of a task, an end one *must* (try to) attain, whether the end is merely the doing of something quite simple, such as stamping and mailing the day's mail, or the more difficult responsibility of bringing about, maintaining, or preventing a certain desirable and complex state of affairs, such as getting the business out of the red, keeping it out, or preventing it from slipping into it. A task is one of my duties only if I am *required*, and not merely encouraged or asked, to perform it. This means that certain other people, *to whom* I have the duty, may *insist* that I perform it, and may, if they wish, impose certain burdens on me if I fail to perform it without justification or adequate excuse. We can thus normally distinguish between the person who *has* a duty (the "duty-bearer"), the person *to whom* he has it (the "duty-principal"), *the task* in which the duty consists (the "duty-content"), the *reason why* a duty-bearer has a certain duty (the "duty-ground"), and *what may be done to* the duty-bearer if he fails to carry out his duty without an exculpatory explanation (the "duty-sanction").

Our main question is, of course, *what* (if any) duty a given person has at a given time. To answer this, we must know how people acquire specific duties. But this, in turn, gives rise to a second problem, namely, what we are to say when the method for telling what specific duties a given person has acquired ascribes conflicting duties to him. We must deal briefly with this second problem before looking into how we acquire specific duties.

§4 TYPES OF DUTY-CLAIM

Our talk of duties is designed to answer the question of what, morally speaking, one *must* or *ought to* do here and now — what one has here and now a duty to do, all things *considered*. We arrive at this answer by examining the various things it *appears* one has a duty to do and by eliminating those that are mere appearances or compounding those that are real but only partial duties into an overall, final duty, a duty, all things (that is, all apparent duties) considered.

Suppose Jones has a role-duty to advance the sales of his firm's products. Suppose also that his firm manufactures lawn mowers that are hazardous and that he knows to be so. And let us finally also suppose that we all, including of course Jones, have a duty to refrain from knowingly doing what would put someone else at serious risk of harm. There is, then, a clash between Jones' duty not to put anyone at such risk and his employee role-duty to advance the sales of his firm's lawn mowers. The conflict arises because his duty to his firm amounts to doing something that would be a case of knowingly putting someone at serious risk of harm.

Duties that conflict in this way can be said to be *contradictory*, since one would be contradicting oneself if one claimed that one had carried out both. If two duties are contradictory, then one of them is not a real but a merely apparent or presumptive duty. The circumstances are such that there is a presumption (an appearance) of there being a duty, but the appearance is illusory, the presumption has been rebutted by the existence of the other contradictory and stronger duty. Claiming a presumptive (or apparent) duty is noncommittal about whether or not it is a real duty. If the claim can be rebutted in this way, then the duty is a *merely* presumptive (or apparent) duty.

Consider now another way in which apparent or presumptive duties may come into conflict. Suppose Jones has concluded a contract with an African customer to deliver five thousand machine guns in June. Then we think that he, and through him his firm, have a duty to do so, unless some other "stronger" or "more stringent" duty incompatible with this one requires the firm to set this one aside. Suppose that, for a variety of reasons beyond its control, Jones' firm has fallen behind in its production of tanks, which it has contracted to supply to its own government in May, and that it could, by suitably redeploying its labor force, meet on time either the government or the African contract but not both. Such duties are practically incompatible duties. If, in the example at hand, the government contract imposes a *more stringent* duty, as we may assume, then Jones' employer has a duty to redeploy his work force so as to discharge his commitment to the government and postpone delivery to the African customer. But that is not the end of the matter. Jones', and his firm's, failure to do their duty by the African customer now creates a new, substitute or successor duty: to send an explanation and apology, to promise and make supreme efforts to deliver as soon as possible, and to make amends in various ways, perhaps by a reduction in price, by supplying an additional machine gun or two, by a promise of free maintenance and spare parts, by a suitable present for the colonel, or by whatever would seem to be appropriate compensation for non-performance of duty.

Philosophers call Jones' duty to the African customer a "prima facie duty"[4] (or a "duty other things equal") *but not* an "overall duty" (or a "duty all things considered"), and they call Jones' (and his firm's) duty to the government *both* a "prima facie duty" *and* an "overall duty." This distinction between two senses of "having a duty" allows us to say that a person, at time *t*, has both a (prima facie) duty to do A and an (overall) duty to do B, although doing B is practically incompatible with doing A at the same time. Of course having a prima facie (unlike having an overall) duty to do A at time *t* does not entail that one *must* do A at that time.

Thus, what someone's duty at a particular time actually is, that is, what that person at that time must actually do, is determined by compounding in a suitable way the various prima facie, that is, *partial* duties he has acquired into a total, overall, final duty, much as the resultant force impressed on a body is compounded out of the various partial forces impressed on it. However, prima facie duties do not merge or fuse into an overall duty in the additive way in which partial forces merge or fuse into a resultant force; the final duty is not a fusion, compound, or amalgam of his prima facie duties. The duty-bearer must therefore rank-order, suitably reschedule, and adequately supplement them. For by (quite correctly) setting aside the less stringent prima facie duties, the duty-bearer may nevertheless incur a "new" prima facie duty to compensate the innocent duty-principal whose right to some benefit had to be overridden in order to honor the more stringent right of another duty-principal, as occurs, for example, when Jones' firm offers a reduced price to its African customers.

The main difference between these two kinds of conflict is that, whereas in the case of two practically incompatible prima facie duties, the *overridden* duty still imposes *some* task on the duty-bearer, in the case of contradictory duties the less stringent duty is revealed as really never having imposed any task. The less stringent duty is not merely set aside for the moment to be carried out later, but is exposed as mere appearance. A specific prima facie duty that has been overridden must still be honored somehow, perhaps by being carried out later or by some substitute performance, but a rebutted presumptive duty, that is, a *merely* presumptive duty, need not be honored at all.

Thus Jones' duty to advance the sales of his firm's lawn mowers and his duty not to put someone else at serious risk of harm are not just two practically incompatible prima facie duties, but contradictory ones. Jones's duty not to put anyone at risk implies the duty not to sell the dangerous lawn mowers and so contradicts his duty to advance their sales. The less stringent one is a merely presumptive duty. Unlike an *overridden* prima facie duty, the *rebutted* presumptive duty plays no part in determining the overall duty.

Contrary to linguistic appearance, the distinction between presumptive, prima facie, and final duties is not one between types of duty — such "duties" are merely candidates for that position and may be defeated by other stronger (more stringent) rivals — but between duty-claims of different degrees of abstraction. Presumptive duties are the most, final duties the least abstract. The claim that an action is a *final duty* says that all relevant matters have been considered, that nothing further could come to light to defeat the claim that this is what must be done here and now. That an action is a *prima facie duty* says merely that it is a real candidate for being what a specific person must do here and now, but that it may yet be defeated by some other equally real but stronger candidate. That an action is a presumptive duty is more abstract still. It says only that the task *appears* to be a candidate for being what that person must do, but implies that the appearance *may be* deceptive. That an action is a *merely* presumptive duty says the same thing, except that it implies that the appearance *is* deceptive.

These distinctions throw light on our title question. Plainly it does not concern the overall duty of employees to their employer at a particular time, for that would involve weighing their various prima facie duties to their employer against one another as well as against their prima facie duties to other people, such as their customers, their family, or society at large. Clearly, we cannot hope (at any rate in this paper, if indeed anywhere) to produce a *general* answer to this most concrete and context-dependent question about employees' duties to their employer.

Our title question, therefore, must mean, "What are the presumptive duties one has *as* an employee to one's employer?" or in other words, "What are employees' *role*-duties to their employer?" An answer to this more abstract and considerably narrower question can leave entirely open what, if any, other (non-employee-role) prima facie duties specific employees have to their employers, and which of these various prima facie duties are the most stringent.

§5 TYPES OF DUTY

As we have seen, presumptive, prima facie, and final duties are best thought of, not as types of duty, but as duty-claims of different degrees of abstractness. Any type of duty can appear in duty-claims of any of these types. However, for purposes of determining someone's final duty, we need to know the various grounds that generate presumptive duties and the degrees of their stringency. It will, therefore, be helpful to survey some of the most important types of duty distinguished in our morality and the degree of relative stringency we ascribe to them.

The most general duty-ground is that of having the capacities of a duty-subject (e.g., the ability to think impartially). This ground gives rise to what are often called unconditional duties. They are called that because no condition beyond being a duty-subject, which is taken to be normally satisfied, is necessary. Unconditional duties are universal in the sense that all duty-subjects have them and have them as long as they retain the relevant capacities. Thus, cats and babies, because they do not have these capacities, also do not have unconditional duties (or, for that matter, any others). However, as soon as a child becomes a duty-subject, he or she becomes a duty-bearer of all unconditional duties.

It follows from this that everyone who can have duties at all always has some presumptive duties, namely, the unconditional ones. And these will be overall duties in a given case unless rebutted or overridden by others. Of course, if as is widely believed, all unconditional duties are negative ones, such as "Thou shalt not kill," "Thou shalt not lie," and so on, then this is not usually much of a constraint on us, since usually we shall not be tempted to do these things. Such negative duties, since they do not tell us what we must but only what we must not do, usually merely close off certain specific lines of action, leaving everything else open. As we shall see more fully below (§6), however, serious questions arise regarding whether the duties some employees have to their employers ever rebut their unconditional duties.

By contrast, *conditional duties*, those that arise only under certain conditions, require more than the capacity involved in being a duty-subject. Such duties can be acquired in three different ways. They can be incurred, imposed, or assumed. Like unconditional duties, incurred ones are acquired independently of anyone's say-so, whereas imposed and assumed duties are acquired because of someone's say-so. Unconditional and incurred duties, because they do not come into being by someone's will, are sometimes lumped together as *natural* or will-independent duties, whereas imposed and assumed duties are classified together as *artificial* or will-dependent duties.

Here are two examples of incurred duties. First, if, on a little-traveled country road, one passes someone who has had an accident and who needs help, one then incurs the (so-called Good Samaritan) duty to extend that help. Second, if, for instance, one manufactures and sells lawn mowers made of materials that tend to shatter and cause injuries to the user, one then incurs the duty to compensate those who have suffered injuries and also the duty to stop selling this type of lawn mower until that flaw is remedied.

Will-dependent duties, by contrast, are acquired through someone's say-so, either the duty-bearer's or the duty-principal's. The duty to keep a promise is illustrative of the former. Because, in our morality, every duty-subject has the authority to *assume* duties by his or her own say-so, each can (within certain limits) be the author of exactly the duty each wants to acquire.

In our morality, duties can also be *imposed*, that is, acquired by someone else's say-so. Legislators, officers, employers, and teachers have such "ex-officio" authority over their subjects, subalterns, employees, and pupils. That is to say, these authority-principals may, of course only within the scope of their authority, give directives to their authority-subjects, who, as a result, acquire duties to do what they have thus been directed to do. Each such duty ends when it has been discharged, though one's general duty to carry out the directives (if any) of the authority remains in existence as long as one is subject to that authority. Whether one has a particular imposed duty thus depends on whether one is subject to such an authority and whether that authority has directed one to do something (within its competence) that one has not yet done.

In an employment contract, the two will-dependent ways of acquiring duties are combined. Employees undertake to carry out not only the duties from a certain specific list in the employment contract, but also whatever further duties, within a certain acknowledged range, employers may from time to time impose on them by their explicit instructions.

§6 THE RELATIVE STRINGENCY OF NATURAL AND ARTIFICIAL DUTIES

It is plausible to think that natural duties are more stringent than artificial ones. We should think of a promise or an order that violated a natural duty as immoral and, therefore, as not giving rise to a duty or obligation to keep the promise or obey the order. The professional hit man who has freely undertaken or has been ordered by his Mafia boss to assassinate someone has not acquired an (artificial) prima facie duty to do so. The fact that he has made a promise or been given an order by his boss merely gives rise to the presumption that he has a (prima facie) duty to keep his promise or carry out this order. But as soon as the duty-content comes to light, it becomes clear that the presumption is rebutted, because his natural duty not to kill anyone precludes that artificial duty from coming into existence, that is, precludes a claim that he has a prima facie duty with that content from being true.

Are natural duties always dominant over institutional role-duties? We can think of institutional ethics as the part of ethics dealing with artificial, including institutional role-duties, and of general ethics as the part dealing with natural duties. It may then be argued that general ethics is concerned with the demands that, as *independent moral agents*, we can in reason make on one another. Independent moral agents are people interacting with one another without being enmeshed in institutional nets, such as those created by the family, the law, or the world of business. In the capacity of independent moral agents, we pursue the ends whose attainment we think worthwhile. In that "non-institutional role," we can in reason demand essentially two things of one another: non-interference and mutual aid. We want non-interference so that we can better carry out our various life projects and so that we need not devote any of our resources to removing impediments other people have put in our way. But we also want assistance from one another when we cannot attain our ends by our own unaided efforts. Since we are making these demands on one another on a basis of reciprocity, we shall want and need guidelines that fairly balance our wish to be helped against other people's wishes not to be diverted from their pursuits by helping us with ours, and our wish not to be interfered with by others, against theirs to interfere when that is necessary for the attainment of their ends. Our basic moral precepts—not to kill, not to lie, not to inflict harm, or to help others in need—are such natural duties derived from general ethics, that is, from ethics dealing with the interrelationships between independent moral agents.

Plainly, most if not all actual moralities go beyond general ethics. Even relatively simple societies regulate more than that. The Ten Commandments, in addition to "Thou shalt not kill" and "Thou shalt not lie," also include "Thou shalt not covet thy neighbor's house" and "Thou shalt not commit adultery," which spell out the institutional duties arising out of the institution of property and marriage. Such positive moralities, in other words, give their backing to society's institutions with their peculiar role-ends, duties and rights. From the moral point of view, such institutions are thus seen as ways in which members of the society may legitimately interact with one another to mutual benefit. Conformity with the role-rights and role-duties is expected to promote the role-ends, and the attainment of the role-ends is seen as making possible or facilitating a good life for all. Institutional role-rights and role-duties thus extend mutual help beyond the limited positive duty of the Good Samaritan, which alone comes out of general ethics. A great deal of mutual help is thus provided by the discharge of voluntarily assumed role-duties, because it is provided mainly by those who stand to others in special institutionally determined relationships, such as those of parent and child or those of employer and employee. And such role-duties normally are acquired only by the duty-bearer's having entered the role voluntarily, thereby assuming these role-duties.

Given this perspective on institutional ethics, it is quite plausible to think, as surely we do in our morality, that natural duties are more stringent than artificial ones. For it is plausible to think that our social institutions are ways of facilitating the achievements of what independent individuals would themselves want to achieve with as little mutual interference and as much mutual assistance as can in reason be demanded, namely, the good life as they conceive of it. The division of labor made possible by the existence of cooperative social institutions is intended to enable members of society to develop their special talents and to cater to individual tastes, as well as to free them from those tasks, necessary for the attainment of their respective ends, for the accomplishment of which others are better suited by their different talents and tastes than they are themselves. As a consequence, each of us can leave to others the provision of some of the things necessary for the good life as long as some institution—in our case mainly the market—provides for the transfer of the various necessities from those who produced them to those who need them. Of course, as is often emphasized by opponents of extreme individualism, such social institutions do not merely facilitate the attainment of ends already aimed at prior to the creation of these institutions, but often *create* entirely new pursuits, bring into existence new tastes, and call for new skills, thus providing for individuals wider ranges of attractive "career choices," greater scope for finding suitable niches and so greater opportunities for fulfillment. By the same token, they also create greater dangers that some will be excluded from worthwhile lives by being shunted into life patterns (such as those of slaves, untouchables, or members of a permanently unemployed underclass) in which they cannot find fulfillment.

The main requirement on the design of cooperative institutions would thus seem to be the coordination for common ends of many activities people find worthwhile on their own account or as means to these common ends. The ends are those that can have a place in the conception of the good life developed by members of the community. Entering on a career of teaching or business involves ends that are acceptable in our community. Making a living by prostitution or selling heroin, though widely embraced, are (rightly or wrongly) regarded as unacceptable by our morality.

A second requirement on institutional design is that the institutions attract an adequate number of people, either because they find the institutional roles created by the institutions intrinsically attractive or because they appreciate the desirability or necessity of filling these roles if certain other desired ends are also to be attained. Thus, the role of soldier satisfies this second requirement if a sufficient number voluntarily join the armed forces either because the role of soldier appeals to them on its own account or because people think it necessary or desirable to join in order to insure an adequate defense of the country, or perhaps because they cannot in any other way acquire the money they need or the skills they desire.

Viewed from this perspective, our institutions merely extend the scope of the natural duty of mutual aid by encouraging people to become enmeshed in special relationships with one another and attaching to these relationships additional (role-) duties whose performance provides direct or indirect mutual assistance. If general ethics deals with what we may in reason demand of one another as independent moral agents, institutional ethics deals with what we may in reason demand of one another as moral agents enmeshed in institutionally defined relationships. From this perspective, the primary moral question about institutional role-duties concerns their consistency with natural duties. For, on this view, the role-ends that are served by role-duties and role-rights must fit in with natural duties and rights. If the role-duties of an institution, such as those of slavery, untouchability, or suttee, violate natural rights and natural duties, as we think they do, then that institution is itself morally objectionable. Hence, on this plausible view, natural duties are more stringent than institutional role-duties. And this means that if an institutional role-duty *contradicts* a natural duty, the former is a *merely presumptive* duty; it does not amount to a genuine prima facie duty.

If this plausible view is sound and if, for instance, there is, as we all think, an unconditional natural duty not to put anyone at risk of serious harm, then the Contract Thesis (CT) cannot be sound even in the relatively weak interpretation we gave to it in §2. For, as we have seen, CT would imply that if Jones undertakes in his employment contract to promote the sale of his firm's products, then he has a prima facie duty to do so and must take it into account in determining his overall duty, even if the content of that duty is inconsistent with the content of his unconditional natural duty not to put anyone at serious risk. CT, in other words, implies that (artificial) employee role-duties are more stringent than natural duties, and so rebut them where they contradict them.

But does this really dispose of CT? Are natural duties really *always* more stringent than artificial ones? On closer inspection, it may not seem so. For example, are not the role-duties of the executioner and the soldier to kill certain people more stringent than the unconditional natural duty not to kill anyone? Well, perhaps (more on this in a moment). But even if these artificial duties are more stringent than the *unrestricted* natural duty against killing, that would not force us to abandon the general claim that natural duties are more stringent than artificial ones. We can maintain the greater stringency of natural duties if we suitably restrict their scope. For example, if the natural duty against killing is restricted to *innocent* persons, then the executioner can be held to be doing his real duty when he carries out his role-duty to kill persons properly found guilty of a crime and sentenced to death. Similarly, we can say that the role-duty of soldiers is only to kill the enemy and those only in a just war, that is, a war of self-defense, and that killing in self-defense is not a violation of our natural duty, because it does not involve killing the innocent. To restrict the scope of the natural duty against killing in this way will not cover some other roles, however, such as that of the spy and the counterespionage agent, for their roles involve the duty to obey orders to kill spies, counterespionage agents and government officials of other countries even *in times of peace*. Hence there is no case for saying that these people are not innocent.

Thus, instead of saying that our natural duty is "not to kill *any* human being" we can restrict the scope to "any *innocent* human being." And if even that reformulation fails to salvage one of the advocated artificial duties, as in the case of spies whose duty it may be to kill innocent persons, then we can say that our natural duty is "not to kill any innocent human being *except when*, as secret agents, we have been ordered by our superiors to do so." We can, that is, maintain the plausible and useful universality and superior stringency of natural over artificial duties by suitably reformulating the content of natural duties. For this reason, we cannot simply argue that, because natural duties are universal and more stringent than artificial ones, an artificial duty that contradicts a natural duty, as currently formulated, *must be a merely* presumptive one. The real issue is not whether our natural duties *in their current formulation* do or do not contradict a given institutional role-duty, such as that of the executioner or the secret agent, but rather whether there is an *adequate justification* for that institution and for its institutional roles, which give rise to prima facie role-duties contradicting natural duties in their current formulation. In the case of the executioner's role we need a justification of the death penalty; in the soldier's, a justification of war; in the secret agent's, a justification for spying on others and preventing others from spying on us. If we can provide these justifications, then these role-duties are more stringent than those natural duties that they contradict in their current formulation. But then we need suitably to contract the scope of natural duties so as to make them consistent with these more stringent role-duties.

There is thus reasonable doubt about the soundness of the commonsense view that natural duties (in their current formulation) are always and from their nature dominant over artificial ones. Its great plausibility may rest on the fact that this principle of dominance is a merely regulative one — one telling us to adjust the scope of natural duties in such a way that the principle of dominance remains sound. If the principle of dominance is a merely regulative one, then it does not follow from the fact that there is a natural duty not to kill human beings that it cannot be anyone's role-duty to execute a man condemned to death, for it may be that the scope of that natural duty should be restricted to innocent human beings. The same question arises even in the cases of the killing of innocent civilians in wartime, and even in peacetime when the killing is done, say, by counterespionage agents in the course of an important mission. It also applies to our case of employee role-duties, for what should be dominant depends on the legitimate scope of our natural duties and the employee role-duties with which they conflict. To this topic we must now turn.

II. A DEFENSE OF THE CONTRACT THESIS

§7   THE ROLE-DUTIES OF BUSINESS EMPLOYEES

We must now turn to our main question, namely, "What are the role-duties specifically of employees in business?" To answer it, we must have some idea of how role-duties are determined. Clearly role-duties and role-rights depend on the nature of, and the function served by, the institution in which the roles in question are embedded. We must therefore say something about that nature and that function and spell out the part each of the relevant role-players is supposed to play in the performance of that function. In our case, the institution of business, the main roles could be said to be the employer, the employee, the customer, and society at large, if the last can be said to be a role. Since we are concerned only with employees' role-duties to their employers, I shall concentrate on the first two roles and their relationship.

How exactly can an understanding of the nature and function of the institution of business help us to determine the role-duties of the roles embedded in this institution? Clearly, the roles should be so designed that the exercise of the role-rights and the discharge of the role-duties adequately serves the performance of the function of the institution. We must, therefore, raise four critical questions. The first is whether the duties imposed are relevant or irrelevant to the performance of the role-function. The second is whether, though relevant, the duties are objectionable on other, more general grounds — for example, because they affront the dignity, autonomy, or self-respect of the role-players (especially, of course, those of employees and perhaps customers, who have the more vulnerable roles). The third is whether, though relevant to that function and not objectionable on these general grounds of respect for the person and protection of the underdog, they unfairly burden some and relieve others. The fourth and most difficult is whether the very function the institution is supposed to serve is morally acceptable, as perhaps that of the executioner or the spy or the agent-provocateur is not.

Suppose, then, that such an investigation of the nature and function of business can yield an answer to our main question about the role-duties of employees to their employer. Suppose, furthermore, that this method for dealing with our question can yield a correct answer in each case. Even if both these controversial assumptions were granted, it might still be desirable to have someone entrusted with the task of using this method with the understanding that his judgment would fix these duties, somewhat as a judge's verdict based on statute and precedent authoritatively fixes the legal rights and duties of the parties in the case before him. It may be desirable to have such authoritative settlements, because the method for determining these duties may result in different answers when used by different people. The need for such an authoritative decision-maker is, of course, even greater when the method does not always, even in theory, yield a correct answer. There appear to be the following major alternatives: (i) that the determination of employee role-duties should be left entirely to the individual employment contract (the principle of contractual freedom); (ii) that the law should spell out these duties for those and only those cases in which the individual employment contract is silent; (iii) that the law should lay down *minimal* duties, that is, those which employers and employees may not at will contract away, but that employers and employees should be free to settle on *additional* employee duties; (iv) that the law should lay down *maximal* employee duties, that is, those beyond which employees may not validly commit themselves by contractual stipulation, but that any employee duties *less onerous* may be freely agreed on between employer and employee; (v) that the law should lay down both the minimal and the maximal set of duties, leaving contractors free to fix by contractual stipulation only the range and the level of burdensomeness of employee duties within these outer bounds; (vi) that the law should determine all employee duties. For reasons already indicated we shall consider only the first arrangement, which is presupposed by the Contract Thesis.

§8 CONTRACTUAL FREEDOM AND LAISSEZ-FAIRE CAPITALISM

The nerve of the moral justification for this first arrangement is the contention that complete freedom from restrictions in the economic domain, including complete contractual freedom between employer and employee, apart from being intrinsically desirable, is also the best way to increase individual and social wealth, and, through it, individual and social good. In a famous passage, Adam Smith, the patron saint of laissez-faire capitalism, reasons as follows:

> As every individual . . . endeavours as much as he can both to employ his capital in the support of domestic industry and so to direct that industry that its produce may be of the greatest value, every individual necessarily labours to render the annual revenue of the society as great as he can. He, generally, indeed neither intends to promote the public interest, nor knows how much he is promoting it. By preferring the support of domestic to that of foreign industry, he intends only his own gain; and he is in this, as in many other cases, led by an invisible hand to promote an end which was not part of his intention. Nor is it always the

worse for the society that it was no part of it. By pursuing his own interest he frequently promotes that of the society more effectually than when
he really intends to promote it. I have never known much good done by
those who affected to trade for the public good. It is an affectation, indeed, not very common among merchants, and very few words need be
employed in dissuading them from it.[5]

Adam Smith here highlights three features of a laissez-faire capitalist
system that he thinks should recommend it to every rational person.
Such a system, Smith claims, promotes the good of society more effectually than other systems in which people are actually required to aim at
it. Next, it is not a utopian ideal since it makes very modest demands on
individual motivation. Indeed, all one is required to do is to promote
one's own best interest. There may be some who find it unpalatable to
follow the dictates of self-interest when doing so imposes great hardships
on others, but Smith thinks that few are so squeamish and that when
they are, it is only affectation and will not take more than a few words to
overcome. And, lastly, this system liberates people from the many legal
shackles previously thought necessary for the good of society. Smith's
reasoning exposes such constraints on the untrammeled pursuit of self-
interest not merely as superfluous but as positively harmful to society.
Thus both what we called the Doctrine of Freedom (§2) and CT are in
harmony with laissez-faire capitalism.

§9 CAPITALISM AND THE GOOD OF SOCIETY

Classical economists have developed an impressively precise theory
closely akin to Adam Smith's, and their conclusion, unlike Smith's, is
rigorously demonstrated. They can show that, under certain clearly formulated conditions, called *perfect competition*, a capitalist economy tends
toward a state of equilibrium that is also in a certain sense an optimal
state, called a Pareto-optimum. Such an equilibrium state is optimal
because in it everyone is as well off as possible, in the sense that no one
could be made better off without someone else being made worse off.

There is an obvious connection between this proof of the economists
and a utilitarian justification of laissez-faire capitalism. Utilitarians consider anything morally justified if and only if it "promotes the good of
society." But they attempt to give a clear and workable account of that
rather obscure idea. They think of something as promoting the good of
society if and only if it "maximizes utility." Classical utilitarians think of
utility as pleasure or happiness, contemporary utilitarians as maximal
preference satisfaction.[6] Despite important differences, there is an element common to all versions of utilitarianism: Something is morally justified if and only if it maximizes the overall "pay-off," however that pay-
off is to be construed. If we can say that an economic system that tends
toward a Pareto-optimal equilibrium state ipso facto maximizes the
utility of the relevant persons, then the economists' proof amounts to a
utilitarian justification of laissez-faire capitalism.

Before we can state the economists' argument succinctly, we must say
a few words about the workings of a capitalist economy under perfect

competition. This will enable us to understand the premises required for the economists' proof and the utilitarians' justification.

Consider first how such an economy is organized. It features three major economic roles: (i) producers, organized as firms, that is, legal entities engaged in hiring the factors of production (land, capital, labor, and entrepreneurial skill) for the production of goods and services; (ii) the various owners of these various factors of production who sell factor services to firms; and finally, (iii) consumers, organized as households, who use the money earned form the sale of factor services to purchase what is sold by firms. Of course, any one person may play more than one of these roles.

All goods (apart from a few "free goods," which are not scarce, such as air), including also the factors of production, have a price. That price is determined, essentially through supply and demand, in the markets in which they are bought and sold—the commodity or output market for goods and services, and the factor or input market for the factors of production. This circulation of commodities and factors of production from producers to consumers and from consumers to producers, by way of the relevant markets, is often called "The Wheel of Wealth."

How do employers and employees fit into this scheme? Firms are composed of employers and employees, but their roles in them are rather different. Following the economist Jacob Marshak, we can think of the firm as an organized group of people with the character of a "foundation" rather than a "team" or a "coalition."⁷ A team comes into and remains in existence solely for the purpose of attaining an end common to all team members. A coalition is an organized group of persons, having a variety of ends, only some, and possibly none, of which are shared though all are mutually tolerated. It is so organized that their mutually coordinated activities no longer hinder but actually promote the attainment of their respective ends. A foundation comes somewhere between the two. It is a group organized to achieve a given purpose, which is the purpose of some members, but not of all; those who join a foundation do so not because their aim is the aim of the foundation but because they are rewarded for their efforts to achieve the foundation's purpose.

If a firm is a foundation, then clearly its purpose is also the purpose of the entrepreneur, but not that of the employees. The interest of employer and employee are related in a complex way. As sellers of labor in a factor market, the main interest of employees is the wage they receive in return. They have no primary interest in the firm's output, since they do not appropriate it. They are in principle willing to leave the firm the moment another firm offers them a better wage. Of course, they are interested not only in the wage, but also in the working time and the other conditions of work, including safety, paid annual leave, sick leave, and so on. I shall call all these things together their "reward." Suppose that the extent to which they discharge their role-duties has an impact on the revenue of their firm, and that their reward is a function of that revenue.

Then employees have an indirect role-interest, mediated by their vary-ing reward, in the primary aim of the firm, and therefore indirectly an interest shared with their employer, but potentially in conflict with that of consumers and competing firms. As employees, they will, therefore, also have this indirect role-interest in granting the employer all the powers over employees needed in order to insure that he has at his dis-posal sufficiently pliable and effective instruments for carrying out his specific plans. At the same time, employees will have role-interests directly opposed to those of the employer, since, from the employer's point of view, the employees' rewards reduce the profits employers can pocket. Nevertheless, because the capitalist economy we are considering is under perfect competition, we can make the following assumption. If employers and employees fix employee role-duties by common agree-ment, then because employers may threaten to hire other workers will-ing to agree to duties more favorable to the employer and because work-ers may threaten to find other employment more favorable to them, employee role-duties will tend to be fixed in such a way that the con-scientious discharge of these duties will increase not only the firm's profits but also the employees' real wages. If this assumption is sound, then we have here the outline of an argument for the principle of con-tractual freedom, even if the duties employees freely acquire are oner-ous. For it may really be in *the best interest of employees* freely to agree to those role-duties to their employer, such as hard and conscientious work, a reasonably long working day, prohibition of absenteeism, re-strictions on work breaks, and so on, that contribute to greater produc-tivity and profits, which in turn will enable and, under perfect competi-tion, force the employer to increase employee rewards.

How weighty is this argument for contractual freedom, considered from the moral point of view? Plainly, it depends at least on the follow-ing two factors: (i) whether the role-interest of employees in increasing their reward is promoted in the morally most acceptable way (that is, most fairly or justly) by the firm's performing its assigned function, namely, maximization of its profits and the resulting increase of the em-ployee reward, or by some other arrangement, and (ii) whether the maximization of the firm's profits and the employees' getting a fair re-ward is most effectively achieved by letting employee role-duties and employee rewards be determined by a free bargain in the factor market. We shall look into this shortly.

First, however, we must examine the conditions required for perfect competition, for which alone this argument is valid. Under perfect com-petition, there must be such a large number of buyers and sellers in the markets that the transactions of none of them can change the conditions under which the other transactions are made.

Furthermore, under perfect competition, every buyer and seller has perfect market knowledge. Thus, everyone has knowledge of product and factor availability, and knowledge of the profitability of economic projects. And all firms sell non-differentiated, standardized products.

Thus, there are, for example, no brand name products preferred by customers merely on account of their brand.

Next, all goods are purely *private*: If one unit of the good is consumed by one person, then the same unit cannot also be consumed by another. Public parks, roads, and museums are not purely private goods.

Under perfect competition, there also are no external economies or diseconomies: It is not possible for someone to consume goods without a return in factor services, that is, money, labor, and so on. (Thus, it must not be possible for a manufacturer to pollute the air without paying for it.) Similarly, it is not necessary for anyone to provide factor services without being able to consume goods in return. (Thus, it must not be the case that people pay taxes for amenities they cannot or do not want to use.)

We next assume perfectly rational individuals in the economists' sense, that is, individuals motivated always to maximize their own interest, and totally indifferent to the interests of others, that is, neither envious nor compassionate. As rational individuals in this sense, all the economic actors always pursue their own best interest as determined by the structure of the capitalist economic system. Firms arrange their business activities so as to maximize their profits, owners of the factors of production sell factor services at the highest possible price, and consumers make purchases so as to maximize their satisfactions.

Finally, all individuals are *free* to produce, consume, and sell factor services, as they see fit. Thus, there must, for instance, be no legal patents keeping some from producing the patented commodities of others, and no economic obstacles to obtaining the needed capital, which could keep some from starting a new business.

Under these conditions free production and exchange tend toward a state of equilibrium. No one will be able to improve his position by further exchanges, because, given what other people are doing, what he is doing already is in his best interest. Hence, as a rational person, he has no reason to make any changes. Since this is true of everybody, the system tends to remain in or return to equilibrium. Classical economists can also prove that this equilibrium is Pareto-optimal. They can show (a) that it is productively efficient (given the factors employed, no greater quantity of goods can be produced); (b) that it is distributively efficient (no further mutually profitable exchanges can be made); and (c) that the available factors of production have been put to the best possible use (no alternative bundle of goods and services, if produced from these same factors, could have made some individuals better off without making others worse off than they now are).

Suppose, then, that a given capitalist economic system is perfectly competitive and that, therefore, every subject, by promoting his individual best interest, as defined by his economic role, thereby also necessarily promotes a Pareto-optimal social equilibrium. Suppose, furthermore, that such an equilibrium is a *social optimum*, a state of society that cannot be bettered. Since, in that case, such an optimum is achieved by allowing every individual to promote his own best economic interest, it is not implausible to maintain that society should permit every individual to act as he sees fit. As far as our limited question is concerned—What role-duties do employees have to employers?—this would mean that society should subscribe to the principle of contractual freedom, that employers and employees should settle their conflict of economic interest by free bargaining, and that, therefore, morally speaking, employee role-duties to employers are all and only those tasks on which employees and employers have freely agreed in their employment contract. But this amounts to CT (the Contract Thesis).

One might further support this conclusion as follows. Under a private enterprise system, the key economic role on which economic progress and social wealth depends is that of the entrepreneur. As an entrepreneur, Jones either succeeds in producing goods and services consumers want to purchase at a price profitable to him or he is driven out of business and superseded by a more astute competitor, who has better anticipated the public demand. To play this socially useful but also very risky role, Jones must set up a large entity, the firm, consisting of him and, typically, other people under his direction, whose activities he coordinates so that they work harmoniously together, much as if they were one single superperson. In his role of head of the firm, Jones has the responsibility for the direction of the common enterprise, the obligation to pay his employees the agreed wages or salaries, the right to reap the profits, if any, and the liability for the losses if he fails. To have a reasonable chance of avoiding failure, he must have authority over his employees sufficient to coordinate their activities toward his business goals. Moreover, since he is bearing the risk of failure, and since his employees stand to benefit from his success, it should be up to him to stipulate the scope of the authority he thinks he needs for success. This seems all the more reasonable since, under the rule of contractual freedom, prospective employees are free either to accept his conditions of employment, if they are to their taste, or to seek employment elsewhere under more attractive conditions.

If this is sound, then the acceptance of contractual freedom not only produces the best possible results; it would also be the arrangement most likely to induce entrepreneurs to shoulder the grave risks necessary for society to increase its wealth as rapidly as possible, and fairly to compensate the entrepreneur for shouldering these grave risks.

This view implies that the private enterprise system under perfect competition is so beneficial to all that as far as the economy is concerned, the sole function of law and conventional morality must be to maintain the system in existence and to prevent any obstruction to its smooth working. Law and morality, therefore, are not required to impose any constraints on its natural operations.

In particular, on this view, the smooth working of the system requires the removal of most traditional legal and moral constraints on the terms of the employment contract, such as those that fix a "fair" wage or a "fair" price, which religious thinkers and some economists (perhaps under their influence) had erroneously thought necessary to curb egoistic (and, in their view, antisocial and immoral) impulses. These constraints, on the contrary, only made matters worse, since they suppressed those self-interested pursuits that, with the help of the "invisible hand," most "effectually" promote the social good. So these regulations should be abolished and conventional morality, always on the side of "the underdog," should now cease to approve of them.

Of course, self-interested economic activities can flourish only in a social climate of security, trust, and social peace. So the law must prohibit and reduce as much as possible the incidence of murder, crime in the street, larceny, burglary, robbery, and similar ways of promoting one's own best interest. And morality must also (continue to) condemn them.

The freedom to engage in these self-interested economic activities would, of course, be entirely useless if the self-created contractual bonds now made possible by the removal of past legal and moral impediments were not just as reliable as the impediments previously imposed by law. The law must therefore uphold the sanctity of the contract and the courts must enforce the freely assumed contractual obligations. And conventional morality should strongly commend fidelity to contract and strongly condemn any breach of it. As Adam Smith put it, "In the race of wealth . . . he may run as hard as he can, and strain every nerve and every muscle, in order to outstrip all his competitors. But if he should jostle, or throw down any of them, the indulgence of the spectators is at an end. It is a violation of fair play, which they cannot admit of."[8]

On this view, then, law and conventional morality must not interfere with the unfettered working of free enterprise itself. Therefore, the economy itself, conceived as a self-contained system, isolable from the other sectors of society, must be guided by the doctrine of contractual freedom. There may be doubt about how to deal with questions of shoring up the structure of the private enterprise system itself by legal and moral pressure, such as whether or not to pass anti-trust legislation and have it administered by the government to insure at least a high degree of (if not perfect) competition, or legislation forbidding, say, child labor to protect those who cannot yet protect themselves in free market transactions. But these are borderline cases between what is necessary to preserve the structure of free enterprise itself and what interferes with its smooth functioning. The doubts about them do not touch the basis of the argument: If the good of society is our supreme moral consideration, and if everyone's pursuit of individual best interest (as defined by the particular role each person is at a given time playing in the free enterprise system) most effectually promotes the good of society, even when no one is aiming at it, then neither law nor morality can rightly constrain that sort of self-interested activity. There are morally justifiable constraints on contractual freedom, namely, those alluded to by Friedman and Levitt (see above, §1), but they are only those necessary for or helpful to the smooth functioning of the capitalist economy itself.

§10 THE JUSTIFICATION OF THE CONTRACT THESIS

We must now put in more perspicuous form the argument for CT that rests on the economists' account of the way the good of society is promoted in a capitalist economy under perfect competition and the role of business employees in that promotion. We shall begin with short definitions of the key concepts involved, which have been explained in greater detail in previous sections.

Definition (1), the (Weak) Doctrine of Utilitarianism: the doctrine that something is morally justified only if, or morally desirable to the extent that, it satisfies the Principle of Utility.

Definition (2), the Principle of Utility: the principle that requires people to do whatever maximizes the utility of the relevant persons. (Different versions of this principle give different accounts of utility and of relevant person.)

Definition (3), the Doctrine of Freedom: the doctrine according to which something is morally justified only if, or to the extent that, it satisfies the principle of freedom.

Definition (4), the Principle of Freedom: the principle that allows people to do whatever they see fit, provided only that their actions do not violate certain moral constraints (such as those on force, fraud, and deception) that are necessary for or helpful to the smooth functioning of the morally acceptable institutions of society.

Definition (5), the Principle of Contractual Freedom: the principle that allows people to assume duties by voluntarily entering into contracts with one another, provided only that these contracts do not violate the moral constraints mentioned in the principle of freedom.

Definition (6), Human Society: an entity that, like a person, persists for a certain time and that throughout that time is capable of reidentification as well as change in character but that, unlike a person, consists of persons living under a system of social institutions.

Definition (7), Pareto-optimality: the property of a state that yields to those in it "as much utility as possible" in the precise sense that no one could be getting more utility without someone else's getting less.

Definition (8), Perfect Competition: a complex ideal state in which all economic roles are filled by wholly self-concerned and self-interested agents in conditions under which they have free access to all relevant information and their transactions are subject only to those moral and legal constraints required for the smooth working of the economy.

Definition (9), Role-Duties: the presumptive duties people have in virtue of playing a certain role.

Definition (10), the Contract Thesis (CT): the thesis that employee role-duties are all and only those that the employees have voluntarily undertaken in their employment contract, subject only to the moral constraints mentioned in the principle of freedom.

Our justificatory argument for CT could therefore be formulated as follows:

Premise (1): A capitalist economy is morally justified if and only if it satisfies the principles of utility and freedom.

Premise (2): Such an economy satisfies the Principle of Utility if and only if it tends toward a Pareto-optimal equilibrium state.

Premise (3): Such an economy tends toward a Pareto-optimal equilibrium state if and only if it is under perfect competition.

Sub-conclusion (1): Therefore, such an economy satisfies the Principle of Utility if it is under perfect competition. (From premises 2 and 3.)

Premise (4): Such an economy satisfies the principle of contractual freedom if it is under perfect competition.

Premise (5): Such an economy satisfies the principle of freedom if it satisfies the principle of contractual freedom.

Sub-conclusion (2): Therefore, such an economy satisfies the principle of freedom if it is under perfect competition. (From premises 4 and 5.)

Sub-conclusion (3): Therefore, such an economy satisfies the principles of utility and of freedom if it is under perfect competition. (From sub-conclusions 1 and 2.)

Sub-conclusion (4): Therefore, such an economy under perfect competition is morally justified. (From premise 1 and sub-conclusion 3.)

Sub-conclusion (5): Therefore, there is at least one type of capitalist economy, namely, one under perfect competition, that satisfies the principle of contractual freedom and is morally justified. (From premise 4 and sub-conclusion 4.)

Sub-conclusion (6): Therefore, there is at least one type of morally justified capitalist economy, namely, one under perfect competition, in which people are free to do what they see fit, provided only that what they do violates neither the moral constraints mentioned in the principle of freedom nor those arising out of the duties they have assumed in their voluntarily concluded contracts. (From sub-conclusions 2 and 5.)

Sub-conclusion (7): Therefore, in a capitalist economy under perfect competition, people's role-duties are all and only those they have assumed in their voluntarily concluded contracts, subject only to the moral constraints mentioned in the principle of freedom. (From sub-conclusion 6.)

Final conclusion (A): Therefore, CT is sound in *some* morally justified capitalist economies. (From sub-conclusions 6 and 7.)

This is a relatively weak conclusion, for it states only that there are some morally justified capitalist economies, namely, those that are under perfect competition and satisfy the principle of freedom, in which CT is sound. It does not claim that CT is sound in all morally justified capitalist economies. However, we can extract this stronger conclusion by the following steps:

Sub-conclusion (8): Therefore, a capitalist economy satisfies the Principle of Utility if and only if it is under perfect competition. (From premises 2 and 3.)

Sub-conclusion (9): Therefore, a capitalist economy is morally justified only if it is under perfect competition. (From premise 1 and sub-conclusion 8.)

Sub-conclusion (10): Therefore, a capitalist economy is morally justified only if it satisfies the principle of contractual freedom. (From premise 4 and sub-conclusion 9.)

Sub-conclusion (11): Therefore, a capitalist economy is morally justified only if people under it are free to do what they see fit, provided only that what they do violates neither the moral constraints mentioned in the principle of freedom nor those arising out of the duties they have assumed in their voluntarily concluded contracts. (From sub-conclusion 10.)

Sub-conclusion (12): Therefore, in *all* morally justified capitalist economies, people's role-duties are all and only those they have assumed in their voluntarily concluded contracts, provided only that these role-duties satisfy moral constraints mentioned in the principle of freedom.

Final conclusion (B): Therefore, CT is sound in *all* morally justified capitalist economies.

This is a stronger conclusion, for it says that there are *no* morally justified capitalist economies in which CT is *not sound*. It is important to note that this conclusion rests on the claim that a capitalist economy cannot satisfy the principle of freedom or the Principle of Utility without satisfying the principle of contractual freedom, and that the soundness of CT in such an economy depends on that economy's satisfying the principle of contractual freedom.

Despite its great plausibility and attractiveness, this justification has been attacked from many sides. Its basis is the claim that a capitalist economy is the most effectual way of promoting the good of society. Accordingly, there are four major lines of attack. One is to argue that individual freedom and the good of society are not (contrary to the assumptions of premise 1) the only, the most important, or the decisive moral considerations; thus, it is claimed, for instance, that respect for individual rights, or the requirements of social or economic justice, ought to have precedence over individual freedom and the good of society. A second is to concede that the good of society is the decisive moral consideration, or together with freedom, one of the two decisive ones, but that the good of society cannot be identified with social wealth, particularly as measured by economists, namely, in terms of GNP; thus, it is claimed, for instance, that the good of society involves many more important goods than wealth, such as the quality of life, self-respect, love, friendship, justice, and many others. A third is to argue that even on its own terms, laissez-faire capitalism cannot make out its claim that it most effectually promotes the good of society; thus, it is claimed that what it really does promote, namely, Pareto-optimality, cannot (contrary to premise 2) be the greatest social good, by its own showing. Lastly, it is argued that laissez-faire capitalism can justify itself only under the assumption of perfect competition, but that this assumption was never realistic and is less so now than ever. Thus, it is claimed that the justification is irrelevant to our society because our economy operates under conditions that do not tend toward Pareto-optimality, as is required by premises 2 and 3. I shall deal with some of these objections in the next few sections.

§11 PARETO-OPTIMALITY AND THE GOOD OF SOCIETY

As already mentioned, laissez-faire capitalism is often defended along utilitarian lines. Some of those who believe in utilitarianism believe that they can meet the first two of the above four objections by construing the good of society in terms of overall social utility. Overall social utility, they say, includes not only wealth but all the various so-called goods, such as respect for rights and justice, the prevalence of love, friendship, freedom, and so on. With this construal of utility they think they have met the first two objections, because they have made the good of society so general that no goods at all can have been left out. On this construal, social utility is not too narrow a notion to serve as the basis of justification.

To keep things manageable, let us concede this initially plausible point. On this construal of utilitarianism, then, the good of society is overall social utility. But what is that? Utilitarians think of overall utility as the sum of the utilities of the various individuals in a society. Given the differences in individual abilities and tastes, different individuals may well derive different amounts of utility from a given social state of affairs. From their different prespectives, then, their individual greatest utility may well be derived from quite different social states. We cannot, then, assume that the social utility of a given social state will coincide with the greatest utility derived from that state by any one individual. It is then plausible to think of social utility as the utility of a total social state when calculated from a neutral, impartial, no-man's point of view. Utilitarians construe this neutral point of view as that of a person unconcerned about the utilities of any particular individual member of the society in question, but concerned only with increasing the "sum total" of these individual utilities, whatever may be the utility outcome for this or that individual member. Utilitarians hold that morally speaking we should adopt this neutral point of view and so should compound *into an overall magnitude* the utilities severally derived from various alternative possible social states by the members of the society in question. Then the best social state, the state everyone should, morally speaking, try to bring about is the one that produces the greatest such compound of individual utilities. Of course, for this to make sense, utilitarians must devise a method for comparing and compounding the utilities of different people into an overall utility. I shall simply assume, as many utilitarians do, that such a comparison and summing of the utilities of different people is possible.[9]

The possibility of constructing such a sum total of the utilities of different people does, however, create the following problem for laissez-faire capitalism and the principle of freedom. Laissez-faire capitalism, which, as we have seen, rests on the principle of freedom, assumes that economically rational behavior leads to a Pareto-optimal equilibrium. But it does not seem necessarily to lead to the greatest sum of the relevant individual utilities. This opens up the possibility, rejected by premise 2 of our argument on page 83, that Pareto-optimality and the social optimum as conceived by the utilitarians do not necessarily coincide.

John Stuart Mill thought that he had a proof of the necessary coincidence between individual rationality and the social optimum. He argued, in a much-quoted passage, that "each person's happiness is a good to that person, and the general happiness, therefore, a good to the aggregate of all persons."[10] However, this argument is, notoriously, fallacious. What follows from the premise that each person's happiness is a good *to him* is, of course, only that *their own* happiness is a good to all. It does not follow that the general good, the good of society, the greatest total social good or utility, is a good to each and all. Adam Smith was clearer about the issue. He did not rely on a *logical* connection between individual rationality and the good of society, but acknowledged that the operation of an Invisible Hand was required to insure the coincidence. The problem for laissez-faire capitalism is that this Invisible Hand at most insures a *coincidence between individual economic rationality and Pareto-optimality*; it does not show either an identity or a necessary connection between *Pareto-optimality and the social optimum*, as utilitarians conceive of the latter, namely, as the greatest possible social utility. As we have seen, Pareto-optimality means only the highest possible individual utility everyone can reach *given a certain starting point*, that is, given a certain initial distribution (ownership) of the factors of production and their subsequent use in a private enterprise system under perfect competition. Given these two fixed conditions, the outcome is indeed necessarily Pareto-optimal. But it is *not necessarily a social optimum*, that is, the social state with the highest possible *social* utility, given the same individuals and the same factors of production but a different initial allocation. If we start with a different initial distribution of these factors, then the outcome, though a different social state, must still be Pareto-optimal, but it may have a higher or a lower total *social* utility. Thus, in a capitalist society under perfect competition, every social state that is a utilitarian social optimum is necessarily Pareto-optimal, but not every social state that is Pareto-optimal is necessarily a utilitarian social optimum. If this utilitarian reasoning is sound, as I believe it to be, then we must reject premise 2 of our argument on page 83.

Hence, if we are utilitarians and think we ought to promote the utilitarian good of society, that is, maximize social utility, we ought not to subscribe to laissez-faire capitalism. For in order to maximize social utility, we will have to tamper either with perfect competition, and so with Pareto-optimality, or with the initial factor allocation. Supporters of so-called welfare-state capitalism advocate the former, various forms of natural rights theories advocate the latter. I briefly discuss the first in §12 and the second in §13.

§12 WELFARE-STATE AND PLANNED-INITIAL-STATE CAPITALISM

Welfare-state capitalism receives moral support from the utilitarian consideration that Pareto-optimal social states can often be improved upon, that is, changed so as to yield higher social utility, by redistributive taxation. The underlying idea is the so-called law of diminishing marginal utility. It says that a person's utility increases with increasing quantities of a given good consumed, but that the rate of increase in utility diminishes with the consumption of each such unit. Suppose that when you have one dozen eggs and five pounds of potatoes, you are *indifferent* between getting an additional egg and an additional pound of potatoes. Then, the law says that, if you had only eleven eggs but still five pounds of potatoes, you would *prefer* getting an additional egg to getting an additional pound of potatoes; but if, instead, you had only four pounds of potatoes but still a dozen eggs, then you would *prefer* getting an additional pound of potatoes to getting an additional egg. This means that the utility of an additional egg and an additional pound of potatoes is not a fixed quantity but diminishes with each additional unit.

Suppose this plausible principle is sound. Suppose also that in a given Pareto-optimal state, goods have come to be very unequally distributed. Then we could increase the social utility of that social state by suitably redistributing the goods. Suppose someone already has a million dollars; then by taking a thousand dollars from him and giving it to someone else who has only a thousand dollars, we would be increasing total social utility, since the utility loss of the millionaire is much smaller than the utility gain of the pauper. In this way, while allowing the initial factor allocation, welfare-state capitalism, it is claimed, can promote the good of society more effectually even than laissez-faire capitalism. Hence utilitarianism favors welfare-state over laissez-faire capitalism. However, these gains are not purchased without cost. For welfare-state capitalism requires the imposition of redistributive taxation, which forces those on whom it falls to behave in ways in which, if they are economically rational, they do not want to behave. Welfare-state capitalism thus involves significant inroads on the principle of freedom.

There is, however, a third version of capitalism, that can avoid this particular shortcoming; I call it "planned-initial-state capitalism." It, too, encroaches on the principle of freedom, but does so by imposing inheritance taxes, which are also redistributive. However, they are redistributive not as between economic role-players once they have entered the competition, but as between successive generations of role-players. The point of such inheritance taxes is to bring it about that the rational activities of the various role-players in the perfectly competitive economy yield a more nearly equal distribution of resources than would be the case without such taxation, and so to increase overall social utility in accordance with the principle of diminishing utility just explained. Planned-initial-state capitalism thus also relies on the principle of diminishing utility to increase overall social utility, not, however, through redistributive intervention in the rational activities of the economic role-players, but rather through a suitable modification of the initial factor allocation, that is, the competitive starting point. It can thus preserve perfect competition and so Pareto-optimality and so can achieve even greater overall social utility than can welfare-state capitalism, if the cost of bringing about this suitable initial factor allocation is no greater than the cost of the imposition of suitable redistributive taxation.

So far, we have distinguished three forms of capitalism: laissez-faire, welfare-state, and planned-initial-state capitalism. The first necessarily tends toward Pareto-optimality but not necessarily toward a utilitarian social optimum. The second necessarily tends toward a utilitarian social optimum but not necessarily toward Pareto-optimality. The third tends toward both. It is therefore superior to the other two.

It may be objected that the departures of this third form of capitalism from the laissez-faire variety impose two novel restrictions incompatible with the principle of freedom. The first concerns a possible constraint on the wish to bequeathe. If, as seems likely, the practice of bequeathing what one has acquired in one's lifetime to one's chosen heirs does not generate an initial factor allocation that, together with subsequent perfect competition, will produce a utilitarian social optimum, then the law may have to abolish the right of bequest altogether or at least significantly curtail it to achieve the necessary initial factor allocation. But this appears to violate the principle of freedom.

The second constraint concerns education. In order to make the most of the innate talents of the community, at the time when its members are ready to enter the market, the community will want to see to it that these innate talents are fully developed by a suitable education. Freely available but voluntary public education may be the most desirable way to achieve this goal. It may be discovered, however, that compulsory public education, perhaps up to the individual's ability to benefit from it, has results superior to those of voluntary education. The danger of leaving to individuals, that is, in effect, to parents or guardians, the decision whether the child is to have an education, is that parents or guardians, for reasons of their own, may prevent the child from attending school: He may be wanted as a worker on the farm or in the business; she may be thought destined by her sex to become a housewife; the parents may object on religious grounds to the teaching the child would receive in a public school.

However, the inroads on the principle of freedom required by this form of capitalism would not, as far as I can see, impose any restrictions on the principle of contractual freedom in the specifically economic domain (if the freedom of bequest is excluded from that domain). For, as we have seen, under planned-initial-state capitalism, once society has gotten people ready for the market, perfect competition and so contractual freedom prevails. Hence, if utilitarianism is a tenable moral theory, then there is at least one morally acceptable form of perfectly competitive capitalism, namely, planned-initial-state capitalism, which backs contractual freedom in the economic domain. In such a capitalist system, then, CT is sound, and an employee's role-duties to his employer are all and only those he has agreed to in the employment contract, provided, of course, these duties (also) satisfy the moral constraints mentioned in the principle of freedom.

§13 CAPITALISM AND NATURAL RIGHTS

We must now consider an entirely different moral approach to the whole problem, namely, the theory of rights. The Natural Rights theory of John Locke, recently revived by Robert Nozick,[11] claims, in opposition to utilitarianism, that the good of society is not the only or the most important thing, from the moral point of view. It rejects the contention of utilitarians that moral constraints on economic transactions can be justified by and only by their utilitarian results. Natural Rights theory holds, on the contrary, that there are what Nozick has called "side constraints" on the way the good of society may be promoted. As he puts it, "The moral side constraints upon what we may do, I claim, reflect the fact of our separate existences. They reflect the fact that no moral balancing act can take place among us; there is no moral outweighing of one of our lives by others so as to lead to a greater *social* good. There is no justified sacrifice of some of us for others."[12]

From this moral perspective, initial factor allocation is not morally irrelevant, as laissez-faire and welfare-state capitalism maintain, but neither is it to be determined with a view to producing the greatest total social utility, as planned-initial-state capitalism maintains. It must be viewed as subject to side constraints, or natural rights. On this approach to a capitalist economy, people have a right to a certain initial factor endowment as well as a right to use it in their own best interest under the same moral side constraints as everyone else — each enjoying whatever his ingenuity and good fortune enable him to garner. Society, the government, has no right to modify individual factor endowment in such a way as to enhance the overall social good. For, as utilitarians calculate it, that social good is simply the sum of individual goods. But there is no social entity comparable to an individual who sacrifices something now in order to have more later. Tampering with the initial factor endowment of people in order to increase the social good is simply to take from one to give to another in order to make their combined good greater than it would otherwise be. But the person from whom some factors are taken in no way benefits from the increase of this combined good, since she neither shares in the increase nor benefits from it, unless she happens to love the other for whose benefit she was taxed more than she loves herself, and in that case it would surely be preferable if she were free to do the transferring of her own free will.

This is a very plausible argument, but it leaves unanswered the crucial question of exactly what initial factors a person has a right to. In the absence of such an answer, we cannot tell what amounts to tampering with individuals' rights to their initial factor endowments and what to respecting them. Let us look more closely at the initial factors. In economic theory, the economic units, the firms and the households, do not cease to exist at some natural termination point. They are continuing structures defining roles that are filled by new players when the old depart, and so could go on forever. Initial factors are not, therefore, allocated anew at specifiable intervals. By contrast, when we consider the real people who play these various roles, there are natural starting and terminating points: birth or first entry into the competitive economic life, and death or exit from the economic life. Initial factor allocation determined by birth is of two kinds: those factors over which society has (at least as yet) no control, that is, individual genetic endowment, and those over which it has control, namely, inheritance, understood to include education, an especially important initial factor, since one's economic prospects appear to depend to a considerable extent on one's education.

Natural Rights theorists offer various theses about what factors a person has a natural right to. Our focus here is on theorists who agree that natural rights comprise those side constraints on people's pursuit of their economic self-interest that are required for the smooth working of a capitalist economy under perfect competition, such as, in Friedman's view, the prohibition on force, deception, and fraud. Among these theorists we find two groups with diametrically opposed views. The first group—let us call them "freedom of bequest capitalists"—includes those who claim that people have a natural right to bequeathe to whomever they choose whatever they have acquired by their ingenuity or fortune in their competitive struggle for economic self-advancement, and those to whom they bequeathe it have a natural right to start their competitive race with the advantage this inheritance confers on them over others who have inherited less or nothing. Assuming that wealth is passed on within households, such accumulation over a number of generations can make a great difference to the life expectations of persons born into different households, but this theory considers this a consequence that must be accepted if rights are to be respected.

The second and opposed view—let us call it "equal opportunity capitalism"—espouses the principle of equal opportunity. It argues that everyone has a right to the same initial factor allocation, at least as far as these factors can be controlled without excessive cost. This means either that people should not be empowered to bequeathe anything to their favorites or that their bequests should be subject to an inheritance tax for purposes of equalizing initial factor allocation. It also means that society should make available to the young, perhaps force them to submit to, at least a minimal education that would adequately equip them for the competitive economic struggle in which they must eventually engage.

There is much disagreement about how such different approaches can be rationally evaluated. I have space only to sketch the solution that I find most persuasive. It is based on the premise that it is desirable for a social order to be such that everyone has equally good reason to accept its institutions and compulsory rules. Let us say that such a social order conforms to *the principle of equitability*. Its special virtue is that, to the extent that people are rational, they will either voluntarily perform the various social role-duties their roles will impose on them, thus minimizing the costs of enforcing the social order, or recognize that their failure to conform is *unjustified*. Since they themselves have *as good reason as anyone else* to adhere to society's institutions and compulsory rules, and to object to their being generally ignored, individuals have only themselves to blame when they are made to pay the price for non-compliance. On this view, the moral side-constraints that prohibit force and fraud are universally acceptable prohibitions and are morally justified precisely for this reason. Similarly, advocates of the principle of equal opportunity can argue, with some show of plausibility, that the prohibition of or limitation on bequests is a morally justifiable side-constraint, because it gives everyone an equally good reason to support such an order, since this side-constraint does not discriminate against anyone, does not exploit anyone, and is of course not an unnecessary chicanery, benefiting no one.

It might be objected that prohibition of bequests, or limitations on them by inheritance tax, is as much a violation of the conditions of perfect competition as redistributive taxation under welfare-state capitalism. This is not true, however. For, as we have said, economically rational individuals are (by definition) unconcerned about other people's interests, and so would not find it detrimental to their own interest to have their property returned to society after their death for equitable distribution among those starting out in the competitive struggle. To insist that this rationality assumption is unrealistic would perhaps be plausible but such insistence would also undermine the entire argument, which has assumed perfect competition and so economic rationality. I return to this issue in the next section.

Let us, however, waive this point and assume that as a matter of fact all or most people care strongly about at least a few other people, and participate vigorously in the competitive struggle at least in part because they want to provide for their loved ones not only in their own lifetimes but also after their death. Still, if they accept the principle of equitability stated above, they must admit that, given their conception of social life, the prohibition of bequests or their limitation is not exploitative or discriminatory or pointless, since it provides everyone, including their loved ones, with an equally good reason, and indeed a reason as good as *everyone* can have, and so a morally adequate reason, to support such a law. By contrast, the existence of a legal right of bequest tends, especially in the long run, to set up differences, possibly very considerable ones, in the initial factor endowments and thus to give different individuals unequally good reasons for supporting a legal system with the right of bequest. Indeed, those starting their competitive careers with a relative handicap have a self-interested reason to want the system changed, whereas those favored have a self-interested reason to preserve the system. The principle of equal opportunity, backed by the principle of equitability, gives everybody as good a self-interested reason to support the system as everyone can have. For if anyone has a self-interested reason better than that, that is, a reason to think that he will have even better prospects for success in economic life, then someone else has a reason not as good. But a reason as good as *everyone* can have is a reason as good as *anyone* can in reason demand. Hence if a system is supported by such reasons, then everyone has adequate reason to support it and no one has adequate reason not to.

If this line of moral reasoning, based on the principle of equitability, is sound, then it seems that a better case can be made (always, of course, under the assumption of perfect competition) for equal-opportunity capitalism, which allocates initial factors in accordance with the principle of equal opportunity, than for freedom-of-bequest capitalism, which bases itself on the principle of freedom of bequest.[13]

However, ignoring for the moment this apparent moral superiority of equal-opportunity over freedom-of-bequest capitalism, we can say that both these types of capitalism also provide full support for the principle of contractual freedom and CT. The reason is, of course, that both these types of capitalism are envisaged as operating under perfect competition and so imply the moral acceptability of the principle of contractual freedom, as demonstrated in sub-conclusion 5 of our argument on page 83, and therefore the soundness of CT.

§14 EMPLOYEE ROLE-DUTIES UNDER PRESENT CONDITIONS

Can we apply to real life the ethical conclusion we reached in §12 and §13? Clearly, our economy does not at present satisfy the conditions of our simplified and idealized model. However, by itself, that can hardly be a sufficient reason to reject our conclusion based on it. Surely, it all depends on how close reality is to that ideal. So let us try to determine how important the differences between the model and reality are.

In outline, our argument was this. The ideal capitalist economy we just envisaged espouses three ideals: perfect competition, utilitarian social optimality, and initial factor endowment in accordance with the principle of equal opportunity. The first insures that, given any initial factor allocation, the society considered simply as an aggregation of individuals (that is, ignoring the relative individual shares) tends toward an equilibrium in which nobody could be better off without someone else becoming worse off than he now is. The second guarantees that this Pareto-optimal equilibrium is also a utilitarian social optimum, yielding the greatest possible aggregate of individual utilities. The third insures that this doubly optimal equilibrium also represents the outcome of a contest between individuals who, though endowed by nature with different assets, have entered the contest with equal social factor allocation, so that the eventually different rewards each receives are based on what each contributes by his or her own effort. (We assume, here, what may not be true, that all three ideals can be attained by a given capitalist economy.)

In such a social order the smooth functioning of the firm is necessary and sufficient for the attainment of that equilibrium with those desirable characteristics. That smooth functioning in turn is best insured if all employers are able to impose on their employees those role-duties employers think necessary for success in their business. But the best way to insure that employees have these necessary role-duties is their determination in compliance with the principle of contractual freedom. At the same time, contractual freedom is the intrinsically most desirable way of fixing employee role-duties, since it conforms to the principle of freedom.

However, our present economic system falls short of all three of these ideals. It certainly does not operate under perfect competition and does so less now than it did, say, a hundred years ago. For there has been a considerable increase in the areas in which large firms dominate market conditions, in which labor unions prevent willing workers from offering their labor at wages below those set by the unions, and in which employers impose external costs on the community. Again, although our legal system makes some effort to redress inequalities of opportunity by taxing inheritance, thus reducing the greater initial factor endowment of the heirs of the better off, it does little to improve the initial endowment of those who inherit nothing, and so fails to determine initial factor allocation by the principle of equal opportunity. Lastly, the social state produced by our economy can be seen not to be a utilitarian social optimum, if we assume the law of diminishing marginal utility in application to monetary reward. Given the considerable disparity at present in monetary incomes, the law of diminishing utility implies that those with a high income receive much less utility for each dollar than those with a lower income. Thus, the maximization of total social utility would seem to require redistributive taxation on a much larger scale than we now have.

How does this affect our ethical conclusion in §12 and §13? If the ideal economy sketched there is morally preferable to our current one and if there is no other economic ideal preferable to it, then this would seem to mean that we should aim at bringing our economy closer to this ideal, close enough to justify applying that ethical conclusion to our improved economy.

Here, however, we encounter major uncertainties. It is not clear, for instance, whether bringing the economy closer to perfect competition is desirable or even possible. Can we make individuals more rational than they now are? Can we, should we, break up the many giant firms whose economic power has created widespread oligopoly or monopoly conditions incompatible with perfect competition? Once a firm is so large that it is not merely a "price-taker"[14] but also can influence the market price of its products by its own supply decisions, it can maximize its profits by restricting output and raising its prices and thus can do so without having to produce the socially optimal quantity of goods.[15] To maintain perfect competition in the economy, such dominant firms would have to refrain from maximizing their profits, or the state would have to break them up to prevent any one from dominating the market. However, one of the reasons firms become giants in a competitive economy is that they can, by so-called economies of scale (mass production), become so efficient that they can profitably sell their product at a price that drives their smaller competitors out of the market. Thus, a policy of breaking up such a giant and restoring competition by many smaller businesses may actually reduce total output. Perfect competition is thus not a self-maintaining system. On the contrary, it requires constant supervision and frequent state intervention to prevent its destabilization by the inherent tendency of firms to become so large as to dominate the market.[16]

There are many other problems with raising the level of competitiveness of our economy and with bringing it closer to the other two ideals. But we need not here concern ourselves with them, for even if it is feasible and desirable for the government to take the relevant corrective measures, producing the desired change will presumably be a complex and lengthy job. The question, therefore, is what role-duties employees have in the meantime.

Much must depend on the function of the firm in our actual economy. But what is that function? In our ideal economy, entrepreneurs, taking their cues from the various relevant markets, seek to organize the production and sale of goods and services with a view to maximizing their profits. Similarly, consumers are to pursue their economic interest by spending their money so as to maximize their utility. The role of employees in this scheme is a purely subsidiary but equally self-interested one: they are to pursue their best economic interest by selling their labor to entrepreneurs in return for undertaking to carry out the tasks the latter deemed necessary for the success of the firm. The justification for this unfettered pursuit of economic self-interest by all, constrained only by the fairly generous limits set by the moral and legal prohibition on force, deception, and fraud, is that the greatest social good could be achieved by and only by that pursuit.

However, without perfect competition, without utilitarian social optimality, and without conformity to the principle of equal opportunity, the whole economic enterprise assumes a very different complexion. We now have people in several roles, each trying to promote his or her own best interest, within the relatively undemanding constraints of a ban on force, deception, and fraud, but without the help of the various Invisible and Visible Hands mentioned in §12 and §13 to insure that all this self-promotion would also promote the good of society.

How does this affect the principle of contractual freedom? Clearly, it has lost nothing of its intrinsic attractiveness, but it has lost its support as an essential factor in the promotion of the good of society (premise 4 and sub-conclusion 5 on page 83), and therefore its claim to the virtually unlimited supremacy we granted it. There is now no guarantee or even likelihood that the good of society and so the good of the other role-players will be best promoted if the firm is best able to increase its profits. There is, therefore, also no justification for limiting the moral constraints on employer and employee to the prohibition on force, deception, and fraud. Since society has not provided an economic framework capable of so channeling the self-interested pursuits of the economic role-players that they will automatically promote the social good, these economic role-players are no longer exempted from the moral constraints of general ethics. Therefore, they must be regarded as subject not only to the prohibition on force, fraud, and deception but also to the whole range of those constraints, just like everyone else.

Thus, if the imposition of certain external diseconomies on the community, such as the dumping of poisonous chemicals in Love Canal, is harmful to it, and if harming the community is wrong, then the entrepreneur who has ordered this dumping cannot justifiably claim exemption from this moral constraint on the ground that he did it in his role of entrepreneur, a role that requires him to maximize the firm's profits in all possible ways, excluding only fraud, force, and deception, *and* that dumping the chemicals was one of these ways. This argument will not work now for, although nothing has been said to show that maximizing the firm's profits is no longer a role-duty of the entrepreneur, it is now plain that it is only a presumptive duty (see §4). And since, in an imperfect economy such as ours, the utilitarian and the natural rights case for exempting the firm from universal moral constraints is undermined, in the absence of some other moral justification the presumption is rebutted that the entrepreneur has a right, let alone a duty, to harm the community whenever that maximizes the firm's profits.

The upshot of all this is that under our present economic conditions, employers and employees would seem to be subject not only to the prohibition on force, deception, and fraud, but also to exactly the same moral constraints as everyone else. This includes the top-level managers of corporations, even if they are the employees of the stockholders and they in turn the owners of the firm rather than mere investors in it. Managers thus cannot claim that they are morally required by the role-duty to their employers to maximize profits and dividends in every possible way, short only of force, deception, and fraud. Thus, exactly what moral limitations are imposed on the principle of contractual freedom depends on what are the *natural* duties (see §5) of the firm to its customers in particular and to society in general. In our economy, employers cannot legitimately impose and employees cannot legitimately assume role-duties that are contradictory to the firm's natural duties. For, as we have seen (§6), natural duties must be presumed to be more stringent than contradictory artificial ones, unless this presumption can be rebutted in the case in hand. We examined such attempted rebuttals in §11, §12, and §13. We concluded that certain ideal forms of capitalism do indeed give strong support to the principle of contractual freedom and through it to CT. If this conclusion could be applied to real-life capitalism and real-life employees, then indeed we would have rebutted the presumption that employee role-duties (because artificial duties) are less stringent than any contradictory natural duties in their current formulations. But we also saw in this section that these rebuttals in §11, §12, and §13 hold only under certain unrealistic assumptions, such as perfect competition. Hence our efforts to justify CT under real-life conditions have failed. This does not, of course, show that some other justification of CT is impossible. But it does show that those usually offered are inadequate, and that the burden of proof is on those who uphold CT. In the meantime, the absence of such an alternative justification and the difficulty of producing one would seem to justify us in rejecting CT.

There still appears to be widespread belief, not only in the business community but also among others who have given extensive thought to the ethics of business, that CT is sound, even under present economic conditions and despite the fact that the primacy of natural duties has not been satisfactorily rebutted. It may be instructive to end this paper with a very recent expression of this popular opinion by a distinguished thinker[17]: "Neither corporate nor governmental officials can ethically be compassionate. A corporate officer who, *on his own hook* [emphasis added], withdraws a dangerous product, is nevertheless stealing from his company even if he gains no personal advantage. Laudable as the public benefit is, the corporate officer is behaving unethically." The speaker clearly implies that, regardless of whether a company has the moral right to harm its customers, its officers have a contractual moral duty to obey their superior even if he orders them to market a dangerous product. Those who hold this view probably do so mainly because it has not occurred to them that contractual agreements do not generate moral duties if they transgress the boundaries drawn by natural duties. Thus, the speaker just quoted went on to say: "We have two rights in conflict; two opposing goods. For several millennia this conflict in ethics has been handled chiefly by the State. In part, the State has been interested in preventing fraud, as in the English law on the baker's dozen. Since the rise of the corporations, however, one of the functions of the State has been to set up a hierarchy of ethical values. Those who complain of meddlesome regulations are either motivated by greed, or they do not see the conflict between private and public ethics. Agribusiness, as a whole, involves so many diverse products and such different sizes of business that a single ethical code seems impractical. Great corporations, and even small ones, may require the coercive rules of the State. If corporations are both heartless and witless, it may stem in some part from the fact that no corporate officer can ethically exercise his conscience. Not that anyone has accused many of them of wanting to exercise their conscience. To those who want to, however, the recourse must be to laws and regulations which require upright behavior."

Now, there may indeed be other good reasons for state regulations, but that otherwise corporate officers would be unethical if they disobeyed their superiors whatever their orders is surely not one of them. We simply do not have good reason to think that, in the absence of laws forbidding it, corporate officers are duty-bound to market dangerous products if ordered to do so by their superior. There is, therefore, no reason to think that corporate officers would be unethical if they refused to obey such orders. And marketing dangerous products is not, of course, the only thing corporate officers may, perhaps ought to refuse to do when ordered. Plainly, the next and most important step would be to determine what natural duties employers and employees have and thereby to bring to light the moral limitations we must impose on CT, but that inquiry would take us into the territory of other papers in this volume.*

NOTES

1. For an interesting discussion, see Jack G. Kaikati, "The Phenomenon of International Bribery," *Business Horizons* (February 1977), reprinted in Vincent Barry, ed., *Moral Issues in Business* (Belmont, Calif.: Wadsworth, 1979), pp. 216–26.

2. Milton Friedman, *Capitalism and Freedom* (Chicago: University of Chicago Press, 1962), p. 133.

3. Theodore Levitt, "The Dangers of Social Responsibility," *Harvard Business Review* (September–October 1958), reprinted in Tom L. Beauchamp and Norman Bowie, eds., *Ethical Theory and Business* (Englewood Cliffs, N.J.: Prentice-Hall, 1979), p. 141.

4. This term was invented by the twentieth-century English philosopher W.D. Ross, *The Right and the Good* (Oxford: Clarendon Press, 1930), chs. 1 and 2. For a more extensive discussion, see Robert K. Shope, "Prima Facie Duty," *The Journal of Philosophy*, Vol. LXII, no. 11 (May 27, 1965), pp. 279–87. The term is rather misleading, because it suggests that such duties are mere appearance, that on closer inspection it is simply a mistake to think that the person in question has a duty, but this is not what Ross means to say. However, the term is so well established that I have adhered to it. Accordingly, I have used another term, "presumptive duty," for what is literally meant by Ross' term, but not by Ross himself.

5. Adam Smith, *An Inquiry into the Nature and Causes of the Wealth of Nations*, reprinted in *Adam Smith's Moral and Political Philosophy*, Herbert Schneider, ed. (N.Y.: Harper Torchbooks, 1948), p. 399.

6. I here largely ignore the classical, Benthamite version of utilitarianism, which identifies utility with pleasure and happiness, that is, with introspectively quantifiable, perhaps measurable, psychological pay-offs. I consider only the modern version, which identifies an individual's utility with his observable preferential choice patterns. Unlike Benthamites, modern utilitarians do not determine an individual's utilities independently of his preferential choices, and then judge him rational or not, depending on whether his preferential choices maximize his utility. Modern utilitarians determine whether a person is rational and what his utilities are by a single step, namely, by an evaluation of his observable preferential choice patterns. A person can be said to have a so-called "utility function" if and only if his preferential choice patterns are consistent with one another. But if they are, he has necessarily chosen rationally because in the modern utilitarians' construal of utility, he has also ipso facto maximized his utility: Having consistent preference patterns *is* having a utility function, *is* maximizing one's utility, and *is* choosing rationally. Having a utility function *is* having the particular consistent preferential choice pattern one has. Knowing someone's utility function is knowing his (consistent) preferential

*I am greatly indebted to my colleague, Shelly Kagan, who has carefully read an earlier version of this paper. He was particularly helpful in showing me that my argument on page 83 could be simplified and strengthened in various ways. I have gratefully accepted his suggestions, but he is not, of course, responsible for any errors that may have remained. I also want to thank the editor, Tom Regan, whose many excellent suggestions for reorganization, clarification, and stylistic improvements I have gladly accepted.

choice pattern — knowing when he prefers tea to coffee, a concert to a play, a tax increase to a tax reduction, and so on.

7. Jacob Marshak, "Towards an Economic Theory of Organization and Information," in *Decision Processes*, R.M. Thrall, C.H. Coombs, and R.L. Davis, eds. (N.Y.: John Wiley & Sons, 1954), ch. 14. Quoted by Jerome Rothenberg, *The Measurement of Social Welfare* (Englewood Cliffs, N.J.: Prentice-Hall, 1961), pp. 310ff.

8. Adam Smith, quoted by Thomas Donaldson, in *Corporations and Morality* (Englewood Cliffs, N.J.: Prentice-Hall, 1982), p. 65.

9. The problem is that the modern account of individual utilities allows them to be measured in terms of a so-called interval, not a ratio scale, but this means that utilities so measured do not permit interpersonal comparisons, hence utilities so measured cannot be added in a straightforward fashion. For a simple explanation of this, see Anatol Rapaport, *Two-Person Game Theory: The Essential Issues* (Ann Arbor: University of Michigan Press, 1966).

10. John Stuart Mill, *Utilitarianism*, reprinted in Samuel Gorovitz, ed., *Utilitarianism, with Critical Essays* (N.Y.: Bobbs Merrill, 1971), ch. 4, p. 37.

11. John Locke, *Second Treatise of Civil Government* (N.Y.: Everyman's Library, Dutton, 1924). Robert Nozick, *Anarchy, State, and Utopia* (N.Y.: Basic Books, 1974), esp. pp. 174–82; 280–92.

12. Nozick, op.cit., p. 33. See also pp. 28–33. For a similar view, see John Rawls, *A Theory of Justice* (Cambridge, Mass.: Belknap Press, 1971), §12, esp. pp. 66–72, 39, and 565–67.

13. I lack space to discuss the question of whether these two types of capitalism should perhaps be evaluated on the basis of their respective ideals of human life, one favoring a meritocratic ideal that is strictly individualistic, the other one that rests on a family line. The first insists that every individual enter the race from the same starting line and then lets individuals be rewarded in accordance with their innate assets. The second insists that individuals enter the race with the assets conferred by heredity and inheritance and lets individuals garner rewards that reflect the assets of a family line. For an interesting discussion, see Rawls, op.cit., §17, esp. pp. 106ff.

14. See Paul Samuelson, *Economics. An Introductory Analysis*, 6th ed. (N.Y.: McGraw-Hill, 1964), chs. 3, 4, p. 451.

15. Samuelson, op.cit., pp. 496–97.

16. Samuelson, op.cit., p. 507.

17. John T. Schlebecker of the Smithsonian Institution, "Ethics and Agribusiness." This was one of the lead papers in a multidisciplinary conference on Agriculture, Change and Human Value, held at the University of Florida at Gainesville from October 18 to 21, 1982. Mr. Schlebecker's permission to quote from his paper is gratefully acknowledged.

SUGGESTIONS FOR FURTHER READING

For a general introduction to business and professional ethics, see Norman Bowie, *Business Ethics* (Englewood Cliffs, N.J.: Prentice-Hall, 1982); Richard T. DeGeorge, *Business Ethics* (N.Y.: Macmillan, 1982); Thomas Donaldson and Patricia H. Werham, eds., *Ethical Issues in Business* (Englewood Cliffs, N.J.: Prentice-Hall, 1979); Michael D. Bayles, *Professional Ethics* (Belmont, Calif.: Wadsworth, 1981); Manuel G. Velasquez, *Business Ethics* (Englewood Cliffs, N.J.: Prentice-Hall, 1982).

For a discussion of the social responsibility of the corporation, see Neil H. Jacoby, *Corporate Power and Social Responsibility. A Blueprint for the Future* (New York, Macmillan, 1977), and Thomas Donaldson, *Corporations and Morality* (Englewood Cliffs, N.J.: Prentice-Hall, 1982).

Section I. For a searching discussion of the current "rules of the game" alluded to by Friedman and Levitt, see Joan Robinson, "What Are the Rules of the Game?" in Virginia Held, ed., *Property, Profits, and Economic Justice* (Belmont, Calif.: Wadsworth, 1980), and Christopher McMahon, "Morality and the Invisible Hand," *Philosophy and Public Affairs*, Vol. 10, no. 3, Summer 1981, pp. 247–77. On the question of recent changes in employees' legal rights and duties, see Alan F. Westin and Stephan Salisbury, eds., *Individual Rights in the Corporation* (N.Y.: Pantheon Books, Random House, 1980). On the nature of the employment relationship, see any textbook in business law, e.g., Lowell B. Howard, *Business Law*, Barrow's Educational Series, 1965, chs. V, VI. On the question of the employee's duty of loyalty, see, for instance, Phillip I. Blumberg, "Corporate Responsibility and the Employee's Duty of Loyalty and Obedience: A Preliminary Inquiry," *Oklahoma Law Review*, Vol. 24, no. 3, August 1971; reprinted in Tom L. Beauchamp and Norman E. Bowie, eds., *Ethical Theory and Business* (Englewood Cliffs, N.J.: Prentice-Hall, 1979), pp. 304–17. On the question of rights, duties and obligations, see Joel Feinberg, *Social Philosophy* (Englewood Cliffs, N.J.: Prentice-Hall, 1973), and Richard A. Wasserstrom, ed., *Morality and the Law* (Belmont, Calif.: Wadsworth, 1971).

For a discussion of social ethics, see John Rawls, *A Theory of Justice* (Cambridge, Mass.: Belknap Press, 1971), and Robert Nozick, *Anarchy, State, and Utopia* (N.Y.: Basic Books, 1974).

Section II. For a lucid statement of neo-classical capitalist economic theory, see Paul Samuelson, *Economics. An Introductory Analysis*, 6th ed. (N.Y.: McGraw-Hill, 1964). For an illuminating discussion of the conditions of perfect competition and other matters relevant to this section, see Charles E. Lindblom, *Politics and Markets* (N.Y.: Basic Books, 1977). For a discussion of welfare economics, see A.C. Pigou, *The Economics of Welfare* (N.Y.: Macmillan, 1962), or for a more technical review of the problems, Jerome Rothenberg, *The Measurement of Social Welfare* (Englewood Cliffs, N.J.: Prentice-Hall, 1961). For an excellent discussion, from which I have borrowed extensively, of the various kinds of capitalism distinguished, see the already mentioned paper by David Gauthier, "Economic Rationality and Moral Constraints," *Midwest Studies in Philosophy*, Vol. III (Wien: University of Minnesota Press, 1978), pp. 75–96. I have discussed the relation between classical and modern conceptions of utility in "Maximization and the Good Life," in *Akten des 5. Internationalen Wittgenstein Symposiums*, 25. bis 31. August 1980 (Vienna: Hölder-Pichler-Tempsky, 1981). For a simple explanation of the problems of the measurement of utility, see Anatol Rapoport, *Two-Person Game Theory* (Ann Arbor: University of Michigan Press, 1966), ch. 2. For a theory that allows interpersonal comparison, see John Harsanyi, *Rational Behavior and Bargaining Equilibrium in Games and Social Situations* (Cambridge: Cambridge University Press, 1977), ch. 4, esp. pp. 51–60.

For a discussion of Mill's views, see John Stuart Mill, *Utilitarianism*, reprinted in Samuel Gorovitz, ed., *Utilitarianism, with Critical Essays* (N.Y.: Bobbs Merrill, 1971), ch. IV, p. 37. For a discussion of the principle of equitability in the defense of "equal-opportunity capitalism," see my "Moral Reasons," in *Midwest Studies in Philosophy*, Vol. III (Minneapolis: University of Minnesota Press, 1978), pp. 62–74.

4

Individual Rights in Business

PATRICIA WERHANE

〈〉

I. INTRODUCTION

A society such as ours grants and enforces important political rights to its citizens, for example, the rights to freedom, to privacy, and to due process. These rights are part of the fabric of our political institutions. The same is not true of the workplace, however, as the following cases illustrate.

> A salesman for U.S. Steel, George Geary, was fired for protesting to his superior about a defective steel casing he was asked to sell. Although the casing was later proved to be faulty, Geary was fired for speaking out, and the courts upheld his dismissal, relying on the principle known as Employment at Will. According to this principle, an employer has the right, unless specified to the contrary by contract or law, to hire, demote, fire or promote "at will" whom and when it wishes.[1]

> A social worker, Daisy Alomar, was fired for not changing her political views. This firing was not rescinded by the courts, again because of the principle of Employment at Will.[2]

These cases illustrate how individual rights that are taken for granted and legally protected in society at large often seem to be neither acknowledged nor protected by the courts in the workplace. In fact, workers can be dismissed *because* they exercise their political rights.

In this country not all employees are without protection from arbitrary employer actions, as were Geary and Alomar. At least one-fifth of all workers are covered by collective bargaining agreements that protect against unfair dismissal and guarantee rights to grievance hearings and fair procedures when a worker is demoted or fired. Moreover, many employees who are civil servants employed by local, state, or national government, in what is called the public sector of the economy, have, by statute, the right to due process. They cannot be dismissed without a hearing. According to a recent study at least sixteen percent of public sector workers in this country fall in this category, and in some states veterans receive comparable employment protection under the law.[3] But even assuming that the group of unionized employees protected by collective bargaining and those protected by civil service statutes do not overlap, only thirty-six percent of all employees in this country would have those due process and other rights as workers, which the law grants them as citizens. At least sixty-four percent of all employees, most of whom are in private industry (called the private sector of the economy), lack legally mandated protection in the workplace against, for example, arbitrary invasions of free expression or privacy by their employers. Nor are these rights of these employees protected by legally enforced due process procedures.

Despite this paucity of legal protection, most employers do not mistreat their employees. Many places of employment are decent places to work, jobs are pleasant, most employers treat employees with respect, and many workers receive fair treatment in the workplace. But none of this is an adequate substitute for workers' *rights* to free expression, to privacy, to due process, and the like, if the case can be made for recognizing that employees have these rights. Whether employees have these rights, and, if they do, what their limits are, are important questions for both employees and employers. If employees have rights that extend to the workplace, they should not have to depend merely on the kindness of their superiors for fair treatment, but neither should employees be able to take advantage of employers at the slightest provocation by waving the banner of "workers' rights."

Whatever the present condition of employment practices, the central conclusion to be argued in the pages to follow is that employees have moral rights that should be recognized in the workplace. I shall contend that it is inconsistent to take steps to guarantee these rights in society at large and not to do so in the workplace. But to make a general case for employee rights is too vague an assignment. So this essay will analyze three specific rights—the rights to due process, to free expression, and to privacy—and we shall show how these are legitimate employee claims in the workplace. The choice of these three rights is not arbitrary. They constitute the most basic political claims of any democratic society. Therefore their institution in the workplace should be the first order of business in a democratic capitalist economy. Moreover, if one can make a rational defense for the institution of these rights in the workplace, the same sorts of arguments can be used to plead for other important, but less basic, employee rights. To defend the rights of employees, it will be argued, is not to call the justice of capitalism into question. It is, as we shall see, merely to require consistency in the ideas that make a private free enterprise economy possible.

In what follows the terms "employee" and "worker" will be used interchangeably to refer to any person in the employ of another. For the sake of abbreviating the argument, the term "employer" will refer to any person or institution who has the power to hire or fire another person. In this context "employer" could refer to an individual, an owner, a corporation, a personnel officer, a manager, a supervisor, or a foreman.

II. MORAL RIGHTS

The argument that employees have rights is based on a more general thesis that all human persons have certain moral rights. To defend this thesis fully would require much more than an essay, even one devoted exclusively to the topic of moral rights. Fortunately we can avoid the rigors of this inquiry here. For the thesis that persons have rights is hospitable to defenders of capitalism since all standard defenses of this economic philosophy rest on the thesis that all persons have certain rights, including rights to liberty and to property. So, in arguing that those humans who are employees have rights, we are merely making use of a tenet of standard defenses of capitalism. What rights employees have and how these rights are to be understood remain to be discussed.

§1 DEFINING RIGHTS

The idea of a right has been defined in a variety of ways. A right might simply be a liberty or privilege to do what one wants, for example, to get a Coke from the refrigerator. Yet rights sometimes involve more than a mere permission or an absence of constraint. A right might also be a claim to something (for example, money) against someone else (for example, a debtor). Rights also might involve powers, as in the case of the powers of the president of a university to confer degrees. At other times rights are claims to immunities or protection; the right to police protection is such a right. Immunity rights might be thought of as rights not to be deprived of other rights, such as the rights to freedom or to property. Finally, rights are sometimes thought of as entitlements to something, for example, to life or to property.[4]

Most rights involve more than one of these elements. The right to work, for example, is a permission involving, in the first instance, the absence of constraint in looking for a job. But the right to work might include the right to be given a job — a privilege or power conferred on the rights claimant, that is, the person claiming the right, by another. In all of these characterizations, however, the right in question is at least implicitly a claim (for example, a claim to liberty or non-interference) and sometimes, but not always, the right in question involves a claim against a particular individual or some group, as in the case of debts, rights to power, or immunity rights.

To assert that one has a right to something is not merely to say that one wants it or even that one wants it a lot. Rights must be validated independently of appeals to one's preferences. One way to validate a rights claim is through appeal to the law. *Legal rights* are claims that are shown to be valid by appeal to rules, laws, or constitutional systems. And sometimes legal rights are validated on the basis of an interpretation of the law — what *should* be recognized by those who accept such rules or systems. Of course not all rights defined or implied by laws are *morally* just. For example, in South Africa it is against the law to give equal pay to whites and nonwhites who do equal work. Most of us think that that is an unjust law, because it does not respect the rights of all persons equally. But to criticize this and other laws we must appeal to something other than legal rights; we must appeal to the rights we have as persons. This is to appeal to a notion of moral or human rights — rights that every person has and that every legal system should recognize and protect, despite the peculiarities of particular social or legal conventions, local customs, or historical traditions. Human rights are called moral rights, as distinct from legal rights, because the former are not contingent on legal authority, or on the particular customs or mores of a given time and place. Such rights are normative, because they concern how individuals morally *ought* to be treated. And such rights are human rights, because they are possessed equally by all human persons. For example, to say that the right to freedom is a moral or human right is to say that all persons everywhere, despite particular social, political, or legal circumstances, have a valid claim to exercise their autonomy just because, as persons, they are autonomous. When, as in South Africa and Russia, this right is denied, we say that the laws of these countries fail to respect human rights.

§2 INDEFEASIBLE AND DEFEASIBLE RIGHTS

Overarching the distinction between legal and moral rights is a further distinction, that between indefeasible and defeasible rights. *Indefeasible rights* are of two kinds. First, a right might be an exceptionless right, that is, a right that could never be overridden or outweighed no matter what the circumstances. If the right to liberty, for example, was exceptionless, no one would ever be justified in limiting another's freedom. Few will find the idea that rights are exceptionless a credible view. Second, indefeasible rights might be absolute rights, rights that hold without exception within a restricted set of circumstances or for certain classes of persons. For example, the contemporary philosopher H.L.A. Hart argues that the equal right to freedom is an absolute right for all autonomous, rational adults. Every rational adult, according to Hart's thesis, has an absolute right to as much freedom as every other rational adult, and there are no valid exceptions to this right. In other words, we cannot limit one person's autonomy *merely* as a means to accomplishing a desirable end, even the end of increasing the amount of autonomy for others.[5]

Though some human rights *might* be absolute, most seem to be *defeasible rights*, or what are called prima facie rights, rights that can be justifiably overridden in some cases. The right to freedom is normally thought of as a defeasible right, one that is justifiably outweighed in some circumstances, such as in times of national emergency. But the justice of overriding any right will involve considerations about other moral rights (that is, the valid claims of others), not merely the power or prejudices of another person or an institution.

§3   RIGHTS AND DUTIES

If rights are valid claims, they are claims to something, and sometimes they are claims against a particular individual or group. Worries about rights, then, will naturally arise in a social context. The hermit on a desert island has rights and so may make claims based on them. But his claims would be empty of import, since there is no one to recognize or overrule these claims, nor is there any way his rights could conflict with other similar claims made by others. Because human rights are often claims against others, and because human rights are moral rights, one person's rights are connected with the obligations or duties of other persons. For example, if I claim the right to a debt owed me, and if my claim is valid, then my debtor has a duty to pay me my due. Because of this connection between one person's rights and the obligations of others, some thinkers maintain that when one person has a moral right, some other person or persons have corresponding obligations.

Some philosophers contend that *every* right is defined by, or at least correlated with, a duty of another person or other persons, and, conversely, that every duty is identified by, or at least correlated with, someone's right. But there are exceptions to this idea [the correlativity-thesis]. For example, people may have a duty to contribute some of their money to charitable organizations, but no one charitable organization, such as the Crusade of Mercy, has a *right* to anyone's contribution. Moreover, some rights do not have correlative duties. For example, if two persons find a ten-dollar bill, both parties have an equal right to the money, but neither has a duty to respect the other person's right.[6] Thus, most, but not all rights, are correlated in some way or another with the obligations of other persons.

§4   THE UNIVERSALITY AND EQUALITY OF RIGHTS

Because of the shortcomings of the correlativity-thesis, some philosophers appeal to the notion of the universality of moral rights as at least a partial test of the validity of a rights claim. The universality of moral rights is best explained by the idea that rights, whether defeasible or indefeasible, are equal rights. All who have a given moral right have that right equally. Jack's moral rights to life, liberty, and fair treatment are neither more, nor are they less, than Jill's comparable rights. The fact that Jack is male and Jill is female, for example, makes no difference to the equality of their individual rights.

Moreover, this equality also holds independently of skin color, religious beliefs, place of birth, and present domicile. A black worker in South Africa has different legal rights than a white worker in South Africa. But both persons have the same equal moral rights, and the moral rights they have are the same as those of a white or black worker in, say, Chicago. One test of whether a given rights claim should be understood as affirming a *moral* right, then, is to ask whether one is prepared to universalize one's claim. What is meant by "universalize" is simply that, when one claims to have a moral right, it is understood that *every other person* must be conceived to have that same right (for example, the right to be paid what one is due) and to have it *equally*. If a claim to "rights" cannot meet the universality requirement—that is, if one is unwilling to recognize that all persons have the right one claims for oneself, and have that right equally—then the right one claims is not a moral right. Thus one test of the validity of a rights claim is universality.

Now, because of the equality of moral rights, employers cannot claim some privileges as their moral rights, or argue for changes in the law by appeal to their moral rights, unless they are willing to acknowledge these same equal rights in the case of their employees. And the same argument holds true for the rights employees might claim. To see this much is not to settle any question about what rights employees have or how rights can be used to argue for changes in employee-employer relations. But it is to see one way these important matters *cannot* be settled.

§5 POLITICAL AND ECONOMIC RIGHTS

In discussions of human rights a distinction sometimes is made between political rights and economic rights. Political rights are viewed as claims that must be recognized and protected in any just political state. The right to life, the rights to freedom of speech, assembly, movement, and the press, the rights to due process and a fair trial, the right to equal opportunity, and the right to vote—all are considered political rights. These are sometimes contrasted with economic rights, which are moral rights bound up with survival or subsistence. This distinction is not altogether clear-cut. The right to life, for example, a vital political right, is connected with survival and subsistence. And the rights to equal opportunity and property are important rights both politically and economically. Despite this overlap, we shall follow custom and distinguish between political and economic rights. While keeping in mind that this distinction is somewhat arbitrary, one of this essay's aims is to argue for the recognition and protection of employees' political rights in the workplace, including the rights to free expression, to due process, and to privacy. Other important moral rights, for example, the rights to life, to equal opportunity, to work, and to fair pay will not be addressed. We shall assume, for the sake of argument, that the latter are valid moral claims that should be recognized everywhere, but we do not have space to defend this view here. This omission is somewhat justified, however,

because the economic rights to work and to fair pay have been widely
treated in the literature on employment (in fact, the right to fair pay is
discussed in this volume by Henry Shue), while political rights in the
workplace have been by and large neglected. The right to equal opportunity is a very important right, and it, too, is discussed at length in
another essay in this volume, by George Sher.

§6 THE RIGHT TO PRIVATE OWNERSHIP

As mentioned earlier, the notion of a moral right to property is at home
in discussions of capitalism, since standard defenses of capitalism assume
that all persons have this right. Employers own businesses — land, factories, advertising agencies, banks, and the like — and they are thus in
the position to hire people to work in those businesses. Through employment, employees develop and improve the business of employers, and
employees in turn are provided with jobs and pay. The *right* to private
ownership is important because it is the basis for the employee-employer
exchange in any capitalist system. Critics of capitalism, especially Marxist critics, argue against the justice of private property and private ownership. These arguments certainly deserve reflective consideration. But
for the sake of this essay we shall assume the justice, in principle, of a
private free enterprise system and the notion of private ownership that is
implicit in that system.

Some non-Marxist readers of this essay might question the importance given to the notion of private ownership. These readers, primarily
contemporary economists, will argue that the notion of private ownership is an idea that, though it was important in the history of the development of a capitalist economy, is outmoded as descriptive of modern
property arrangements. We have moved from a private ownership economy to a collective, organizational and communal society, they will say.
The regulation of property "affected with a public interest" has meant
that owners cannot dispose of their things as they see fit. "Ownership" of
property has been dispersed, because many businesses are corporations
owned by thousands of stockholders. These stockholders do not control
what they own. Rather, the corporations are run by "hired hands,"
managers who have power much exceeding the owners'. Thus, the notion
of private property in our contemporary economy just is not important.[7]

In responding to this criticism, the importance of the organizational
and communal component in our society cannot be dismissed. However,
this view overlooks three crucial aspects of the institution of private
ownership that remain operative in contemporary society. These are: (a)
the recognition of the individual moral right to property ownership; (b)
the powerful institution of private property still enjoyed, albeit with restraints, by individuals, stockholders, and corporations; and (c) the notion
that an owner, whether an individual, a corporation or government, has
a moral right to dispose of his, her, or its property freely, as the owner
pleases. The last notion, (c), is still invoked in employee-employer rela-

tionships, as we shall see in the following section. In short, the rights to ownership and disposal of private property remain a cornerstone in any private free enterprise system, and one must recognize the existence of those rights in order to deal adequately with employee rights within that system.

III. THE RIGHT TO DUE PROCESS

§7 EMPLOYMENT AT WILL

The principle of Employment at Will, referred to in this essay's introduction, is an unwritten common-law idea that employers as owners have the absolute right to hire, promote, demote, and fire whom and when they please. The principle, hereafter abbreviated as EAW, was stated explicitly in 1887 in a document by H. G. Wood entitled *Master and Servant*. Wood said, "A general or indefinite hiring is prima facie a hiring at will."[8] But the principle behind EAW dates at least to the seventeenth century and perhaps was used as early as the Middle Ages. EAW has commonly been interpreted as the rule that all employers "may dismiss their employees at will . . . for good cause, for no cause, *or even for causes morally wrong*, without being thereby guilty of legal wrong."[9]

The principle of EAW is not self-evident and stands in need of defense. The most promising lines of defense involve appeals to the right to freedom, to the common notion that property is defined as private ownership (for example, of land, material possessions, or capital), to the supposed moral right to dispose freely of one's own property as one sees fit, or to the utilitarian benefits of freely operating productive organizations. Let us briefly characterize the main elements of each defense.

The first justification for EAW in the workplace, at least in the private sector of the economy, involves both appeals to the right to freedom and considerations about the nature of places of employment in a free society. Places of employment are privately owned, voluntary organizations of all sizes, from small entrepreneurships to large corporations. As such, it is claimed, they are not subject to the same restrictions governing public and political institutions. And, as they are voluntary organizations, employees join freely and may quit at any time. Political procedures, needed to safeguard citizens against arbitrary exercise of power in society at large, do not apply to voluntary private institutions. Any restriction on the principle of EAW, those who argue in this way conclude, interferes with the rights of persons *and* organizations not to be coerced into activities that either are not of their own choosing or limit their freedom to contract.

The principle of EAW is also sometimes defended purely on the basis of property rights. The rights to freedom and to private ownership, we are assuming, are equally valid claims, and the latter right entitles owners, it is argued, to use and improve what they own, including all aspects of their businesses, as they wish. According to this view, when an employee is working for another, this activity affects, positively or negatively, the employer's property and production. Because employers have property rights, and because these rights entitle them to control what happens to what they own, the employer has the right to dispose of the labor of employees whose work changes production. In dismissing or demoting employees, the employer is not denying *persons* political rights; rather, the employer is simply excluding their *labor* from the organization.

Finally, EAW is often defended on practical grounds. Viewed from a utilitarian perspective, hiring and firing "at will" is necessary in productive organizations if they are to achieve their goal of maximum efficiency and productivity. To interfere with this process, it is claimed, would defeat the purpose of free enterprise organizations. We shall consider each of these arguments more fully in the following section.

§8 THE RIGHT TO DUE PROCESS IN THE WORKPLACE

Due process is a procedure by which one can appeal a decision or action in order to get a rational explanation of the decision and a disinterested, objective review of its propriety. In the workplace due process is, or should be, the right to grievance, arbitration, or some other fair procedure to evaluate hiring, firing, promotion, or demotion. For example, Geary and Alomar were fired without a hearing. Should they have been given some warning, a hearing by peers, a chance to appeal? The call to recognize the right to due process in the workplace extends the widely accepted view that every accused person, guilty or innocent, has a right to a fair hearing and an objective evaluation of his or her guilt or innocence. Those who deny due process in the workplace could argue (a) that this right does not extend to every sector of society, or (b) that rights of employers sometimes override those of employees and do so in this case. However we decide the merits of these arguments, the absence of due process in the workplace is not merely an oversight, as witness the principle of Employment at Will discussed in the last section. An employer, according to this principle, need not explain or defend its employee treatment in regard to dismissal nor give a hearing to the employee before he or she is dismissed.

In order to support the validity of the claim to the right to due process in the workplace, we must examine the defenses of the principle of EAW given in the previous section. First, EAW was defended on the ground that every person has the right to own and accumulate private property and, relatedly, every person, and analogously every corporation, has the right to dispose of what they own as they see fit. To say that employers have the right to dispose of their property "at will" is a legitimate claim, which follows from the right to ownership. To say that employers have this same right to "dispose of," that is, to fire for *any* reason, their employees is quite another sort of claim. The right to private ownership gives one the right to dispose of *material possessions* as one pleases, but it in no sense implies that one has the right to dispose of *persons* as one pleases. Employees, although they work on, and labor to improve, the business of their employers, are not themselves property. They are autonomous persons. Their employers do not own them, just as the employers do not own members of their own families. So the right of an employer to hire or demote "at will" cannot be defended simply by appealing to employer ownership rights, because employees are not the property of employers.

A second attempted justification of EAW, we saw earlier, appeals to an employer's right to freedom. Voluntary private organizations in a free society rightly argue that they should be as free as possible from coercive and restrictive procedures. Due process might be thought of as such a procedure, since it requires checks for arbitrariness on the part of employers. However, one needs to evaluate the role of the employer and the coercive nature of "at will" employment in voluntary organizations more carefully before accepting a negative view of due process in the workplace.

Though private businesses are voluntary organizations which employees are free to leave at any time, employers are in a position of power relative to individual employees. This by itself is not a sufficient reason to restrict employer activities. But the possible abuse of this power *is* what is at issue when we question the principle of EAW. By means of his or her position, an employer can arbitrarily hire or fire an employee. The employee can, of course, quit arbitrarily too. But an "at will" employee is seldom in a position within the law to inflict harm on an employer. Legally sanctioned "at will" treatment by employers of employees, on the other hand, frequently harms employees, as the following observations confirm.

When one is demoted or fired, the reduction or loss of the job is only part of an employee's disadvantage. When one is demoted or fired, it is commonly taken for granted that one *deserved* this treatment, whether or not this is the case. Without an objective appraisal of their treatment, employees are virtually powerless to demonstrate that they were fired, demoted, and so forth, for no good reason. Moreover, fired or demoted employees generally have much more difficulty than other persons in getting new jobs or rising within the ranks of their own company. The absence of due process in the workplace places arbitrarily dismissed or demoted employees at an *undeserved* disadvantage among persons competing for a given job. Viewed in this light, the absence of due process is unfair because workers who do not deserve to be fired are treated the same as those who do, with the result that the opportunities for future employment for both are, other things being equal, equally diminished.

To put the point differently, a fired employee is harmed, at least prima facie. And this raises the question, Do employers exceed their right when they fire or demote someone arbitrarily? For it is not true that one has the right to do just anything, when one's activities harm those who have not done anything to deserve it. In order to justify the harm one does to another as a result of the exercise of one's freedom, one must be able to give good reasons. And good reasons are precisely what are lacking in cases where employers, by firing those in their employ, prima facie harm these people for "no cause, or even for causes morally wrong." It is difficult to see how a defense of EAW can elicit our rational assent, if it is based exclusively on an appeal to an employer's liberty rights, because the unrestrained exercise of such rights may cause undeserved harm to those employees who are the victims of its arbitrary use.

Worse, "at will" practices violate the very right the principle of EAW is based on. Part of the appeal of the principle of EAW is that it protects the employer's right not to be coerced. According to the libertarian thinker Eric Mack, a coercive act is one that renders individual or institutional behavior involuntary.[10] Due process might be thought of as a coercive procedure because it *forces* employers to justify publicly their employment practices. But some of the employment practices sanctioned by EAW also are, or can be, coercive, according to Mack's definition. Persons who are fired without good reason *are involuntarily* placed in disadvantageous, undeserved positions by their employer. It is, therefore, difficult to defend "at will" employment practices on the basis of avoidance of coercion, since these practices themselves can be, and often are, coercive.

Defenders of EAW might make the following objection. EAW, they might claim, balances employee and employer rights because, just as the employer has the right to dispose of its business and production, so the employee has the right to accept or not to accept a job, or to quit or remain in a job once hired for it. Due process creates an imbalance of rights, this defense continues, because it restricts the freedom of the employer without restricting the freedom of the employee.

This objection lacks credibility. It supposes that the rights of employees and employers are equal when EAW prevails, but this is not the case. The principle of EAW works to the clear advantage of the owner or employer and to the clear disadvantage of the employee, because the employee's opportunity to change jobs is, other things being equal, significantly impaired when the employee is fired or demoted, while the employer's opportunity to hire is not similarly lessened. The employee's decreased opportunity to dispose of his or her labor, in other words, normally is *not* equal to the employer's decreased ability to carry on his business activities. So the operation of EAW, judged in terms of the comparative losses normally caused to employers and employees, does not treat the two, or their rights, equally.

"At will" treatment of employees is also advocated on the basis of maximizing efficiency. Unproductive or disruptive employees interfere with the business of the employer and hamper productivity. Employers must have the liberty to employ whom and when they wish. But without due process procedures in the workplace, what is to prevent an employer from making room for a grossly unqualified son-in-law by firing a good employee, for example, an action which is itself damaging to efficiency? And how inefficient *is* due process in the workplace really? Due process does not alter the employee-employer hierarchical arrangement in an organization. Due process does *not* infringe on an employer's prima facie right to dispose of its business or what happens in that business. The right to due process merely restricts the employer's alleged right to treat employees arbitrarily. Moreover, would not knowledge that employees are protected against arbitrary treatment go some way toward boosting employee morale? And will anyone seriously suggest that employee morale and employee efficiency are unrelated? In spite of the fears of some employers, due process does not require that employees never be dismissed on grounds of their inefficiency. Due process merely requires that employees have a hearing and an objective evaluation before being dismissed or demoted.

Finally, proponents of EAW will argue as follows. Ours is a free-market economy, they will say, and government should keep out of the economy. To heed the call for legally mandated due process in the workplace, which is what most critics of EAW seek, is to interfere with the free enterprise system. The government and the courts should leave employees and employers to work out matters on their own. Employees have the freedom to quit their jobs "at will." Therefore, the freedom of the employer to fire "at will" should be protected.

This is a peculiar defense. The plain fact is that employers, at least when they have the status of corporations, have not been reluctant to involve the government and the courts in the name of protecting *their* interests. The courts have recognized the right of corporations to due process while by and large upholding the principle of EAW for employees in the workplace. This at least appears to contravene the requirement of universality (§4). For if corporations have a moral right to be treated fairly, and this moral right grounds legal rights to due process for them, then one would naturally expect that employees would also have this moral right, and that the law should protect employees by requiring fair grievance procedures in the workplace, including, in particular, legal protection against arbitrary dismissals or demotions. Yet the situation is not as expected. *Employers* have a legally protected right to due process. Employees hired "at will" do *not*. The universality we expect and require in the case of moral rights is missing here.

The difference in the status of employers and employees under the law is defended by the courts by the claim that corporations, all of which have state charters, are "public entities" whose activities are "in the public interest." Employees, on the other hand, are not public entities, and, at least in private places of employment, the work they perform is, so the courts imply, *not* in the public interest. Now there are celebrated problems about conceiving of corporations as public entities, and one might want to contest this defense of EAW by challenging the obscurity of the difference on which it is based. The challenge we should press in this essay, however, is not that the distinction between what is and what is not a public entity is too obscure. It is that the distinction is not relevant. The *moral* importance of due process—of being guaranteed honest attempts at fair, impartial treatment—has nothing to do with who is or is not a public entity. Fundamentally, it has to do with the rights of the private citizen. The right to due process is the right to a fair hearing when the acts or accusations of others hold the promise of serious harm being done to a person who does not deserve it. To deny due process of employees in the workplace, given the prima facie harm that is caused by dismissal or demotion, and given that those who are harmed in these ways may not deserve it, is tantamount to claiming that *only some* persons have this right. Such a conclusion conflicts with the view, widely held in our society, that due process is a *moral* right, one that is possessed by *everyone* in *all* circumstances.

To make what is an obvious point, due process is an essential political right in any society that respects just treatment of every person. When people who do not deserve it are put at risk of being significantly harmed by the arbitrary decisions of others, the persons put at risk ought to be protected. Indeed, if those who make decisions are powerful, and those who are the recipients of these decisions are, by comparison, both weak and in danger of significant harm, then we must insist *all the more* on measures to protect the weak against the strong. Paradoxically, therefore, precisely in those cases where workers are individually weak—precisely, that is, in those areas where EAW prevails—is where it should not. Thus, the democratic political ideal of fairness is threatened if the principle of EAW is allowed.

There is, then, for the reasons given, a very strong presumptive case to be made against EAW and in favor of the right of employees to impartial grievance procedures in the workplace, independently of the presence of a contractual guarantee of such procedures. Let us give a summary statement of the right.

> Every person has a right to a public hearing, peer evaluation, outside arbitration or some other mutually agreed upon grievance procedure before being demoted, unwillingly transferred or fired.

The arguments given in favor of recognizing the right of employees to due process in the workplace were characterized as being strong presumptive arguments. It was not contended that the reasoning given "proves" this right conclusively. Rather, the arguments collectively provide a set of reasons that make it logical to recognize this right, while allowing that objections might be raised that show that there are better reasons against recognizing the right to due process in the workplace.

According to strong advocates of employee rights, the right to due process does not go far enough. It does not give an employee much in the way of *rights*. It simply precludes dismissal without a formal hearing. However, the worker's right to due process would, if appropriately institutionalized, make progress in the area of employee rights. This is because due process helps to prevent arbitrary treatment of persons in the workplace by making the cause and reason for the employee treatment public and by guaranteeing the opportunity to appeal. Respect for the rights of employees as persons will not be satisfied with anything less, even if it is true, as some contend, that genuine respect requires much more.

§9 POLICIES FOR THE INSTITUTION OF DUE PROCESS IN THE WORKPLACE

Though such procedures are hardly universal, a number of companies employ a variety of grievance procedures in the workplace. The most successful and objective of these include some or all of the following elements.

1. Written contracts between employees and employers drawn up at the time of hiring where the rights and responsibilities of each party are spelled out.
2. Written due process policies drawn up and made public to all employees.
3. "Open door" policies of employee complaints instituted where complaints are truly welcomed and promptly resolved. An anonymous complaint procedure is very effective. An ombudsman or an employee advocate is helpful because employees have fewer fears of retaliation if there are designated persons available for such purposes.
4. Any employee who has an unanswered complaint against an employer or who feels he or she has been demoted or fired without good reason has the right to appeal through a formal set of procedures, which, in outline, are as follows.

Formal Procedures:

5. (a) Formal appeals begin with a written complaint, where possible. (b) The person issuing the complaint appoints an employee advocate or co-worker to attend each hearing. (c) The complaint is heard first by one's immediate supervisor, next by a department head.
6. A peer review committee reviews complaints not settled by the above procedures.
7. An appeals committee, consisting of representatives from management, from the peer committee and a co-worker, reviews the decision of the peer committee.
8. If all the foregoing fail, and if the employee persists in his or her grievance, independent arbitrators are brought in to evaluate the decision.
9. All parts of this process are open and prompt.
10. Any person unjustly demoted or fired is reinstated with back pay or equal compensation.

Employer Rights:

11. Any employer who has a complaint against an employee is similarly entitled to go through these formal procedures.
12. When the grounds for dismissal or demotion are upheld, the employer may demote or fire the employee, without penalty to the employer.

IV. THE RIGHTS TO FREE EXPRESSION AND PRIVACY

Since workers can be fired even if their right to due process is protected, one needs to establish what constitutes good reasons for their dismissal. Poor job performance, drunkenness on the job, and criminal behavior in the workplace constitute such grounds. But often employees are fired or demoted because they have exercised their political rights in the workplace. Assuming, as we have, that freedom and privacy are not only constitutional but also moral rights, people have these rights *everywhere*, including the workplace. Still, assuming that these rights are not absolute, they may be justifiably overridden in some cases. As will be argued shortly, however, neither the economic interests of the employer nor the employer's right to freedom to contract override the rights to freedom and privacy in the workplace. Employees should not be dismissed or demoted for responsibly exercising these rights on the job any more than they should be punished for doing so in society at large.

§10 FREE EXPRESSION AND WHISTLE-BLOWING

It will be recalled that George Geary was fired by the U.S. Steel Corporation for calling attention to a faulty product. Similarly, Dan Gellert, a pilot for Eastern Airlines, was demoted and grounded for speaking out to his superiors and to the Federal Aviation Administration about defects in the autopilot mechanism of the Lockheed 1011 airplanes he was asked to fly.[11] Geary and Gellert proved to be right in their assessments, respectively, of the casing and the Lockheed 1011. They felt it was their duty to dissent and "blow the whistle" on their employer. Later, however, they were fired for speaking out.

Geary and Gellert are "whistle-blowers." Whistle-blowing in business is the activity where an employee makes known, or sounds an alarm about, either within the corporation or publicly, business activities he or she feels threaten individuals, the organization, or the public. It is a form of free speech prompted by an event or condition that the whistle-blower views as in some way morally objectionable and that would probably otherwise go unnoticed. Both Geary and Gellert began their protests by voicing these sorts of objections within their respective organizations; only later did they move to a public forum.

Cases of whistle-blowing arise in different circumstances, including the following. (1) Some have to do with differing views regarding the fairness of one's treatment by one's superior. Such was the case of Olga Monge, an employee for the Beebe Rubber Company, who was fired for objecting to what she regarded as unfair treatment by her foreman, who made "granting him favors" a condition for promotion.[12] (2) Others have to do with questions about efficiency or product quality, the type of conflict illustrated by the Geary case. (3) Some conflicts concern consumer or product safety, as in the Gellert case. (4) Yet other conflicts arise when employees challenge the propriety of their employer's treatment of other employees. Let us look more fully at an example of (4).

The Polaroid Corporation is a transnational organization with operations in a number of countries, including a distributor in South Africa. In 1970 a group of black employees at Polaroid's headquarters in Massachusetts formed a movement to protest the existence of Polaroid in South Africa, because of that country's position on human rights. Polaroid responded to the group by sending employee representatives to South Africa and by enforcing improved treatment of nonwhite South African employees by their distributor in that country, in direct violation of South African law regarding treatment of blacks. However, one of the leaders of the group of protesters at Polaroid was eventually fired for allegedly disrupting company work and "for conduct detrimental to the best interests of the company."[13] This case illustrates both an instance where a crucial moral issue is at stake, and an instance where an employee's militant views about the issue were felt to conflict with the economic well-being of the company. Can the employee's right to free expression be defended in this instance?

Like other questions about individual rights, this one cannot be answered in a vacuum. To answer it, we must consider the more general question of the scope of the right to free expression.

§11 THE RIGHT TO FREE EXPRESSION IN THE WORKPLACE

The right to free speech is taken for granted in our society. This right is not absolute, however, and so may be justifiably overridden in some cases. In the particular case of whistle-blowers in the workplace, what are the arguments, and how strong are they, for overriding their exercise of this right? Among the possibilities, the following arguments should be considered. (1) Employees are not autonomous adults and so lack the right to free expression; (2a) efficiency and, thus, a greater economic good or more satisfaction of needs is possible by limiting free speech in the workplace; (2b) greater harm to the corporation or to society is produced by allowing free expression in the workplace than without free expression; (3) the employee right to free expression conflicts with employer rights and the rights of the latter override the rights of the former. Let us examine each of these possibilities.

Argument (1) is clearly unacceptable. If one assumes that employees are not rational adults, one's definition of a "rational adult" would have to be such that it applied only to managers and owners. Such a definition is patently absurd. Both forms of argument (2) are utilitarian in character. They assume that rights are connected with personal or societal benefits. If a business is more efficient without employee dissent, then employees have no *right* to dissent. That implies, however, that a person has a right to free expression only if the recognition of this right benefits some group or society generally. And that sort of basis for individual rights could pave the way for many abuses of rights. If enslaving some class of persons, for example, were more beneficial to society than allowing them freedom, those persons would justifiably lose their freedom in the name of "the general welfare." Indeed, by appeal to this basis, *any* moral right could be overridden for the sake of *any* collective good. The workplace would be merely a special case of collectivist benefits "trumping" individual rights; only there it could be done in the name of "the corporate welfare."

Although the issues are complex and controversial, a utilitarian basis for moral rights seems highly unsatisfactory. If the notion of a moral right makes any sense, one must recognize that persons have such rights, if they do, *just because they are persons*, that is, *just because they are rational, autonomous individuals*. They cannot have such rights as the right to life or to liberty because, and only so long as, acknowledging these rights promotes the general welfare. One could then justify sacrificing the rights of a small minority in a society in order to promote the general welfare. Of course, recognizing and enforcing these moral rights might promote the general welfare, and it would be very nice if this occurred. But it need not, and the existence of such fundamental rights cannot depend on whether collective interests are enhanced. Those moral rights persons have, as persons, are independent of the social utility that stems from recognizing them. These rights are possessed by all persons and possessed equally, wherever they might live and—and this is the crucial reminder in the present context—whatever their role in a free market. Employers have these rights. But so, too, do employees. And both have them independently of considerations about "corporate utility." If that much is granted, it should come as no surprise that the moral rights of the individual "trump" utilitarian calculations, both outside and inside the workplace. To put the same point differently, the only thing that can override a given moral right is another moral right. Rights are never to be overridden merely in the name of promoting increases in social or corporate utility, including, then, corporate profits. Assuming, as our society does, that all persons have an equal moral right to free expression, no employer has the right to override this right of an employee *merely* on the grounds of profits and losses. Both forms of argument (2), therefore, fail to justify overriding employee rights to free expression.

Argument (3) is more difficult. It states that if a worker's free expression interferes with employer rights, the latter justifiably prevail. An employee's right to free expression, that is, is outweighed *by other rights*, not by utilitarian considerations. A number of rights could be at issue here. Let us consider two that are of special importance to employers: first, property rights to private ownership, and second, the right to freedom, including freedom to contract.

In the case of property rights, do they outweigh the right to liberty that underlies the right to free expression? It is difficult to see how this could be so. If property is understood as one's material possessions, then the right to ownership could not be thought to override the right to liberty without absurdity, since the former right presupposes the latter. Unless we assume that, as persons, we have the *liberty* right to acquire, keep, and dispose of material possessions (our property), the very idea of our having a right to property becomes unintelligible. Viewed in this light, and seen against the backdrop of a private free enterprise economy, therefore, property rights, while they are valid claims, cannot themselves override the right to liberty, a right that must be respected if there is to be such a thing as a right to private property in the first place. Moreover, since the right to free expression is itself part of the larger right to liberty, there is no reason to suppose, and good reason to deny, that property rights can, or should, outweigh the right to free expression.

In cases of conflicting employer-employee claims to freedom, the right to free expression *can* be set aside when the "greater harm" might be the loss of some other important moral right such as the loss of some other person's right to freedom. In the workplace, restrictions on the equal right to free expression are justified when, for example, an employee engages in slanderous accusations that create greater harm to the rights of employers. But one cannot restrict employee freedom of expression to protect an employer's freedom to contract if that restriction (a) creates an imbalance of rights such that the employee is coerced to a greater extent than the employer, or (b) allows the employer to engage in activities harmful to others, as in the Geary and Gellert cases. When one restricts or punishes employees for speaking truthfully about issues clearly physically or morally harmful, an employer is coercing an employee into behavior not of his or her choosing, while at the same time abetting preventable harmful activities.

If this last argument is sound, we can now see that the employees at Polaroid acted within their political right to free expression when they protested the company's operations in South Africa. However, once the company took those steps it could to correct its own operations, assuming that it did this, the continued agitation on the part of a particular employee would be a case where that individual exceeded her rights. Even corporations can be obligated to do only what they can reasonably be expected to do. After Polaroid had done what it reasonably could be expected to do, as, let us assume, it did, it did not have any obligation to do more. For an employee to persist in urging the company to do what it could not do, especially if this agitation was detrimental to the company's economic interests, would be grounds for dismissal.

In summary, every person has a prima facie right to free expression in the workplace, employers and employees have *equal* rights, and one set of freedoms can be set aside when other equal rights are at stake. But an employee's freedom cannot be overridden for the sake of property rights, greater employer freedom, or larger economic interests.

§12 MORAL DILEMMAS OF WHISTLE-BLOWING

The right to free expression is often called an active right. Possession of this right entails, of course, possession of the right not to be coerced by others. But in order to enjoy freedom fully one must exercise that right: One must *do* something—speak out, practice religious freedom, or print controversial news items. In the workplace the right to free expression ordinarily is not an issue except in cases where an employee's *exercise* of freedom appears not to be in the interests of the employer. And these very instances often involve whistle-blowing. The whistle-blower, having to initiate this activity, often faces moral dilemmas where the choices are not simple. The difficult questions facing potential whistle-blowers include: Is blowing the whistle the best action to take, all things considered? Will this action result in a balance of benefits over harms, or will whistle-blowing in this instance accrue little in the way of positive results?

When an employee perceives an activity in the workplace to be illegal or morally wrong, and when it appears that the questionable activity will not be corrected, one is tempted to say that, in principle, the employee should always make public this activity. But this oversimplifies the whistle-blowing situation. First a potential whistle-blower must be sure of his or her facts, must believe *with good reason* that the employer (or another employee) is engaging in an illegal or an immoral activity, and must be able to document any charges that are made. Many times whistle-blowers sound false alarms, thus violating employer rights and giving a bad name to whistle-blowing.

Second, the whistle-blower must determine the harm done by the employer activity in question and weigh that harm against (a) possible benefits accrued by blowing the whistle and (b) possible harms created by the action. Third, the whistle-blower must evaluate conflicting duties to society, profession, employer, family and self.

All of these judgments are interrelated. In weighing benefits against harms, the whistle-blower has certain loyalties to the employer, and, often, conflicting loyalties to her profession. The whistle-blower also knows that her action will, in all likelihood, disrupt the economic activities of the employer, which, in turn, might economically harm other employees. The whistle-blower, then, must weigh loyalties and harms to the employer and to other employees against her duties to uphold professional standards and to prevent societal harm where possible. And surely the circumstances of each individual case must be weighed by the responsible whistle-blower. Whistle-blowing also presents serious personal moral choices for the whistle-blower. Often whistle-blowers are demoted or fired, and sometimes they are prevented from getting other jobs in the industry. Whistle-blowing, then, may cause economic and psychological harm to the whistle blower or her family.

Finally, whistle-blowing is not always the best course of action, all things considered. Sometimes simply to blow the whistle when a wrong is committed, while within one's moral right to free expression, might not be the most responsible course of action nor achieve the desired result. Returning to Dan Gellert, had there not been a strong pilots' union, Gellert would have been fired summarily from Eastern Airlines, he would not have been hired by another airline, his family and self-esteem would have suffered, and, in all probability, the automechanism in the Lockheed 1011 would have gone unrepaired until some serious accident had occurred. Because Gellert could stay at Eastern and continue his protests within the company, he was successful. Sometimes, then, taking another course of action within the company, without blowing the whistle, might achieve the desired result without jeopardizing either one's job or the public welfare.[14]

This discussion of whistle-blowing is not meant in any way to underestimate the importance of the right to free expression nor to downplay the value of whistle-blowing. Its purpose is simply to remind ourselves that the decision to blow the whistle in particular cases is not easy and should never be taken lightly. Having said that, however, it is morally imperative that clear-cut and open policies for free expression and the protection of legitimate whistle-blowers be instituted in the workplace.

§13 POLICIES FOR PROTECTING FREE EXPRESSION IN THE WORKPLACE

A fair policy for free expression and whistle-blowing would include the following:

1. The right of any employee to speak out freely in protest of a product, employee treatment, or other organizational activity should be protected without risk of reprimand, demotion, or job loss.
2. Because of the right to due process, the whistle-blower is to be initially protected from employer retaliation. However,
3. To honor the employer's right not to be slandered, the whistle-blower must be able to document the charge. If this is not achieved, the matter should be dropped.
4. Documented cases that are, or are likely to be, ignored by the corporation should be aired through a public medium. If the charges are true, the employee blowing the whistle should be protected by statute from employer retaliation or discrimination.
5. Slanderous or clearly false accusations that threaten the equal right to freedom of other employees or the employer should result in the dismissal of the employee making such charges and, when appropriate, legal punishment.

§14 THE RIGHT TO PRIVACY

In 1890 two then little-known lawyers, Samuel D. Warren and Louis D. Brandeis, wrote an essay for the *Harvard Law Review* entitled "The Right to Privacy." In this article Warren and Brandeis argued that the right to life includes the right to enjoy life. This right in turn includes the right to be left alone, that is, the right to privacy. Warren and Brandeis argued further that the right to be left alone includes intangibles, such as one's ego, one's personality, and one's thoughts. A person's right to privacy, according to these thinkers, is an unconditional right of all humans.[15] But *why* is the right to privacy such an important entitlement?

Privacy is a privilege particularly valued in our society. Norms against the invasion of privacy protect a person's autonomy as an adult individual and help guarantee the opportunity of persons to maximize their control over their own lives. Respect for privacy fosters respect for persons as free moral agents who can, and should be allowed to, decide for themselves what they will do. A lack of respect for privacy, in turn, breeds a lack of respect for persons. Moreover, the right to privacy underpins social relationships, particularly those involving mutual respect between persons, such as trust and love. Finally, respect for privacy prevents possible control or coercion of one group by those who have, and might use, intimate information. Protection of the right to privacy is, therefore, necessary if one values individuality, personal freedom, and autonomy, and the institution of this right helps prevent possible harms arising from those who misuse personal information.

We see, then, that the right to privacy defended by Warren and Brandeis is a moral right that, like the equal right to freedom, cannot be overridden except when another right is threatened. In the workplace, therefore, the right to privacy, like the right to free expression, cannot be set aside merely by appeal to the economic interests of the employer. Nor can employee privacy be overridden by an employers' exercise of his right to freedom (for example, his voluntarily deciding to share employee information with some person or agency outside the workplace), if this action shows lack of respect for the employee as an autonomous adult. The legitimacy of these restrictions will be seen more clearly when we note how workers' rights to privacy find expression in the workplace.

§15 CONFIDENTIALITY

Employees often have little privacy about their personal lives. Employers request personal information, which, they say, is necessary if they are to hire the right person and thereby prevent unnecessary dismissals. A lack of employee personal data, it is claimed, turns out to be expensive for the employer and unfair to prospective employees who are hired for jobs they cannot perform, as well as to those who, though amply qualified, are not hired. Now it is true that employers *need* information about their employees. Yet a major objection to the demand for employee information is that there is little confidentiality. Personal information intended for the employer sometimes finds its way to creditors, banks, and other interested or curious persons. When this happens, the worker's right to privacy is violated.

This strong claim can be defended as follows. An employer's *right* to personal information is coupled with that employer's *obligation* to safeguard that information. Otherwise the employer undermines respect for the worker as a person by making his or her personal life a subject for public scrutiny. An employer might argue that personal information is "voluntarily given" by job applicants and employees. But one must be careful of the term "voluntary." If one needs, or wants to keep, a job, economic pressures often win out over one's self-respect. And the applicant or employee is in a disadvantageous position, because an employer can withhold a job on the basis of lack of personal data. Because of this, the employer has an obligation not to demand more information from an employee or a potential employee than is necessary to evaluate the employee's likely contribution to the workplace. And an employer has an obligation *not* to let personal employee information become public. The right to confidentiality needs to be protected in the workplace, perhaps with legal measures if necessary, so that employee autonomy is safeguarded.

What *legal* rights of privacy do employees have? In a recent case the Supreme Court decided that eavesdropping on employee telephone conversations was a violation of privacy. The Fair Credit Reporting Act allows persons to know why they are turned down for credit and to have access to the source of the creditor's information. The Freedom of Information Act allows employees to examine their own files and letters of recommendation. Additional protection of employee rights to privacy is found in the Privacy Act, which protects public, but not private, employees from employer intrusions in their private lives. This act, in brief, protects the employees from eavesdropping on private conversations, from compulsory or surreptitious investigations of their personal life, from the requirement to give irrelevant information, and from the release of personal material by the employer in the employee's file. What the act suggests is that there should be a *minimum of intrusiveness* by employers in the private lives of their employees and a *maximum of confidentiality* regarding the facts the employer feels are necessary to hire someone. In view of what has been argued to this point, we might summarize our conclusion by stating that what is needed is a privacy act that protects the privacy of *all* employees, those in the *private*, not just those in the public, sector of the economy.

§16 THE PRIVACY OF OUTSIDE ACTIVITIES

The controversy about a worker's right, as a private citizen, to engage in outside activities of one's choice is illustrated in the case of Daisy Alomar, who, it will be recalled (see the opening paragraphs of this essay), was fired as a social worker because she would not change her political affiliation. This case demonstrates that the right to privacy has not been clearly established in the workplace or in the courts. As in the case of free expression, outside activities are seldom questioned unless they somehow conflict with employer's goals. Most employers do not want to know what people do in their leisure time. But the issue of the *right* to privacy raises the question: In principle *should* employees have the right to engage in outside activities if these activities might hurt the reputation, status, or even the business activities of the employer?

The right to engage in outside activities of one's choice is part of the respect for individuality so highly valued in our society. Moreover, it is an extension of the right to freedom that we discussed in §10 and §11. There it was argued that an employee has an equal right to express himself or herself freely except when (a) the employee engages in slanderous activity or (b) there is an overriding threat to the rights of others. The same conditions limit an employee's right to engage in outside activities of his or her choice. There is little to support the view that one's political views damage one's abilities as a social worker, for example, as was claimed in the case of Ms. Alomar. More generally, no employer has the right to deny employees their right to engage in political or social activities of their own choosing, and no employer has the right to dismiss an employee *merely* because of employee political or social activities. Nor should any person be dismissed for protesting against a company program that that person thinks is immoral or illegal so long as the basis for the protest can be documented. On the other hand, the right to engage in outside activities of one's choice is a prima facie right that *can* be overridden by the equal rights of other persons. When an employee's activity literally competes with his employer's business or damages her workplace, for example, it is difficult to imagine how limitations on such employee activities could be viewed as arbitrary or a violation of employee rights. For example, if a Klu Klux Klansman slanders fellow employees, such an action threatens to undermine the personal working relationships necessary for the normal operation of a business. The employer thus acts within his or her rights when taking disciplinary action against the employee in such a case. Like other rights in employment, the right to the privacy of one's own activities can be abused and is limited by respect for the rights of fellow employees and one's employer.

§17 THE POLYGRAPH AND PRIVACY

The right to privacy is seriously threatened by the prolific use of the polygraph in employment. The polygraph is used in every area of the workplace, from local taverns, where it is used to "make sure" bartenders are turning in all the cash they receive, to department stores, where employees are routinely interrogated about stolen merchandise or money. Employers argue that use of the polygraph is sometimes the only method that insures a reduction in lying and stealing in their places of employment. Moreover, it is in the interests and job security of honest employees, it is claimed, to submit to a polygraph test in order to "weed out" dishonest employees. Yet the polygraph, I shall argue, violates the right to privacy of both honest *and* dishonest employees.

No person has a right to the thoughts and feelings of another person. The polygraph invades a bastion of privacy unique to persons — the self. Without the privacy of one's thoughts, one's autonomy as an individual is forfeited. Normal social relationships break down when individuality and norms of privacy are threatened. The polygraph interferes with self-control over one's own life by allowing very personal information to get into the hands of others. Employers seldom misuse this information. But if the right to the most private elements of one's personality can be set aside to protect employer or even employee economic interests, then the right to privacy could be overridden to protect other collective interests — for example, a societal interest in knowing who has dissident political thoughts or who engages in socially questionable but harmless activities. The use of the lie detector in the workplace threatens workers' moral rights to freedom and respect, because it allows economic interests or collective welfare to override these rights. In §11 we argued that moral rights in general cannot be justifiably overridden by appeal to utilitarian concerns. Thus, by the same reasoning, if we are to *protect* these rights, including the rights to freedom and respect, as we should, we must not allow use of the polygraph in the workplace.

In addition to these general moral considerations, there are many other factors that strengthen the moral case against the use of the polygraph. First, while taking a lie detector test is supposedly voluntary according to the law, a refusal to take the test is often interpreted by an employer as a sign of guilt. Therefore, the "voluntariness" of the test is questionable, at best. Second, there is the practical problem of test accuracy. The polygraph is accurate between sixty-five and ninety percent of the time. Let us suppose the test is ninety percent accurate. This means that if one tests one hundred employees and ten out of that hundred are found guilty according to the polygraph results, at least one out of the ten found guilty is likely to be innocent under the best of testing conditions. By relying on polygraph results, one therefore runs the risk of using untrustworthy evidence against innocent people. The economic interests of the employer or even of employees are not sufficient reasons for allowing this risk to be run. Indeed, some estimate that the inaccuracies of testing may be such that up to thirty-five percent of the persons shown to be guilty by the polygraph are, in reality, innocent![16] There is also a problem with the nature of the questions asked by the polygraph tester. Although in principle the questions are supposed to be factual in content, many are put in words that can arouse deep emotions, emotions that trigger reactions on the lie detector that can easily be misinterpreted as signs of guilt.

If one outlaws the polygraph, what should an employer do when there is excessive employee theft? How can the employer's place of business be protected without the lie detector? There are viable, although not pleasant, means other than the polygraph which protect private property. For example, personal searches and video surveillance are two alternatives that, while coercive, do less harm to freedom and autonomy than the polygraph, if done with the foreknowledge of employees. Dismissal with hearing and criminal prosecution of suspected employees are also very effective measures that, if practiced, would help deter employee theft. Many companies dismiss employees caught stealing, but seldom does any company take guilty employees to criminal court. Sometimes these employees are even given bland letters of recommendation! And these employees return to the workplace. This lack of punitive action simply encourages more employee theft. Employers do have a right to protect their property and ought to be, if anything, more severe in their punishment of anyone who steals or maliciously damages their business. But this laudable end does not justify every means of achieving it. Use of the polygraph, in particular, should be abolished in the workplace.

§18 POLICIES FOR PROTECTING PRIVACY IN THE WORKPLACE

The following highlights some of the key elements of policies that will help protect privacy in the workplace.

1. To protect privacy and thus confidentiality in the workplace, the privacy act should be adopted for *all* employees, *both* in the public *and* in the private sector.
2. The polygraph should be outlawed. Its invasion of privacy and freedom is not outweighed by its possible viability as a protection of the economic interests of employers.
3. Employees proven guilty of theft or other employer property damage should be dismissed and brought before the law.

V. CONCLUSION: GUARANTEEING RIGHTS IN EMPLOYMENT

The widespread and persistent nonrecognition of employee rights in this country is inconsistent with the primary importance our nation places on the rights of the individual. This non-recognition remains one of the most questionable elements in the political and economic structure of our society. If the arguments in this essay are sound, standardly accepted individual rights need to be recognized and honored in the workplace. The rights to due process, to freedom, and to privacy are moral rights honored politically in public life. To deny them a place in the workplace is to assume that employer rights or economic interests always take precedence over the rights of employees. Neither assumption is tenable.

How does one institutionalize the recognition of rights in employment? In many European countries employee rights are recognized by law and enforced by the government. In West Germany, for example, after a trial period, employees acquire a right to their jobs. Persons may be dismissed for job-related negligence, absences, or disruptive and criminal activities, but the grounds for dismissal must be documented and hearings must be conducted before an employee can be fired. The United States is the only major industrial nation that offers little legal protection of the rights of workers to their jobs. It has been suggested that what is needed in this country is statutory protection for employees against unjust firing, an idea that embodies some of the principles of the German model. It has been further suggested that this statutory protection should include rights to expenses incurred in finding a new job, and rights to back pay for those unjustly dismissed.[17]

A second fruitful way to institutionalize recognition of employee rights is through written contracts between employers and employees, contracts that state the exchange agreement, the rights of each party, and the means for enforcing these rights (for example, arbitration, peer review, or outside negotiators). If properly done, such contracts could be relied upon to help give meaning to the sometimes loose talk about the moral rights of each party and would help settle, without the intervention of the courts, many disagreements about employee *and* employer rights.

A third, most propitious and less coercive way to institutionalize recognition of employee rights is simply for employers to do this voluntarily. This suggestion is not as preposterous as it may seem. Increasingly, employees are demanding rights in the workplace. Correspondingly, employers are beginning to recognize the expediency and, sometimes, the fairness of such employee demands. And the courts are beginning to take interest in employee rights. There is an obvious way for employers to avoid "coercive intervention" by government and the courts. This is for employers *voluntarily* to institute programs that respect and protect employee rights on their own.

There are many employee rights that remain to be considered in another essay. The rights to work safety, information, and participation in management decision-making, for example, are essential for employee autonomy and job development. And the question of meaningful work cannot be dismissed if employees are to be considered as autonomous individuals. (This question is explored at length in Adina Schwartz's essay in this volume.) The continuation of a private free enterprise economy set within a democratic free community where individual rights are viewed as fundamental requires that employee rights be fully and fairly recognized *and* protected in the workplace.

NOTES

1.   *Geary* v. *U.S. Steel Corporation*, 457 Pa. 171, 319 A 2nd 174 (1975).
2.   *Alomar* v. *Dwyer*, 404 U.S. 1020 (1972).

3. Mary Ann Glendon and Edward R. Lev, "Changes in the Bonding of the Employment Relationship: An Essay on the New Property," *Boston College Law Review* (1979), pp. 457–84.

4. Wesley Hohfeld, *Fundamental Legal Conceptions* (New Haven: Yale University Press, 1919, rpt. 1964), pp. 35–64.

5. H.L.A. Hart, "Are There Any Natural Rights?" *Philosophical Review*, 64 (1955), pp. 175–91.

6. Hart, op. cit., p. 177.

7. See George Cabot Lodge, *The New American Ideology* (N.Y.: Alfred Knopf, 1975), Chapter 7.

8. H.G. Wood, *A Treatise on the Law of Master and Servant* (Albany, N.Y.: John D. Parsons, Jr., 1877), p. 134.

9. Lawrence E. Blades, "Employment at Will versus Individual Freedom: On Limiting the Abusive Exercise of Employer Power," *Columbia Law Review* 67 (1967), p. 1405, quoted from *Payne* v. *Western*, 81 Tenn. 507 (1884), *Hutton* v. *Watters*, 132 Tenn. 527, S. W. 134 (1915).

10. Eric Mack, "Natural and Contractual Rights," *Ethics*, 87 (1977), pp. 153–59.

11. Dan Gellert, "Whistle Blower: Dan Gellert, Airline Pilot," *The Civil Liberties Review* (September–October 1978).

12. *Monge* v. *Beebe Rubber Company*, 114 N.H. 130, 136 A. 2nd 519 (1974).

13. Charles E. Summer and Jeremiah H. O'Connell, "The Polaroid Corporation," *The Managerial Mind* (Homewood, Ill.: Richard D. Irwin, 1973), pp. 822–44, quotation from p. 830.

14. Frederick A. Elliston, "Anonymity and Whistleblowing," *Journal of Business Ethics*, 1 (1982), pp. 167–79.

15. Samuel D. Warren and Louis D. Brandeis, "The Right to Privacy," *Harvard Law Review*, 4 (1890), pp. 193–220.

16. George Brenkert, "Corporations, Polygraphs and Privacy," *Business and Professional Ethics Journal*, 1 (1981), pp. 19–26.

17. Clyde W. Summers, "Individual Protection Against Unjust Dismissal: Time for a Statute," *Virginia Law Review*, 62 (1976), pp. 481–532.

SUGGESTIONS FOR FURTHER READING

A great deal has been written on the subject of rights, but little has been written on the subject of employee rights from a philosophical point of view. The following are suggested readings that are pertinent to each individual section of the essay.

§§1–2.   Joel Feinberg, "The Nature and Value of Rights," *Journal of Value Inquiry*, 4 (1970), pp. 243–57.

Joel Feinberg, *Social Philosophy* (Englewood Cliffs, N.J.: Prentice-Hall, 1973).

Wesley Hohfeld, *Fundamental Legal Conceptions* (New Haven: Yale University Press, 1919, rpt. 1964), especially pp. 35–64.

H. J. McCloskey, "Rights—Some Conceptual Issues," *Australasian Journal of Philosophy*, 54 (1976), pp. 99, ff.

Rex Martin, "Human Rights and Civil Rights," *Philosophical Studies*, 37 (1980), pp. 391–403.

Gregory Vlastos, "Justice and Equality," *Social Justice*, Richard Brandt, ed. (Englewood Cliffs, N.J.: Prentice-Hall, 1962).

Carl Wellman, "Upholding Legal Rights," *Ethics*, 86 (1975), pp. 49–60.

§3.   Richard Brandt, *Ethical Theory* (Englewood Cliffs, N.J.: Prentice-Hall, 1959), p. 436, especially.

Braybrooke, David, "The Firm But Untidy Correlativity of Rights and Obligations," *Canadian Journal of Philosophy*, 1 (1971), pp. 351–63.

David Lyons, "The Correlativity of Rights and Duties," *Nous*, 4 (1970), pp. 45–55. (See also Braybrooke's reply in the same issue.)

§4. S. J. Benn and R. S. Peters, *The Principles of Political Thought* (New York: Free Press, 1965).

Ronald Dworkin, *Taking Rights Seriously* (Cambridge: Harvard University Press, 1977).

Alan Gewirth, *Reason and Morality* (Chicago: University of Chicago Press, 1978), especially chapters 2 and 3.

R. M. Hare, "Universalisability," *Proceedings of the Aristotelian Society*, LV (1954–55), rpt. in *Essays in the Moral Concepts* (Berkeley: University of California Press, 1972), pp. 13–28.

Hillel Steiner, "The Natural Right to Equal Freedom," *Mind*, 83 (1974), pp. 194–210.

§5. Isaiah Berlin, *Four Essays on Liberty* (Oxford: Oxford University Press, 1969).

Richard Flathman, *The Practice of Rights* (Cambridge: Cambridge University Press, 1976).

Charles Fried, *Right and Wrong* (Cambridge: Harvard University Press, 1978).

Henry Shue, *Basic Rights* (Princeton: Princeton University Press, 1980).

§6. Milton Friedman, *Capitalism and Freedom* (Chicago: University of Chicago Press, 1962).

Thomas Jefferson, "A Summary View of the Rights of British America," *The Papers of Thomas Jefferson*, Julian Boyd et al., eds. (Princeton: Princeton University Press, 1950–), Vol. 1, pp. 121–35.

John Locke, *Second Treatise on Government* (Indianapolis: Hackett, 1980).

C. B. McPherson, "A Political Theory of Property," in *Democratic Theory* (Oxford: Oxford University Press, 1973), pp. 120–35.

Robert Nozick, *Anarchy, State and Utopia* (New York: Basic Books, 1974), especially Chapter 7.

Charles Reich, "The New Property," *Yale Law Journal*, 73 (1964), pp. 733–71.

For an interesting collection of contemporary philosophical views on property and property rights see J. Roland Pennock and John W. Chapman, eds., *Nomos XXII: Property* (New York: New York University Press, 1980), especially essays by Thomas C. Grey, Lawrence Becker, and Hillel Steiner.

§§7–9. Mary Ann Glendon and Edward R. Lev, "Changes in the Bonding of Employment Relationships: An Essay on the New Property," *Boston College Law Review*, XX (1979), pp. 457–84.

James O. Greenebaum, "Two Justifications of Property," *American Philosophical Quarterly*, 17 (1980), pp. 53–61.

Thomas C. Grey, "Procedural Fairness and Substantive Rights," in *Nomos XVIII: Due Process*, J. Roland Pennock and John W. Chapman, eds. (New York: New York University Press, 1977), pp. 192–205.

A.M. Honore, "Ownership," *Oxford Essays in Jurisprudence*, A. G. Guest, ed. (Oxford: Clarendon Press, 1961), pp. 107–47.

Philip Levine, "Towards a Property Right in Employment," *Buffalo Law Review*, 22 (1972–3), pp. 1081–1110.

Charles R. O'Kelley, Jr., "The Constitutional Rights of Corporations Revisited: Social and Political Expression and the Corporation after *First National Bank v. Bellotti*," *Georgetown Law Review*, 67 (1979), pp. 1347–84.

Theodore A. Olsen, "Wrongful Discharge Claims Raised by At Will Employees: A New Legal Concern for Employers," *Labor Law Journal* (1981), pp. 265–97. This essay contains a list of legal articles on Employment at Will for students interested in pursuing this issue further.

Edmund L. Pincoffs, "Due Process, Fraternity, and a Kantian Injunction," in *Nomos XVIII: Due Process*, pp. 172–81.

John Rawls, *A Theory of Justice* (Cambridge: Harvard University Press, 1971).

Thomas Scanlon, "Due Process," in *Nomos XVIII: Due Process*, pp. 93–125.

J. Peter Shapiro and James F. Tune, "Implied Contract Rights to Job Security," *Stanford Law Review*, 26 (1973–74), pp. 335–69.

John R. S. Wilson, "In One Another's Power," *Ethics*, 88 (1978), pp. 266–315.

§§10–13.   Christian Bay, *The Structure of Freedom* (Stanford: Stanford University Press, 1958).

Philip I. Blumberg, "Corporate Responsibility and the Employee's Duty of Loyalty and Obedience, A Preliminary Inquiry," *Oklahoma Law Review*, 24 (1971).

Ralph Nader et al., *Whistleblowing* (N.Y.: Grossman Publishers, 1972).

Alan Weston, *Whistleblowing* (N.Y.: McGraw-Hill, 1981).

§§14–18.   Elizabeth Beardsley, "Privacy: Autonomy and Selective Disclosure," *Nomos XIII: Privacy*, J. Roland Pennock and John W. Chapman, eds. (N.Y.: Atherton Press, 1971), pp. 56–70.

Stanley I. Benn, "Privacy, Freedom and Respect for Persons," in *Nomos XIII: Privacy*, pp. 1–26.

Charles B. Carver, "The Inquisitional Process in Private Employment," *Cornell Law Review*, 63 (1977), pp. 1–64.

Martin Flics, "Employee Privacy Rights: A Proposal," *Fordham Law Review*, 47 (1978), pp. 155–202.

Charles Fried, *An Anatomy of Values* (Cambridge: Harvard University Press, 1970).

James Rachels, "Why Privacy is Important," *Philosophy And Public Affairs*, 4 (1975), pp. 323–33.

Jeffrey H. Reiman, "Privacy, Intimacy and Personhood," *Philosophy and Public Affairs*, 6 (1976), pp. 26–44.

Thomas Scanlon, "Thomson on Privacy," *Philosophy and Public Affairs*, 4 (1975), pp. 315–23.

Robert Ellis Smith, *Privacy: How to Protect What's Left of It* (Garden City: Anchor Press/Doubleday, 1978).

Judith Jarvis Thomson, "The Right to Privacy," *Philosophy and Public Affairs*, 4 (1975), pp. 295–315.

Alan Westin, *Privacy and Freedom* (N.Y.: Atheneum Press, 1967).

Conclusion.   Donald L. Martin, "Is an Employee Bill of Rights Needed?" *Individual Rights in the Corporation*, Alan F. Westin and Stephan Salisbury, eds. (N.Y.: Random House, 1980), pp. 15–20.

Thomas Scanlon, "Rights, Goals and Fairness," in *Public and Private Morality*, Stuart Hampshire, ed. (Cambridge: Cambridge University Press, 1978), pp. 93–112.

On the general subject of employee rights see David Ewing, *Freedom Inside the Organization* (N.Y.: McGraw-Hill, 1977), Michael Hoffman, ed., *The Work Ethic in Business* (Cambridge: Oelgeschlager, Gunn & Hain, 1981), and Alan Westin and Stephen Salisbury, eds., *Individual Rights in the Corporation* (N.Y.: Random House, 1980).

5

Autonomy in the Workplace

ADINA SCHWARTZ

═══════════════ 《〉》 ═══════════════

A commonplace of political discourse in our society is that all people should be respected as autonomous agents. What does this mean when applied to the workplace? Are individuals stripped of autonomy or, in other words, of independence whenever laws restrict the conditions of employment they can accept? For example, does this occur when there are minimum wage or maximum hours laws? Or, is just the opposite true? Must restrictions be imposed for the sake of autonomy, to insure that people do not work under conditions that destroy their control over their lives? For example, are minimum wage and maximum hours laws needed for the sake of enabling workers to control their lives? For the same reason, should legal measures be taken to *democratize the workplace*, that is, to give all employees a significant "say" in deciding how their jobs should be performed and what their enterprise's policies should be?

Let us start thinking about these issues by focusing on an important period in the history of our country's Supreme Court, what is commonly known as the Lochner era.

I. THE LOCHNER ERA AND AUTONOMY

§1 THE LOCHNER DECISIONS

During the Lochner era (1905–1937), the United States Supreme Court repeatedly struck down labor laws, or, in other words, declared them unconstitutional. The era gets its name from the 1905 case *Lochner* v. *New York*.[1] There, the Court struck down a New York State law making

129

it illegal to employ bakers for more than sixty hours a week or ten hours a day. In subsequent cases, the Court went on to strike down federal and state minimum wage laws, laws outlawing "yellow dog" contracts (contracts in which workers agree not to join a union as a condition for holding their jobs), and so forth.

What reasons did the Court give for deciding that it was unconstitutional for the federal and state governments to make these laws restricting the employment agreements that people could make? It claimed that these decisions were required by the two due process clauses of the American Constitution. The Fifth Amendment clause prohibits the federal government from depriving any person of life, liberty, or property without due process of law. The Fourteenth Amendment clause extends the same prohibition to the states. In order to argue that these clauses prohibited the federal and state governments from legislating restrictions on labor agreements, the Lochner era Court had to answer the question: What liberties do these clauses protect? By making it unconstitutional for people to be deprived of liberty without due process of law, the Fifth and Fourteenth amendments obviously do not invalidate *all* laws restricting people's freedom to do whatever they want. If they did this, one of the absurd conclusions that would follow is that it would be unconstitutional to have laws against rape and murder. These are, after all, things some people sometimes want to do. Might there be certain types of conduct, nonetheless, that should always be free from legal restrictions? What, if any, types of conduct might (or should) judges see as included in this privileged area of freedom that the due process clauses of the Constitution protect?

In the Lochner era, the majority of the Supreme Court judges gave an answer to this question never given by the majority on the Supreme Court either before or since. They claimed that a fundamental component of the freedom from legal restrictions that the due process clauses protect is *freedom of contract*. This means freedom for people to make any agreements to which all parties voluntarily consent and to have these agreements enforced at law. According to the opinions issued by the majority of the Supreme Court in the Lochner era cases, an especially valuable part of freedom of contract is freedom of contract with regard to employment. Employers and employees should be free to have any arrangements to which they mutually consent enforced at law. Now that we see the distinctive answer that the majority of the Supreme Court judges in the Lochner era gave to the question "What liberties do the due process clauses protect?" we can understand why they claimed that these clauses make minimum wage laws, maximum hours laws, and other restrictions on labor contracts unconstitutional. These laws make it illegal for people to work under certain conditions (for example, working more than sixty hours a week as a baker) *regardless* of whether they or their employers voluntarily agree to those terms. Thereby, they impinge, so this reasoning affirms, on both employers' and employees' freedom of contract with regard to employment. In other words, they abridge a fundamental part of the privileged area of freedom that the Lochner era claimed the due process clauses protect.

The Lochner era ended dramatically with the 1937 case *West Coast Hotel* v. *Parrish*.[2] There, the Supreme Court ruled that the minimum wage law of the State of Washington was constitutional. In its argument for this decision, the majority on the Court took a highly unusual step. It stated explicitly that it was reversing precedent. It claimed that the minimum wage law of the State of Washington that it was ruling constitutional was substantially similar to the minimum wage law of the District of Columbia that the Supreme Court had ruled unconstitutional in a 1923 case, *Adkins* v. *Children's Hospital*.[3] It indicated, moreover, that the *Adkins* decision was only part of the precedent it sought to overturn. What it sought to reverse was the Lochner era's central contention that the due process clauses invalidate labor laws. The grounds for this reversal demand an explanation.

We have seen that the majority opinions in the Lochner era cases supported the contention that the due process clauses invalidate labor laws on grounds that the privileged area of freedom protected by due process includes freedom of contract, especially with regard to employment. These grounds were dismissed swiftly in Chief Justice Hughes' opinion for the majority in *West Coast Hotel*. "What is this freedom?" he wrote. "The constitution does not speak of freedom of contract."[4]

Until very recently, the *West Coast Hotel* decision seemed to have dealt a final blow to the Lochner era's position on labor laws. Within the legal profession, it became a cliché to claim that the mistakes of Lochner must be avoided. "'Lochnerizing' has become so much an epithet," noted constitutional scholar Laurence Tribe warned in his 1978 treatise on constitutional law, "that the very use of the label may obscure attempts at understanding."[5]

The view that the Lochner decisions were a mistake is called into question, however, by the widespread recent questioning of the interventionist political philosophy that has shaped American life since Franklin Delano Roosevelt's New Deal. The halt to government intervention demanded by President Ronald Reagan, philosopher Robert Nozick,[6] economist Milton Friedman,[7] and many other politicians, scholars, and ordinary citizens includes a halt to workplace regulations. Current objections to such particular regulations as minimum wage laws and federally enforced standards for occupational health and safety often seem based on a more general, Lochner-like presumption against all State interference with agreements between employers and employees.[8] Would it be desirable for our government to end its past forty-odd years' policy of making and enforcing laws about the conditions under which people can be employed? *Contra* Reagan and his supporters, might our problem instead be not too much but too little government intervention in the workplace? In particular, might it be desirable for our government to follow Japan, West Germany, the Scandinavian countries, and others in legally intervening in an area in which it has yet to intervene —

taking legal measures to institute *workplace democracy?* For example, should our government make and enforce laws similar to the West German laws requiring "co-determination" — worker representation on the boards managing firms? Or, should our laws require all factories, offices, and service operations to give all their employees still more significant opportunities than electing representatives for deciding how their individual jobs should be performed and what their workplace's overall policies should be? To answer these questions, we need to consider the main philosophical question raised by the Lochner era and *West Coast Hotel* decisions: Is freedom of contract with regard to employment so valuable a liberty that it should be protected from government infringement?

To answer this last question completely, we would have to analyze and evaluate all plausible arguments for and against according this value to freedom of contract with regard to employment. This is too large a task for this essay to pursue. Instead, we will consider only one argument, an argument that has been and is advanced not only by philosophers, but also by lawyers, economists, politicians, and ordinary citizens. To put the argument very generally first (a more detailed statement is given in §2), it states that if we accord fundamental importance to personal autonomy, we must accept the Lochner Court's position that freedom of contract with regard to employment should be preserved.

How are we to decide whether this argument works? One suggestion is to count heads — to see who agrees or disagrees with it and then to side with the majority or with those we like. The problem is that this procedure asks *who* supports the argument, but we need instead to examine *what reasons* support it in order to tell whether it works. To see whether there are good reasons for accepting this argument, we will need to answer the following philosophical questions. What must people mean by "autonomy" if they are to claim that valuing it commits us to preserving freedom of contract with regard to employment? If autonomy is given this meaning, is it coherent and realistic to claim that it is possible for people to be autonomous? If not, can we make sense of the widespread conviction, among members of our society, that people can be autonomous by developing an alternative interpretation of what it means to be autonomous? On this alternative interpretation, does valuing autonomy commit us to the Lochner Court's or to some other position on labor laws? Let us start considering these questions by examining the connections that the judges' opinions in the Lochner cases and in *West Coast Hotel* suggest between autonomy and freedom of contract with regard to employment.

§2   THE LOCHNER ERA'S ARGUMENT FROM AUTONOMY

In order to understand how the notion of autonomy entered into the judges' opinions in the Lochner cases and in *West Coast Hotel*, we must qualify our description of the Lochner Court's interpretation of the Constitution's due process clauses. As we have seen, the Lochner era judges were able to use these clauses to invalidate labor laws because they claimed that freedom of contract, especially with regard to employment, is a fundamental liberty that those clauses protect. We must recognize, now, that these judges distinguished the freedom of contract protected by due process from absolute freedom of contract. Absolute freedom of contract means that people may have any agreements that they make legally enforced regardless of who they are, what measures any of them use to cause any of the others to agree, or what they agree to do. "There is, of course, no such thing as absolute freedom of contract,"[9] the Lochner Court argued, because the state and federal governments must exercise their "police powers," or, in other words, their powers to make and enforce laws relating to the "safety, health, morals, and general welfare of the public."[10] The legitimate exercise of these police powers demands, the Lochner Court claimed, that agreements not be enforceable at law if they are made by those not competent to make them (for example, children), under certain sorts of pressures (for example, under severe psychological stress), or for purposes that the State ought not to condone (for example, contracts of enslavement). In sum, then, the Lochner era's rulings against labor laws were not based on the position that the due process clauses make *all* legal restrictions on contracts unconstitutional. The underlying legal doctrine was, instead, that these clauses make freedom of contract "the general rule and restraint the exception, and the exercise of authority to abridge it can be justified only under exceptional circumstances."[11]

How was the Lochner Court able to use this doctrine to justify its presumption against labor laws? In other words, how could it argue that anyone who accepted this doctrine must agree with it in finding most, although not all, minimum wage laws, maximum hours laws, and other restrictions on contracts of employment unconstitutional? Why didn't the majority of the Lochner judges hold, instead, that the overall quality of people's lives tends to be so greatly affected by the conditions under which they work that contracts of employment ought to be excepted from the general rule favoring contractual freedom? One important philosophical argument against this position is sketched, although never as clearly developed as a philosopher would wish, in many of the opinions that the judges wrote. Let us reconstruct this argument, or, in other words, formulate it more clearly than the judges did. Let us call it the *argument from autonomy*, although autonomy is a word that their opinions never use. The opinions of the Lochner era judges instead use several terms that we can take to be synonymous with the term "autonomy." They speak of people being "independent," "taking care of themselves," "protecting themselves," and "rationally judging what is in their best interests and acting to further it." Bearing in mind that each of these terms can be interchanged with the term "autonomy," the following can be seen as the Lochner Court's main philosophical argument for its presumption against labor laws, or, in other words, in favor of freedom of contract with regard to employment.

The Argument from Autonomy.

Premise 1: Workers generally have the capacity for being autonomous, or, in other words, independent.

Premise 2: It is extremely desirable for people to exercise the capacity for being autonomous.

Premise 3: Workers who have the capacity for autonomy are hindered from exercising it whenever laws prevent them from contracting to work under conditions to which they would otherwise agree to contract.

Sub-conclusion 1: Therefore, from premise 1 and premise 3, laws restricting contracts of employment (i.e., labor laws) tend to prevent workers from exercising the capacity for being autonomous or independent.

Sub-conclusion 2: Therefore, from premise 2 and sub-conclusion 1, labor laws tend to prevent workers from exercising a capacity that it is extremely desirable that they exercise.

Sub-conclusion 3: Therefore, from sub-conclusion 2, labor laws tend to have an extremely undesirable effect.

Main conclusion: Therefore, from sub-conclusion 3, there ought to be a presumption against labor laws.

It is important to realize that this argument does not conclude that there ought not to be *any* laws restricting contracts of employment. It argues only for a presumption against such laws. According to premise 1, workers *generally, but not always*, are capable of being autonomous, or, in other words, of rationally judging what is in their best interests and acting to further it. From premises 2 and 3, labor laws are objectionable because they prevent workers *who have* the capacity for autonomy from exercising it. Joining these statements together, we see that the argument from autonomy itself implies that it is possible to override the presumption that it establishes against labor laws. That presumption is overridden if a labor law is shown to apply only to a class of workers who lack the capacity for autonomy and who therefore cannot be hindered from exercising it by that law. When, if ever, is it possible to show this? Let us examine the answers to this question that the majority of the Supreme Court gave in three of the most interesting Lochner era cases: *Lochner* v. *New York, Muller* v. *Oregon,*[12] and *Adkins* v. *Children's Hospital*. Let us also examine the answer that the majority gave in the case that brought the Lochner era to a close, *West Coast Hotel* v. *Parrish*.

We saw above that *Lochner* v. *New York* struck down a New York State law prohibiting bakers from being employed for more than sixty hours a week or ten hours a day. One of the major arguments that the majority gave for this decision was that bakers, as a class of people capable of autonomy, do not need State protection against agreeing to excessive hours of work. "There is no contention," the majority wrote, "that bakers as a class are not equal in intelligence and capacity to other men, or that they are not able to assert their rights or take care of themselves without the protecting arm of the State, interfering with their independence of judgment and of action."[13]

How could the Court go on to conclude, in *Muller* v. *Oregon* in 1908, that a law restricting women's hours of employment was constitutional? In particular, how could it hold that this decision was consistent with the 1905 *Lochner* v. *New York* decision that we have just described? One of the major premises from which it reached these conclusions was that sexual differences correlate with differing capacities for autonomy. The law at issue in *Lochner* v. *New York* applied to bakers, who, as males, have the capacity for autonomy not had by the women to whom the law in *Muller* v. *Oregon* applied. "History discloses the fact," the Court asserted in *Muller* v. *Oregon*, "that woman has always been dependent upon man . . . looking at it from the viewpoint of the effort to maintain an independent position in life she is not upon an equality."[14] The Court contended, moreover, that woman's dependence is not a product of history. It is a trait inseparable from her sex.

> Even though all restrictions on political, personal, and contractual rights were taken away, and she [woman] stood, so far as statutes are concerned, upon an absolutely equal plane with him [man], it would still be true that she is so constituted that she will rest upon and look to him for protection.[15]

It is because *Muller* v. *Oregon* saw women as differing from men, then, in being incapable of autonomy or of caring for themselves, that it was able to endorse both Oregon's hours legislation for women and *Lochner* v. *New York*'s overturning of a law restricting male bakers' hours.

The Court repudiated this view of the differences between men and women in *Adkins* v. *Children's Hospital* in 1923. After noting that the Court had sought to justify its decision in *Muller* v. *Oregon* by "the fact that historically woman has always been dependent upon man," Justice Sutherland argued for the majority in *Adkins* v. *Children's Hospital* that "these differences have now come almost, if not quite, to the vanishing point . . . woman is accorded emancipation from the old doctrine that she must be given special protection."[16] Differences in the two sexes' capacities for autonomy have been caused to disappear, Justice Sutherland wrote, by "the great—not to say revolutionary—changes which have taken place since that utterance [*Muller* v. *Oregon*] in the contractual, political, and civil status of women, culminating in the Nineteenth Amendment."[17] On this basis, he asserted that "we cannot accept the doctrine that women of mature age . . . require or may be subjected to restrictions upon their liberty of contract which could not lawfully be imposed in the case of men under similar circumstances."[18] *Adkins* v. *Children's Hospital* therefore struck down a federal law fixing minimum wages for women in the District of Columbia.

Was *Adkins* v. *Children's Hospital* a victory for women? Can we criticize it for depriving women of protection against excessively low pay and yet applaud it for denying that being dependent is a necessary part of being a woman? We saw above that in 1937 in *West Coast Hotel* v.

Parrish, the Court affirmed the constitutionality of a minimum wage law for women that it claimed was substantially similar to the law that *Adkins* had overturned. One of the main reasons that the majority in *West Coast Hotel* gave for this reversal of precedent was that *Adkins* had credited women with an independence that they do not have. Women need "protection," the majority wrote, "from unscrupulous and over-reaching employers."[19] Unlike the Court opinion in *Muller* v. *Oregon*, which we examined above, however, the majority opinion in *West Coast Hotel* v. *Parrish* did not claim that women need protection because of their sex. Instead, the majority wrote that "women in employment" need protection because of "the fact that they are in the class receiving the least pay." Workers in this class need protection because "their bargaining power is relatively weak." They are therefore "the ready victims of those who would take advantage of their necessitous circumstances" by agreeing to employ them only if they work for hours too long for health, "at wages so low as to be insufficient to meet the bare cost of living,"[20] and so forth.

We saw above that *West Coast Hotel* v. *Parrish* did not merely reverse the Court's decision in *Adkins* v. *Children's Hospital*. It did this as part of overturning the Lochner era's basic presumption in favor of freedom of contract with regard to employment. Looking at the argument just outlined, we can now see that *West Coast Hotel* did this by rejecting one of the three premises in the argument from autonomy reconstructed above—the main philosophical argument that the Lochner era judges gave for their presumption against labor laws. The premise that *West Coast Hotel* rejected was premise 1: Most workers have the capacity for being autonomous, or, in other words, for rationally judging what is in their best interests and acting to further it. Instead, the majority's position there implied that economic inequalities between employees and employers tend to place most workers in a "take it or leave it" position where they are unable to act on their judgments of their interests. Workers

> are often induced by the fear of discharge to conform to regulations which their judgment, fairly exercised, would pronounce to be detrimental to their health or strength. In other words, the proprietors lay down the rules and the laborers are practically constrained to obey them.[21]

On this basis, *West Coast Hotel* v. *Parrish* dismissed the Lochner era's central argument that there ought to be a presumption against labor laws because they tend to prevent workers from being autonomous or independent. Instead of admitting, as the Lochner majority did, that this presumption may be overridden *occasionally* by laws that apply only to *exceptional* workers, such as women, who lack the capacity for autonomy, the majority in *West Coast Hotel* implied that this presumption *generally* does not hold. Since *most* workers lack the capacity for effecting their rational judgments of their interests and thus lack the capacity for being autonomous, it makes no sense to object to laws restricting contracts of employment on grounds that they tend to prevent workers from exercising that capacity.

Is this a good way of dismissing the Lochner era's argument from autonomy? To evaluate it, we need to see that it is only one of three main arguments that might be used. To show that the argument from autonomy does not work, one might take *West Coast Hotel*'s route of arguing for the falsehood of premise 1 of that argument: Most workers have the capacity for autonomy. Alternatively, one might seek to disprove premise 2: It is extremely desirable for people to exercise that capacity. Or, one might argue against premise 3: Workers who have the capacity for autonomy are hindered from exercising it whenever laws prevent them from contracting to work under conditions to which they would otherwise agree to contract. Once we see that these three strategies are available, we can appreciate the problems with the one that *West Coast Hotel* used.

This strategy can be criticized for only considering the claims of one party to contracts of employment. *West Coast Hotel*'s argument that most workers are incapable of autonomy is consistent with and might even be taken to suggest the claim that, in contrast, most employers are capable of autonomy. If this were not so, why would employees need to be protected against employers? Granted that this difference between employers and employees exists, is it not possible to argue for a further difference? On the one hand, since most workers lack the capacity for autonomy, restrictions on contracts of employment cannot be objected to on grounds that they tend to prevent them from exercising that capacity. On the other hand, since most employers *have* the capacity for autonomy, restrictions on contracts of employment *can* be objected to on grounds that they tend to prevent them from exercising that capacity. This shows, it seems, that *West Coast Hotel*'s strategy of arguing only against the argument from autonomy's first premise that most workers have the capacity for autonomy does not suffice to dismiss the Lochner era's central contention that there ought to be a presumption against labor laws. Why should employees be protected when the cost of doing so is hindering employers from exercising *their* capacity for autonomy?

Both the Lochner cases and *West Coast Hotel* suggest that a decision to protect workers is a decision to further some value other than autonomy. This suggestion follows from a generalization of premise 3 of the argument from autonomy: All people who have the capacity for autonomy, whether they are employers or employees, are hindered from exercising it whenever laws restrict the contracts of employment that they can make. If we grant this and nonetheless seek to dismiss the Lochner era's strong presumption against labor laws, we need first to ask just what value other than autonomy makes it desirable to protect workers. Is this desirable, for example, because it is likely to increase the total happiness of the members of society? Or is it desirable because it is likely to contribute to the goal of reducing economic inequality? Is some value(s)

other than happiness or economic equality the value(s) that makes protecting workers worthwhile?

After developing answers to these questions and backing them by
reasons, it would then be necessary severely to qualify the argument
from autonomy's premise 2: It is extremely desirable for people to exercise the capacity for autonomy. An argument would have to be constructed to show that this is less desirable than furthering the value(s)
determined to be the one(s) that makes protecting workers worthwhile.
Although it might be possible to complete these tasks, it would be at the
least extremely difficult to do so. Might there be a way of avoiding these
tasks and yet giving strong philosophical reasons for viewing the
Lochner era as a mistake?

The way out would be to show that a decision to protect workers
need not be based on any value other than autonomy. We would need
to show, more precisely, that the very kinds of restrictions on freedom of
contract that the Lochner Court opposed can be justified without subor-
dinating autonomy to any other value. In order to do this, as indicated
above, we would need to disprove the generalized version of premise 3 of
the argument from autonomy: All employers and employees who have
the capacity for autonomy are hindered from exercising it whenever
laws restrict the contracts of employment that they can make. Against
this, we would need to argue that certain restrictions on contracts of employment, including those that the Lochner Court opposed, are needed
if all members of our society, employers as well as employees, are maximally to develop and exercise their capacities for autonomy.

Could this argument be made to work? Doing so would take us far
towards a compelling reply to today's frequent suggestion that the interventionist social policies that have shaped America since the New Deal
are unjust because they violate personal autonomy. We would have
shown that this charge does not hold when it comes to much of our government's post–New Deal intervention in a major area of life: labor relations. Might it be possible to advance from this to the more radical claim
that those who care about autonomy must demand that our government
take a more activist role than it has yet taken in labor relations? To
answer these questions, let us see if there are reasons for rejecting the
generalized version of premise 3 of the argument from autonomy.

§3 A CRITICISM

The premise that all people who have the capacity for autonomy are hindered from exercising it whenever laws restrict freedom of contract with
regard to employment seems, initially, to be obviously true. Imagine a
society with no such restrictions. Since relations between employers and
employees would there be settled only by mutually agreed-upon contracts, it seems that the contents of those agreements would in no way be
influenced by that society's institutions. The sole determinants of what
pay workers would receive, what hours they would work, and so forth

would seem to be the interests and abilities of individual employers and employees. Thus, both parties to contracts of employment would seem to be left completely free to exercise their ability to be autonomous, or, in other words, to take care of themselves.

We need to look more closely, however, at what happens when a government legally enforces all employment agreements that both parties wish to have legally enforced. The above scenario to the contrary, this policy of preserving freedom of contract with regard to employment does influence the kinds of agreements that are made. By adopting this policy, a government insures, on the one hand, that bargaining power is not in the hands of workers. The reason for this is that they by and large cannot afford to wait for job offers that suit them. If they are to survive economically, they must be employed fairly immediately. On the other hand, adopting this policy places bargaining power in the hands of the more economically powerful employers. The reason for this is that they can afford to wait for workers to accept their terms, to eliminate jobs by automation if workers do not comply, and so forth. In short, a government decision to enforce contractual freedom with regard to employment is a decision to bias the contents of labor contracts in favor of the economically powerful.

Would it be possible to avoid biasing the contents of the labor agreements that people make? To understand the connections between autonomy and freedom of contract with regard to employment, we need to realize that no society can avoid having policies that favor people's reaching some, rather than other, labor agreements, regardless of what restrictions it enforces or fails to enforce. What people choose, including what work conditions they choose, must always be pervasively influenced by the social institutions of the particular society in which they live.

This is so because human action takes place within particular cultural and institutional frameworks, within given economic systems, technologies, linguistic systems, and so forth. No person ever creates the cultural and institutional framework(s) within which he or she acts entirely on his or her own. At the same time, any such framework severely limits what the people acting within it can choose to do. (For example, no one could choose to pick up a phone in ancient Greece.) In addition, it pervasively pressures them to choose to do some, rather than others, of the things that they can choose to do. For example, why don't middle-class Americans choose not to have phones installed in their homes? Finally, human beings are not born knowing how to participate in cultural and institutional frameworks, or, in other words, how to speak and understand a language and behave in other distinctively human ways (for example, to play games according to rules, to distinguish people who are relatives from people who aren't, to distinguish between their wishes and reality). If they are to learn these things, they must be raised among adults on whom they model their behavior. They must be subject to these adult's approval and disapproval and instructed only in skills that these adults value and have. As a result of this early education, normal children have no choice but to acquire values, beliefs, and abilities strikingly similar to those of the people who raise them, people whom children of course do not choose. In turn, the result of being inculcated in their childhoods with these values, beliefs, and abilities is that normal people are throughout their lives predisposed to choose some, rather than other, things.

Once we recognize that what people choose must always be at least partially explained by their particular childhood educations and by the particular social pressures and opportunities to which they are subject as adults, we can appreciate the difficulty of the question: Is freedom of contract with regard to employment or some set of restrictions on this freedom the policy that gives employers and employees most scope for exercising their capacities for autonomy? On the one hand, freedom of contract seems to be the obvious answer only if we accept an unrealistic account of autonomy. We must assume, as the first paragraph of this section showed, that people are autonomous only if what they choose is in no way influenced by social institutions. It follows from the account just presented of human social dependency that no human being can make such choices. In other words, it is impossible for people to be as independent as that paragraph assumed autonomous people must be.

On the other hand, we now face the questions: Can we still make sense of the claim that people can be autonomous or independent? Does not our account of human social dependency instead imply that autonomy is an ideal that people cannot achieve? Must we not therefore conclude that it is senseless to distinguish between social policies that do and do not enable people to be autonomous?

Our account of human social dependency does seem to imply that there can be no such thing as an autonomous person if, on our definition, autonomous people differ from others in being *free from the influence of social institutions*. At the same time, it seems that people can be autonomous if, on our definition, autonomous people are distinguished from others by the sorts of *abilities and traits of character that they are influenced to form*. More specifically, might a realistic definition not state, in the first place, that autonomous people are distinguished by *acting so as to control their lives significantly*? Might it not add that autonomous people have and exercise the abilities and traits of character that enable them to exert significant control over their lives partly as a result of their particular early educations and of the particular social pressures and opportunities to which they are subject as adults? To show that this definition is realistic, we need to answer the question: What abilities and traits of character can enable people significantly to control their lives when they must be socially dependent in the ways we have seen all humans must be? We shall attempt to do so in the next major section of this paper. After developing this new account of autonomy, we will be in a position to answer the question: If we accord fundamental importance to personal autonomy, what labor policy or policies must we endorse?

II. A REALISTIC ACCOUNT OF AUTONOMY

§4 SHAPING ONE'S CIRCUMSTANCES BY ONE'S GOALS

How must people act if they are to be autonomous, or, in other words, significantly to control their lives? The key, it seems, is that they must act so as to make their lives become the sorts of lives they want to lead. Since they must do this, autonomous people must form relatively clear over-all conceptions of the sorts of persons they want to be: of what they wish to achieve at various stages of their lives, of the priorities that they accord to various of their goals (for example, do they wish to become parents? Do they believe it's less important for them to devote time to parenting than to pursuing certain professional goals?) They must be both capable of and firmly committed to acting so as to realize these over-all conceptions of their goals.

In economics and other branches of social theory, people's attempts, actions, decisions, or plans are standardly defined as rational or intelligent to the extent that they are the ones most likely, given the information available to them, to satisfy their goals to the greatest extent at the least cost. To understand this standard definition, imagine a person who considers no goal remotely as important as the goal of making as much money as possible. This person's decision to go to law school is, according to the standard definition, rational or intelligent to the extent that, given the information available to him or her at the time that he or she makes it, no alternative course of action (for example, going to business school) is likely to contribute more to his or her earning power. Returning from this example, we can now see another way of putting this standard definition of rationality. People rationally or intelligently attempt to realize a goal when and only when they act so as to realize it. Joining this definition with the claims in this section's first paragraph, it follows that autonomous people must be both capable of and firmly committed to striving *rationally* to achieve their over-all conceptions of their goals. Since they have both the requisite abilities and inclinations, they must regularly engage in this rational striving. To do this, autonomous people must consistently exercise sophisticated intellectual abilities. Let us describe their exercise of these abilities, throughout understanding the words "rational" and "intelligent" as bearing the standard definition just presented.

In order rationally to attempt to achieve their over-all conceptions of their purposes in life, autonomous people must carefully observe their emotional dispositions, abilities, and social situations. They must rationally consider how these must be changed if they are to become the sorts of persons they want to be. On this basis, they must intelligently plan to act in ways that will enable them to effect these changes. They must proceed to execute these plans.

As an example of this, consider a person who realizes, as he interacts with his children, that he has less emotional rapport with them than he aspires, as a parent, to have. As part of rationally striving to make his life conform to his over-all conception of his goals, he searches for the causes of this emotional distance and decides it may well be the result of his extensive professional traveling over the past several years. On this basis, he considers how he might most decrease his travel load without sacrificing valued aspects of his career (for example, knowledge of colleagues' work, emotional ties with colleagues). Having decided that the most effective plan would be to refuse certain kinds of invitations to work away from home and to attempt to schedule certain professional meetings nearer to his home, he attempts to carry through this plan.

Considering this example, we can now see that any realistic account of autonomous conduct must recognize a crucial feature of human life: Even the best laid plans go astray. Given the limits of human intelligence and the diversity and complexity of people's behavior, the person in our example could not be expected accurately to predict just how he, his children, and his colleagues would react to his decreased travel load. Even the most careful and intelligent planning could not guarantee, for example, that his colleagues would not react by increasing their demands on his time, thereby causing him to invest even less emotional energy than previously on his relationship with his children.

This example shows, it seems, that if people are to be autonomous, or, in other words, to act so as to make themselves become the sorts of persons they want to be, they must be alert, as they execute their plans, to the possibility that their actions will have unexpected or unwanted consequences. More generally, they must be alert to changes that may occur in their circumstances as they attempt to perform the actions they planned. On the basis of these observations, autonomous people must rationally consider whether and how their plans need to be changed if they are to become the sorts of persons they want to be. Thus, the person in our example must examine whether his relationship with his children might be improved by telling them about his colleagues' demands, by spending slightly more time traveling, and so forth. As they pursue the plans that they devise to remedy their previous plans' failures to enable them to achieve their goals, autonomous people must remain alert to the possibility that these plans, too, will need to be changed.

When people act in these ways, they do not act only in response to the actions of others and to the requirements of social institutions. In addition, they plan to influence what these actions and requirements will be (in our example, how one's children will act towards one; how much time on the road one's job will require). Similarly, they are not only caused to act in certain ways by their own abilities and temperamental proclivities. In addition, they deliberately influence what physical, emotional, and intellectual traits they will have (in our example, how close one feels towards one's children). Once we recognize this, we can see the point of our central claim that autonomous people must be both able to plan and strongly committed to planning rationally to achieve some over-all conception of their goals. This claim implies that they do not passively accept their circumstances but instead effectively strive to change them. By doing this, autonomous people exert significant control over their lives.

Claiming that autonomous people control their lives in these ways is compatible with recognizing that they must be socially dependent in the ways we earlier saw all humans must be. In the first place, *whether* people exert this control is crucially affected by their early educations and by the social pressures and opportunities to which they are subject as adults. Only certain types of childhood and adult experiences make it possible for a person to develop the intellectual abilities and emotional inclinations necessary for planning rationally to achieve some over-all conception of his or her goals. For example, people are hindered in developing these traits if, in their childhoods, their parents and siblings continually undermine their self-confidence. In the second place, *how* people exert this control is similarly affected crucially by their childhood and adult experiences. What goals they include in their over-all conceptions (for example, whether or not they aim to have children and what sorts of emotional ties they seek to have with them) and what means they use when they attempt to conform to those conceptions (for example, whether they use money as a means for making their children depend on them) are pervasively influenced by their past interactions with others in various institutional contexts (for example, with their parents and siblings at home and in the family business).

Important qualifications must be appended to this second claim. People are autonomous, we have argued, only if they are both capable of and firmly committed to planning rationally to achieve aims integrated into systematic conceptions of the lives they want to lead. While people develop these dispositions only if their interactions with others predispose them to pursue particular goals and to do so by using particular means, having these dispositions at the same time involves being disposed rationally to criticize and create alternatives to one's own and others' means.

People plan rationally to achieve their goals only if they recognize when and how their own and others' methods have been inefficient. This follows from the standard definition of rationality given above and from the standard definition of an efficient method as one that realizes its goals at the least cost. From these definitions, it also follows that rational planners must realize how differences between their own and others' personalities and situations may prevent them from successfully following procedures that others efficiently use. For example, a woman professor must realize that, because of her sex, methods that male colleagues use for gaining undergraduates' respect (for example, demonstrating athletic prowess) will not work for her. Since, on our account, autonomous people are rational planners, they have these perceptions and respond to them by intelligently devising and pursuing new means for achieving the goals included in their over-all conceptions. Thus, in our previous example, the professor may decide to rely exclusively on scholarship and teaching to gain undergraduates' respect.

This is not to say that autonomous people make all and only the changes that it is rational for them to make in their means, or that they change them in all and only the ways that best further their goals. In the first place, there are severe natural limits on the intelligence of any single human being. In addition, any culture predisposes its members to notice some, rather than other, problems with the methods they and others use. It also limits the alternatives they can conceive of pursuing. For example, in a culture where people generally live in extended families, people may question and suggest alternatives to the ways extended families raise children. They may be unable to see any problems, however, with raising children in this rather than some other (for example, the nuclear) family structure. It is within these individual and cultural bounds that people can and do learn rationally to criticize both their own and others' methods for pursuing certain goals and rationally to devise alternative means. Acting consistently in accord with these considerations, people can to a significant extent shape their circumstances by their aims.

Might it not be important, however, for us now to distinguish between two types of people? On the one hand, consider people who shape their circumstances so that they come to achieve aims that they have played a role in shaping. On the other hand, consider people who shape their circumstances so that they come to achieve aims totally defined for them by others. Do not people of our first type control their lives more significantly than do people of our second type? Must we not therefore claim that people are autonomous only if they satisfy two conditions? In addition to satisfying the condition described in this section (namely, planning rationally to achieve over-all conceptions of their goals and thereby shaping their circumstances by their goals), must not autonomous people also shape their over-all conceptions of their goals?

§5 SHAPING ONE'S GOALS

a. Preliminary Objections   There is an obvious objection to the suggestion that shaping one's goals be part of our definition of being autonomous. By adding this condition, do we not define autonomous people as more independent than any human can possibly be? This objection arises, in the first place, because, as we saw in §3, human action takes place within particular cultural and institutional frameworks. Although no person is ever the sole creator of the framework(s) within which he or she acts, any framework within which a person acts favors the pursuit of some, rather than other, goals. For example, the "publish or perish" system in American universities means that career advantages are more likely to accrue to faculty who pursue scholarly distinction than to those who aim primarily at improving their teaching. In the second place, children only learn to engage in distinctively human behavior if, as explained in §3, adults instill them with particular values, beliefs, and abilities and thereby lead them to form some, rather than other, goals (for example, to seek or not seek academic distinction). Since changes that people make in their goals must always be made from the standpoint of goals they already hold, the aims that people have are necessarily derived from and constrained by aims that their childhood educations instilled.

From these two claims, it follows that autonomous people cannot shape their goals in the sense of choosing them *entirely* on their own. We have just argued, however, that although autonomous people's social interactions predispose them to use particular means for achieving their goals, they at the same time influence them rationally to criticize and create alternatives to those means. Could not autonomous people similarly be influenced rationally to question and change their goals? Would not a realistic definition therefore include two conditions for being autonomous — (1) shaping one's circumstances by planning rationally to achieve some over-all conception of one's goals and (2) shaping one's goals by criticizing and revising them rationally?

This is the definition that I believe we should give. To show that it is viable, however, we need to disarm two major objections. In the first place, the two conditions in the definition might seem inconsistent. How can people be *both* able to doubt and revise their aims *and* committed to investing the time and effort needed for rationally planning to achieve their aims? Is not commitment possible only at the cost of a critical attitude and *vice versa*?

In the second place, it might seem impossible to make sense of the definition's second condition that autonomous people *rationally* criticize and revise their aims. The standard definition of rationality presented above (§4) gives us a way of judging the rationality of people's attempts to criticize and devise alternatives to their means. Invoking their ends, we ask whether they are right to believe that certain means cannot be used to realize their goals or can be used only at unnecessary cost. Similarly, we ask whether the alternative methods that they have devised more efficiently realize their goals. In contrast, when people criticize and change not their means but their ends, there seems to be no standard by which to judge the rationality of what they do. Since there seems no way of judging this, there seems no point to stipulating that autonomous people criticize and change their goals rationally as opposed to irrationally.

b. How and Why Autonomous People Change Their Goals These objections can be dismissed by a closer consideration of how people must act in order to satisfy our first condition for being autonomous — planning rationally to achieve aims integrated into systematic conceptions of the lives they aim to lead. They must, we saw above, intelligently frame, revise, and pursue plans in order to change their social situations into ones that maximize their opportunities for achieving the component aims of their conceptions. They must also intelligently frame, revise, and pursue plans so as to change their physical, emotional, and intellectual dispositions into ones that maximally enable them to conform to their conceptions of the persons they should be. We can now see that by requiring autonomous people to make these changes, the first condition in our definition requires them to meet the second condition's requirement of being able to change their conceptions.

To appreciate these connections, we need to recognize that people's personal dispositions and social situations change as they interact with others in the course of framing, revising, and pursuing their plans. From the preceding paragraph, it follows that people can satisfy our first condition of planning rationally to achieve over-all conceptions of their goals only if they respond to these changes by further specifying their aims. Specifically, as they come to face new social situations (for example, a tighter academic job market), they must define the changes they aim to make in their social situations or their abilities and emotional dispositions (for example, adding a J.D. to one's Ph.D.) in order to have opportunities for achieving what their conceptions require (for example, being part of a scholarly community, having a stable family life, participating in politics). Similarly, as they come to have changed physical, emotional, and intellectual propensities (for example, coming as one grows older to have less rapport with one's students and younger colleagues) they must define the changes in their propensities or the social situations at which they aim (for example, doing more "adult division" teaching) in order to become the sort of person they want to be (for example, being an effective teacher, having egalitarian relations with one's colleagues, having one's social life integrated with one's work life). In defining these aims, people who satisfy our first condition for autonomy are on the one hand guided by their existing systematic conceptions of the persons they should be. On the other hand, as they define these aims, they extend their conceptions to circumstances to which they did not previously apply (in our examples, to a tighter job market, to an "age gap" with one's students and colleagues). By extending them to new circumstances, they in effect change their over-all conceptions by more completely specifying their component goals (in our examples, getting a J.D., doing "adult division" teaching).

People must also be able to make more radical changes in their over-all conceptions of their goals if they are to satisfy our first condition for autonomy. To see this, we need to recognize how difficult it is for people to make their lives conform to their conceptions of the lives they want to lead. On the one hand, they are highly unlikely to achieve this conformity by the simple route of copying others' plans. They must instead adjust their plans to their unique personal dispositions and social situations and must continue to do so as their circumstances change. On the other hand, people's ability to perform these intellectually demanding tasks is both naturally and culturally restricted. Humans can develop their innately limited capacities for acquiring and using information only within cultural and institutional frameworks that limit both the ends they can imagine pursuing and the means they can conceive of using.

For these reasons, it is likely that as people attempt to satisfy our first condition for autonomy (namely, planning rationally to achieve over-all conceptions of their goals), they will often fail to devise adequate means for achieving aims that they specify as components of their over-all conceptions (in the first example just above, not getting admitted to law school and therefore not realizing the aim of earning a J.D.). This includes situations in which they believe two or more aims essential to their conceptions but can only devise methods for achieving some at the cost of others. For example, a person who believes the kind of scholarly life she wants can be attained only by teaching at a large university and the kind of family life only in a rural setting may nonetheless be able to get job offers only from small colleges in rural settings or large universities in big cities. In addition, individuals may believe that the only way to achieve certain aims required by their conceptions is to undergo experiences likely to deprive them of the physical and psychological wherewithal for continuing to plan rationally to achieve component aims of their conceptions. For example, a person may believe that becoming a partner in a large law firm is the only way to achieve the prestige and financial security he desires. He may also believe that the pressures of striving for partner status are likely to threaten his emotional stability.

People satisfy our first condition for autonomy only if in these situations they rationally search for alternative methods that will enable them to achieve their goals (in the preceding paragraph's first example, strengthening one's law school application by writing a better essay, asking different people for recommendations, and so forth). Opposing people's limited intelligence to the almost limitless diversity and complexity of their situations, however, we see that these rational efforts may often not succeed. Must a person's repeated failures to devise adequate means to aims that he or she specifies as part of his or her over-all conception prevent him or her from satisfying our first condition for autonomy? It seems to me that they need not. People can nonetheless plan rationally to achieve over-all conceptions of their goals if, in the preceding paragraph's situations, their rational attempts to revise their means go hand in hand with rational attempts to revise their specifications of the aims composing their over-all conceptions. They must seek to replace the individual goals that they fail to achieve with goals that resemble them in being consistent with their over-all conceptions but differ in being easier to achieve. Thus, the person in the second of the preceding paragraph's examples may decide that her scholarly interests can be served as well by teaching in a small college as by teaching in a large university.

The limits on human intelligence and the diversity and complexity of people's situations make it possible, however, that even if people rationally change both their means and their specifications of their over-all conceptions, they may nonetheless fail to make their lives conform to their conceptions of the lives they want to lead. If they are to satisfy our first condition for autonomy, they must respond to persistent failures of this kind by changing not the component aims of their conceptions but their conceptions themselves. They must reject and devise alternatives to their fundamental assumptions about what they should achieve at various stages of their lives, about the relative importance of their various goals (for example, deciding that prestige and financial security are much less important to them than they previously believed). Their aim in making these revisions must be to replace their over-all conceptions by alternatives that they believe themselves more likely to be able to plan rationally to achieve. Given this aim, it follows that autonomous people commit themselves to new over-all conceptions of their goals only when they commit themselves to certain courses of action. The courses of action to which they commit themselves are intelligently defining, revising, and pursuing means and aims so as to make all aspects of their lives conform to their new conceptions of the lives they aim to lead.

c. Answers to Our Preliminary Objections   The preceding account of how and why autonomous people change their goals allows us to dismiss the objections raised above to the two conditions that we gave for being autonomous. Our first condition, it will be recalled, was shaping one's circumstances by planning rationally to achieve some over-all conception of one's goals. Our second condition was shaping one's goals by rationally criticizing and revising one's over-all conception.

A major objection raised was that these two conditions are inconsistent. How can people have the requisite commitment for planning rationally to achieve over-all conceptions of their goals if they are disposed to criticize and change them? In effect, the preceding section answers this objection by showing that autonomous people are motivated to change their conceptions *precisely because* they are committed to planning rationally to achieve over-all conceptions. People can continue to act on this commitment despite changes in their circumstances and displays of their human fallibility only if they are able to make changes in their over-all conceptions of their goals, either by specifying their conceptions' component goals, *or* by revising these specifications, *or* by replacing their conceptions as wholes by systematic alternatives.

Once we see this, we can also answer the objection that since there is no standard for judging whether people criticize and change their goals rationally or irrationally, there is no point to our making doing this *rationally* a condition for being autonomous. The key is to realize that autonomous people guide their actions by a *hierarchical structure of aims*. Although they commit themselves to planning rationally to achieve aims integrated into systematic conceptions of the persons they should be, autonomous people never ultimately aim to have lives that conform to any particular conception. Rather, they aim above all else at shaping their lives rationally by their goals. Another way of putting this is that their ultimate aim is to lead rational, planning lives. Autonomous people intelligently frame, revise, and pursue plans directed at achieving particular over-all conceptions because they believe doing so is the best means to their ultimate goal of being the rational shapers of their lives.

It follows, on the one hand, that autonomous people do not lightly abandon their over-all conceptions of their goals when they fail to realize aims that they believe these conceptions require. To the contrary, they attempt to make their lives conform to these conceptions by devising alternatives to their means or redefining their conceptions' component goals. They are motivated to do this precisely by their major reason for accepting the particular over-all conception of their goals that they accept – the belief that intelligently planning to achieve these over-all conceptions is the best way for them to achieve their ultimate goal of leading goal-directed lives.

On the other hand, autonomous people are never committed no matter what to their over-all conceptions. Their own and others' persistent failures to achieve goals taken to be components of a particular conception lead them to wonder whether intelligently planning to achieve that conception will indeed enable them to shape their lives to accord with their goals. Since autonomous people are above all else committed to shaping their lives rationally by their goals, these doubts lead them to search for alternative conceptions that they believe they are more likely to achieve through their rational plans.

Once we see this, we realize that there are indeed standards for judging the rationality of the changes that autonomous people make in their aims. On the one hand, consider the changes they make *within* the context of their over-all conceptions of their goals. They further specify the aims that they take to be components of those conceptions and revise their views of what aims are components. Their aim in doing this is rationally to shape their lives to conform to the particular over-all conceptions of their goals that they accept. Thus, in one of the examples above, a person forms the new aim of doing "adult division" teaching because he believes pursuing this aim will make him more able to achieve such crucial components of his over-all conception of his goals as being an effective teacher and having egalitarian relations with others. This granted, and given the standard definition of rationality presented above (§4), saying that autonomous people make these changes rationally means that they conform to a two-part standard. They choose aims that are consistent with the conceptions they have so far defined of the lives they aim to lead. In addition, they choose aims that, in the light of the knowledge available to them, it is possible for them to plan rationally to achieve.

On the other hand, consider the changes that autonomous people make *of* their over-all conceptions of their goals. They reject and devise alternatives to their fundamental assumptions about what they should achieve at various stages of their lives, about the relative importance of their various goals. They do this in order to achieve their ultimate goal of rationally shaping their lives by their goals. Thus, continuing one of the examples above, a person concludes that the cost of attaining the prestige and financial security that he takes to be crucial components of his over-all conception of his goals is subjecting himself to job pressures (for example, those associated with working in a large law firm) that threaten his emotional stability and hence his ability to lead a rational, planning life. Motivated by the aim of shaping his life rationally by his goals, he decides that prestige and financial security are much less important to him than he previously believed. From this and from our standard definition of rationality, it follows that autonomous people rationally decide whether to continue attempting to realize a particular conception or to seek to replace that conception by some alternative if and only if they conform to a certain standard. They make the decisions that seem most likely, given the knowledge available to them, to enable them rationally to make their lives conform to their conceptions of the lives they want to lead.

§6 SUMMARY

Having answered the objections raised above to our second condition for being autonomous, we have now completed the task set for Section II of this paper. We sought to develop a realistic account of autonomy, or, in other words, to show that and how it is possible to take account of human social dependency and yet make sense of the claim that people can be autonomous or independent. This section's discussion proceeded from the premise that autonomy is not a matter of being free from social influences, but of acting so as to control one's life significantly. It argued that in order to act in this way, people must satisfy two conditions. The first is shaping one's circumstances by planning rationally to achieve some over-all conception of one's goals. The second is shaping one's goals by rationally criticizing and changing one's over-all conception. People can satisfy these two conditions, we argued, even though all humans are fallible and have their methods and goals crucially shaped by their early educations and by the social pressures and opportunities to which they are subject as adults. Indeed, we indicated that people need to be subject to some, rather than other, types of social influences if they are to develop the abilities and traits of character needed for satisfying our two conditions for being autonomous.

Let us now embark on a closer consideration of the social conditions that aid and hinder people from achieving autonomy. Specifically, let us return to the question that led us to pursue this section's investigations. What labor policy or policies must our society pursue if it is to respect all its members as autonomous agents? Section I of this paper concluded, it will be recalled, that we would have an adequate basis for answering this question only if we developed a realistic account of autonomy. By appealing to the present section's account, we can now evaluate the answer that the majority of the Lochner Court gave. Were those judges right to assume that all people who have the capacity for autonomy are hindered from exercising it whenever laws restrict the contracts of employment that they can make? If we accord fundamental importance to personal autonomy, must we therefore endorse the judges' strong presumption in favor of freedom of contract with regard to employment? As indicated above, we need to answer these questions if we are intelligently to respond to a pressing contemporary issue. Are Reagan and his supporters right to condemn the interventionist social policies, including labor laws, that have shaped American life since the New Deal on grounds that they violate personal autonomy?

III. AN ALTERNATIVE TO THE LOCHNER ERA'S POLICIES

§7 A FINAL REJECTION OF THE LOCHNER COURT'S POSITION

In order to evaluate the Lochner era's view of the relations between autonomy and labor laws, we need first to state, in very broad terms, the implications for social policy of the preceding section's discussion. A crucial implication is that respecting people as autonomous is not equivalent, as commonly assumed, to leaving them as free as possible from social influences. Instead, a society respects all its members as autonomous to the extent that it assists them in leading a certain kind of life. People achieve autonomy, the preceding section argued, to the extent that they develop and act on the ultimate goal of shaping their lives rationally by their goals. It follows that a society respects all its members as autonomous when its institutions are arranged maximally to influence them all to lead such rational, planning lives. Would a return to the Lochner era's policies enable our society to do this?

A negative answer becomes obvious once we realize that there are material prerequisites for achieving autonomy. People clearly need to enjoy a certain amount of leisure and a certain level of health and material comfort if they are to become and remain able and inclined intelligently to frame, revise, and act on their answers to the questions: What sort of person do I aim to become? How should I attempt to achieve my goals? Just as clearly, our earlier examination of the Lochner cases shows that employees are likely to be deprived of these material conditions when no laws restrict the contracts that they can make with employers. A government decision to preserve freedom of contract with regard to employment is, we saw in §3, a decision to place bargaining power in the hands of the economically powerful — generally, in the hands of employers rather than employees. This allocation of power tends to leave many people with no choice but to work unhealthily long hours, at wages that can only pay for crowded and unsanitary housing, and so forth. To say that the preservation of freedom of contract tends to leave many people with no choice but to accept these conditions is equivalent to saying that it tends to leave many people without the material conditions that humans standardly need for leading rational, goal-directed lives.

Can we conclude, on this basis, that our government must impose the very sorts of restrictions on freedom of contract that the Lochner Court opposed if it is to respect all its citizens as autonomous? Before we can reach this conclusion, we need to disarm a major objection. Might restrictions on freedom of contract, such as minimum wage and maximum hours laws, assure workers the material prerequisites for autonomy only at the cost of depriving both workers and employers of legal freedoms that they need for achieving autonomy? Might the Lochner era's policies therefore still be the ones that we must endorse if we accord fundamental importance to personal autonomy?

To dismiss this argument, we need to recognize a crucial implication of Section II's discussion. Being autonomous is not a matter of being able to achieve whatever goals one forms. On the contrary, in any ordinary life, both one's personal dispositions (for example, limited intelligence) and social situations (for example, being among people whose goals conflict with one's own) prevent one's achieving certain of one's goals. Being autonomous is a matter of continuing to be a rational planner despite these failures of some of one's plans. Another way of putting this is that autonomous people continue to frame, pursue, and *revise* their methods *and* aims intelligently as their personal dispositions and social situations change.

Once we see this, we can draw a crucial distinction among material conditions, educational opportunities, and legal freedoms. There are certain material conditions (for example, owning a leather pants suit), educational opportunities (for example, taking a Charles Atlas bodybuilding course), and legal freedoms (for example, freedom not to wear a helmet while riding a motorcycle) that people must have in order to achieve certain goals (for example, to project a certain type of "macho" image) but do not need in order to achieve autonomy (that is, to develop and act on the ultimate goal of shaping their lives rationally by their goals). In contrast, there are certain material conditions (as indicated above, a certain amount of leisure and a certain level of health and material comfort), educational opportunities (for example, being raised in a family atmosphere that supports, instead of severely undermining, one's self-confidence), and legal freedoms (roughly, a society's legal restrictions must not be so extensive that its citizens lack significant opportunities for making decisions and for considering alternative beliefs and lifestyles) that are prerequisites for autonomy. People standardly need these material conditions, educational opportunities, and legal freedoms in order to become and remain able and inclined intelligently to frame, revise, and act on their answers to the questions: What sort of person do I aim to become? How should I attempt to achieve my goals?

This distinction between material conditions, educational opportunities, and legal freedoms that are and those that are not prerequisites for autonomy gives rise to a further classification of legal freedoms. There are certain legal freedoms that people do not need in order to achieve autonomy and whose exercise is likely to deprive others of legal freedoms, material conditions, or educational opportunities without which these others cannot lead the rational, planning lives of autonomous agents. Clearly, people have legal freedoms of this kind when no laws prevent them from killing or injuring others or from depriving their children of all instruction. Must we not similarly classify freedom to have employment agreements enforced at law regardless of their effects on the physical well-being of employees? On the one hand, does not our discussion of the Lochner cases show that employees are likely to be deprived of material prerequisites for autonomy as a result of others' exercise of this freedom? On the other hand, cannot employers as well as employees continue to frame, revise, and pursue methods and aims intelligently even if laws prevent their making employment contracts that pose a general threat to health and physical well-being?

Once we see this, we can dismiss the Lochner judges' main philosophical argument for their presumption against labor laws, the argument from autonomy reconstructed in §2. That argument does not work because there is no reason to accept the generalized version of its premise 3: All people who have the capacity for autonomy are hindered from exercising it whenever laws restrict the contracts of employment that they can make. We have shown, to the contrary, that the types of restrictions on freedom of contract that the Lochner Court opposed deprive people of freedoms not needed for leading rational, planning lives in order to guarantee people a level of material well-being without which it is virtually impossible to lead such lives. *Contra* Reagan and his supporters, then, we can conclude that our society can give all its members maximal scope for achieving autonomy only if it continues to reject, instead of returning to, the Lochner era's non-interventionist labor policies.

Might it be the case, in addition, that our government needs to pursue a kind of intervention that it has yet to take? In addition to being affected by what hours they work and what pay they receive, people's ability to lead rational, planning lives is clearly affected by whether their jobs give them opportunities to frame, revise, and pursue methods and aims intelligently. That much conceded, we can show that all members of our society can achieve autonomy only if the current arrangement of employment is radically changed. We can suggest that our government needs to restrict freedom of contract with regard to employment in order to insure that these changes are made.

§8 A PROBLEM WITH OUR SOCIETY'S ARRANGEMENT OF EMPLOYMENT

We can understand how and why the arrangement of employment in our society needs to be changed only if we recognize that a distinctive type of division of labor has so far existed in all industrial societies, including our own. In all societies, whether industrial or non-industrial, where people produce goods and services for exchange, there is a social division of labor. Different members of society specialize in producing different goods and services (for example, hunting, fishing, being a medicine man), and what they produce is exchanged within their society as a whole. Only in industrial societies, however, has there also been a significant development of what the great nineteenth-century social theorist Karl Marx called the detailed division of labor, a division that we may also appropriately term the hierarchical division of labor.[22]

Labor is hierarchically divided or divided in detail only when different members of society specialize in performing various tasks that join together to produce a good or service that can be exchanged within their society as a whole (for example, working at different positions on an automobile assembly line and performing the associated engineering, machine repairing, and supervisory jobs). Under this division, the specialists who cooperate to produce a good or service are always divided into those who decide and those who execute others' decisions. On the one hand, a small group of managerial experts coordinates and schedules others' activities, deciding what people will do in their jobs and the precise manner in which they will execute their tasks. On the other hand, a much larger group of detail workers performs the actions that managerial experts precisely specify.

The nature of the subordinate, or detail workers', jobs created by the hierarchical, or detailed, division of labor can be more concretely grasped by considering a famous eighteenth-century description of a pin-making factory. In the opening pages of his pathbreaking work *The Wealth of Nations*, philosopher and economist Adam Smith wrote "one man draws out the wire, another straights it, a third cuts it, a fourth points it" and so on to eighteen distinct operations.[23] Some workers may perform two or three of these routine tasks; many repeatedly execute only one operation. In addition to assembly line jobs, contemporary analogues of the detail workers' jobs that Smith described include watchman's jobs in automated oil or chemical refinery plants. These jobs consist only in repeatedly reading simple dials in an order and at intervals specified by others. To appreciate the role that the detailed division of labor plays in our economy, we need to see that it extends to offices and service operations as well as factories. To give only a few examples, the subordinate, or detail workers', jobs created by this division include being a typist in a typing pool, a keypunch operator, a bank teller or a server in a fast food line.

We are now in a position to see that there is a conflict between (1) the widely held view, among members of our society, that all people should be respected as autonomous agents and (2) the detailed or hierarchical division of labor that extends to virtually all branches of production in our society.[24] The many people in our society who are employed at the subordinate jobs created by this division do not decide the over-all goals of the factories, offices, or service operations in which they work. In addition, they do not decide how to perform their particular jobs. Instead of being hired to achieve certain goals and left to select and pursue adequate means, they are employed to perform precisely specified actions.

Even the order in which they perform these operations, the pace at which they work, and the particular bodily movements they employ are largely determined by managerial experts' decisions. Since detail workers' jobs consist almost entirely of such mechanical activity, they are in effect paid for blindly pursuing ends managerial experts have chosen, by means that such experts judge adequate. Joining this with our account of autonomy, it follows that detail workers cannot act as autonomous agents while performing their jobs.

The fact that the detailed, or hierarchical, division of labor extends to virtually all branches of production in our society means that many people in it can be remuneratively employed *only* if they accept the subordinate jobs just described. The additional fact that most adults in our society *have no choice but* to devote significant amounts of time to remunerative employment means that many people in our society are prevented from intelligently framing, revising, and pursuing methods and aims, or, in other words, *from acting autonomously while at work*. The tension between these facts and the view that our social institutions should be arranged to aid all people to lead the rational, planning lives of autonomous agents is sharpened by the existence of a carryover effect. From Adam Smith's time to our own, the empirical literature has consistently argued that people are hindered from leading autonomous lives on the whole when they are prevented from acting autonomously while at work.

More precisely, the scholarly consensus has been that when people work, for considerable lengths of time, at jobs that mainly involve mechanical activity, they tend to become less capable of and less interested in rationally framing, pursuing, and adjusting their own plans *when they leave the workplace*. As Smith wrote in 1776 in *The Wealth of Nations*,

> The understandings of the greater part of men are necessarily formed by their ordinary employments. The man whose whole life is spent in performing a few simple operations . . . has no occasion to exert his understanding, or to exercise his invention in finding out expedients for removing difficulties which never occur. He naturally loses, therefore, the habit of such exertion . . . His dexterity at his own particular trade seems . . . to be acquired at the expense of his intellectual virtues.[25]

As Arthur Kornhauser wrote in his classic study of Detroit automobile workers in 1964,

> Factory employment, especially in routine production tasks, does give evidence of extinguishing workers' ambition, initiative, and purposeful direction toward life goals.[26] . . . The unsatisfactory mental health of working people consists in no small measure of their dwarfed desires and deadened initiative, reduction of their goals and restriction of their efforts to a point where life is relatively empty and only half meaningful.[27]

Once we see, however, that the detailed division of labor in our society insures that many people are prevented from acting autonomously while performing their jobs, and once we also realize that people who are prevented from doing so are hindered from leading autonomous lives on the whole, we are forced to reach the following conclusion. *All members of our society can lead the rational, goal-directed lives of autonomous agents only if the detailed or hierarchical division of labor is eliminated.* Would it be possible, however, for our society to eliminate this division? In particular, could it do so without depriving people of other conditions they need for achieving autonomy? Only answers to these questions will allow us to determine whether and how the arrangement of employment in our society could be changed to aid all people to shape their lives rationally by their goals, or, in other words, to be autonomous.

§9 SOME CURRENT REFORMS

To decide whether it would be possible to eliminate the conflict between our society's arrangement of employment and the view that all people should be respected as autonomous, let us start by considering certain contemporary proposals for reform. Often, routine clerical or factory jobs are enlarged by a process of horizontal integration: Each worker is made responsible for a number of routine operations instead of being assigned one mechanical task. An example of this is having assembly line workers rotate jobs so that each worker can follow a product through all the stages in its production.[28] Or, bank tellers may be assigned to sort returned checks when the loads at their counters are light.[29]

The problem is that all these horizontal restructurings do is make detail workers' work more various. Their jobs consist, exactly as before, in performing actions managerial experts precisely specify. Thus, horizontal integration does nothing to eliminate the vice ascribed in §8 to the detailed division of labor. People are still divided, at work, into those who decide and those who execute others' decisions. This means that many people's jobs still prevent them from acting autonomously and thereby stunt their autonomous development on the whole.

The vice of the detailed division of labor is also not eliminated when structures of democratic decision-making are imposed on factories, offices, or service operations whose employees are still distinguished into detail workers and managerial experts. Such parliamentarism may only involve, as in West German co-determination, consulting selected workers about management's policies. Or it may extend, as in Yugoslav workers' self-management, to allowing all employees to vote on policies. Similarly, parliamentarism may only consist, as in many American experiments, in allowing workers to decide relatively trivial matters, for example, the colors of their offices or the pace of the assembly lines on which they work. In contrast, parliamentarism may mean, as in the Yugoslav experience, that major policy questions are decided by all employees.[30]

We can see that workplace parliamentarism is by itself inadequate if we consider the most radical version of this reform. Even if all employees vote on administrators, mergers, hiring and financial policies, and so forth, the relations between managerial experts and detail workers remain hierarchical. On the one hand, the managerial experts are employed to decide how to implement policies. On the other hand, the detail workers are hired to effect those decisions. Their role is to perform precisely those operations that the managerial experts judge the best means to the workplace's goals. This distinction between those whose daily job is to decide and those whose daily job is to execute others' decisions seems to carry over to a distinction between the use that detail workers and managerial experts make of their opportunities to participate in parliamentary decision-making. Under Yugoslav workers' self-management, at least, the managerial experts' control of relevant information and their greater experience in making decisions appears to give them a powerful advantage in having their proposals accepted by others.[31] Should we not have expected this, given the connection described in §8 between being prevented from intelligently framing, revising, and pursuing plans while performing one's job and becoming less able and inclined to do so during the rest of one's time?

If our society's arrangement of employment is to be changed, then, to make it possible for all people to achieve autonomy, detail workers cannot simply be assigned greater numbers of routine operations and formal democracy cannot simply be imposed on workplaces whose division of labor remains hierarchical. Rather, jobs must be democratically redesigned, tasks must be shared out to abolish the distinction between those who decide and those who execute others' decisions. A start in this direction was made in a dog-food plant opened by the General Foods Corporation in Topeka, Kansas, in 1971.[32] There, each worker was hired to be part of a small group of people, each group was made responsible for intellectually demanding functions (for example, maintaining and repairing machines, quality control operations), and all groups of workers shared in the routine work that was not eliminated by automation. Within each group, work was also democratically distributed. All workers were given opportunities to perform all the tasks assigned to their group, no group member was mainly assigned to routine operations, and all the members in the group shared in supervising its operations, democratically deciding on job assignments, on pay raises, on breaks, and so forth.

As a result of this sharing of supervisory functions and of routine and intellectually demanding production work, no person in this plant was mainly employed to perform actions that others precisely specified. All people's jobs gave them significant opportunities for rationally framing, pursuing, and adjusting plans. A closer look at this General Foods experiment should now enable us, on the one hand, to dismiss certain doubts about the possibility of changing our society's arrangement of employment. On the other hand, it should allow us to indicate how extensively that arrangement must be changed if many members of our society are not to be denied the opportunity to achieve autonomy.

§10 THE REQUISITE CHANGES

In §8 it was noted that the detailed, or hierarchical, division of labor has existed so far in all industrial societies. It would obviously be extremely difficult, if not impossible, for our society to eliminate the routine jobs created by that division if the cost of doing so was eliminating its industrial base. The General Foods experiment suggests that this change need not have this cost. Although no employee in the dog-food plant mainly performed routine operations, together the employees nonetheless operated a highly sophisticated industrial plant. This clearly is strong evidence for the frequent scholarly claim that today's machine systems can be operated without a detailed division of labor. The machinery itself does not dictate that employees be divided into those who perform the routine tasks involved in assisting machine operations and those who decide how the machines are to be used.[33]

Hand in hand with suggesting that our society could eliminate the routine jobs created by the detailed division of labor without substantially lowering its level of technology, the General Foods experiment suggests that our society could do this without so lowering productivity as to deprive some people of material conditions for autonomy. We need not choose, in other words, between an arrangement of employment that gives some people jobs that stunt their autonomous development and one too economically unproductive for all people to enjoy the leisure time, health, and general material comfort requisite for leading rational, planning lives. *Business Week* reported in 1977 that unit costs in the General Foods dog-food plant were "5% less than under a traditional factory system. . . . This . . . should amount to a saving of $1 million a year."[34] The unusual productivity of this plant accords with a conclusion reached by a special task force to the United States secretary of Health, Education, and Welfare in 1973. "The redesign of work," the task force argued,

> *can* lower such business costs as absenteeism, tardiness, turnover, labor disputes, sabotage and poor qualities. . . . The evidence suggests that meeting the higher needs of workers can, perhaps, increase productivity from 5% to 40%, the latter figure included the "latent" productivity of workers that is currently untapped.[35]

The General Foods experiment does not contain the solution, however, to all the problems with our society's current arrangement of employment. The title of the *Business Week* article just mentioned was "Stonewalling Plant Democracy." Despite the dog-food plant's unusual productivity and workers' uniform enthusiasm for it, *Business Week* reported that its democratic division of labor had "been eroding steadily" because of "indifference and outright hostility from some GF managers." "The problem," the report argued,

> has been not so much that the workers could not manage their own affairs as that some management and staff personnel saw their own posi-

tions threatened because the workers performed almost too well. . . . Personnel managers objected because team members made hiring decisions. Engineers resented workers doing engineering work.[36]

The reasons for the erosion of the General Foods experiment seem to be similar to the reasons for Polaroid's liquidation of a profitable worker participation project in the 1960s. According to Polaroid's training director, the project

was too successful. What were we going to do with the supervisors—the managers? We didn't need them anymore. Management decided it just didn't want operators that qualified.[37]

Why was the opposition of managerial experts sufficient to cause the elimination or severe curtailment of these attempts at giving workers significant control over decisions? Why weren't these democratic reforms instead continued despite managerial opposition because of their productivity and because of the enthusiasm for them that workers displayed? Restricting ourselves to the General Foods experiment, we see that the managerial experts were able to act on their resentment precisely because the arrangements were not democratic enough, not because they were too democratic. Within the dog-food plant, management *unilaterally* decided what should be produced, how profits should be used, what hiring policies should be, and whether its democratic reforms should continue. In short, the plant's reform consisted solely of sharing functions so that no person was mainly employed at routine operations. It did *not* extend to eliminating the distinction between those who decide and those who execute others' decisions. The workers in the plant could only plan to implement policies that the managerial experts set. It follows that if all members of our society are not to be denied the opportunity to achieve autonomy, labor must be divided still more democratically than it was by General Foods. In addition to sharing out functions so that no person is mainly employed at routine operations, information must be shared and opportunities provided so that all people can participate in shaping their enterprise's policies.

Could this democratic alternative to the detailed, or hierarchical, division of labor possibly be instituted, however, on a society-wide basis? In particular, would it be possible for our society to do this without depriving people of other prerequisites for leading the rational, goal-directed lives of autonomous agents? It might be suggested to the contrary that the economic success of the General Foods experiment need not carry over to the more democratic reform we urge. On this basis, it might be argued that the widespread institution of our democratic alternative in our society would so lower productivity as to deprive some people of material prerequisites for achieving autonomy. It might therefore be concluded that no efforts to institute this reform are incumbent on those who accord fundamental importance to personal autonomy.

To meet this objection, it is first necessary to locate the burden of proof. Our discussion has established that in the absence of attempts to institute our democratic alternative to the detailed division of labor, some members of our society are *certain* to be denied the opportunity to achieve autonomy. It follows that if we accord fundamental importance to personal autonomy, the call to attempt to institute our democratic reform cannot be rebutted by citing the mere *possibility* that this attempt might lead to some people's being deprived of material prerequisites for autonomy. To the contrary, to rebut this call, defenders of the existing detailed division of labor must show that this is a *certain, or at least a highly probable*, consequence of making the attempt in question.

The difficulty of showing this becomes evident once we recall (§7) that the material prerequisites for autonomy are the leisure time and level of health and over-all physical comfort that people standardly need if they are intelligently to frame, revise, and act on their answers to the questions: What sort of person do I aim to become? How should I attempt to achieve my goals? Clearly, people can enjoy these material conditions without having as much wealth as they could possibly want. In order to show, then, that there is a conflict between instituting our democratic alternative to the detailed division of labor and insuring all members of our society the material prerequisites for autonomy, it is not sufficient to show that the institution of this alternative must so lower productivity as to necessitate some people's suffering a decrease in wealth. It must be shown to the contrary that the institution of this alternative will certainly, or at least will highly probably, decrease total social wealth so severely as to make it impossible for all members of our society to enjoy the leisure time and level of health and material comfort that humans standardly need for leading rational, planning lives.

The available evidence does not support this conclusion. Although reforms as democratic as the one we urge have yet to be instituted, we saw at the beginning of this section that the few attempts so far made to democratize the workplace in our society have *generally* tended to increase rather than decrease productivity. In addition, there is a crucial similarity between the economically successful General Foods experiment and the more democratic reform we urge. While arguments for the economic unfeasibility of instituting an alternative to the detailed division of labor often assume that any alternative would require deindustrialization, neither the General Foods experiment nor our proposed reform does. Just as today's machine systems do not by themselves dictate that some people be exclusively assigned to routine operations, so they do not by themselves rule out sharing information and providing opportunities so that all people can participate in shaping their enterprises' policies.

It might be argued, however, that even if there is no conflict between instituting our democratic alternative to the detailed division of labor and insuring all members of our society the material prerequisites for autonomy, there is a conflict between instituting this alternative and preserving the legal freedoms that people need for achieving autonomy. The basis for this argument might be the claim that our democratic alternative would only come to replace the detailed, or hierarchical, division of labor throughout our society if people were legally prevented from contracting to work under the detailed division of labor. Would not this restriction of freedom of contract with regard to employment insure all employees the democratic workplace conditions they need for achieving autonomy only at the cost of depriving *both* employers *and* employees of legal freedoms that they need for achieving autonomy? Must we not therefore condemn such legal restrictions if we accord fundamental importance to personal autonomy?

To the contrary, we can now see that respect for all people as autonomous commits us to urging, instead of condemning, such government measures. Thus, we can show that no conflict obtains between instituting our democratic alternative to the detailed division of labor and preserving the legal freedoms that people need for achieving autonomy. Let us start by recalling a crucial distinction drawn in our refutation of the Lochner era's position on the relations between autonomy and freedom of contract with regard to employment (§7). There are certain material conditions, educational opportunities, and legal freedoms that people may want in order to achieve certain goals but do not need in order to lead lives that they shape rationally by their goals, or, in other words, to be autonomous. In contrast, there are other material conditions, educational opportunities, and legal freedoms that people standardly do need if they are to become and remain able and inclined to lead the rational, planning lives of autonomous agents. Against the claim that the Lochner era decisions preserved a legal freedom that people need for achieving autonomy, we urged that both employers and employees can continue to frame, revise, and pursue methods and aims intelligently even if laws prevent their making employment contracts that pose a general threat to health and physical well-being. Can we not similarly dismiss the claim that freedom to have the law enforce agreements to work under the detailed division of labor is a legal freedom that people need for achieving autonomy? Cannot people continue to lead rational, goal-directed lives even if laws prevent them from hiring others or being hired for the unquestioning pursuit of ends managerial experts have chosen, by means that those experts judge adequate?

So far, however, this argument only shows that we need not condemn government measures to democratize the workplace if we accord fundamental importance to personal autonomy. Would it be possible to show that we are committed to urging such measures? To this end, let us recall a further classification developed above (§7) to show that our government must impose the very sorts of restrictions that the Lochner Court opposed if it is to respect all its citizens as autonomous. Freedom to have employment agreements enforced at law regardless of their effects on the physical well-being of employees belongs, we argued above, to the class of freedoms that people do not need in order to achieve autonomy *and* whose exercise is likely to deprive others of material conditions, educational opportunities, or legal freedoms that these others need for achieving autonomy. Should we not similarly classify freedom to use the law to enforce agreements for people to work under the hierarchical, or detailed, division of labor?

Must we not draw this conclusion because the existence of that division implies that some people's jobs demand their unquestioning pursuit of ends that others have chosen, by means that others judge adequate? Must we not also draw it because the existence of the detailed, or hierarchical, division of labor influences even more people not to work towards changing that state of affairs? On the one hand, people employed in the managerial positions created by that division of labor seem, as suggested by our discussion of the General Foods and Polaroid experiments, to develop a stake in retaining their responsibilities. They therefore tend to oppose reforms that give workers significant control over decisions. On the other hand, as we saw above (§8), the subordinate, routine jobs created by the hierarchical division of labor tend to "extinguish . . . workers' ambition, initiative, and purposeful direction towards life goals."[38] Thus, although "Workers on repetitive jobs feel deprived and stultified by the endless dull routine . . . [and] poignantly wish for more interesting and challenging work in which they could use their abilities and derive a sense of worth and self-respect,"[39] their work itself tends to decrease their capacities for rationally planning to effect these implicit desires for a democratic alternative to today's arrangement of employment.

Once we urge, however, that our government intervene to change this situation, we are urging that it pursue a truly revolutionary task. To this day, the hierarchical division of labor has existed in all industrial societies. It is difficult to imagine what a society-wide democratic alternative to it would look like. It is even more difficult to see how best to pursue that change. Is the change we are urging any more radical a departure from recent policy, however, than the anti-interventionist revolution that Reagan and his supporters urge? Must not our change rather than theirs be supported by all who accord fundamental importance to personal autonomy and who ground that commitment in a realistic answer to the question: What can it mean for people to be autonomous, given the socially dependent nature of all human beings?

IV. SUMMARY

There is a widespread agreement, within our society, that all people should be respected as autonomous agents. This essay explored some of that view's implications with regard to labor policy. We started by considering a position that the majority of the United States Supreme Court took during the Lochner era (1905–1937) and which Reagan and his supporters come close to reaffirming today. This position is that a strong commitment to personal autonomy goes hand in hand with a strong presumption against State intervention to restrict the contracts of employment that people can make. We showed that this connection between autonomy and freedom of contract with regard to employment seems obvious only if we mistakenly assume that autonomous people are free from the influence of social institutions. In order to have rational grounds for deciding whether this connection obtains, we proceeded to develop a realistic account of autonomy, or, in other words, to explain what it can mean for people to be autonomous or independent given the socially dependent nature of human beings. On the basis of our account, we showed that the Lochner Court gravely misunderstood the relations between autonomy and freedom of contract with regard to employment. The principal kinds of restrictions on contractual freedom (minimum wage and maximum hours laws) that that Court opposed, on grounds that they violate personal autonomy, must to the contrary be imposed if all members of our society are to achieve autonomy. In addition to demanding these traditional kinds of labor laws, we suggested, in conclusion, that respect for autonomy demands a kind of workplace intervention that our government has yet to take. Measures are needed to democratize the workplace: to abolish the hierarchical division of labor that currently divides the members of our society into the few who decide and the many who execute others' decisions.

NOTES

1. 198 U.S. 45.
2. 300 U.S. 379.
3. 261 U.S. 525.
4. 300 U.S. 391.
5. Laurence H. Tribe, *American Constitutional Law* (Mineola, N.Y.: The Foundation Press, 1978), p. 435.
6. Robert Nozick, *Anarchy, State, and Utopia* (N.Y.: Basic Books, 1974).
7. Milton and Rose Friedman, *Free to Choose: A Personal Statement* (N.Y.: Harcourt Brace Jovanovich, 1980) and Milton Friedman, with the assistance of Rose Friedman, *Capitalism and Freedom* (Chicago: University of Chicago Press, 1962).
8. For a discussion of how current Labor Secretary Donovan's attempt to eliminate laws against home labor is grounded in a general presumption against labor laws, see "A Stitch in Time for Labor," *The New York Times* (October 17, 1981), p. 22.
9. *Adkins* v. *Children's Hospital* 261 U.S. 546.
10. *Lochner* v. *New York* 198 U.S. 53.
11. *Adkins* v. *Children's Hospital* 261 U.S. 546.
12. 208 U.S. 412 (1908).
13. *Lochner* v. *New York* 198 U.S. 57.
14. 208 U.S. 556.
15. Ibid.
16. 261 U.S. 553.
17. Ibid.
18. Ibid.

19.   300 U.S. 398.

20.   300 U.S. 398–399.

21.   300 U.S. 394.

22.   Marx establishes and explores the concept of the detailed division of labor in Part IV of Vol. I of *Capital*. See, especially, ch. XIV, sec. 4, pp. 350–59 in Karl Marx's, *Capital: A Critique of Political Economy* (N.Y.: International Publishers, 1967). Harry Braverman's *Labor and Monopoly Capital: The Degradation of Work in the Twentieth Century* (N.Y.: Monthly Review Press, 1974) is the most detailed and illuminating work available on the development of the detailed division of labor since Marx's time.

23.   Adam Smith, *An Inquiry into the Nature and Causes of the Wealth of Nations*, Vol. I (Chicago: University of Chicago Press, 1976), p. 8.

24.   For a detailed argument for the claim that the detailed division of labor now extends to virtually all branches of production in our society, see Braverman, op. cit. In particular, see ch. 9 of that book for a discussion of the extension of that division to automated oil and chemical refinery plants, ch. 15 for a discussion of its extension to clerical occupations, and ch. 16 for a discussion of its extension to service occupations.

25.   Smith, op. cit., Vol. II, pp. 302–303. For a recent study that confirms Smith's conclusions, see Melvin L. Kohn and Carmi Schooler, "The Reciprocal Effects of the Substantive Complexity of Work and Intellectual Flexibility: A Longitudinal Study," *American Journal of Sociology*, Vol. 84 (July 1978), pp. 24–52.

26.   Arthur Kornhauser, *Mental Health of the Industrial Worker: A Detroit Study* (N.Y.: John Wiley and Sons, 1964), p. 252.

27.   Ibid., p. 270. For discussions of Kornhauser's work and of other studies that confirm his results and extend them to workers in other industries, see pp. 81–92 of *Work in America: Report of a Special Task Force to the Secretary of Health, Education, and Welfare* (Cambridge, Mass.: MIT Press, 1973), and Charles Hampden-Turner, "The Factory as an Oppressive and Non-Emancipatory Environment," in Gerry Hunnius, G. David Garson, and John Case, eds., *Workers' Control: A Reader on Labor and Social Change* (N.Y.: Random House, 1973), pp. 30–45.

28.   For this example and a general account of horizontal integration, see Elwood S. Buffa, *Modern Production Management: Managing the Operations Function*, 5th ed. (N.Y.: John Wiley and Sons, 1977), p. 230.

29.   For this example, see Braverman, op. cit., p. 37.

30.   For descriptions of West German co-determination and Yugoslav workers' self-management, see in Hunnius, Garson, and Case, op. cit., "Co-Determination in the Federal Republic of Germany," pp. 194–210; Helmut Schauer, "Critique of Co-Determination," pp. 210–24; and Gerry Hunnius, "Workers' Self-Management in Yugoslavia," pp. 268–321. For descriptions of American experiments with workplace parliamentarism, see Buffa, op. cit., pp. 232–33; Daniel Zwerdling, "Workplace Democracy: A Strategy for Survival," *The Progressive* (August 1978): 16-24, pp. 18–19; and Richard Edwards, *Contested Terrain: The Transformation of the Workplace in the Twentieth Century* (N.Y.: Basic Books, 1979), pp. 155–56.

31.   Hunnius, op. cit., p. 297.

32.   For descriptions of this plant, see pp. 96–99 of *Work in America*; Zwerdling, op. cit., pp. 17–18; and "Stonewalling Plant Democracy," *Business Week* (March 28, 1977); pp. 78–82.

33.   See ch. 9, especially pp. 230–31, of Braverman, op. cit., and, in Louis E. Davis and James C. Taylor, eds., *Design of Jobs: Selected Readings* (Harmondsworth, Middlesex, England: Penguin Books, 1972), Nehemiah Jordan, "Allocation of Functions between Man and Machines in Automated

Systems," pp. 91–99, and James G. Scoville, "A Theory of Jobs and Training," pp. 225–44.
34. "Stonewalling Plant Democracy," p. 78.
35. *Work in America*, p. 27 (their italics).
36. "Stonewalling Plant Democracy," p. 78.
37. This quotation and an account of the Polaroid project are in Edwards, op. cit., p. 156.
38. Kornhauser, op. cit., p. 252.
39. Ibid., p. 285. This general claim is supported by the interviews with American workers recorded in Studs Terkel's *Working* (N.Y.: Avon Books, 1975). People employed at routine jobs consistently objected to being treated like "machines," "robots," or "monkeys" (Terkel, especially pp. 57–60, 221–27, 239–43, 256–65, 344–51, 713–21). Similarly, the authors of *Work in America* found that "Workers in all occupations rate self-determination highest among the elements that define an ideal job. Content of work is generally more important than being promoted" (pp. 94–95).

SUGGESTIONS FOR FURTHER READING

Further readings are mentioned below in connection with the sections of the essay to which they are most pertinent.

I. §§1–2. Constitutional theorists Gerald Gunther and Laurence H. Tribe present interesting accounts of the Lochner era in, respectively, *Cases and Materials on Constitutional Law*, 10th ed. (Mineola, N.Y.: Foundation Press, 1980), pp. 502–44 and *American Constitutional Law* (Mineola, N.Y.: Foundation Press, 1978), pp. 427–55. For an extremely clear account of what a contract is and of why one might value contractual freedom, see Gordon Tullock, "The Logic of the Law," in Anthony T. Kronman and Richard A. Posner, eds., *The Economics of Contract Law* (Boston: Little, Brown, 1979), pp. 22–26. For a masterly account of the historical origins and development of contractual freedom, see nineteenth-century social theorist Max Weber's "Forms of the Creation of Rights," in Vol. II of his *Economy and Society: An Outline of Interpretive Sociology*, Guenther Roth and Claus Wittich, eds. (Berkeley: University of California Press, 1968), pp. 666–752.

I. §3. For sensitive accounts of how the enforcement of freedom of contract with regard to employment affects workers, see the section "Freedom and Coercion" in Weber's "Forms of the Creation of Rights," pp. 729–31 and Book V, ch. XI, sec. 12 of John Stuart Mill's *Principles of Political Economy with Some of Their Applications to Social Philosophy* (Fairfield, N.J.: Augustus M. Kelley, 1976), pp. 963–65.

II. It is important to distinguish the notion of autonomy developed in this section from two widely accepted notions. The first is the notion criticized in §3: Autonomy is a matter of choosing one's individuality, of being the sole author of the values, beliefs, and abilities that make one the particular person that one is. The second is the strictly Kantian notion that contemporary philosophers (most prominently John Rawls, in *A Theory of Justice*, Cambridge, Mass.: Harvard University Press, 1971) often invoke. Autonomy, on the Kantian view, is a matter of freedom from individuality, of abstracting from one's contingent personal history. One is autonomous to the extent that one chooses solely on the basis of considerations that are common to all rational agents, or, less strictly, to all rational human beings.

For an attempt to criticize these two widely accepted notions of autonomy and to exhibit the superiority of the socially bounded notion that Section II of this essay develops, see my "Against Universality," *The Journal of Philosophy*, Volume LXXVIII, Number 3 (March 1981), pp. 127–43. For one of the most interesting recent discussions of autonomy from a non-Kantian point of view, see Joel Feinberg's "The Idea of a Free Man," collected in his *Rights, Justice, and the Bounds of Liberty: Essays in Social Philosophy* (Princeton, N.J.: Princeton University Press, 1981).

III. Harry Braverman's *Labor and Monopoly Capital: The Degradation of Work in the Twentieth Century* (N.Y.: Monthly Review Press, 1974) is the most valuable available guide to understanding the current arrangement of employment in our society. The theoretical underpinnings of Braverman's work are contained, as he notes, in Part IV of Vol. I of Karl Marx's *Capital: A Critique of Political Economy* (N.Y.: International Publishers, 1967). Other useful empirical works include Elwood S. Buffa, *Modern Production Management: Managing the Operations Function*, 5th ed. (N.Y.: John Wiley and Sons, 1977), pp. 207–36; Louis E. Davis and James C. Taylor, eds., *Design of Jobs: Selected Readings* (Harmondsworth, Middlesex, England: Penguin Books, 1972); and *Work in America: Report of a Special Task Force to the Secretary of Health, Education, and Welfare* (Cambridge, Mass.: MIT Press, 1973). Studs Terkel's *Working* (N.Y.: Avon, 1975) contains fascinating interviews with American workers.

Karl Marx's discussion of alienated labor in the *1844 Manuscripts* is indispensable philosophical reading. See Karl Marx, *Early Writings*, translated and edited by T. B. Bottomore, ed. and trans. (N.Y.: McGraw-Hill, 1964), pp. 120–34. For a philosophical position radically opposed to Marx's and to the one advanced in this section of this essay, see Robert Nozick, *Anarchy, State, and Utopia* (N.Y.: Basic Books, 1964), pp. 246–53.

6

Justice and Injustice in Business

DAVID BRAYBROOKE

〈〉

In business, questions of justice press for attention as urgently as anywhere, and more variously. Important injustices can occur in sports (Who gets to play? Who is judged the winner?), the arts (Who gets attention? Who gets praised?), even in science (What lines of research are encouraged? Who is credited with the discovery?); but the injustices are not so various there. They are not even, I think, so various in politics or in family life, the only spheres that rival business in variety of applications for justice. Philosophers have as much to learn from reflecting on business as people in business have to learn from philosophers' reflections on justice.

I shall begin, in Part I, with a survey of the basic features of justice, for present purposes drawing my illustrations from business.

There is some fun to be had from observing business; often, for many people, there is fun to be had taking part in it. We may be tempted, in the course of the proposed survey, to think of business as a game. It allows certain moves and disallows others; and the moves have consequences that, among other things, open up further moves for the players or close them off. Yet business, if it is a game, is a game that is played for keeps: Justice, when it is an issue in business, is likely to be a vital issue.

Business is also a game that people must play whether they want to or not. You and I have to play it almost every day. Even if we get our income from other sources, business is where we spend it. How we fare in business, moreover, depends even more on what we bring to the game than it does in other, less consequential games, for the resources of the players differ much more in business. I would not stand much of a chance playing basketball against Wilt Chamberlain; but at five foot ten inches I am more than five-sevenths of his height, I am at least half as fast in a short sprint, I can dribble a basketball, and I have on occasion sunk one through the basket. That makes us an even match, by comparison with the discrepancy between me and Exxon or even Henry Ford II. In assets relevant to business—take any asset you like—Exxon has a million times what I do; you are probably in much the same situation. Is business a fair game? If it is not fair, will justice be done you and me and other players?

Two further parts of the essay will follow Part I, which itself falls into three sub-parts. In Part II, I shall take up a number of kinds of injustice that frequently occur in business, but which (as I aim to show) can be remedied without doing more than restore the status quo ante from which they wrongly depart, or at least can be remedied without substantially changing the basic arrangements of the business system. Finally, in Part III, I shall consider what might be done about charges that those arrangements—private property in the means of production; the power (founded on such property) of private firms; the market, perfect or imperfect—are unjust generally, and with them the positions that people are assigned in the status quo to begin with.

I. BASIC FEATURES OF JUSTICE

In the last dozen years or so, philosophers have been remarkably active discussing what is traditionally called "distributive justice," that is to say, justice in the way the benefits available to a society and the burdens of arriving at them are shared among its members. These discussions have brought a great deal of new light on the subject. However, concentration upon distributive justice has, I think, somewhat confused and distorted our notions about justice in general. Distributive justice itself cannot be fully understood if its place in a general picture of justice is not appreciated.

Justice, in general, has to do with equality: on the one hand, with equality in departures from the status quo; on the other hand, with equality in the status quo. If we look upon business as a game, this is a difference between a condition on how moves are to turn out and a condition on (among other things) the power to make them.

§1 DEPARTURES FROM THE STATUS QUO

The status quo with which justice is concerned in a market society, where business as we know it is practiced, is the distribution at any given instant of resources, including talents, skills, health, influence, and privileges, as well as the sorts of things (consumers' goods, producers' goods and financial assets) that can be held as private property. I shall be primarily concerned with the distribution of these resources among persons, though I recognize that some of them are in the effective possession of firms rather than of persons, and others are held, both formally and effectively, by other private organizations, or by the state.

Some people may have in their possession resources that they did not acquire legitimately. For the time being I shall raise no questions on that score. I shall first consider how departures from a given *status quo* may be just or unjust, and if unjust, worsen matters. Then (§2) I shall consider how departures (some of them otherwise just) may give some people unfair advantages in future status quos, which it would be just to prevent or remedy. Only then, by the natural route of discussing unequal advantages, will I come (§3) to consider the justice of the received distribution of resources, as we might find it in the status quo that we began with.

One way in which departures from the status quo may occur is exchange. You bring me ten beaver pelts; I give you, in return, a blanket, a rifle, and two jugs of whiskey. Or you, a merchant in a genteel suburb, take some of my money; I carry away one of your lawn mowers. We have both departed from the status quo, but so long as we end up both better off, and indeed equally better off, the results are in accordance with justice. Sometimes such results — equal results — are perfectly unambiguous. If my tomatoes ripen before your apples do, my helping you pick apples for a day will give you exactly what you give me if you help me pick tomatoes for a day, that is to say, the same amount of help when it is needed. Not very different, so far as establishing equal results goes, is a case in which you and I alternate week by week in fetching the same amount of drinking water for each of us; over time, any advantage that one has on the first round from being able to wait and go second will vanish as a proportion of the total benefit, however measured.

Usually things are more complicated. What I give you is, as in the instances first mentioned, something very different from what you give me.

We can always say, if the transaction is voluntary, that the parties agree in treating the value of what is exchanged as equal: You, the hardware dealer, and I, the suburban householder, agree to treat the lawn mower as having the same value as $159.99. Moreover, we are both better off: You wanted the money more than the lawn mower; I, the lawn mower more than the money.

Yet in some ways we may not be equally better off; and thus the results may not be equal in every respect. You may have gained more than I by comparison with the ordinary prices of the things exchanged, or of comparable things. Other people regularly buy the same lawn mower for $79.99. As prices of high-rise buildings go, three squashed beer cans do not seem to be equivalent in value to the Empire State Building. You do not get equal results if I persuade you to make over the Empire State Building in return for them. If we could compare the utilities obtained by different people, we might expect to find that in many transactions one party gained much more utility than the other. Even without comparing utilities, we might find in some cases that one party doubled her already superior holdings of the good that she took in exchange, while the other got barely more than one percent to add to his inferior holdings of the good that he received.

These inequalities would raise questions about justice. Their existence would not settle the questions. Inequalities in addition to holdings (or to consumption) may be troubling when they are very substantial, as gross inequalities in utilities would be. In a market society, however, great weight will be given to the consideration that both parties are satisfied with the deal, as they may perfectly well be, regardless of such inequalities. Justice seems to many to require no more. In their view, the results of an exchange are equal, so far as justice goes, by the agreement of the parties to treat them as equal.

Deviation from the ordinary price is more troubling. One is compelled to ask whether both parties to the transaction had the same information, or the same bargaining power in other respects. Even here, however, if the price was arrived at through bargaining, and both parties were reckoned to be adults competent to bargain (though not necessarily equal in skill), the deviation would be accepted. If the buyer did not know what the ordinary price was, perhaps he did not think the effort to find out worth making. If he knew, but decided to pay the extraordinary price anyway, because there was at least for the time being no one else to buy from, the price would reflect monopoly power on the part of the seller. However, monopoly power is often accepted without question (think of someone selling an heirloom, an antique chair). It would be accepted by many — though here an abnormal strain on ordinary moral convictions becomes visible — even if the party who pays more, perhaps much more, than the ordinary price has no real alternative to doing so, being in dire need of a good (say, potatoes) of which there is suddenly a dearth.

Some exchanges take place under contracts. Breaches of contract are involved in some flagrant instances of injustices. A woman arranges to have her house painted for $1,200 plus the paint; when, after five days' work, the painter comes for his money, the owner refuses to pay more than $950, giving as a pretext not liking the color after all. The English philosopher Thomas Hobbes (1588–1679) thought the connection between justice and contracts so important that he defined injustice as the not keeping of promises. However, the injustice consists rather in the inequality of results than in the breach itself (breaking the rule about keeping promises) — in other words, in the same failure of the departures from the status quo to match as occurs in any instance of unfair exchange. Here it was agreed, in the contract, that the departures would match if $1,200 was exchanged for five days' work by the painter and his crew. The actual results are unequal, with the owner giving up less than a matching amount, and the painter giving up more.

That it is the unequal results that are crucial, not the breaking of the promise, is proved by the fact that justice will call for setting aside the promise, if the results of keeping it — carrying through the exchange — would be catastrophic to one party, in a way that no one could have anticipated, or in a way at least that the party in question was in no position to weigh sensibly earlier.

This holds even when the party that stands to gain was quite innocent of any wrongdoing herself. She may not have done anything to mislead the other party; she may not have cheated on entering into the contract; she may not be about to cheat now. External events (for example, a sudden, gigantic rise in the price of gold) may with no help from her have brought about the change in prospects. It will still, if the catastrophe is big enough, be unjust to require keeping the promise (though some compensation for the prospective beneficiary may be called for). If (as may happen) a court upholds a contract when it turns out, unexpectedly, ruinous for one party (giving up the family farm, all his valuable possessions, half his income for the rest of his life), our respect for the courts will be severely strained. There may be some temptation, following the treatment of such cases offered by the Scottish philosopher David Hume (1711–1776), to consider that this only shows that injustice may at times be at odds with human welfare. In fact it shows more: It shows that the letter of the law may be at odds with what justice requires.

Usually, the person who stands to gain from an injustice in an exchange or a contract is not innocent. Perhaps—outside the ambit of legitimate business—he uses force to extort the exchange or the promise. Or, much more commonly in a market society, and common enough in business even though it is not legitimate either, he cheats. He omits to reveal something about the goods that he offers that he should normally reveal; or he deliberately misrepresents the character of the goods to the other party.

Cheating is the more specific charge; we readily make it in many connections where we would much less readily speak of "injustice." It seems that we reserve the term "injustice" for cases in which one party is specially vulnerable and the other exploits the vulnerability. Yet even in the case of the house-owner's failure to pay the full contracted price, where the painter, after the work is done, is in a specially vulnerable position, and it seems natural enough to speak of an injustice being done him, it may be even more natural to say that the painter has been cheated. Here the cheating may not have involved deception, for the owner may have decided not to pay the full price only at the last moment; nevertheless, the painter's legitimate expectations were defeated by an act of the owner, he was misled, and thus he was cheated.

"Cheating" rather than "injustice" seems even more appropriate, indeed the uniquely favored term, if we suppose that the painter is not just a local man, in business for himself, but a large national concern—a chemical combine, say, with a division that makes paints and through its retail branches contracts for house-painting. In general, when there is a great inequality of power between the parties to an exchange or contract, the term "unjust" is reserved for misdeeds of the more powerful party. You can cheat in your dealings with Union Carbide; you cannot be unjust to it. A treatment of the concept of justice that aimed to represent ordinary usage accurately would reflect this fact, as well as the displacement of the term "injustice" by the term "cheating," or another term, like "theft," in many cases where the parties are equal, and in some where they are not. However, for present purposes, it seems accurate enough, and it certainly is simpler, to treat all cases in which exchanges, whether under a contract or not, have unequal results as cases of injustice, including cases in which the party profiting from the inequality has cheated to obtain such results, sometimes in the face of a party much more powerful.

Unequal results are the basic consideration again in the injustices arising from injuries that come as it were out of the blue, imposed by departures that are not preceded or launched by striking a bargain. There is a nicety that I shall disregard here and elsewhere: The injustice may be said to lie rather in letting the unequal results stand than in reaching them in the first place. I borrow your truck to haul a load of manure from the race track. I attend a drinking bout with some cheerful loose women and end up smashed. So does the truck, which I turn over on top of a wayside pizza parlor. Or you begin manufacturing margarine from pig fat in your backyard. Living next door, I am forced to keep all my windows closed. Even that does not do much to keep away the oily stink; moreover, there is a lot of horrible greasy smoke coming my way in ever greater, ever more depressing quantities.

In each of these cases, one person has done some harm to the other, gaining something for himself (at least some moments of whoopee), but leading the other to depart for the worse from the status quo. We can think of either case as amounting after all to an exchange, an exchange with unequal results, and therefore objectionable; or to an exchange that has to be completed if injustice is to be avoided. I must restore your goods intact; or, if I cannot do that, I must pay you compensation — the value of the truck. You must compensate me for making my house uninhabitable; or, as well, perhaps instead, you must be subjected to punishment for violating a city ordinance. Restoration and sometimes compensation are means of balancing the departures from the status quo so that no one loses by the departures. One or more people may even gain: The value of the margarine may exceed the compensation that has to be paid for the damage to my standard of housing. Punishment, if it is adequate, makes the departures match by making them both negative: I lose in worsened housing; you lose just enough in fines or imprisonment to make it not worth your while to have done the worsening. Sometimes compensation has a negative result on one side, and thus again leads to a social loss overall: I perhaps sadly conclude, when the time comes to pay up, that the whoopee was not worth the price of the truck (to say nothing of the spoiled pizzas and the disconcerted pizza patrons).

When we shift our attention from cases of a single person being dealt with by another person (or a firm) to a larger social perspective, matching departures and equal results again figure decisively. A person does something to benefit society—perhaps by doing a good job arranging for businessmen to cooperate in a downtown improvement scheme. It will be unjust to withhold from her the reward, which she has grounds to expect, normally given for such contributions (which may be just praise); and especially unjust if other people who did no more are rewarded simultaneously. If the contribution was negative—an injury to society rather than a benefit—justice calls for matching the departure by restoration or compensation or punishment. When a judge requires a juvenile delinquent to repair the shop windows that he vandalized, and perhaps some more besides, restoration and punishment run together, creating an especially satisfactory instance of justice accomplished. The status quo is regained; and the negative departure, balanced, negatively, by the unwilling effort.

In a social perspective, justice and injustice often visibly generalize over whole social groups. Blacks or Indians or women put in the same effort, conferring equal benefits on society, but do not get as much recognition, or as much pay, as white men doing the same work, whether it is plucking turkeys, assembling generators, or processing life insurance applications. Blue-collar workers find the courts much readier to jail them for making off with some extra engine parts than to jail executives for genteelly conspiring to fix the prices of toaster-ovens. These aberrations are, moreover, not just a matter of objectionable departures at any one time. The groups that suffer disproportionately many such departures suffer disproportionately time after time. One may infer that social arrangements which persist from one status quo to the next continually engender the injustices in question.

§2 UNEQUAL ADVANTAGES IN THE NEXT STATUS QUO

The results of departures in one period establish a changed status quo from which departures will be made in the next. The game begins again on different terms. If the results were unjust, enriching some people at the expense of others, and there are no compensating changes, they bring about a distribution of resources (in private property and in other resources like influence) that raises the prospects of injustice in further departures. For rich men can more easily wriggle out of contracts than poor men—they can hire more expensive lawyers. They can also deploy, in the negotiations that lead to transactions and contracts in the first place, more refined skills and more comprehensive information; so they can get away with more at that stage, too. The new status quo will itself be more unjust because it lends itself more readily to creating injustices.

Moreover, results unjust in one period will, by increasing the advantages in bargaining that some people have over others, increase the chances of troubling results in the next—results accepted by convention as equal by agreement of the parties on the value of the goods exchanged, but unequal, maybe very unequal, by comparison with ordinary prices or in terms of proportionate gains. Troubling results in one period will themselves have the same effect. As the advantages of some people accumulate from status quo to status quo, it will become more and more difficult to suppress questions about whether bargaining, with such unequal advantages, uncorrected in procedures, can be fair to all parties. Fairness is a matter of procedures, while justice is a matter of results; but, of course, the two are closely connected (so much so that the terms are sometimes interchangeable). Increasing trouble about the fairness of procedures is bound to lead to increasing misgiving about the justice of results.

Disconcertingly, even under fair procedures, advantages that are questionable on the point of fairness can creep in; unless they are corrected for, the procedures will no longer be fair. To put the point another way, we may say that just results from past departures may, when looked upon as resources available for further departures, give some persons unacceptably unequal advantages. Consider a professional basketball player who can attract thousands of fans each willing to pay five dollars to see him play. If only a fraction of the five dollars finds its way into his pocket, he is likely to become rich — much richer than most of his fans. The transaction between him and each of his fans may not quite fit the model of a fair exchange, even if we disregard the intervention of third parties like the club owner: What the basketball player gives up to any one fan is nothing substantial or even distinguishable. Nevertheless, each fan may be perfectly satisfied that it was worth as much as five dollars to have a part in seeing the player's performance. There is honest dealing all around; and no question that the player is doing anybody an injustice in collecting his share of the ticket prices paid so cheerfully by his fans.

What then could be wrong from the point of view of justice? A number of quite serious things. First, one should notice that having become extraordinarily rich, the basketball player is in a position to restrict other people's freedom and exercise power over them, in any of a number of ways, from hiring henchmen to beat them up to influencing politicians to disregard their claims. None of the fans, in paying five dollars for admission, consented to this power; it is an unintended overall consequence of a lot of single actions in which nothing of the sort was intended. It is also a consequence that no one fan could prevent by refusing on his own to buy a ticket. Second, being extraordinarily rich, the basketball player now has greater bargaining power than many of the people with whom he may choose, one by one, to exchange goods. They will need to trade with him more than he needs to with them. Third, the basketball player, if he keeps his riches, will have a great advantage henceforth in competing with other people to meet his needs and follow his preferences. He may already be in a position to buy up all the remaining seashore, or the last pears of the season. If hard times come, he will be able to go on meeting his needs, when some or all of his fans have lost the capacity: Their reserves will not enable them to hold out through a time of famine; they will not be able to bid as much as he can for what supplies remain.

These points could be interpreted to imply that the exchanges between the player and the fans were not so fair as they looked: The fans were giving up, not just five dollars each for admission and whatever else they might have bought for the five dollars, but increments of power and advantage, and not getting anything in return for these unintended and unnoticed consequences.

There is a conflict in our ways of thinking about these matters. What we consider justice in acquiring and holding private property does not consort happily with what we consider justice in the subsequent status quo, considered as a distribution of direct power over other people and of advantages in bargaining. In this respect, results that are not troubling pair by pair become troubling when they are aggregated for one person from his belonging to many pairs. Results that are troubling to begin with add troubles on this point to the more obvious troubles about discrepancies in the immediate gains for the two parties.

Here, too, the ways in which the results are unequal may be overridden in many people's view by the fact that the parties have agreed to treat the value of what is exchanged as equal. The preeminence given to this consideration leads people to ignore, or to give little weight to, the increased power and increased advantages in bargaining that, with private property, parties may take away from transactions. Moreover, the preeminence leads people to neglect questions about the unequal advantages that the parties will bring to further transactions.

Would it be any different if the advantages came, not from exchanges cumulatively specially favorable to any person with the advantages, but from work done on his own? I have been treating justice as a matter of departures in which more than one person is immediately involved. It is possible, however, for a person to depart from the status quo and gain advantages in the next one by accumulating resources out of the product of his own labor. Imagine a farmer, who perhaps works harder than most, grows more, and has in the end more than his household requires, a surplus to which he adds in effect another surplus every year, so that he can operate on an ever larger scale. It is hard to see that he is doing anything unjust in creating and keeping these surpluses; indeed, he seems to deserve praise for being unusually provident. Can there be anything objectionable in the advantages that he gains thereby?

That there is may be more disconcerting, and harder to accept than before; but essentially the case is the same. The farmer, like the basketball player, has done, item by item, nothing illegitimate; but both, through saving some of their gains, have acquired power that in the three ways enumerated pose a threat to other people. Someone could do this, in fact, without having a rare talent or working harder than most people, simply by saving more.

In all these cases, if the resources saved were acquired without any current objection, there would be an affront to justice in expropriating them afterwards. Nor would this affront be merely an effect of the present attachment, so far as it goes, of our thinking about justice to the institution of private property. Any change in social rules that upsets expectations legitimately formed under the rules as previously understood and defeats actions that people have taken with those expectations is an affront. It is a negative departure from the status quo, which cannot be compensated for so long as the change is to remove advantages in resources.

The affront to justice would not occur if the rules were changed long enough in advance (*ex ante*, as economists say) so that people could adjust their affairs and escape losses disproportionate to those of other people. If all changes in the rules for acquiring, keeping, and using property, for example, were announced a generation in advance, the injustices springing from upset expectations would for the most part disappear. Moreover, it would be intolerable for society at large not to be able to change the rules at least with notice of a generation. In practice, it is accepted that the rules (for example, about the rates and incidence of taxes) can be changed with much less notice. In an emergency, where some people's very existence is threatened, a government will be expected to move at once: It will not, for example, accept in a famine the prices that the merchants who hold the only stocks of potatoes might wish to charge, even though hitherto, under the rules, the merchants were free to accumulate such stocks and charge varying prices for them.

The injustice done to the provident might be done a small business-man—someone who had spent years building up a foundry or making a success of a restaurant. However, it is appropriately thought of as injustice done to a farmer. Our notions about justice still reflect the arrangements of the agrarian society in which most of our ancestors lived, even in what are now heavily industrialized countries, until some time in the nineteenth century. Under those arrangements, or rather under an idealized form of them, typical citizens were individual farmers assigned land on which it was their responsibility (with the help of their households) to raise pretty much everything that they needed. If farmers worked hard, they could prosper; if they chose to be idle, what claim could they have upon the products of those who had not, who might in fact, in spite of hard work, have little to spare?

Yet accumulated resources create difficulties even in these circumstances of minimal interdependence. Not only do the resources still constitute advantages—which may lead to some farmers losing their independence. What is to be done about farmers who work hard, but are unlucky about floods and lightning? Can they justly be simply left to starve? Will it be unjust for them, if they get no help, to seize what they need from others? What is to be done about the children of the farmers who have in idleness or folly wasted their resources?

In a society in which a great deal of interdependence exists—for example, a fully developed market society—the conflict between giving the present scope to private property and accepting the status quo as just in every respect is bound to be more acute. Such is the society in which yonder basketball player is becoming rich: He could not devote himself to playing basketball unless a lot of other people grew tomatoes, stitched shirts, shingled roofs, drove buses, felled trees. Are their contributions to society not so worthwhile as the basketball player's? Why should their contributions be less worthwhile because their skills are not so rare? Their skills may be as complex and as hard-won. Should they not keep more or less abreast of him in the resources that they command? Surely there is a very powerful impulse in us to say "Yes"; and that impulse springs from one side of our sense of justice. It comes the more strongly when the discrepancies in resources persist and accumulate, favoring some people to such an extent that the rest can never hope to catch up.

A market society, however, will persist in finding it congenial to value contributions at the prices that can be got for them in the market and to reward people accordingly. The conceptual situation is further complicated by the fact that private property also counts, in a market society, as a source of contributions to production. Our notion that it is just to reward people for their contributions, which has its roots in our appreciation of their personal efforts, is generalized in our ordinary thinking to cover contributions that people make by putting their property to use—raising crops on it, building mills on it, investing it in processing equipment, or simply cashing it in to buy shares in going firms (which supposedly sooner or later releases funds for new investment). Thinking like this aggravates the conflict with the idea that no one should be able to increase—indefinitely—his or her advantages over other people.

§3 UNEQUAL ADVANTAGES AT THE START, IN THE PRIOR STATUS QUO

The opposition that our sense of justice presents to the accumulation of unequal advantages in departures from the status quo—unequal advantages in political power and in bargaining power, increasing the frequency of unjust results and troubling results—readily converts into opposition to any unequal advantages that already exist in the status quo. So we come at last to raise questions about the justice of the status quo that we imagined starting with—the present status quo, let us say, present at whatever instant we take up the discussion of justice.

Insofar as those unequal advantages in the present status quo are taken to be unfair advantages, they make the procedures by which departures will be made from the status quo unfair, too, implying that the status quo is systematically biased against reaching just results in those departures. On that ground, the status quo may be said to be unjust. Or the status quo may be called unjust simply in anticipation of the unjust results that will be forthcoming from it, and in anticipation of troubling results, too, to the extent that these are lumped together with the unjust ones. And will they not be lumped together, whenever it turns out that they, too, are consequences of unequal resources? We are not to suppose, however, that all that justice or injustice signifies for the present status quo can be captured by considering how the distribution of resources positions people to maintain or increase their resources (and their advantages) in the next one. To do so would be to omit to consider why in the end these advantages—and justice itself, implying approval or disapproval for them—are prized.

Justice requires us to consider, as well, how people are currently faring in the status quo. Are their needs being met, right now? If their needs are met, are their preferences being heeded?

The question whether everyone is in a position to meet his needs is a relatively easy question to answer, if we take a strict view of needs, that is to say, count as a need only something that must be met if a person is to function normally, and count as meeting it the minimal provision that will enable a given person to function. Food, clothing, shelter, companionship are such needs; sex is for many people; we may add education and recreation. Inevitably what are defined as minimum provisions for any of these needs will have conventional features that vary between cultures. In any given culture, however—in our own—general agreement can be attained on perfectly definite minimum provisions, at least if the minima are set low enough. For example, people need enough clothing to move about out-of-doors without shivering. This agreement can be extended, moreover, to cover variations of minima among persons. If some people cannot maintain the same weight or same level of energy without more food, they need more food.

Supposing that there are resources to spare after meeting everyone's needs, the question next arises, are the spare resources distributed so that people have substantial chances, if not equal chances, to have their preferences heeded? Some preferences will almost surely have been heeded in choosing provisions to meet needs. There would be no point in providing everybody with cheese-and-macaroni dinners when almost everybody liked minced collops better. People commonly have more refined preferences than that, however, even in respect to their basic diet; and these go far beyond what is required to meet their needs. Many would never eat minced collops at all if they could have things like fillet of sole with shrimp stuffing, and on the side a nice bottle of chilled *Gewürztraminer.* Some would cater less to their palates, but care about preferences in other matters, delighting in jewelry, mink stoles, fine editions, and porcelain whatnots.

It is difficult to answer in any precise way the question about equal chances to have preferences heeded. Will heeding a few important preferences compensate a given person for disregarding a number of less important ones, and if so, which and how many? The economists' notion of "utility" does not lay these questions to rest; even at its most sophisticated, it eludes practical measurement as an empirical datum for social policy. How are importance and number of preferences to be balanced when we try to heed the preferences of several people at the same time? Deep logical problems stand in the way of finding a satisfactory system of combining preferences through voting; and formidable practical problems would beset any attempt to enable masses of people to express through voting a detailed variety of preferences. The market may do better than voting as a practical device for this purpose; yet it does not, in practice, live up to the theoretical claims for it, and those claims cannot be fully justified, even in theory, once it is acknowledged that public goods (lighthouses, law and order, pure science) must be considered as well as private ones.

Nevertheless, it is often possible to discern gross discrepancies in provisions for preferences. A real estate operator in Vancouver bulldozed a French Regency mansion (including eight bathrooms and a swimming pool), worth $1 million after renovation, to make way for a $4-million palace, built as a present for his new wife. "Whether or not I knock down a house," he told reporters, "is about as important as what color pants I put on." Meanwhile, one may safely assume, a number of women in that same city, deserted wives, mothers with children to support, were laboring for minimum wages all day, day after day, washing pots or plucking turkeys.

The questions that I have formulated as questions about current faring in the present status quo can easily be turned into questions about a succession of status quos and their common properties. Are everybody's needs met time after time? Does everybody have a substantial chance of getting preferences heeded? Or are there respects in which some people at least are continually treated less than equally? If there are, we may well, in judgments about the justice of these respects, revert to the view of possessions in which they are looked upon as advantages in replacing and increasing personal resources during the succession of status quos. However, we can persist in the perspective that highlights current faring. In that perspective, even if temporary discrepancies were accepted without distress, perhaps as matters of luck, the continual repetition of the discrepancies, with one set of people always faring well, and another always faring badly, would seem unjust. Some people, and their children, would be living their lives out—very possibly shortened lives—without having any chance to live decently; others would be surfeited with pleasures.

Such discrepancies would seem unjust to many even if no one had deliberately produced them, so long as they were capable of being remedied. Can it be just for a mining financier to have seventy pairs of Gucci loafers (the same style loafers) and to stand thirty friends at Las Vegas five rounds of triple bullshots at eighteen dollars a drink, while turkey-pluckers and their children scrape by in poverty? The resources wasted in those loafers and triple bullshots could be drawn upon to meet their needs and lighten their lives. Moreover, it is not simply a matter of resources being available that could be used to reduce the discrepancies. If we have in view members of the same society, some in luxury, some in dire need, the people involved in the discrepancies have places in the same network of mutual responsibilities. Everybody in the network is expected to do her part in maintaining society; in particular, everybody is expected to forbear from attacking other people and making off with their goods even when she can get away with doing so. The people who are faring ill may be doing more than forbear. They may be working as hard (or harder) and as skillfully (sometimes more skillfully) than most of the people who are enjoying luxury.

These considerations cumulate in a powerful argument for regarding discrepancies in current faring, and with them the society and the status quo in which they occur and persist, as unjust. It must be granted that this argument, as well as the earlier argument from the dangers of unequal power, conflicts with views widespread in a market society. Not only do those views by and large accept the market as conferring justice upon its results; they waive any searching questions about the distribution of resources with which people, owning greater or lesser amounts of property, enter the market. One cannot justify waiving those questions merely by citing the possibility that the inequality of resources in the present status quo did not come about through unjust actions on the part of the people who have more resources. Nevertheless, it is true that any attempt to equalize current faring by redistributing resources would, like attempting to equalize power (or check growing inequalities) by the same means, do a number of people injustices by upsetting hitherto legitimate expectations, under which they were led to make departures that now turn out to be for the worse.

If one is to choose sides in this conflict, I think one does better to choose the side of the first of the two arguments. The upset to expectations, which is the most serious point about justice on the other side, since it is a point that follows from perfectly general considerations of principle, can be mitigated by giving as much advance notice of reforms as possible. On other points, the other side either argues from a theory of the market that ignores imperfections in the real world or simply affirms an uncritical acceptance of current practices.

To some extent, however, the conflict even on these points is far from being completely irreducible. The injustices of particular departures from the present status quo can be remedied by measures that do not substantially jeopardize the operation of the market in the real world. Indeed, as I am about to show in Part II of this essay, such measures already exist, though they are in some connections painfully incomplete. Moreover, they could be made completer without jeopardizing the market; on the contrary, making them completer would bring the market in the real world closer to the ideal market of theory, or otherwise fulfill the views cherished on the other side.

Even the farther-reaching reforms, designed both to make current faring more equal and to check the dangers of power, that I shall discuss in Part III can be carried through without abandoning private property and the business system. The nature of the reforms—an inheritance tax, a progressive income tax—is already familiar. The reforms have even been formally enacted without in practice unsettling the business system in any fundamental way. It is true that the enactment has been so limited and qualified that the reforms have been far from achieving their purposes. I shall argue, however—renewing the arguments for these reforms—that even effective legislation would, if it were brought in step by step, leave the business system standing.

II. CHECKING PARTICULAR SORTS OF UNJUST DEPARTURES

Many people, including people active in business but disillusioned about it, incline to think that injustice and unethical conduct generally are inherent in business. I have known professors to declare, "There is no such thing as ethics in business." But this is not so. One might as well say that injustice was inherent in social life. That is where it is found, because that is where the opportunities for it arise. Similarly, lots of different opportunities for injustice arise in business, but except in specially difficult cases where whatever one does will be unjust, these opportunities for injustice are also so many opportunities for justice, and may be so approached, even by parties that have the advantage in bargaining power. At the very least, whatever unfair advantages business may accept in the status quo, there are a lot of injustices that can be avoided in departures from it. In the three subdivisions of this part, I shall consider, first, the injustices that persons may do to firms and the injustices that firms may do in transactions with consumers; next the injustices that firms may do in transactions with firms; finally, the injustices that firms may do in the employment relationship.

§4 PERSONS UNJUST TO FIRMS; FIRMS UNJUST TO CONSUMERS

So many of my previous examples have involved persons dealing with persons that at this point there is no need for me to do more than mention that many opportunities for justice and injustice occur in such dealings, even nowadays. Nowadays, however, most persons do most of their business with large firms and very likely it is toward firms that they act unjustly in business, when they do. In this connection, too, there is no need for me to mount an extended discussion. The facts are familiar, and seeing their import for justice requires at most a few verbal adjustments. We may acknowledge, as we did earlier (§1), that more specific words like "cheating" or "stealing" preempt the part that on general grounds "injustice" is entitled to play here. We can refuse to let pop terms like "rip-off" delude us into looking on cheating and stealing with an amused, indulgent view when firms are the victims. Some people, "ripping off" the Bell telephone system by evading long distance telephone charges, contrive to think of themselves simultaneously as playing a high-spirited prank and as striking a blow to redress social grievances against rich, powerful, and allegedly insensitive corporate giants. In fact, they are cheating; they are doing, in general terms, an injustice by bringing about a departure that gives unequal results favoring their own interest.

There is no need, either, for me to treat at length the ways in which firms can be unjust to consumers. The ways in question are susceptible of infinite variation, but most of them fall into one or another familiar category: such as deceptive sales tactics; extortionate prices; defective goods; refusal of redress. These matters have not gone unnoticed. The status quo in market societies has always provided consumers with some power to redress injustices when they have occurred. When the damages are very great, the present status quo provides for bringing suit against offending firms in regular courts. When the damages to any one victim are otherwise too small for litigation, it provides for legal remedies in part by setting up small claims courts and in part by entertaining class actions that bring together the small claims of a number of consumers.

The present status quo also has provisions for increasing beforehand the capacity of consumers to avoid being taken in by careless or unscrupulous firms. Consumers are empowered to denounce sales contracts within a few days of signing them. They are supplied with information assisting them in the precautions that they need to take. Some of the information is supplied by reputable firms, some through Better Business Bureaus, some through industry-sponsored testing laboratories. Some of it is supplied by consumers' magazines. A great deal of it is supplied by the government, which tests and grades all sorts of products, and continually monitors the output of industry, especially for safety.

Can it be maintained that these provisions have interfered with the market so much as in effect to do away with it? In the past—indeed, to this day—courts have hesitated to interfere with exchanges and contracts knowingly entered into on both sides by competent parties; but they have always been prepared to restrain fraud and misrepresentation. The theory of the (ideal) market itself assumes that participants are fully competent and knowledgeable. The enlarged provisions now existing in the status quo for information (on packages and elsewhere), and for reflection (after signing contracts) increase the chances of realizing the sort of market envisaged by the theory.

The justification of regulating certain prices (electricity, telephones, railroad service) is different, but still consistent with the theory of the market. The theory concedes that certain goods are most efficiently supplied by monopoly producers; there the competitive market necessarily fails and fair exchanges cannot be ensured without regulation. Inevitably, regulation of this sort is concerned not simply with the justice of the departures, but with the justice of the status quo itself—with the justice of the powers assigned at the points of departure. The same, however, can be said of the other provisions just surveyed, and of provisions for dissolving monopolies—in favor of a more vigorous market—by antitrust actions. They are provisions for redressing or avoiding certain departures, but to accomplish these things they modify the resources, including bargaining power, otherwise assigned in the status quo.

The modifications need not be thought of as superimposed on the present system without compensating changes. If, for example, what alarms people about the modifications is that they would increase the burden and complications of a body of regulations already complicated and burdensome, it would be possible in principle to calm them by removing some existing regulations at the same time. Notoriously, not all existing regulations have worked out well in achieving the purposes for which they were adopted; some of them have actually been counterproductive. But if some old regulations on private property and the free operation of the market are removed as the new regulations aiming at greater justice are introduced, the net effect in increased restrictions on business may be negligible.

§5 FIRMS UNJUST TO FIRMS

Firms can treat other firms, as well as people, justly or unjustly. The particular departures, or sorts of departures, from the status quo can be identified, and—when they involve injustices—in many cases remedied without raising questions about fundamental changes in the status quo. Again, the status quo already embodies some provisions for remedy. When the provisions are absent, or present but in one way or another burdensome, suggestions will arise about taking away powers to impose such departures, and about creating powers to avoid them or to have them redressed. We arrive, again, at questions about modifying the status quo. They are still, however, questions that arise about checking particular sorts of departures rather than about reforming the status quo in a general way.

Some firms act as sales agents of others. They are the "authorized dealers" for certain brands of stereo equipment; they have the local franchise to pump a particular brand of gasoline or the franchise to sell Hupmobiles. The firms that sell through them—the manufacturers of stereo equipment, gasoline, and Hupmobiles—look in their turn to yet other firms for supplies. However, the firms in the middle may have both the agent-firms and the supplier-firms under their thumb.

The agent-firms have clienteles that look to them for brand-name products. The firms in the middle can threaten not to supply the products; not to renew the franchises; not to renew the loans of capital that went with the franchises. Accordingly, they can force the agent-firms to accept unfavorable terms—for the products, or the franchises, or the loans. The terms may get more unfavorable with each renewal, since the dependency of the agent-firms is likely to increase over time. Oil firms have sometimes treated the (nominal) owners of service stations in such ways; and automobile manufacturers have similarly treated their dealers. The agent-firms have little recourse.

Supplier-firms, confronted with demands for lower prices, have even less. The supplier-firms have often specialized in making things, like auto parts, designed for use by just the firms that they supply; or those firms form most of the market, perhaps all the market, for the things that the supplier-firms produce. However, the courts will not compel the firms in the middle—the Hupmobile firm, for example—to renew contracts, much less to go on buying from the supplier-firms in the absence of a contract. Yet in all these cases, the departures from the status quo are negative for the agent-firms and the supplier-firms, and non-matchingly to the advantage of the firms in the middle.

Dependency, and injustice, may run the other way. The supplier-firms, big or little, may have monopolies, perhaps through patents that they hold, perhaps because no would-be rivals can easily assemble the expensive plant required to enter their industry. Firms in the agent position sometimes represent such large proportions of the market for the goods produced by the firms in the middle that they can exact uncomfortably large amounts of rebates from them. Big grocery chains, for example, often drive hard bargains with the bakeries and canneries that supply them.

If the discounts are passed on in lower prices to consumers, however, will there not be something to be said for what the firms in the middle do in all these cases? The firms in the middle may have gained something—part of what they saved in the bargains that they reached stuck to their fingers—but the public may have gained even more. If the supplier-firms make no profits, however, or less than they normally would, the public has gained (along with the winning firms) at their expense. Efficiency and justice have not been reconciled.

In real-world business, efficiency may pull one way and justice the other even when the firms taking the lead in efficiency do not squeeze their agents or their suppliers. They may do nothing flagrantly unfair in competing with their rivals either. A nationwide grocery chain may get lower prices from its suppliers; the suppliers may be glad to offer such prices to be able to do business on a large scale. Furthermore, the chain may do nothing deliberately intended to drive smaller groceries out of business, like temporarily lowering prices below costs in a given vicinity while it continues to take in profits elsewhere. (That is a classic example of unfair competition.) The economies of scale passed on to consumers may be just as fatal to the small stores, however, and almost as quick-acting. Mom and Pop just can't sell bread or canned ham or soap as cheaply; they can't compete; even long-established groceries that used to be the biggest in town can't.

People with a business frame of mind outside the losing firms may be inclined to write off their fate as caused by their own inefficiency. They are, it would seem, either justly punished for their slackness, or justly denied their former rewards because they no longer make so useful a contribution to society. Yet, in fact, those firms may have been as efficient as ever, given the old terms of trade; and the people in them—decent people, who deserve a decent life—may have worked more diligently than most. What has happened is that the terms of trade have been changed; the grocery chain has innovated in operating on a larger scale. The ruined firms have done nothing to be punished for.

Should they be compensated? Taking a more sophisticated view, people with a business frame of mind, and other people too, might still say "No." Would economic progress be possible at all if every innovation capable of increasing efficiency had to bear the burden of compensating every firm that would lose business because of the innovation? One can easily imagine that a comprehensive system of providing compensation, with hearings and appeals, would give full-time employment to a host of lawyers and bureaucrats, but slow innovation down to a crawl. In practice, innovation has more often than not been pretty much allowed its head, in the belief that sooner or later everybody will benefit from it. Yet this belief has only vague and shaky foundations. Often enough, some firms have to close up shop and the losses imposed on them are not made up in any distinct and visible way, if at all. Have not the firms and the people involved in all probability suffered from an unremedied injustice?

Forms of compensation could be envisaged for them, and forms of protection, too. If we rule such measures out as inefficient, that is because we care more for efficiency than for justice in some of its aspects —more even than we do for private property, specifically property in the losing firms, whose assets as well as expectations may be much diminished. Innovations could be phased in, so that the old-time small grocery firms might have several years to shift to other lines of business. Or they might be kept going with subsidies until, a few years later, the people chiefly involved in them were ready to retire anyway. Firms not in a position to wind up their affairs at any early date might be given special privileges. In Quebec, for example, where alcoholic beverages for home consumption were long sold only through publicly owned outlets, Mom and Pop stores sell beer.

Some forms of protection already exist, most notably in anti-trust legislation. The main rationale for such legislation, of course, is that large firms with something approaching monopoly power are likely to charge prices higher than competitive ones. Part of the support for the legislation, however, seems to come from a widespread feeling that big firms, even when they are charging low prices, have an unfair advantage over small rival firms. Some of the prosecutions undertaken under the legislation seem to express this feeling, attacking firms just because of their unique relative size in their industry, whatever their record in prices and competitive practices.

Over-all, however, at present the status quo seems to allow for processes of innovation and forms of competition that do time and again lead to unequal results, unjust for some firms as well as for some people.*

---

*Firms may be the victims of injustice not only on the part of other firms (and other persons) but also on the part of governments. Sometimes firms that have made the most reliable bids for government contracts are passed over because governments unjustly favor other firms; sometimes firms are singled out for harassment by governments. These are important matters; but I already have enough to discuss in treating justice and injustice among people and firms in the private sector.

§6 THE EMPLOYMENT RELATIONSHIP

Some of the things that firms do, justly or unjustly, in dealing with agents and suppliers are done to people rather than firms. Firms also, as we have seen, affect people as consumers through the transactions that they have with them; and affect people again, taken as members of the public with interests in public health, a safe and attractive environment, and a vigorous cultural life. I shall not treat the impact of their activities on the public as raising questions of justice and injustice. The impact can certainly be good or evil, but the impact is diffuse, and cannot be pictured readily as conveyed in transactions with individual agents, where the concept of justice is most at home. The one other connection in which I shall treat firms as doing justice or injustice is the employment relationship. Firms are not, even nowadays, the only employers in business. Many people are employed by individual persons, who may act as justly or unjustly in the employment relationship as firms. But individual persons are no longer the most typical employers. Most people are employed by firms.

The employment relationship, so far as doing justice or injustice is concerned, runs both ways. Employees can "rip off" firms; or betray them; or sabotage their operations. These are all—in the general way in which we are using "injustice"—forms of injustice, at least apart from revolutionary situations. There are laws for dealing with them one by one, person by person. Whether the employment relationship goes right or wrong in the other direction, too, may be something that falls to the lot of individual persons without systematically affecting whole classes of people. A machinist, working for a small firm making brake drums, may be denied the prevailing pay for his sort of work, even though he is a white Anglo-Saxon Protestant in good standing; he may not get the same privileges in vacations and hours of work as other workers not senior to him in employment by the firm; he may not have the same security of employment. Let us suppose he is a prickly fellow and the boss dislikes him. In all these connections, what other people in comparable positions—the most comparable being other machinists employed by the same firm—are getting in return for their work establishes in a roughly adequate way what results in the wage-contract are to be accounted equal on the side of the employee. A famous theory—the theory of exploitation set forth by Karl Marx (1818–1883)—holds that even when the results are equal by this sort of comparison, workers are giving up something (the labor that is the source of the employer's profit) for which, under market arrangements, they are not compensated. One does not have to accept or reject this theory to recognize that results unequal for the machinist in any of the ways mentioned earlier would be objectionable on grounds of justice. In each case, there is a departure in which the machinist gives up time and effort and does not get a matching compensation; and a move toward justice if the inequalities are avoided or rectified.

Avoiding or redressing such injustices might be looked upon as something to be worked out person by person, in individual cases. Noticing the discrepancies between the way in which he is being treated and the way in which other workers are, the machinist goes to the boss and points out the injustice. No doubt something like this sometimes succeeds. When it doesn't, one may have to accept it. There is a limit to what can be done by social procedures. Pair by pair, people are inevitably going to be often so ill-assorted in information, temperament, and cunning that one will do an injustice to the other. This will be true so often that only when substantial damage is done will it be worthwhile to set in motion a system of remedies.

It is apparently quite a different matter when whole classes of people can be identified who are subjected time and again to the same injustices. Blacks, Hispanics, Indians, and women have been denied equal chances with WASP males to get jobs in the first place. When they have had jobs, they have had less chance of keeping them and less chance of being promoted. They have also, especially in the case of women (and of blacks in South Africa), got less pay when they have been doing much the same work. In the United States and Canada, systematic measures now check such injustices and provide redress for them. Prominent among the measures are laws that give people rights not to be discriminated against, in respect to employment (and in other connections), on grounds of race, sex, or religion.

I have not hitherto mentioned rights. It may seem that rights and justice are so intimately connected that one cannot get very far with the discussion of justice without discussing rights. Certainly, failing to respect people's rights is flagrant injustice; taking them away or purporting to do so may be even worse. Yet I have in fact gone on as long as this, discussing justice without discussing rights. That is no accident. The rights against discrimination just mentioned came into being as legal devices—new sets of rules—to remedy specific injustices. Evidently the injustices could be detected and condemned in the absence of the devices. They could also conceivably be remedied in their absence. In part, they are so remedied: Among the current measures taken against discrimination, for example, is the prescription that the proportion of people from minority groups employed by a given firm shall not vary greatly from the proportion of such people in the general population.

Although justice can be conceived, and done, without instituting special rights, the device of rights nevertheless has certain advantages over alternative devices like prescribing proportions or quotas. It gives employers and employees more room to match jobs with people who have relevant qualifications. It enlists the people affected by discrimination in the task of combating it. They are given new resources, which so much strengthen for them the points of departure from the status quo that they now have the power to revoke certain departures unfavorable to them.

Whether the injustices of discrimination are remedied by rights or otherwise, remedying them can be looked upon, once again, not as an interference with the market, but as a modification tending to perfect it. One of the chief arguments for such rights is that the people who are being discriminated against could do just as well as the people favored by the discrimination, sometimes even better, if they were only given a chance to do the same sort of work, whether it is heaving coal or writing computer programs. If this is so, firms practicing such discrimination are behaving irrationally and jeopardizing their own efficiency. They are cutting themselves off from part of the supply of suitable labor.

Blacks, women, and the other minority groups mentioned are classes of people readily defined, independently of any injustices done them. It has taken a good deal of agitation to make them visible as victimized groups. Even so, the ease of identification facilitates making the case that they have been, as groups, systematically subject to injustice; and hence facilitates making the case that they deserve to have systematic remedies instituted on their behalf. Are the other injustices that firms may do to employees to be left to measures not taken on behalf of any independently defined social groups? There might still be rights to be resorted to; but, like legal provisions for disallowing unconscionable contracts, these would have been designed to assist any persons who on occasion needed them, regardless of the social groups to which they belonged.

Yet at least one other social group may be held to be in need of measures specially designed for it. Let us return to that prickly machinist. Suppose the boss refuses to act on the discrepancies that the machinist points out. Are we really going to write off the outcome as the sort of petty injustice that must be put up with now and then, given the imperfections of human nature and of social arrangements? In fact, the machinist belongs to a visible social group—nowadays by far the majority of the working population—that is systematically vulnerable to injustices of this kind—namely, employees, or more precisely, people who depend on employment for their livelihoods.

Compared to employees, employers, even in the private sector of the economy, are relatively few to begin with; and a few of those few are employers of large concentrations of work-people. There are thus very many fewer alternative parties to a bargain struck about employment on one side of the bargain; and on that side of the bargain there are resources that no employee has enabling the employers to wait out the bargaining process. The laws against discrimination fall very far short of protecting employees, even employees in the groups most victimized previously by discrimination, from all the injustices that abuses of the employers' greater power can lead to.

Other measures of protection do exist. In Canada, the courts will do something to protect employees against arbitrary dismissal. They may not restore the employees' jobs; but they will exact some form of compensation, in some cases up to a year's salary. Through unionization, employees themselves have taken their own measures of protection: not only arrangements for collective bargaining, but also provisions for hearing and settling, during the life of a collective agreement, the grievances of individual workers. All the points on which the machinist considers himself unjustly treated could be brought forward as grievances. Unfortunately, for many workers, indeed for most, including professional people and people in managerial positions, no reliable grievance procedures exist. They remain vulnerable to a great variety of injustices at the hands of the firms that employ them.

III. REFORMING GENERAL FEATURES OF THE STATUS QUO

In Part II, we were concerned with particular sorts of departures, just or unjust, or troubling enough to be taken as unjust, and with features of the status quo that lend themselves variously to fostering, preventing, or rectifying such departures. I left aside the basic question whether the present status quo is currently meeting people's needs equally and giving people substantial chances of having their preferences heeded. I also left aside the threat to justice posed by increases in the inequality with which resources are distributed, and the general threat, in the form of unequal power, posed by the present inequality of distribution. The importance of these considerations to the achievement of justice was made plain in the outline of the theory of justice that I gave in Part I, however; and one cannot assume that modifications in the status quo that check particular sorts of injustice will take care of them. Such piecemeal modifications may leave gross inequalities in current faring standing, even increasing. Nor do they remove the pervasive dangers of unequal power, which may be applied in subtle ways (for example, in selecting political candidates and shaping political issues so as to favor people with unearned income), and which continually find new forms of expression.

It is now time to take up, with these considerations, reforms directed at inequalities of resources and income as such, quixotic as it may be to attack them directly. People, even people who have some reason to be dissatisfied with the present inequality of advantages, may currently have little interest in achieving justice. We may be going through a period in which most people are content—some people, very content—to live again under the nineteenth-century bourgeois banner "Enrichissez-vous!"* Yet some unrest about justice, including basic justice, persists; and even people who are not going to be moved in the slightest to act against received injustices in the distribution of resources will understand the unrest, and the context of their lives, better if they consider what measures of reform they are rejecting.

---

*The phrase means exactly what it seems to mean, even to a speaker of English. But if a translation is required, "Doonesbury" suggests, "Getting yours."

§7 BASIC JUSTICE RESPECTING NEEDS AND PREFERENCES: THE PROBLEM

If departures from the status quo adverse to people's meeting their needs and giving effect to their preferences are prevented or rectified, no people will be made worse off by such departures. Some people, however, may have been badly off to begin with, and they may, in spite of these protections, stay badly off, even if social product (GNP) per capita remains the same or, rising, is accompanied by adjustments that maintain everybody's relative positions. With these inequalities, could the status quo be basically just? Does justice require that anything be done about them? The Harvard philosopher Robert Nozick, in a widely read recent book inspired by born-again faith in "possessive individualism," has held that justice does not require reducing the inequalities, though his position is qualified to a degree when needs rather than preferences are in question. At any rate, in his view, justice does not require this, if the inequalities have come about, as we allowed in the basketball player's case (§2), through fair exchanges of resources themselves fairly acquired.

There is, Nozick acknowledges, a case for reducing the inequalities, if they stem in part from past departures themselves unjust. Should we then trace the history of each present item of property and rectify all the injustices done at earlier stages? But this is absurd (Nozick himself recognizes that it would be very difficult): We are in no position to do all the tracing required, and even if we were, it would not be determinate how present claims to property would be rearranged, since rectifications at earlier stages in the past would open up different possibilities for bargaining at later stages, and hence many different possible sequences of fair exchanges. If we could identify uniquely what the present arrangement should be, nothing would be more disruptive to society than to try to bring it about.

Worse, we can also infer from Nozick's position and our knowledge of history taken together that in all probability the history of acquisition and exchange behind almost every substantial accumulation of private property is thoroughly tainted. Even if on his side the basketball player (§2) accepted in good faith all the cash offered him by his adoring fans, many of them were not entitled to offer the cash. Either they had done someone an injustice in getting it or they in turn had got it following an injustice done someone earlier.

Should we just disregard the claims to resources with such tainted histories? In principle we might be justified in doing so, but, mindful of the social disorders that sudden changes in institutions and expectations generate, proceed very cautiously and slowly in reducing them. We might even, on the same ground, let them stand for the time being. On the other hand, just letting them stand will not save us from disorder. The world of business, indeed the general life of society in the United States, Canada, Britain, and other countries is continually being disrupted by strikes and other forms of agitation for higher wages, which imply that present inequalities are not accepted as just.

Unions are not content with simply keeping abreast of wages elsewhere in the industry, or of the wages paid people in occupations that have in the past had wages comparable to the wages of the union members. They aim, whatever the inflationary consequences that sometimes follow, to improve the relative position of the members, as compared with other workers who seem no more deserving, or as compared with people living on income from property. Unions may settle disputes on the basis of received notions of comparability, and on terms that permit firms to make (and distribute) as much profit as before, but they are always ready to start up the disputes again. They do not see why air traffic controllers should not do as well as air pilots, or as judges on the bench; and, without necessarily fuming about the privileges of property owners, they do not see why profits should not be reduced if wages could thereby be made bigger. How can they be expected to look upon the distribution of resources—income and wealth—in the status quo otherwise, so long as they are not convinced that the distribution is in accordance with justice, much less prescribed by it? In the continuing unrest about wages and the inflationary pressure that the unrest implies, business as it is currently conducted continually touches upon issues about the basic justice of the market and of private property.

§8 BEARING WITH THE PROBLEM OR TRYING TO RESOLVE IT

Workers and unions may be aware, in many cases, of doing quite well from the unrest, and they may hope to do even better in further rounds of agitation and bargaining. (Unionized workers in particular may have chances to improve their positions relative to workers in sectors of the economy not unionized.) People on the other side—for instance the people who are doing well as property owners—may complain about the unrest, treating every strike as a threat to national survival. In reality they may be content to bear with the unrest rather than undertake stringent measures to bring about anything like a basically just distribution of resources. Moreover, serious efforts to deal with the problem might lead to bitter social conflict. The quest for basic justice, even the quest for agreement on a principle of justice, would very likely break up into as many partisan arguments as there were distinct interests to rationalize and defend.

Is there no hope even within the limits of a philosophical discussion of finding a principled solution to the problem? What does justice prescribe (so far as it gives a determinate prescription) regarding the distribution of resources? Some people would say that the principle is simply that resources in any given status quo should be equal; or, more subtly, that, given the variation among people in the amounts they need to be provided with to meet the same needs, that they should give everyone an equal chance of meeting his or her needs. Equality in resources will not be generally convincing, however, at least as things stand, even among people who might gain from it. For not only do some people need more than others, but some people are outstanding either in contributions to society or in derelictions. Most people believe that they should be re-warded or punished accordingly in matching departures. Equality in meeting needs, while it is perhaps a principle that more people would find convincing, takes care of only one of these points. Moreover, it does not say what is to be done with what is left over after meeting needs, which in an affluent society is a lot, and can generate a lot of controversy.

At this point the Difference Principle, made famous in our day by another Harvard philosopher, John Rawls, might come forward. The Difference Principle says that there shall be equality in acquiring new material resources (money, income) so long as there is no way of increas-ing everybody's resources by giving some people more resources than others, as a reward for contributing to the increase. It prescribes (under certain safeguards respecting rights and opportunities that are to be equalized for everybody) inequality if those who will be worst off will be better off than they would be otherwise.

I am going to use the Difference Principle in a rough-and-ready way as the means of arriving at a principled solution to the problem of basic justice. Even in this rough-and-ready use, it requires a good deal of ad-justment. For instance, workers as well as managers will join in insisting that it must be adapted to discouraging anyone inclined to from idly free-riding on the contributions of the rest. The most attractive way of checking such inclinations would be to instill in everyone a steady desire to contribute, which might in fact be consistent with everyone's accept-ing equal rewards. Unfortunately, no large or complex society has yet succeeded in instilling the desire in everyone, much less in making peo-ple content with equal rewards; even small communes often have trouble doing so. On the other hand, attempting to police people strictly enough to detect and punish every lapse into idleness is invidious, inimi-cal to freedom, and counterproductive. Idleness becomes a gesture of de-fiance. Moreover, few even among these who are most excited about the abuses of public support are prepared to let people go without food, shelter, and clothing, whether they are idle or not. The worst of crimi-nals in prison are given those things.

A possible solution would be to grant that everyone's needs are to be met, though whether they are met in ways that accord with anyone's preferences, and whether anyone's preferences are heeded in other mat-ters, would depend on the person's making, given the opportunity, at least a normal contribution to production. In other words, the Differ-ence Principle would apply to discretionary income—the wherewithal for giving effect to preferences. This income would vary with the contri-bution made. So far as external incentives were required for normal ef-forts, let alone extra efforts, on the part of members of the society, the in-centives would be furnished by discretionary income. This solution ac-cords at least roughly with present practice, and with improvements on present practice that might well win general agreement—finding jobs for those who want work; encouraging people who are receiving public support to earn some discretionary income.

Major questions about the use of the Difference Principle remain. One of them is what should count as a contribution? According to received ideas, a person contributes simply by putting something on the market; or by investing some money in a going corporation. These do not seem to suit the Difference Principle as well as exertions of special talent. Yet it is difficult to reject entirely the suggestion that people make a contribution by using their property or making it available. In his explanation of the Difference Principle, Rawls himself mentions the contributions of entrepreneurs who bring in innovations beneficial to everybody. But entrepreneurs make their contributions by the use of property; and often, if they did not have property of their own to use in this way, they might not be free to take the risks involved.

I shall take the Difference Principle to allow for contributions by the use of private property only when the property is used as a means of making a full-time effort in which the owner's skills and talents are exerted. When she needs more capital than she herself can supply, I shall suppose that she can recruit other property owners to work with her. This move clearly allows the Difference Principle to embrace private property in the means of production. On the other hand, it does not go all the way with private property as now conceived and accepted. Some people—for example, people living idly on inherited property—attached to the present way of doing things and able to invoke in their favor some of our received notions about justice, will not wish to go further: For them, in effect, if they subscribe to the Difference Principle, they will do so only on terms that may lead simply to endorsing the present status quo.

Applied to productive contributions, the Difference Principle is compatible with inequalities of discretionary income as great as those existing now in such countries as the United States and Canada. It might even, given the facts about incentives, call for larger inequalities. Most people who have discussed it, however, incline to think that the facts about incentives are such that the Difference Principle will sanction only much smaller inequalities of income. I shall so assume, as part of my rough-and-ready use of the principle. I shall also assume that fulfilling it will reduce the general threat to justice posed by inequalities in the present distribution of resources to a level not only more comfortable but also tolerable in itself (should the present level not be tolerable), and keep the threat in check at that level.

Many people (including members of the intelligentsia) who might persist with the Difference Principle past this point will almost surely fall out soon hereafter, when their own present privileges come under threat. On the other hand, we are still well within the bounds of the received rationale of the status quo insofar as that rationale argues from incentives for personal efforts (such an intense concern when it was a question of idlers on "welfare"). Furthermore, if instead of asking for agreement by everybody in present circumstances, we ask, "Whose agreement, from the point of view of justice, is it most important to have?" we can find a way to go ahead that at least in theory has a prospect of rising above rationalizations of opposed interests.

Surely it is most important, as regards the basic justice of social arrangements, to have the agreement of those who do least well in benefits from them. Those are the people who are most likely to be victimized by the arrangements, other things being equal—most likely to have uncomfortably small discretionary incomes; most likely to be intimidated or overreached in bargaining or other conflicts of power. (Other things being equal: that is to say, rebutting one by one such charges as folly, idleness, criminal behavior, which might imply that their disadvantages were their own fault.) If they freely consent, mindful of their own interests, to arrangements under which they get less in material resources than other people, that is a powerful non-partisan argument, approaching being a necessary and sufficient condition, for thinking the arrangements just. Arrangements comforming to the Difference Principle would invite this consent, for there, by allowing those who get more than their extra rewards, the people who get least still get more than they would otherwise.

However, just what do people require in extra rewards to make extra efforts, or full use of their talents and skills whether or not they make more than a normal effort? It would obviously invite a number of abuses to allow them simply to set their own rates of reward. On the other hand, placing upon them the burden of proof, while justified as a precaution against abuses, does not give them a fully defined question to deal with, or at any rate a question that theory in the social sciences has mastered. People will not know how to go about proving in advance that they will not, if they gain less than they aim at in bargaining, do the work in view unless they get a certain level of rewards. How can they, or anyone else, tell that they are not distorting their prophecies to suit their present bargaining position? An objective answer of sorts is provided by the market in cases where the work involved is something that a number of people compete to do (just as firms compete to have them do it): For then, without any distortion from monopolistic bargaining power on the part of the worker, the worker can expect to get as much as her marginal (revenue) product. It is far from clear, however, that having this amount in wages is indispensable as an incentive.

The Difference Principle does not make it clear either on just what terms the people who get more resources are to keep them. Are they to keep them—to go on accumulating them—during their lifetimes, without regard to the increase in power over other people and in other advantages respecting command over goods? Are they to be able to pass them on, as gifts or inheritances? The Difference Principle seems to sanction these things if they continue to contribute to incentives. Yet over time they, like similar effects from fair exchanges and personal providence, may make the points of departure in succeeding status quos ever more unequal, and pose grave dangers of injustice in departures and of troubling results. Under other principles, about liberty and opportunity, Rawls calls for measures to offset these dangers, but those other principles might not in practice hold their own against the processes and effects of accumulation.

Could we not take an experimental approach to these issues? One may doubt whether the possibility of leaving accumulated property to successors of one's choice is an essential part of the greater incentive to be offered everyone who is to make a greater contribution. One may doubt, likewise, whether the range of income covered in offering incentives need be as great as it currently is in the United States and Canada, where the top incomes for people who work for their incomes (as not all do) may be as much as two hundred times the median income of the lowest-paid tenth. Perhaps a range up to twenty times, or even three or four times, would suffice to call forth the entire amount of effort now being put forward in business. It suffices for natural scientists and for engineers actually employed as engineers. Is it to be supposed that they work less hard or less intelligently than financiers? (Their skills may be just as rare, too.)

If a narrower range would suffice, however, the Difference Principle does not justify a wider range; on the contrary. Nor does it permit being able to pass on accumulations of private property if being able to do so is not an essential part of the incentives to be offered. Maybe it leads to a quandary if inheritance must be allowed for: Were it essential as an incentive to the legators, it could hardly be essential as an incentive to the legatees. As some thoroughgoing champions of capitalism—more thoroughgoing than most—have remarked, inheritance seems to take away the legatees' incentive to contribute.

We arrive, as predicted, at familiar measures—a tax on inheritances and a progressive income tax (that is to say, a tax that takes proportionately more the higher one's income). The measures may be familiar. However, they have yet to be made effective; the will to make them effective may have faltered, as current proposals in the United States for a flat-rate income tax suggest. So it has been of some importance to renew—in the perspective of current faring as well as in the more novel perspective of threats to justice from unequal power—the arguments for the measures.

How far the Difference Principle, as a means corresponding to those arguments, and the taxes mentioned, as means serving the Difference Principle, will actually carry in effective reforms depends on experiment. Taking an experimental approach, governments might proceed in stages to eliminate inheritance (except maybe to allow widows to stay on in the family home, or farmers' children to carry on the family farms). The stages might be taxing away half any inheritance received in a first period, then taxing away three quarters of any received in a second. After each period one could look to see whether the social product or the rate of innovation had fallen. Again proceeding in stages, governments might reduce by a system of progressive income taxes (that is to say, taxes that take proportionately more the higher one's income) the range of net incomes, first from two hundred times to one hundred times, then from one hundred times to fifty times, and so on. No attempt would be made to lower or to raise people's ranks in income, but the increments of income ascending the ranks would diminish; and the discretionary incomes of those at the bottom might rise from transfers.

After each stage, again, one would look at various statistical indicators to see whether net adverse effects were occurring. Some effects might be favorable to overall social income and to the rate of innovation: Less resentful, people whose incomes had risen relatively might put forward more effort; less willing to be harried, people might work less stressfully—and live to work longer. Other effects would not be favorable. When, in either connection, inheritance or income, adverse effects began substantially and persistently to outrun the favorable effects, the society would have arrived in the vicinity of correctly applying the Difference Principle.

Would these experiments be feasible? There are difficulties about measuring the effects (though if there are, they argue as much against supposing that the present distribution of income and wealth is a commensurate return to contributions as against trying to find another distribution that would do better). The effects may be too subtle, too mixed with the effects of other causes, or too slow in coming, to detect at every successive stage. If the composition of social income changes as an effect of the changes in the distribution of income and wealth, price-index problems about comparing the social product at one time with the product at another would come up. There are, furthermore, very likely to be grave difficulties about carrying through the changes in distribution in the first place: Those who stand to lose property or income would emigrate; or evade taxes if they stayed at home; or refuse to work as a protest against the experiments.

These difficulties, however, might be considerably reduced by proceeding very slowly, so that at no stage was the change big enough to provoke emigration or evasion or "job action," and every change was fully digested and adapted to before proceeding to the next. The difficulties about measurement, too, would be mitigated by allowing time to sort out the effects of bringing in the Difference Principle from the effects of other causes and time to establish which effects were after all persistent. Price-index problems might become intractable as time passed, but with any luck, they would not undermine comparisons of social income after one stage of the experiments with social income just before that stage, and they would not become intractable at any greater rate than they would in the absence of the experiments.

Something might be made of the Difference Principle even if it were not possible to go all the way with it: Social policy might be required, if it made any move on the subjects that the principle applies to, to move in the direction of applying it, rather than in some other direction. I do not think, however, that full application, so far as the experiments outlined with inheritance and income amount to full application, would be infeasible, given time and care and steady resolution.

It may be objected that even with the range of incomes greatly deflated—brought down, say, to five times the minimum—some of the people drawing top incomes may not be making commensurate contributions, while some of the people making incomes at the bottom may be contributing incommensurately much. This is true, and it shows that though deflating the range until adverse statistical effects appear might bring the society closer to applying the Difference Principle than before, it would not have come close enough to eliminate all injustices in the status quo. Yet the magnitude of the injustices would have been substantially reduced; and if it was desired to eliminate the injustices that remained, headway could be made in doing so by various supplementary measures. In some cases, it might help to correct for imperfections in the market: for example, to make sure of an adequate supply of people with protracted professional training, a commission on long-run manpower (personpower) requirements might take actions to encourage or discourage people from entering upon such training in any given year. Among the actions would be measures to vary the lifetime income to be expected after completing the training; or to vary the terms on which student loans were to be repaid.

It may be objected, too, that even with the range of incomes deflated —indeed, even with the finer corrections just alluded to—the range might still be so great as to give some people troubling advantages in power. In effect, to get more discretionary income (the discretionary income that they had to start with, plus any additions from transfers occurring during the process of deflation), people at the bottom of the range may be risking abuses of power by those at the top. Can we really count on the people at the bottom to be so mindful of their interests as to keep this risk within safe limits? They would have perhaps to be abnormally alert if they are to do so. They might also have to be unexpectedly agreed on the comparative values of more discretionary income and greater safety from power. These problems are too complicated to try to settle here. I shall have to be content with pointing out that successful application of the Difference Principle in the experiments that I have described would reduce existing inequalities of power, so far as these depend on unequal wealth and income.

Would a society in the vicinity of correctly applying the Difference Principle, with measures being taken to refine the application, find itself outside the bounds of capitalism and private business? I do not think so. It would even be within the bounds of capitalism and private business as most people in the United States and Canada currently conceive of it—in theory. To be sure, the United States and Canada have not eliminated inheritance; not even Great Britain has. Canada, except for Quebec, does not now have any tax at all on inheritances; and the tax in the United States is, I believe, easily circumvented. Nor do the United States and Canada have fully effective progressive income taxes (to say nothing

of having tax systems that taken as wholes are genuinely progressive).
The idea of having both inheritance taxes and progressive tax systems is,
however, familiar, and even, in theory, generally accepted. The theory
of the market economy, as it applies to the effects on incentives of inherited wealth, has already been alluded to. The theory applies in favor of a
progressive income tax insofar as such a tax corrects for imperfections of
the market, which is the case here, since the measures mentioned (when
they do not in effect reintroduce the market) correct for imperfections
that lead to people getting more income than they require in incentives.
(A progressive tax on expenditures, which would encourage capital accumulation and treat earned incomes more fairly, might be even more
effective, though it is less familiar.) To prevent the government from
putting its hands on more funds than it has the capacity to use wisely, furthermore, all of these taxes might be modified to include devices to encourage the diffusion of resources in private hands, including credits for
gifts to charities and (within limits for each recipient) to private persons.

Whether any sustained drive to achieve justice under the Difference
Principle will ever be generated is an entirely different question. Most
people, especially when, as assumed, their needs are met, would not
want to consume their lives in pursuing justice to the end; and a good
deal of injustice will probably persist to the end of time because of this
lack of zeal. People in business might ask themselves now and then
whether they do not benefit from this accident of circumstances. If they
do, would it not be good grace on their part to adopt a more generous attitude toward egalitarian reforms of the distribution of income and
wealth? Should they not also recognize that, so long as they are not
ready to carry through measures to make the status quo fully just, and
just again after correcting for the relevant effects of future departures,
they have no grounds for holding that strikes and other forms of pressure
for higher wages are out of place?*

Acknowledgements: Colleagues and students of the Department of Philosophy at
Dalhousie University heard me deliver a preliminary version of Parts I and III of this essay
at a departmental colloquium in September 1981. I am grateful to them for their comments,
and especially to Robert Martin, Brian Penrose, Peter K. Schotch, and Terrance Tomkow. I
am grateful also to Alasdair Sinclair of the Department of Economics at Dalhousie and
Gregory Kavka of the Department of Philosophy at the University of California, Irvine, for
reading through my draft on impossibly short notice and forestalling some egregious errors
and omissions. (Others may have appeared since.) I must also thank Tom Regan, the editor
of this volume, for many useful suggestions; and Nicholas Rongioni, whose comments,
several of them well-taken, I have responded to during final revising. Another discussion of
some of the central ideas of the present article, viewed in a different perspective and developed in ways not attempted here, can be found in my paper, "Making Justice Practical," in
Michael Bradie and David Braybrooke, eds., *Social Justice* (Bowling Green State University
Series in Applied Philosophy, 1982). It was written after the present article reached near-
final form, though it has come into print first.

NOTES

§1. Hobbes actually says, "The definition of INJUSTICE, is no other than *the not Performance of Covenant"* (*Leviathan*, ch. XV). By "covenant" he means a mutual undertaking for an exchange of goods and services where at least one party has yet to perform. He recognizes, as Kavka has reminded me, that circumstances may change so that one party or the other cannot be expected to perform, in particular so that it might become too dangerous to do so (ch. XIV).

For Hume's contention that single acts of justice upholding claims to private property are "frequently contrary to *public interest,*" see *A Treatise of Human Nature,* Book III, Part II, sec. II.

§2. Notoriously, the example of the basketball player (Wilt Chamberlain) is treated by Robert Nozick, in *Anarchy, State, and Utopia* (N.Y.: Basic Books, 1974), pp. 160–64, to exactly the opposite effect given it in the treatment here. To Nozick it is intuitively clear that justice could in no way require the player to give up any of his gains.

William T. Terrell has impressed upon me the point that governments tend to abandon the market system very quickly when events jeopardize meeting basic needs.

§3. For the logical difficulties of aggregating preferences in direct democracy, see Amartya K. Sen, *Collective Choice and Social Welfare* (San Francisco: Holden-Day, 1970); in representative democracy, Robert A. Dahl, *A Preface to Democratic Theory* (Chicago: University of Chicago Press, 1956), esp. pp. 127–28. Sen gives a comprehensive discussion of the questions about social choice raised by Arrow's startling Impossibility Theorem, published in 1951. On the incapacity of the market to reach an optimum in which public goods are present, see John G. Head, *Public Goods and Welfare* (Durham, N.C.: Duke University Press, 1974), esp. ch. 3.

The Vancouver real estate operator and the mining financier mentioned in this section figured in Peter Newman's recent book *The Acquisitors* (Toronto: McClelland and Stewart, 1981), in passages cited by Alan Fotheringham in his column in *MacLean's.*

§4. James S. Coleman devotes an illuminating short book, *Power and the Structure of Society* (N.Y.: Norton, 1974), to the complications for ethics and behavior imposed upon natural persons by the rise and proliferation of firms and other "corporate actors."

§6. Marx's theory of exploitation can be found in the first volume of *Das Kapital.* Its outline can be quickly and conveniently appreciated by reading the selections from *Das Kapital* in Part II, secs. A and B, of Robert Freedman, *Marx on Economics* (N.Y.: Harcourt Brace, 1961).

A quota for the employment of a racial minority is one of the things aimed at in the prescriptions of the collective agreement at issue in the case of *United Steelworkers* v. *Weber et al.,* decided by the United States Supreme Court in 1979. The decision upheld the agreement, in which the union and Kaiser Aluminum & Chemical Corporation had evidently been strongly encouraged by government officials to adopt the idea of a quota.

Courts in the United States do not seem as ready as courts in Canada to act against arbitrary dismissal, even of long-service employees. Compare Innis Christie, *Employment Law in Canada* (Toronto: Butterworths, 1980), ch. 7, which bears out what I say in the text, with Alvin L. Goldman, *Labor Law and Industrial Relations in the United States of America* (Deventer, The Netherlands: Kluwer, 1979), pp. 72–76. I owe information on this point and the reference to Christie's book to Professor Arthur L. Foote of the Dalhousie University Faculty of Law.

Neil Chamberlain ("The Corporation and the Trade Union," in Edward S. Mason, ed., *The Corporation in Modern Society*, Cambridge, Mass.: Harvard University Press, 1966, pp. 122–40, at p. 133) stresses the establishment of grievance procedures as an undisputed benefit of unionization.

§7. Nozick's book has already been mentioned (see note on §2, above). The phrase "possessive individualism" and the conception are C. B. Macpherson's, made famous in his lively book *The Political Theory of Possessive Individualism: Hobbes to Locke* (Oxford: Clarendon Press, 1962).

§8. On the advantages of unionized workers in "the monopoly sector," see James O'Connor, *The Fiscal Crisis of the State* (N.Y.: St. Martin's Press, 1973), ch. 1.

Rawls treats the Difference Principle mainly in sec. 13 of his book *A Theory of Justice* (Cambridge, Mass.: Harvard University Press, 1971), pp. 75–83. The contribution of entrepreneurs is referred to, for instance, on p. 78. The other principles that Rawls relies on to offset the dangers of injustice arising from the accumulation of wealth are chiefly the principle of equal liberty, treated on p. 61 and (more extensively) in ch. IV, and the principle of fair equality of opportunity, treated in sec. 14, pp. 83–90.

On the present range of incomes in the United States, see Arthur M. Okun, *Equality and Efficiency: The Big Tradeoff* (Washington: The Brookings Institution, 1975), pp. 68–69. My assertion about a range of two hundred times is a safe inference from the data in that passage. For Canadian incomes, see Lars Osberg, *Economic Inequality in Canada* (Toronto: Butterworths, 1981), pp. 15–17.

James P. Sterba, in *The Demands of Justice* (Notre Dame, Ind.: University of Notre Dame Press, 1980), relies as I do on different treatment for needs and for discretionary income, and arrives by a different route at much the same modifications of the Difference Principle. He has some especially interesting things to say about the consequences of allowing for some people at the bottom who may prefer leisure to having any more discretionary income.

I owe to Daniel Cullen the point that the Difference Principle at least thrusts the burden of proof upon those who get greater rewards (or upon their apologists).

Contemporary champions of capitalism who think inheritance must be curtailed include Charles K. Rowley and Alan T. Peacock, *Welfare Economics: A Liberal Restatement* (London: Martin Robertson, 1975), ch. 7. They are also the source (p. 157) of the suggestion that rather than have the government take more in taxes, inheritances might be reduced by encouraging people to spread their legacies more widely and transferring inheritances above specified limits from unduly favored heirs to voluntary charities.

The standard case for supplanting the familiar principle of a progressive income by the principle of a progressive expenditures tax is made by Nicholas Kaldor in *An Expenditure Tax* (London: Allen & Unwin, 1955).

SUGGESTIONS FOR FURTHER READING

The present essay was loosely inspired by St. Thomas' discussion of justice in the *Summa Theologiae*, and in particular by the Reply to Objection 3 in 2a2ae, Q. 58, article 11. The whole of his discussion of justice and injustice in 2a2ae and of law in 1a2ae is worth reading, remarkably topical still, and useful even when detached from his theological premises. The translation most congenial to current readers of English is the Blackfriars translation begun in the 1960s and now largely complete (London: Eyre and Spottiswoode): Vols. 28, 37, 38, and 41 of this translation are the most relevant.

Even more loosely, the present essay was inspired by the *locus classicus* in Aristotle—Book 5 of the *Nicomachean Ethics*—in the sense that I have tried to cover the important points at issue in Aristotle's distinctions without binding myself to exactly those distinctions or to his terminology.

For present-day works on justice, the works cited in my Notes are among the first things that I would recommend. I would add, on the specific topic of private property, Lawrence C. Becker, *Property Rights: Philosophic Foundations* (London: Routledge, 1977); and, on the specific topic of how equality might be reconciled with socially adequate incentives, Joseph H. Carens, *Equality, Moral Incentives, and the Market* (Chicago: University of Chicago Press, 1981). David Miller, in *Social Justice* (Oxford: The Clarendon Press, 1976), offers both an analysis of different aspects of justice and a survey of theories of justice important in the eighteenth and nineteenth centuries. In *Tyranny and Legitimacy* (Baltimore: Johns Hopkins University Press, 1979), James S. Fishkin criticizes a whole range of current theories, concentrating especially on those of Rawls and Nozick.

Most of the most penetrating recent works on justice, like the ones just mentioned, have been preoccupied with over-all social justice, that is to say, distributive justice, rather than justice between pairs of persons. Most of them, furthermore, have been written by people with limited sympathy for capitalism, though they have not always been so unsympathetic as Marx or as R. H. Tawney, the incomparably eloquent author of the two greatest classics of British socialism, *The Acquisitive Society* (1920) and *Equality* (1931), books that, whatever one may think of the performance of British socialism, even the most fervent champions of capitalism have reason to take into account. They might compare Tawney's arguments with the incisive critique of capitalistic practices by Frank H. Knight (himself opposed to socialism notwithstanding) in the title essay of *The Ethics of Competition and Other Essays* (N.Y.: Harper, 1935).

For views of justice more sympathetic to the spirit of capitalism than these authors' (or my own), one might, besides reading Nozick, and Rowley and Peacock, cited in my Notes, seek out F. A. Hayek's *The Mirage of Social Justice*, Vol. II of his three-part work, *Law, Legislation and Liberty* (London: Routledge, 1976). All these last-mentioned authors are in fact robust advocates of capitalism, and Hayek, as his title indicates, is ready to repudiate any notion of achieving social justice as incompatible with carrying on capitalism and enjoying its unique benefits. Even the most fervent critics of capitalism have reason to take his argument into account. (I am indebted to Alistair MacLeod of Queen's University for reminding me of Hayek's book, which, along with Hayek's philosophical work as a whole, has been unduly neglected by philosophers.)

7

Should Business be Regulated?

TIBOR R. MACHAN

I. INTRODUCTION

§1 THE SCOPE OF REGULATION

The topic of government regulation of business concerns the enforcement by governments (federal, state, municipal) of standards, rules, and practices for the conduct of business. Government regulation has its most direct impact on those who produce, manufacture, sell, advertise, market, transport, and otherwise deal with the country's mostly privately traded goods and services — truck drivers, attorneys, barbers, doctors, pest exterminators, toy makers, forklift operators, plumbers, and so forth. Businesses may be regulated in what they may or may not sell, when they may sell some things, how they must manufacture some items, what conditions must be maintained at the workplace, how hiring and firing must be carried out, what may or may not be said in advertisements, what must be worn when traveling on a motorcycle, and so forth.

For example: An ordinance enacted by Westchester County, New York, in 1980 forced two owners to cease the sale of "drug paraphernalia," making it a misdemeanor for "any merchant or other person to knowingly sell, offer for sale or display any cocaine spoon, marijuana pipe, hashish pipe or any other drug-related paraphernalia." A federal appeals court in Manhattan upheld the law, saying it "may constitutionally be applied to prohibit the plaintiffs' sale of certain items clearly within the ordinance's definition of drug paraphernalia."[1]

For example: As of 1975, thirty-three states legally prohibited retail pharmacists from engaging in the advertisement of prescription prices.[2]

For example: The substance variously called "Crazy Glue" and "Instant Glue," which can bind human flesh, was used in Vietnam in emergency surgery, and is badly wanted by hospitals and often smuggled to the United States from Canada, is banned by the Food and Drug Administration. The 3M Company recently discontinued its testing because the FDA continues to ban the substance.[3]

For example: OSHA, the Occupational Safety and Health Administration unit of the Department of Health and Human Services, has issued regulations requiring the placement of fire extinguishers at specific places in various work areas. Regulations have also been issued concerning the number of rolls of toilet paper to be placed in toilets, the stability of ladders, and the levels of exposure to coal dust workers are allowed in coal mines.

Government regulations such as these are in force throughout the United States and most so-called liberal democracies or welfare states, countries that are best regarded as mixed economies, combining the ingredients of a laissez-faire market with state planning. These systems tend to accept the institution of private property in the means of production but do not permit full control of commercial activities along with such ownership and engage in elaborate intervention in the use and disposal of private property when it is related to commerce. Government regulation of business is one facet of such intervention.

There are, of course, different kinds of regulation, some bearing on business affairs more directly than others. But the distinctions are not set in concrete. For example, government regulation of such personal conduct as the consumption of certain drugs has an indirect effect on business because it regulates *how* such drugs can be sold — for example, by means of doctors' prescriptions. Again, government regulation may involve censorship, yet such regulation can also have a bearing on business, as when the United States Supreme Court recently held that billboard advertising may be regulated, even prohibited, by various governmental bodies, except as it relates to political campaigns.[4]

Generally, in many liberal democracies commerce and trade are regulated more vigorously than, for example, writing, speaking, and assembly, yet governments often regulate businesses that engage in publishing, broadcasting, or public entertainment, thus obliterating any supposedly neat division between regulation of business and, for example, regulation of the arts.

It should be noted that government regulation is only one form of government intervention in commerce. Giving various industries like farming and automobile-manufacturing subsidies or government loans, and prohibiting competition in some areas, such as utility services, are also forms of intervention. And government regulation often emerges alongside these other forms of intervention. When the numerous public utilities are regulated, part of this is just the price they pay for being a protected monopoly.

From the legal point of view, the legitimacy of government regulation of commerce turns on the Unites States Constitution's commerce clause, which states the "Congress shall have Power . . . To regulate Commerce with foreign Nations, and among the several States, and with the Indian Tribes" (Article I, sec. 8, par. 3). The legal interpretation of this clause has varied, however, as Walter F. Dodd observes in his widely known textbook on constitutional law.

> The primary purpose of the framers of the Constitution was to prevent state restrictions upon interstate and foreign commerce. Our modern economy places an emphasis upon affirmative regulation by the national government.[5]

This means that while most of those who created the U.S. political and legal system wanted to promote the free flow of commerce, by disallowing the separate states of the Union to regulate interstate commerce by means, for example, of trade restrictions, tariffs, or price supports, eventually the federal government turned away from that goal. It will be useful to sketch the history of this change.[6]

§2 A BRIEF HISTORY OF REGULATION

Contrary to popular generalizations, there has never been an era of pure laissez-faire capitalism, even in the history of the United States. Pure laissez-faire capitalism is that economic system in which there exists full legal recognition and protection of private property rights and of the right to trade goods and services owned privately by individuals or voluntarily associated groups (for example, partnerships, corporations). Abstractly conceived, pure laissez-faire capitalism implies unimpeded, absolute individual discretion on the part of property owners to use, trade, or sell their property without government regulation, even in emergencies, wars, catastrophes, and so forth.[7] That is the form of capitalism we will not find in history. What we do find are more or less impure forms, where governments are not legally permitted to interfere with business, trade, finance, production, manufacture, employment, and other economic endeavors except in such rare and dire circumstances as wars, natural disasters, or civil disorders.

In either its pure or impure forms, laissez-faire capitalism lets business do what it wants outside of such criminal conduct as assult, theft, and murder, and precludes the great bulk of government regulatory measures many citizens now take for granted. Policies such as mandatory government-run unemployment insurance and retirement programs, government-imposed workers' compensation systems, and licensing of such professionals as physicians, psychologists, automechanics, pest exterminators — all these are an infringement upon the principles of laissez-faire. (So are, of course, various pro-business and industry measures of government, such as subsidies, price supports, legally maintained monopolies.) At certain levels of discussion, much debate can ensue about just exactly what may and may not be done by government without upsetting the ideals of laissez-faire. For example, enactment of antitrust legislation has been advocated on grounds that it backs such aspects of laissez-faire as widespread competition. Do mandatory building codes and other measures which aim at safety — such as the requirement that drugs be thoroughly tested before being put on the market for sale — constitute an infringement on laissez-faire, or are they needed measures implicit in the government's role of protecting property rights? If some activities are inherently threatening or dangerous, would not a property-rights–oriented legal system require them to be held in check? (It is usually granted that laissez-faire capitalism would involve laws protecting and preserving the rights to life, liberty, and property, inasmuch as the last is supposed to either grow out of or indeed encompass the former.[8])

With all this said, we can accept some portion of the popular idea that the United States enjoyed laissez-faire capitalism for several decades of its early history, especially when we compare the United States to other societies. Free enterprise is not just Fourth of July rhetoric but a prominent feature of the 1800s, and it still plays a considerable role in American life. While several states have always practiced government intervention, most did so less in the early days of the republic — except, of course, as far as the lives of black slaves were concerned, whose property rights were totally ignored with full legal sanction in the South — than either before its birth or in more recent decades.

If there is a time when the major legal change involving the institution of government regulation itself occurred, it must be placed at a point in the spring of 1877. As historian Johnathan R. T. Hughes tells it, at this time

> The U.S. Supreme Court, still officially sitting in its 1876 autumn term, handed down the fateful decision known collectively as the Granger Cases . . . the basic case, *Munn* v. *Illinois*, concerned the refusal of a Chicago warehouse firm, Munn and Scott, to apply for a state license and to have its service and charges controlled. The Court said that Munn and Scott must comply if they wanted to continue in that line of business.[9]

In this decision one of the several grounds for government regulation is already clearly hinted at by the phrase "affected with a public interest." Later (§5) this and other notions will be discussed more fully, but here let us just note that though the decision marked a departure, even Chief Justice Morrison Waite observed that the power to regulate commerce was very much part of the tradition of government from which America emerged. Citing Lord Chief Justice Hale in *De Portibus Maris*, written two hundred years prior to this ruling, Waite defended the position that "when . . . one devotes his property to a use in which the public has an interest, he, in effect, grants to the public an interest in that use, and must submit to be controlled by the public for the common good, to the extent of the interest he has thus created." Such control is well established in common law, Waite claimed, that very law "from whence came the [private property] right which the Constitution protects."[10]

So as a matter of our nation's heritage in English common law and because of regional practice, government regulation had always been a fact of American economic life. Still, the 1877 decision placed on the federal law books a forceful and explicit interpretation of the United States Constitution. It is this forcefulness and explicitness, rather than the novelty of the developments of the time, that marks this period as so important in the history of government regulation in the United States.

Following the Waite opinion, matters took a fairly normal turn. Gradually state and federal bodies and agencies were established, such as the Interstate Commerce Commission in 1887. In our time the number of agencies at the various levels of government reaches into the thousands. With the development of new forms of technology, new applications of the various sciences in professions and in productive enterprises, the institution of government regulation grew. Since lawmakers attempt to solve problems and judges sanction these attempts to a large extent on the basis of precedent and perceived need, this growth in government regulation should come as no surprise. Whether more is better in this case will concern us as we proceed.

Many people regard the era of President Franklin D. Roosevelt as the watershed marking the serious demise of laissez-faire capitalism in the United States. Again, this is partly justified. Prior to the 1930s, at least the federal government tended to stay away from extensive government regulation and the United States Supreme Court did not accept too many attempts at introducing the federal government into market endeavors. But the Great Depression was seen in large measure as the consequence of laissez-faire. At any rate, people were impatient and understandably panicky. Furthermore, economic theories on the intellectual landscape gave little or no support to the economic wisdom and prospects of laissez-faire. But without the decisive legal precedent of 1877, and the common-law precedent cited by Justice Waite, the severe federalization of the American economy that legitimized President Roosevelt's policies would not have been likely.

To know some of the history of its development is not yet to come to terms with the various arguments for or against government regulation of business. When a measure becomes law, it is rarely because of some one argument, or even one kind of argument, given in its support. Still, the acceptability of or need for some law, or its repeal, may very well be encouraged by ideas and ideals that can be supported or rejected by purportedly serious moral arguments. For example, the First Amendment, which gives legal protection to free expression of at least political and religious ideas, may have been enacted for various reasons, some of them merely emotional—for example, the fear of persecution. But certain ethical arguments would also be instrumental in giving such a measure backing. The view that truth is more likely to flourish if no ideas are suppressed by the authorities has served in giving support to the First Amendment. This argument alludes, clearly, to moral considerations by accepting that truth is very important and therefore worthy of support. Anything so important ought to obtain institutional protection, and since free speech fosters the truth, free speech, too, must be given such protection in our basic legal document.

Similar ideas, more or less complicated, can be found backing or opposing various legal measures in the United States and in other cultures. Liberal democracies, as well as fascist, communist, monarchical, and tribal regimes, rest, in part, on people's ethical beliefs. This is true of that part of the American legal system which is our topic, namely, government regulation of commerce.

§3 A NOBLE COMPROMISE?

The mixed economic system of the Western world are reasonably viewed as attempts to reach an equitable compromise between two ideals — those of individual liberty and the general happiness, with notable stress placed on regulating economic, commercial, or business affairs. This is probably the result of the considerable emphasis placed on the value of prosperity, of being well off from the point of view of so-called material goods and services — food, shelter, medical care, education, transportation, and so forth. But the welfare states of Western-type societies extend their concern for the well-being of people beyond mere "material" benefits, emphasizing the value of art, culture, psychological health, and the like. The attempt to prevent widespread alienation in the workplace, by regulating the employment relationship through such organizations as the National Labor Relations Board, is an example of going beyond mere material concerns. Nevertheless, in general the modern welfare states aim at making sure that in an atmosphere of relative freedom of trade and vigorous business no one seriously lacks basic material provisions in life.

The ideal of liberty, which the welfare state aspires to uphold, means (roughly) that in the running of one's own life, others must not intrude by the use of physical force or its threat, and one's own life includes, variously, one's thinking, talking, and associating with willing others, work projects, commercial endeavors, and the disposal, by sale or by gift, of one's wealth (if one has any). Classical liberalism[11] has upheld the social value of individual liberty, meaning that a person should have authority over his or her life. Not fully and consistently implemented, this ideal did, nevertheless, give support to the promulgation of legal and social institutions that provided official avenues of protest in cases when individual liberty was threatened, infringed, or flagrantly encroached upon.

The most obvious legal exemplification of the spirit of liberalism outside of the idea of economic freedom is the freedom of the press or, more broadly put, freedom of personal expression and conscience: "Congress shall make no law respecting an establishment of religion, or prohibit the free exercise thereof; or abridging the freedom of speech, or of the press; or the right of the people peaceably to assemble, and to petition the Government for a redress of grievances." In the United States, the First Amendment is the most forthright restriction on the power of governments.

At first glance no conflict seems to exist between the ideals of liberty and the welfare state. Just one example will illustrate that this impression is not wholly reliable. In advertising their products, people in the business world are subjected to congressional direction — for instance, in the case of cigarette advertisements, which must include a message of warning about the dangers of smoking. Billboard advertising, too, has come under serious regulation by local governments, mainly for aesthetic purposes. In both cases some speech is regulated. And now that some corporations are beginning to include political and ideological messages in their advertisements, the commercial character of some speech is difficult to separate from the political, as ads from Getty, Mobile, Smith-Kline, and Citicorp illustrate.

One might think that the issue of government regulation could be resolved simply by choosing between the two leading political ideologies presently on the American scene — liberalism or conservatism. Alas, matters are not that simple. Liberals — who tend in the main to favor freedom of speech, civil liberties, and intellectual pluralism while also favoring regulation of business — have supported government regulation of advertising speech. Conservatives — who tend to accept the free market as a workable economic order but find it objectionable to allow full personal discretion in areas such as artistic expression, entertainment, education, and sexual relations — have argued for government regulation of pornography and obscenity. But liberals at times do not tolerate freedom of expression — as when they demanded the removal of the offensive Little Black Sambo figure from front yards and protested speeches of some of their more extreme opponents, such as Professor William Shockley and Governor George Wallace. Conservatives don't always approve of free trade — for example, they wish to prohibit prostitution, topless entertainment, and the sale and purchase of dirty books. Thus no *simple* distinction can be made between civil liberties, on the one hand, and economic liberties on the other, and the full range of the problems surrounding governmental regulation cuts across political ideologies, as is shown by the American legal tradition. Explicit statements of the United States Supreme Court and those who are regarded as the intellectual supporters of the welfare state, both liberals and conservatives, give clear expression to the idea that what a decent society must do is to reach a compromise between the values of liberty and welfare. (One perhaps should say that liberals are more interested in an economic welfare state, conservatives in a spiritual one, depending, probably, on what realm of life, the economic or spiritual, they regard ultimately as more fundamental.)

II. DEFINITIONS AND DISTINCTIONS

§4 REGULATION

To regulate an activity is to adjust and steady its motion at various stages for specific purposes. For example, government regulation aims at the adjustment of people's conduct, and when government regulates business, it aims to adjust people's commercial conduct so as to serve certain ends deemed desirable via the political process. But government regulation involves a crucial ingredient not involved in all sorts of regulation, namely, the use of the threat of force. The Better Business Bureau, the various consumer watchdog groups and "action reporters" may well attempt and even succeed in the regulation of business. They could influence merchants, manufacturers, advertisers, and the like to do as desired. Government regulates by issuing legally enforceable edicts.

Here an initial distinction is important. Government uses or threatens force in many areas, including the criminal law. The difference between plain law enforcement and regulation by government centers on the fact that the latter places limits on conduct deemed generally legitimate, while the former tends to forbid conduct deemed generally illegitimate. The criminal law makes some things illegal to do. Certain aims are not to be pursued, and the law states these in general terms — the killing of another human being, stealing from others, assaulting them, defrauding them, and so forth. In regulation, however, it is conduct that is generally accepted as quite permissible, such as the manufacture of toys, the sale of cars, the lending of money, the building of houses, and so forth, that is circumscribed by rules and standards, which government will enforce. When we speak of regulation, it is the sort practiced by governments that will be referred to, not what may come about by way of persuasion, boycotts, or self-regulation. Occasional overlaps no doubt occur, as when merely to discuss the possibility of regulating some business leads to the reform of the way that business is carried out. But the distinction is generally sound.

§5 SOME IMPLICATIONS OF THE DEFINITION

Government regulation of people's economic activities involves, essentially, giving legally enforceable guidelines and direction to what are regarded as generally proper, legitimate commercial endeavors in a human community. Gaining compliance with such guidance and direction can involve measures ranging from the suggestive to the compulsory. In the last analysis, government regulation can rely on the legal authority of government to use force to implement its edicts. Whenever the achievement of, or at least the attempt to achieve, some purpose is deemed extremely important — for reasons we will examine shortly — the unique instrument, employed by government with legal authority, is called into service: the use, or threat of the use of force (for example, incarceration, fines, censure). Those who refuse to comply with the law as they carry on with their economic activities can be subjected, against their will, to arrest, punishment, or forfeiture (being deprived of the right to carry on).

All this is generally expected of legal measures in a society — they will be enforced. Murder, assault, and theft are deemed such serious misdeeds that to discourage them, and respond to them when they occur, severe punishment is called for. Mere verbal rebuke, ostracism, or even concerted boycott would be insufficient in response to such actions. This would be to do too little. On the othe hand, if someone fails to honor the mores and traditions of the community, for example, by being crude in personal habits, the behavior may evoke resentment and ostracism, but the individual will not be incarcerated or penalized with severe fines. This would be to do too much.

Government regulation of business is clearly deemed to be a needed official response to some otherwise legitimate activities. Such regulation addresses important social issues, as the more severe type of human response is involved in coping with those who fail to comply: Offenders are fined, imprisoned, and so forth. The crucial question for us is whether to allow such regulation is to do too much or whether to forgo it would be to do too little. More precisely, is government regulation of business, with its punitive implications, a morally justifiable way to deal with whatever is regarded as undesirable in society's economic affairs? A historical analogy might make this general question more intelligible. At one time the federal government was enlisted in the effort to stem the consumption and abuse of alcohol. Prohibition was the result and for a while the federal government engaged in the extensive use of its power to accomplish this purpose. It was widely believed to be justified for the government to undertake this task. Subsequently, for various reasons, the government was ordered, via the repeal of the law authorizing its actions against brewers, wine makers, liquor sellers, and so forth, to cease its policy of prohibition. The reasons for believing that government should prohibit alcohol production and consumption are not at issue, only that it was widely believed that it was justified in doing so. But that widely held belief was later rejected.

Perhaps government regulation of people's economic affairs is unjustified, in general, as was true in the case of prohibition in particular, even though it is widely accepted and believed to be justified. Perhaps the commerce clause of the United States Constitution should be repealed. Or perhaps the practice is indeed quite proper, representing neither too little nor too much by way of punitive regulation of commerce. It is to these matters that we will turn in the next section.

III. MORALITY AND REGULATION

§6 THE STRUCTURE OF MORAL ARGUMENTS FOR REGULATION

It was noted earlier that other possible reasons for government regulation can exist besides moral ones. Historians of business, labor, and law all could contribute to understanding the issues before us. But here the focus will be on the moral support for and objections to government regulation.

Debates over government regulation sometimes flounder because of a failure to distinguish between what for lack of a better way of putting it may be called management and regulation. Management can be understood as all those rules and directives that aim at guiding the utilization of public or state properties and funds. For example, in national forests some companies are allowed to engage in mining. But the companies do not own the mines, the public does. And the Bureau of Land Management decides the way the companies must conduct themselves in those areas. When governments administer the rules of highway travel and impose speed limits, place restrictions on the use of cars and motorcycles, forbid the use of bicycles, and so forth, this is not so much government regulation as the management or administration of the publicly owned spheres in a society. When, however, government sets down the rules for the advertising of eyeglasses or the manufacture of toys, no such public spheres and ownership are involved. There is no legal property right that government or the public asserts and has established in the manufacturing plants or the commodities being produced.

This is an important distinction. Ordinarily if someone owns something, that person is understood to have the right of use and disposal over the thing owned.[12] I can give away my tie, my car, or my home, or even destroy these if no one else is endangered in my doing so. If I lend you my money, I can put restrictions on its use, conditions under which you are able to obtain it from me, and so forth. When government lends money to students and requires that this money not be used in such objectionable ways as excluding blacks from enjoying the benefits, it is engaging not so much in government regulation of education as in the management or administration of the public treasury. Most affirmative action programs, whereby government requires colleges, universities, firms engaged in business with the government, and government bodies themselves to seek to aid members of groups that have suffered injustices in the past, are again not so much cases of government regulation as self-regulation or the adoption of administrative rules for running the government itself and the funds paid into it by all taxpayers.[13]

True, in popular discussions this distinction is not often made. That is partly because people tend to lump together support for (and opposition to) government taking any sort of jurisdiction of some areas of concern in society, whether government outright nationalizes (assumes ownership of) the area or merely regulates it. But different arguments either support or raise objections to government ownership, on the one hand, and government regulation, on the other. It may be that government should not appropriate many of the spheres that it in fact has appropriated, but that does not prove that it should not regulate these spheres. Perhaps the forests should not be *owned* by the government, yet it could be true that government should *regulate* what people and companies do in privately owned forests. The Federal Communications Commission administers the use of the broadcast airwaves — the electromagnetic spectrum. The federal government acquired this realm by senatorial declaration in 1927, and broadcasters such as NBC, ABC, and CBS are merely tenants who must reapply for their leases periodically. They do not own the frequencies on which they operate. And the FCC is charged, by Congress, with the responsibility of administrating this public property *in the public interest*. To speak precisely, therefore, much of so-called "government regulation" of broadcasting is the administration or management of public property for the benefit of the public, "in the public interest." Such measures as the "fairness doctrine" or the "equal time rule," both under constant criticism from broadcasters, amount to what in the law is called restrictive covenants — conditions placed by the leasor on the leasee regarding the occupancy of what is being leased. Questions can be raised whether governments should ever own airways, roads, parks, beaches, forests, or the postal system, but these are distinct from questions about whether government regulation of *privately owned* businesses is morally justified.[14]

It is not always easy to detect the distinction between government regulation and government management or administration. To show legal basis for government regulatory activities, defenders of such regulation often make their case by reference to alleged state interest. For example, in opposition to recent efforts to compel restaurateurs in California to establish smoking and non-smoking areas, restaurant owners protested on grounds that this would be an invasion of their private property rights. Advocates of the measure noted, in turn, that restaurants are located on public streets and are licensed by the government. This means that restaurants are unavoidably connected with publicly owned spheres. From this some would infer that regulating them is merely an extension of the government's responsibility to manage its own spheres properly.

However difficult it is to disentangle private from public property, this kind of argument would render the private-public distinction entirely specious. No area of human life could be seen as protected from government management or administration, Bill of Rights or no Bill of Rights, if the justification for government intervention turned on an activity's being connected with a "publicly owned sphere." After all, when a person criticizes the United States government, advocates communism or fascism, or rails against the FBI, the CIA, or even the practice of government regulation, that person is probably in a place that can only be reached by driving or walking the public streets.

There is one final distinction that it will be useful to keep in mind. Various government regulatory bodies actually engage in the administration of fairly distinctive judicial disputes as well. Not only the practice of brokerage firms as they advertise their services or trade stocks, but outright fraud and embezzlement could come under the jurisdiction of the Securities and Exchange Commission. Rules against insider trading — taking advantage of special knowledge for personal gain while also engaging in serving customers — are different from outright fraud, yet both are dealt with by the SEC. The Federal Trade Commission, too, has assumed jurisdiction in the handling of commercial fraud alongside its purely regulatory functions, such as setting rules for the conduct of mail-order shopping.[15]

It was important to stress as precisely as possible the question at issue. What needs to be examined is whether any kind of *genuine* government regulation of any business activity is morally justifiable, at least under normal circumstances. With any social norm there can be exceptions to the most advisable policy in unusual circumstances; we will consider farther on whether such exceptions might be acceptable even if, in usual circumstances, government regulation of business is unjustified. If *some* genuine regulation can be morally defended, as the normal policy in the continuing socioeconomic life of a human community, then there cannot be anything wrong *in principle* with regulating business. On the other hand, if no regulation can be justified as the normal approach to handling problems, then such regulation may well be simply wrong in principle.

Various arguments are available to those who favor government regulation. Though not all of them can be examined here, those that will be are among the most important. All have a common structure, which can be generally characterized as follows:

1. There are certain moral values or principles, these agruments contend, that ought to be respected by a society's economic system.
2. The values or principles, it is claimed, can only be respected if some aspects of a society's economic activity are regulated.
3. Thus, these arguments conclude, some aspects of a society's economic activity ought to be regulated.

Proponents of regulation can differ over *what* principles or values a society's economic life ought to foster as well as what aspects of this life ought to be regulated. Differ though they may in these regards, however, all proponents of regulation agree that it is only by having recourse to regulation that the values or principles they favor can be adequately respected. All defenses of regulation thus have both a normative and a practical or factual component. Normatively they insist on affirming that certain values are worth pursuing or that the observation of certain principles is to be made compulsory for moral reasons, even if this requires limitations on liberty, including business activities, by means of regulation. The practical component consists in the claim that, as a matter of fact, these values or principles will be adequately respected only if government regulates business in certain respects.

The strength of any defense offered for regulation clearly depends on the credibility of both the normative and the factual components. If a given defense fails to make a persuasive case for the values or principles it favors, it will fail as a defense for normative reasons, whereas if it fails to show that, as a matter of fact (judging by past history and sound theory), regulation is necessary if these values or principles are to be respected adequately, it will fail because of its practical unfeasibility. As we shall see in what follows, the leading defenses of regulation fail sometimes for one, sometimes for the other, sometimes for both reasons.

Three defenses can be distinguished: (1) the defense based on ideals; (2) the defense based on utility; and (3) the defense based on rights. Each will be considered, in the order just given.

§7 THE DEFENSE BASED ON IDEALS

One of the earliest and most influential defenses of government intervention, including regulation, is offered by the economist John Maynard Keynes (1883–1946). Conceiving, as he did, of a free-market system along lines usually attributed to Herbert Spencer[16] — that is, as a rather crude version of social Darwinism, where only "the strong" survive — Keynes gave the following characterization of laissez-faire. The idea, he said,

> implies that there must be no mercy or protection for those who embark their capital or their labor in the wrong direction. It is a method of bringing the most successful profit-makers to the top by a ruthless struggle for survival, which selects the most efficient by the bankruptcy of the less efficient. It does not count the cost of the struggle, but looks only to the benefits of the final result which are assumed to be lasting and permanent, once it has been attained. The object of life being to crop the leaves off the branches up to the greatest possible height, the likeliest way of achieving this end is to leave the giraffes with the longest necks to starve out those whose necks are shorter.[17]

The polemics aside, this passage suggests a clear moral argument in favor of abandoning laissez-faire. The moral reason is that the unregulated free market lacks valuable human sentiments, that such a method of arranging a community's economic affairs fosters callousness or insensitivity toward the plight of those who fail in the economic struggle or who, for one reason or another, are unable to take part. A lack of compassion for one's competitors may be acceptable in the jungle but not in human society. Morally, people who are sensitive and compassionate are better people than those who are insensitive and callous. Since these human ideals are destroyed by unregulated business, and since the only way to foster them is to regulate it, such regulation is justified.

Does the unregulated free market in fact lack compassion and foster callousness toward those who fail in the economic struggle or who cannot take part? To a large extent, this is a historical claim, one that is not easy to test. Certainly by many popular accounts, whatever version of laissez-faire capitalism existed in England and the United States during the early 1880s did produce vast numbers of hungry, overworked, and disheartened people. There were booms and busts throughout the markets of these societies, involving unemployment, financial crises, bankruptcies. There was also, in the midst of widespread misery, opulence of such magnitude as to be morally offensive. Granting these large disparities in the quality of life, and ignoring the fact that, prior to the onset of the era of laissez-faire, people in general fared much worse and many died before they could experience unemployment and financial crises, it is difficult to determine whether it was laissez-faire capitalism that was the cause. Serious scholarly disagreement exists on the topic, and Keynes' opinions are not universally shared among social and economic historians. For example, while many attribute the phenomenon of the robber barons (monopolistic business tycoons who wielded enormous economic power over others who were economically dependent upon them, from workers to neighboring small businesses) to laissez-faire, others attribute the robber baron's ascendency to the fact that laissez-faire was not pure enough.[18] It was government intervention, not the workings of the free market, that helped these people attain their exclusive economic power. It was government dispensations, in the form of special protection to some against the forces of competition, that gave privileged protection to the barons' wealth and thus enabled them to engage in monopolistic practices, thereby driving competitors to the brink of disaster. The railroads, for example, gained enormous power as a result of the earliest federal subsidy program, a program that not only made it unnecessary for the people in the industry to raise their own capital through normal business channels but also allowed several lines to forgo bargaining with landowners for rights-of-way because the government gave the owners money from the federal treasury and exercised the right of eminent domain—taking for public use—on behalf of the railroads. Such government protectionism was, of course, carried out in part because government officials believed that the railroads did a valuable public service—for example, built a transcontinental line. Nevertheless, the prior government intervention distorted the laissez-faire character of the society sufficiently to call into serious question Keynes' picture.

Neither must the hardships often associated with industrial capitalism, especially during its early days—child labor, sweat shops, long working days, unsanitary working conditions, repetitive work, lack of adequate health facilities and safety provisions—be laid at the door of laissez-faire capitalism. Only if it could be shown that government regulation, or some more or less socialized market, would have eliminated or lessened these hardships at this time would there be justice in identifying the free market, even in its compromised form, as the cause. But there is evidence — scholarship, at least — that disputes that early industrial capitalism, with its partial laissez-faire structure, fared worse in these respects than did other social systems at the time and, especially, earlier. And in comparison to existing alternative economic systems in our own time, the more or less free-market capitalist systems of Western industrial societies appear to be in better shape than all others concerning the oft-lamented features of laissez-faire Keynes makes reference to.

Finally, even if it is admitted that laissez-faire will produce some cases of neglect of the helpless and the weak, whether government regulation should be introduced to remedy this depends in part on whether government regulation will in fact produce the needed remedies without producing comparable problems. This point is often expressed by reference to the purported exchange of market failures for political failures. If it is demonstrable, as many economists (for example, Sam Peltzman, Thomas Gale More, Milton Friedman) claim it is, that on the whole the measurable costs of government regulation — including the estimated loss of lives, injuries produced, and labor and capital expended — exceed the estimable benefits of the practice (greater safety of the drugs actually allowed on the market, better health for the workers who do obtain jobs, more security for investors who do employ brokers, and so forth) then despite the problems of laissez-faire, government regulation does not seem to offer an adequate solution.

The preceding objections contest the practical elements of Keynes' criticism and suggested alternative. The normative point Keynes makes concerning the moral intolerability of a system that proposes "to leave the giraffes with the longest necks to starve out those whose necks are shorter" may also be contested. Notice, first, that nothing in principle prevents people in a laissez-faire system from lending a helping hand to the unfortunate or the helpless. Because such a system respects the ideal of liberty in general, it respects that ideal in this regard also, and it is highly questionable whether, under an essentially democratic system of government, anything better could be achieved by political coercion. Charity and benevolence, much extolled by Keynes, are not foreign to laissez-faire capitalism, judging by available statistics.[19]

Notice, next, that Keynes mischaracterizes the losers in the marketplace. First, the competition in the market is not like that in a boxing ring, where (normally) there is only one winner and one loser, but rather like that in a marathon race. Between the one at the end and the one up front, there are as many positions as there are participants, many bunched together very close to the front, others a bit behind, some alone in the middle, and so forth. Second, those who do fall far behind are not all "helpless victims." Some are careless, negligent, lazy, slothful, overcome with a greed that sabotages their prudence, or otherwise "victims" of their own character flaws. The analogy with the jungle makes it appear that in human societies those who are losers do not deserve their fate, because the jungle houses dumb animals who are victims of their fate — genes, environment, the comparative physical advantage of their fellow beasts, and so forth. But among human beings another factor needs to be made room for. Human beings are capable of making good and bad choices in their conduct, and they are not helpless when they make the bad ones or the good ones. While no doubt some are unfortunate, indeed totally unprepared — for example, those who are severely crippled, utterly deprived, or abjectly mistreated (sometimes by fellow citizens, sometimes by family, sometimes by the government itself) — most others are probably better regarded as capable of either making the effort or failing to make the effort to make a good showing in "the struggle for survival." Those who can make the effort but fail to do so do not deserve the compassion Keynes seems to believe everyone who fails to succeed deserves. Third, even if it is true that some who fail are helpless and it is the moral responsibility of others to help them, there are serious moral objections to requiring that assistance be given under the threat of force. In morality it is not generally possible that any act of compassion, kindness, generosity, honesty, decency, and so forth be undertaken unfreely, under coercion. Rather, moral conduct must be undertaken as a matter of conscience and free choice; otherwise the act loses its moral worth. A society that forces its citizens, under the threat of punishment, to help the less fortunate, is less, not more, compassionate. Even granting, then, in concert with Keynes, that compassion is a noble human trait, it does not follow that coercive regulation of human behavior fosters its development. Indeed, just the opposite conclusion should be reached.

It might also be observed here that a free society — of which free-market capitalism is a consequence in view of the legal protection and preservation of individual autonomy in all spheres of human life — does not in the least have to take the shape that Keynes assumes it must. There is no requirement, only the freedom, to engage in constant competition in such a society. Also, while it may be true that competition in the economic realm is valuable — involving, as it does, the seeking of more efficient production of goods and services that human beings need and want (most often with all justification, given their own life projects) — it does not follow that competition needs to or will be exported into other realms (science, art, family life, friendship, neighborliness, and so forth). With sufficient pedagogy concerning this matter, the free society would very likely present a balanced picture concerning competition, not the extreme one Keynes puts forth.

§8 THE UTILITARIAN DEFENSE

In response to the deficiencies of the defense based on ideals, it might be argued that what matters is what people do, not why they do it. If one person benefits another out of compassion or generosity, then the presence of these motives makes that person morally admirable, no doubt, but "the virtue of the agent" should be kept distinct from "the virtue of the act"; that is, appraising the morality of what we do (the acts we perform) should be kept distinct from appraising the morality of why we do it (our motives or intentions). That much granted, what is crucial to the defense of government regulation of business, it might be claimed, is a standard that evaluates acts, not motives.

The Principle of Utility provides a standard of this kind. The morality of what we do is to be determined, according to this principle, by the over-all effects this has on the welfare or happiness of those affected by the outcome. On this view, then, government regulation of business would be justified if such regulation brought about better consequences than would result in its absence. In principle, a utilitarian could argue that government should regulate everything, if this was optimizing (that is, if unchecked regulation produced the best results, all things considered). In practice, however, those enamored of the Principle of Utility take a more selective position, arguing only that some, not all, human activities should be regulated by government. The contemporary economist Kenneth Arrow is representative of this more restricted utilitarian position, and his views may be taken as a working example of the utilitarian defense of government regulation.

Like other economists, Arrow tends to eschew making explicit appeals to normative principles. Like others in his field, however, Arrow takes a utilitarian approach to questions of policy decisions, an approach that measures the desirability of any given policy in terms of the contribution it makes to the maximum satisfaction of desires in a society. Since most economists tend to assume that value judgments are meaningful only if they refer to something measurable, the theoretical ideal called Pareto-optimality looms large in the background of their thought. According to this ideal, a society has achieved maximum satisfaction of desires if no one can be made better off without thereby making someone else worse off, the judgment of "better off" and "worse off" to be determined by consulting the preferences of the individuals involved. That is, each individual is the sole and final judge of what is valuable for that individual. Although no one supposes that this ideal of maximum satisfaction will ever be fully realized, the idea that this ideal should guide public policy is quite prominent. Because, given this approach, what people value is what they prefer, and because what they prefer is measurable by determining how they behave, statements about what each person values are meaningful and confirmable. There is, then, no theoretical objection to holding up the utilitarian standard of Pareto-optimality as a bona-fide standard for assessing the moral wisdom of alternative policies. To defend government regulation by reference to this standard, therefore, all that is necessary is to show that regulation will produce results that are closer to achieving Pareto-optimality than the results that would be obtained without it.

Arrow evidently believes that this is true sometimes in the case of government regulation. In a recent essay, "Two Cheers for Government Regulation," he writes as follows:

> For various reasons, it has long been a staple argument among economists that the resulting allocation [in the private sector or free market], while efficient in many areas, will fail in some. The most obvious are the goods that serve society as a whole — defense, justice, police, most roads. . . . More broadly, there are . . . cases in which public intervention, not necessarily expenditure, is necessary to change the way in which resources are used. Take the example of environmental hazards, particularly air- and waterborne pollution. Dumping wastes in a stream may ruin fisheries; this loss should, in a proper economic accounting, be charged against the dumper, but it is impractical to do so. Thus the public must intervene in some way, either by charging the dumper for the costs imposed on others or by regulations. The effects of pollution fall not merely on production but also on comfort, health, and life. . . . I think that while regulation has gone too far or been misdirected in some areas — such as occupational safety — it has probably not gone far enough in those of chemical handling and waste disposal.[20]

When Arrow mentions that the private sector makes efficient allocation possible in many areas but not in others, the measure of efficiency must be the degree to which Pareto-optimality has been achieved — that is, whether the market, given reasonable estimates, has led to greater satisfaction of desires than would result otherwise. This is not true in other cases, in Arrow's view; in particular, it is not true in the case of "defense, justice, police, most roads"; in their case Pareto-optimality justifies government intervention. And the same is true in cases of "environmental hazards, particularly air- and waterborne pollution."

These defenses of government regulation misfire. Arrow views defense, justice, and police as "the goods that serve society as a whole" and thinks that these goods are better provided by governments than by free enterprise. Though some economists would dispute even this, the central point to notice is that these goods do not appear to be economic goods at all, even though some economic problems and activities may be associated with securing them. One simple way to make this clearer is to recall that defense, justice, and police are actually presupposed in the very conception of a free economy; that is, a free market is not possible without those who take part in it agreeing voluntarily to have these goods in place. Defense, justice, and police are not products of the free market, but conditions that make it possible. It cannot be an objection to the free market, any more than it can be an argument for government regulation of business in the market, to argue that the goods that are necessary for the market are not themselves efficiently supplied by the market. A free market presupposes a system of private property rights, and thus a system of justice conceived along certain lines (that is, by reference to a given theory of individual human rights). The government of a laissez-faire capitalist society is established in part to uphold this system of justice, to defend it from foreign aggression, and to enforce, via the police, its edicts (for example, to arrest thieves or violators of property rights). Without this system and the goods Arrow speaks of, no free market is even possible except accidentally. An objection to Arrow's thesis then would be that *of course* the market is inefficient in doing what it could not even embark on doing since the free market presupposes the doing of that thing for its own operations. (It might be noted that the securing of the goods Arrow lists first—defense, justice, police—is not an economic or commercial but a political problem, a problem, as one might naturally put it, of eternal vigilance.)

But aside from these political goods, what about "most roads . . . environmental hazards, etc."? Is it a fact that these goods could not be efficiently produced by the market? Perhaps we cannot really know, though some precedent exists for the idea, both in practice and in theory.[21] Even if roads could not be produced on the scale presently available, however, it is questionable whether this is something inefficient about the market. Given the massive pollution that automobile travel has created, and given that governments (from local to federal) have built most of the roads, partly as a matter of encouraging automobile travel, the question is not academic. It is entirely arguable that had the free market been left to produce roads without government subsidies, while some people might not have been so readily accommodated, on pure Pareto-optimality grounds the result would have been efficient enough. As to the issue of managing the environment, here we encounter the problem of mixing government regulation with government management of public resources (see §4). The air, lakes, rivers, oceans, beaches, and so forth are rarely privately owned, even where they could be (sometimes because of egalitarian measures intended to redistribute their availability). Free-market-oriented environmentalists have argued that any time private property rights can be legally established, the market is more efficient than regulation would be, although the point is difficult to prove. Alternative approaches to regulation, such as tort law, criminal charges for dumping wastes, and similar legal measures, would have to be forced and contrasted with the familiar regulatory mechanisms in order to see whether Arrow's claim about efficiency is true. Where property rights are not feasible—for example, in the airmass—Arrow's recommendation seems sound, but not for purely utilitarian reasons. Rather it is because no "proper economic accounting" is possible without some kind of government management in such realms. So-called regulation would in such cases be a mere substitute for desirable but unfeasible judicial handling of problems of allocation, use, usurpation of rights, and so forth.

From the utilitarian viewpoint, then, the practical points Arrow offers do not provide compelling support for the ordinary sort of government regulation. Arrow himself seems to notice this when he thinks "regulation has gone too far or been misdirected in some areas—such as occupational safety."

To this point we have confined our criticisms of Arrow's ideas to the factual component in his position—the claim that government intervention produces results that better approximate Pareto-optimality than would the results produced by the workings of the free market. Let us now consider the normative component Arrow and many other economists implicity accept—namely, the utilitarian standard of Pareto-optimality. The attractiveness of this view for social scientists should be clear enough. What we are to aim at is maximum satisfaction of preferences, with preferences to be determined by how people behave when they are given the freedom to choose what they want. Public policy decisions, when based on the preferences people reveal through their behavior, give such normative decisions, we are supposed to believe, a basis in fact.

There are theoretical problems at the root of the idea of Pareto-optimality (for example, whether it is meaningful to make interpersonal preference comparisons). We shall not pursue these matters. Here it is enough to observe that, even without an extensively worked-out alternative normative standard, it seems highly questionable that morality should come to no more than "giving people what they want." Suppose that people prefer to purchase pet rocks or Rubik Cubes instead of fostering education, medical facilities, the arts, or science? Would it not seem odd for public policy to be directed toward the production of pet rocks and Rubik Cubes rather than education and health care? Pareto-optimality puts too much trust in the wisdom of individual preference.

In reply it could be said that it is not just what people happen to prefer that is decisive. As Arrow states, "When it comes to economic rather than moral goods, there is no legitimate criterion of policy other than giving people what they want, *or should want if they are properly informed.*"[22] Thus, even assuming that most people happened to prefer pet rocks and Rubik Cubes to arts and letters, it would not follow, given this kind of utilitarian approach to assessing government policy, that the government ought to accede to the preferences of the masses. For though the majority want these things, it is, by Arrow's assumptions, clearly arguable that they would not want them, or should not, if they were properly informed.

But now there is a problem—namely, whether we can possibly measure or establish what people would or should want if they were properly informed. It looks quite hopeless, judged on the methodological grounds at issue (that is, given the assumption that preferences—values—must be quantifiable and thus measurable, if they are to be meaningful). One looks for a theory to measure "what people would or should want, if . . ." and finds none. Moreover, since one virtue generally conceded to the free market is that it communicates information better than any centralized system of economic management would make possible (for example, between consumers and producers),[23] one must also wonder what more information one could reasonably hope to have so as to provide "proper" information.

Even if these criticisms could be overcome—for example, by reference to some idea that what individuals "would or should want, if . . ." can be determined by having experts manage the regulatory process—a defense of government regulation based on what people would or should want, if fully informed, is almost certain to open a paternalistic Pandora's box, one that would have implications that clash with many values that even avid supporters of government regulation of business would not wish to sacrifice, for example, civil liberties that disallow search and seizure. Already quite a few government regulatory measures are seen to be a threat to certain cherished values, such as privacy. Banking regulations, for instance, require that banks make a report of any transaction involving checks over one hundred dollars so that the government may inspect the financial records of citizens who have not been proven to have committed any crimes. City building inspectors are allowed to enter private property with no need of a warrant to investigate whether a home is built in conformity to the building code. Various businesses are subject to on-the-spot, unannounced inspections by agents of OSHA—the Occupational Safety and Health Administration. While many supporters of government regulation dismiss such concerns as alarmist, it is quite arguable that such powerful tools in the hands of government are always a temptation for abuse and should not be placed at the disposal of governments in the first place.

§9 THE DEFENSE BASED ON RIGHTS

A utilitarian defense of government regulation of business, as we saw in the preceding paragraph, has implications that clash with well-considered beliefs about the worth, integrity, and autonomy of the individual. These notions—individual worth, integrity, and autonomy—are allied, both historically and logically, with the idea that people have basic moral rights, including, for example, the rights to life, liberty, and the pursuit of happiness. None of these ideas is simple, and the philosophical case for recognizing the validity of the worth of persons and individual rights is not simple either. We shall have more to say on these matters later (and see §6). The essential point to note at this juncture is how the introduction of the idea of the worth and rights of the individual simply will not and, indeed, cannot find a place in the standard utilitarian cost-benefit analysis favored by many economists. Benefits, according to this approach, are to be measured by what people prefer (or would prefer, if properly informed), while costs are reducible to what people would prefer to do without or avoid (or what they would prefer to do without or avoid, if they were properly informed). The kind of value (or worth) individuals have, however, is not just one benefit competing among other benefits. Your worth as a person is not reducible to whether you happen to be the object of my preference, or of anyone's preference. Your value as a person, in other words, is not to be thought of in terms of whether you are liked, admired, wanted, or valued by anyone. As a person, you have a kind of value that is independent of whether you happen to be the object of anyone's interests. As a person, therefore, the kind of value you have is not reducible to the preferences of others, so that your value will not and cannot show up in any cost-benefit analysis.

The public policy scientist — and former Federal Trade Commission staffer — Steven Kelman has been a persistent critic of cost-benefit analyses for this very reason. Consider the case where some people are injured or harmed by others. "Since the costs of injury are borne by its victims," Kelman contends, "while its benefits are reaped by its perpetrators, simple cost-benefit calculations may be less important than more abstract conceptions of justice, fairness and human dignity."[24] Developing this theme more fully, Kelman writes as follows:

> We would not condone a rape even if it could be demonstrated that the rapist derived enormous pleasure from his actions, while the victim suffered in only small ways. Behind the conception of "rights" is the notion that some concept of justice, fairness or human dignity demands that individuals ought to be able to perform certain acts, despite the harm to others, and ought to be protected against certain acts, despite the loss this causes to the would-be perpetrator. Thus we undertake no cost-benefit analysis of the effects of freedom of speech or trial by jury before allowing them to continue.[25]

The introduction of the ideas of individual dignity and rights in place of cost-benefit analysis means that government regulation of business, if it is morally proper, cannot be justified in the way utilitarians assume. Might it be justified if human rights and dignity are taken into account? Kelman, for one, thinks so, as does Joan Claybrook, former National Highway Transportation administrator. "What about the rights of individuals to breathe clean air, to drink clean water, to secure drugs and food that do not have unnecessary side effects or cause illness, to have a job that does not foster cancer, to drive an automobile without unnecessary exposure to death or crippling injury? These are rights of the citizenry which regulation is designed to defend."[26] In other words, if an unregulated market would violate these rights of the citizenry, then the market should be regulated. And the market should be regulated, not because doing so will bring about better consequences for everyone affected by the outcome (the utilitarian cost-benefit approach), and not because such regulation will foster certain preferred human character traits (the defense based on ideals approach), but because regulation is necessary to insure that consumer rights are not crushed under the wheels of unbridled free enterprise.

Two questions jump out at us. The first is whether people have the sort of rights championed by those who argue for regulation based on rights — the right to "jobs that do not foster cancer," for example. The second is whether, assuming that they have them, there is any reason to believe that an unregulated market would violate these rights, or violate them to any greater extent than a government-regulated market. This latter question is a question of fact — though a difficult one. The former is a normative question. Thus, our assessment of the rights defense of regulation parallels the structure of the earlier discussions of the utilitarian and ideal defenses. The factual question will be examined first.

Does the marketplace violate individual rights? The answer depends on what rights individuals in fact have. Kelman and Claybrook seem to hold that individuals have rights to be spared all sorts of mishaps and protected against all manner of risks. This is highly disputable, a point explored more fully below. However, even if they are correct in supposing that we have such rights, it is unlikely that government regulation is the best way to protect them. In general, there is no reason to assume that the motivations of people in government, from legislators to those who implement and enforce policy, are any more free from vulnerability to temptations than are the motivations of market agents. The "profit motive" is often said to induce great predilection for negligence and lack of care. But are there not equally powerful motivations operating on politicians and bureaucrats to engender "gross abuses"? And since politicians and bureaucrats have at their disposal not only the freedom of the marketplace, as do people in business and industry, but also the legal use of punitive force or its threat, it is arguable that, all things being equal, gross abuses of government power would violate more rights than the free market. Thus, even if the rights claimed by Kelman and Claybrook are accepted as among the rights that individuals possess, there is serious reason to doubt that government regulation could on the whole provide more or better protection for individual rights than the protection offered by a free market.

In response it might be claimed that since people are selfish and greedy,[27] erecting an economic system run by "the profit motive" merely plays into the hands of selfishness and greed, with the predictable result that an unregulated market will violate many more rights than a government-regulated economy. For example, greed is likely to engender recklessness, negligence, even cruelty and callousness. What is called the public interest or the common good is also threatened by such a system, and individual rights as conceived by Kelman and Claybrook will be violated with abandon. But this defense of regulation dies by its own hands. If people are selfish and greedy, as this defense contends, then their selfishness and greed will merely show up at a different place in a regulated market — namely, in the offices of politicians and special-interest groups who stand to gain by abuses of government regulation itself, just as it is contended that business and industry will abuse the marketplace. If persons are selfish and greedy as a general, persistent trait (instead of merely now and then, off and on, depending on goodwill that is just as probable as its opposite), it does not appear that this could be eradicated by passing regulatory statutes and by creating government agencies.

But assume for a moment that this objection could be met and somehow the conduct of politicians and bureaucrats could be made safe from the sort of abuse claimed to be widespread in the marketplace. Defenders of government regulation would still be obliged to explain why business should be regulated, in the name of protection of rights, but not other human institutions (for example, religion, the press, art, and even family life, all of which are vital features of human social life). If, as defenders of regulation maintain, people have a right to have their welfare protected against "gross abuses that the marketplace does not correct," why does this same protection not extend to government regulation of news reporting, writing novels, making movies, and so forth? Why should someone who chooses plumbing or toy-making as a profession be subjected to various government edicts, inspection procedures, and so forth, while those working in the printed news media or publishing are exempt?

One answer might be that the professions of news reporting or publishing are special. Indeed, since these professions involve perhaps the most delicate and precious faculty of human living — namely, the creative mind — and carry out some of the most highly prized human activities, such as the search for truth and the creation of beauty, these activities should not be subjected to coercive political direction. This line of defense of discrimination in favor of some professions is probably based on the time-honored tradition, with roots in ancient Greece, according to which the human mind, spirit, or intellect is regarded as more noble and worthy than the more materialistic aspects of human existence. The human spirit, mind, or intellect is often viewed as something special, something extraordinary and unique to human life, and, as befits its uniqueness as the priceless jewel in the crown of our humanity, as a power meriting special consideration in its various manifestations. Thus are we allowed to regulate business, which is "material," but not art and letters, which are "spiritual."

It is important to note, first, that this argument could just as well support more rather than less political control of the press, arts, and publishing. Such totalitarian politics would suggest that if the search for truth is so vital, it should be guarded or regulated even more carefully than making toys or barbering. But even if we accept that a vital human activity requires greater liberty for those who engage in it, the view that the spiritual, mental, or intellectual aspects of human life are more important than what some regard as the more mundane aspects, such as production, trade, or advertising, is open to challenge. Human beings are, let us agree, unique in being intelligent, rational beings, with minds (or spirits, if you will). But they are, also, living, biological entities. That fact is no less important, even though not unique. Without ample regard for medicine, housing, psychological and sexual welfare, and so forth, human life would be at least as impoverished as it would be without adequate concern for pure science, literature, philosophy, and the arts. It is arguable that the tradition of separating human beings into two parts, the mind and the body, celebrating the former and denigrating the latter—for example, when people's sexual desires were treated as something base and degrading—wrought ill not only for the body but also for the mind.

Instead of accepting the elitist view that some aspects of human life (namely, those having to do with the mind, intellect, or spirit) are more noble than the rest and so should be above government regulation, a less cumbersome and humanely democratic or egalitarian view recommends itself. This is to regard human beings as integrated, whole beings, important through and through, a view that requires a consistent regulatory approach to all human professions in place of the selective regulation of only some professions that characterizes present democratic free markets. If business is to be regulated, why not ballet?

In reply it might be claimed that some human endeavors are so important that government regulation is necessary. Consumer health often is touted as such a concern, as witness Claybrook's claim that people have a right "to secure drugs and food that do not have unnecessary side effects or cause illness." Claybrook's view is not eccentric. Studies referred to by Kelman verify that people are overwhelmingly in favor of government regulation and inspection in the areas of food and drugs.[28] But majority sentiment can be mistaken, and it often has been, prompting such political scientists as the Founding Fathers to guard against unlimited power for majorities. So let us ask whether the public's legitimate interest in consumer health warrants government regulation of food and drugs.

To consider this point we must ask, first, whether it is true that the marketplace fails to eliminate significant health risks. But a full answer would require extensive statistical work, more difficult even than might be supposed initially. This is because for years government has promised to reduce the risks in the marketplace, and the marketplace—that is, the system of interacting firms, corporations, factories, business executives, foremen, shop stewards, carpenters, exterminators, and others involved in commerce—may well have accommodated itself to that promise. Regulation may well have preempted the efforts of those who would have been ready and willing to help reduce significant health risks on their own.

For instance, even today some businesses regulate themselves so as to avoid unnecessary risks. For one, that is a condition for getting better insurance rates. When banks refuse to serve walk-up customers at their drive-up windows, the risk of accidents between pedestrians and cars is reduced; banks that observe this policy in turn receive lower rates from insurance companies as a reward. Such non-governmental regulation does reduce significantly the risk of material health impairment. But when governments take over the field and promise to achieve the same thing, the incentive to do this via the marketplace clearly diminishes. True, if government regulation managed to achieve what it set out to, its record would probably be impressive, but the "cure" of goverment regulation is very frequently worse than the "disease" it is called upon to treat. For example, a recent Brookings Institute study, *The Scientific Basis of Health and Safety Regulation*,[29] demonstrates that scientific findings *are ignored* in all of the five cases of government regulation the authors selected for scrutiny. Are we seriously to suppose that the public's concern about health is served by regulatory mechanisms that ignore the scientific assessment of regulation's implications?

Aside from the difficulty of assessing the success of government regulation, there is evidence from some work on the topic that what government regulation achieves in the way of risk reduction can be achieved by way of a combination of (1) market services for this purpose, and (2) the judicial system, with its ex post facto rather than preemptive approach to actual product liability, pollution, and work safety cases. I merely mention this here, suggesting only that this factual point, too, is open to serious dispute.[30]

The second question we must consider concerns what rights individuals have. This is a difficult question, again, one that will not receive a complete airing on this occasion. Kelman and Claybrook seem to have more than a fair share of confidence about what rights people have, including rights to innumerable deeds and services—for example, not to suffer because of their own mistakes, protection from risks involved in contemporary life. Kelman argues this explicitly when he says that "if a person gets sick or injured, or if he dies, because he purchased an unsafe product, clearly his action in buying the product had external effects on friends and loved ones."[31] The suggestion here is that when these effects are untoward, the friends and loved ones should be viewed as having been deprived or harmed unjustly. Kelman even believes in the duty to render Good Samaritan aid, or so it appears, when he claims that "the person who sees a fire starting in a building and goes on his way without calling the fire department is hardly in a position to say that his failure to act had no external effects."[32] Indeed, Kelman and Claybrook seem to assume that *others have a right, which may even be enforced* (judging by what Kelman and Claybrook infer from their assertion of this right), to the services of such a bystander.

This line of reasoning appears very promising at first, until we consider that Kelman assumes, without argument, that all of us have enforceable duties or legal obligations to help other people and to prevent others from suffering adverse consequences of their own risky associations and actions. *And* they have rights against us in this regard. Such a view threatens to cheapen the idea of individual rights. People who associate with others may wish to enjoy risk-free associations, but do they have a right to a "riskless" life? As long as no contract to avoid risk has been entered into, it is unlikely that simple human associations must involve the security government is asked (by Kelman) to provide against mishaps and even negligence, as a matter of the individual rights of the citizenry. Some kind of "external effect" can be associated with virtually any action we take, especially when we have close personal ties. Kelman himself notes that "if I choose to patronize one business, my action has an effect on other businesses that lose my patronage."[33] But this "effect" is quite ambiguous. The mere truth that I could have gone to the other business but did not is taken by Kelman as having produced an effect. By that line of reasoning any action anyone takes in some respect deprives those who would have benefited if another option had been taken. But, of course, *someone else* would have been deprived *if* another option had been selected. Are we to suppose that we violate someone's rights no matter what we do—or don't do? Such a view is preposterous. In the kind of cases Kelman seems to have in mind—such as not patronizing some business—no injury is done. No one's rights are violated for the simple reason that no one has the rights Kelman seeks to defend.[34]

It is true, of course, that Kelman could fall back on some recent and ancient moral theories to claim some support for holding that we are all bound together by enforceable duties. His view in fact seems to take to the extreme the doctrine of justice-as-fairness made prominent recently by John Rawls.[35] There is some suggestion in that doctrine that, if several ethnic restaurants are available for patronage in one's neighborhood, one's choosing to eat only at one of these is unfair and should be regulated so as to promote justice. But it is very likely that this view flies in the face of the equally plausible doctrine that each person has exclusive jurisdiction over his or her own life, a life that is unavailable, as a matter of morality, for others to make use of as they would wish. Given the plausibility of the extreme priority of personal moral autonomy—the view that persons are *ends* in themselves, not *means* for the promotion of others' well-being (certainly not by force)—the Kelman-Claybrook defense of regulation because an unregulated market violates individual rights no longer carries conviction. If we had the rights they claim on our behalf, there is no good reason to believe that a free market would violate them more often than one that is regulated. And since there is no good reason to believe that we have the extensive rights they claim on our behalf, a defense of regulation based on their position is worse than no defense at all.

§10 WHY REGULATION IS WRONG

I wish now to propose that government regulation of business is, despite some very appealing grounds given in its support, morally wrong. If I am right, deregulation should commence. At any rate, in coming to grips with the issue of whether business should be regulated, the following reflections should be taken seriously.

The points I will raise are, as in the Kelman-Claybrook approach, related to a consideration of human rights. It seems to me that when we appreciate what rights there are, including various types of rights, we should conclude that government regulation is an impermissible violation of people's most basic rights.

There are three distinct types of rights—natural, special, and acquired—each with distinct moral implications for human life and institutions. *Natural rights* are entitlements to liberty (from other's intrusion or forcible interference), which, if we have them, are possessed simply because we are beings who can act autonomously, independently, of our own free will. Such rights are not created by the law. On the contrary, a just society will base its legal systems on these rights and establish the means for their protection and preservation. *Special rights* are almost as firm but obtain selectively, holding, for example, between parents and children. Given the special characteristics of children, as more or less young human beings, and given how they came into the world — by virtue of the voluntary actions of their parents — certain rights and duties emerge when children are born, involving both parties to the relationship. Such special rights may perhaps extend to other members of families; thus, one may have duties to next of kin which one may not have to others (for example, to care for them when they are sick). In general, then, special rights arise because of the special relationships we have to some people. *Acquired rights* differ. They arise because of various choices adults make. When I promise to meet you for dinner, you acquire a moral right to my showing up, a right you would not have if I had not chosen to make the promise. Again, if I agree to sell something to you, you acquire the moral right to the merchandise if you meet my conditions, a right you would not have if I had not agreed to sell it.[36]

Each of these types of rights calls for different ways of handling violations. Violation of a natural right warrants the most severe response, beyond mere verbal rebukes or social ostracism, since respect for natural rights is the minimum requirement for a just society. Without such respect for the autonomy of other human beings, one fails to recognize them *as* human beings. Violations of special rights come close to this, especially in the case of the parent-child relationship. But the choice of bringing a child into the world, however explicit or tacit, is presupposed, so it is not as basic a right as natural rights. Acquired rights, in turn, are quite a risky business. My promise does commit me, and if I break it for frivolous reasons, I certainly am morally condemnable. But no one is justified in taking punitive action in retaliation. Some type of ostracism or rebuke is as much as justice allows.

The one type of right that stands apart from all these is a *legal* or *positive right*, one created by contract or legislation and justified by reference to rights discussed above. It is possible for someone to have a legal right to aid, even though this right would be morally wrong to enforce. Legal rights and contractual rights may or may not be morally well-founded. In any case, such rights presuppose the establishment of government or some third (enforcing) party, apart from those who are subject to the laws or who have entered contracts. Unlike a promise, the minimum parties to a contract are three — the two who contract promises and the third who is hired, invited, or otherwise empowered to enforce, supervise disputes about, or otherwise stand watch over the terms of the contract. A *legal* right, in general, involves *enforceability* and presupposes the institutions required to enforce it, whereas the other rights are independent of these considerations. One's natural rights to be free, the special rights of children, and the acquired rights of promises do not depend on third-party enforcement.

Now, the marketplace does in fact leave room for all these rights to be respected and protected. Government regulation assumes, however, that all types of rights must be like legal or contractual rights, subject to enforcement. And that is the heart of the matter. Our natural, special, and acquired rights do not presuppose the third-party enforcement assumed by legal rights; government, serving the entire public, ought to be appointed to enforce just those rights—namely natural rights—that have the widest scope. No doubt it is a good thing that the products you produce and I purchase prove to benefit me, just as it is a good thing that a father takes his daughter to the show as promised. But no one who respects individual autonomy would assume that the elaborate punitive machinery of the law should be enlisted to coerce the father to keep his promise. In the absence of compelling argument to the contrary, why should we regard the role of the law any differently when it comes to insuring the quality of the products you produce and I purchase? Only if solid moral justification is at hand should we allow natural rights—to life, liberty and property—to be overridden. Such justification is difficult to come by, and though it is arguable that in certain exceptional cases our natural rights would have to be overridden (for example, when we face circumstances in which social life is impossible, as on a life raft or desert island),[37] exceptional cases are not the rule. Our day-to-day commerce does not take place in a state of emergency.

For reasons advanced in §5, the major sorts of justification of government regulation (ideals, utility, rights) fail. Thus ought we to oppose it? This is, in the last analysis, an argument that places the burden of proof on those who would promote the regulation of business. The value of individual liberty is so great that it ought not to be limited in the absence of very strong moral arguments (as is true, for example, in the case of the criminal law). Arguments for government regulation lack the necessary strength. Therefore, they fail to meet the burden of proof. The free market may not be perfect—it would be silly and indeed unnecessary to try to maintain that—but it is one that largely respects the basic, natural rights of individuals (while it also places considerable resposibility on everyone to fend for himself—"caveat emptor"). In the absence of compelling reasons for overriding individual rights as they find expression in the free market, restrictions should not be accepted. Lacking adequate argument to the contrary, we are right to view government regulation of business as wrong.

§11 CONCLUSION

Should business be regulated? I have presented sketches of arguments that reach an affirmative answer to this question and I have myself offered a negative reply. But the issue is very complicated, involving as it does matters of economics, morality, politics, law, considerations of human nature, the psychology of commercial relations, and so forth. Nevertheless, what has been presented here should provide an opportunity for enterprising minds voluntarily to enter into commerce with one of the most active normative public policy issues of our time. In a democratic society, or even one that is but a mild approximation of one, everyone is called upon to help decide what the government *will* do. And it is clearly better if the decision rests on as clear a conception of what government *should* do as possible. The politicians who run to gain our votes, the bureaucrats who will wish to be appointed by these politicians, and the whole array of officials of the various levels of government in a democracy depend on us all for moral guidance. That is what government by the people, of the people, and for the people amounts to. The present discussion has been conducted with this fact in mind.[38]

NOTES

1. *The New York Times* (August 19, 1981).
2. John F. Cady, *Restricted Advertising and Competition, The Case of Retail Drugs* (Washington, D.C.: American Enterprise for Public Policy Research, 1976), p. 1.
3. David A. Mathisen, "Whatever Happened to Human Body Glue?" *Reason* (May 1980), pp. 20–27.
4. *Metromedia, Inc.* v. *City of San Diego*, 101 S.Ct. 2882 (1981).
5. Walter F. Dodd, *Cases and Materials on Constitutional Law* (St. Paul, Minn.: West, 1954), p. 390.
6. For a full treatment, see Bernard Seigan, *Economic Liberty and the Constitution* (Chicago: University of Chicago Press, 1981).
7. My own fuller exposition of the nature and justification of this system is in my *Human Rights and Human Liberties* (Chicago: Nelson Hall, 1975). See, for a diverse selection of support and development of the laissez-faire idea, by *The Libertarian Alternative* (Chicago: Nelson Hall, 1974) and *The Libertarian Reader* (Totowa, N.J.: Rowman and Littlefield, 1982), both edited to cover all major questions.
8. The exception is libertarian anarchism, as represented by Murray N. Rothbard, in *Man, Economy, and State* (Los Angeles: Nash, 1970).
9. Jonathan R. T. Hughes, *The Governmental Habit* (N.Y.: Basic Books, 1977), pp. 3–4.
10. Quoted in Hughes, op. cit., p. 111.
11. This school includes such noted exponents as Adam Smith, John Locke, John Stuart Mill (at times), and Herbert Spencer, and is today represented by such thinkers as Milton Friedman, Karl Popper, F. A. Hayek, and a number of prominent neoclassical economists.
12. Norman Malcolm tells a story about Ludwig Wittgenstein that illustrates the point about property rights. "On one walk he 'gave' to me each tree that we passed, with the reservation that I was not to cut it down or do anything to it, or prevent the previous owners from doing anything to it: with those reservations it was henceforth *mine*." Malcolm calls this one of Wittgenstein's "deliberately absurd or extravagant remarks" in *Ludwig Wittgenstein, A Memoir* (London: Oxford University Press, 1958), pp. 31–32.

13.   Of course, one might still object to such governmental edicts on the grounds that education suffers when they are imposed or that they counter the spirit and letter of existing law. But that is not to challenge the government's proper authority to intervene.

14.   See my *Human Rights and Human Liberties*, and "Rational Choice and Public Affairs,' *Theory and Decision*, 12 (September 1980), pp. 229–58.

15.   Henry G. Manne, "Insider Trading and the Law Professors," *Vanderbilt Law Review*, 23 (1970), p. 547.

16.   Herbert Spencer, *The Principles of Ethics* (Indianapolis, Ind.: Liberty Classics, 1977).

17.   John Maynard Keynes, *The End of Laissez-Faire* (London: Hogarth Press, 1927), p. 40.

18.   Yale Brozen, "Is the Government Responsible for Monopolies?" in T. R. Machan, ed., *The Libertarian Alternative*, pp. 149–168.

19.   Robert Bremmer, *American Philanthropy* (Chicago: University of Chicago Press, 1960); Alfred de Garzia, *American Welfare* (N.Y.: New York University Press, 1961); Frank Greene Dickinson, *The Changing Position of Philanthropy in the American Economy* (N.Y.: Columbia University Press, 1970); and Arnaud C. Marts, *The Generosity of Americans* (Englewood Cliffs, N.J.: Prentice-Hall, 1966).

20.   Kenneth J. Arrow, "Two Cheers for Government Regulation," *Harper's* (March 1981), p. 20.

21.   Robert W. Poole, Jr.., ed., *Instead of Regulation* (Lexington, Mass.: Lexington Books, 1981). For the idea of a free market in roads, see Walter Block, "Free Market in Roads," in T. R. Machan, ed., *The Libertarian Reader*, pp. 163–184.

22.   Arrow, op. cit., p. 19 (my emphasis).

23.   Thomas Sowell, *Knowledge and Decision* (N.Y.: Basic Books, 1980). This is the idea that was pitted against Marxist socialism, and because of which the socialist economist Oscar Lange of Poland wanted to erect a memorial to the famous Austrian economist Ludwig von Mises, who advanced it in his *Socialism* (Indianapolis, Ind.: Liberty Classics, 1981).

24.   Steven Kelman, "Regulation that Works," *The New Republic* (November 25, 1978), p. 19.

25.   Ibid.

26.   Joan Claybrook, "Joan Claybrook Responds," *Regulation* (March/April 1979), p. 4.

27.   This view is inherited from Thomas Hobbes and forms a substantial premise of much of neoclassical economic theory. For a historical sketch, see Albert O. Hirschfeld, *The Passions and the Interest, Arguments for Capitalism before its Triumph* (Princeton: Princeton University Press, 1977).

28.   Seymour Martin Lipset and William Schneider, "The Public View of Regulation," *Public Opinion*, 2 (January 1979), p. 11.

29.   Robert W. Crandell and Lester B. Lave, eds., *The Scientific Basis of Health and Safety Regulation* (Washington, D.C.: The Brookings Institute, 1981).

30.   See Poole, *Instead of Regulation*, and Michael S. Baram, *Alternatives to Regulation* (Lexington, Mass.: Lexington Books, 1981). See also, my "Some Normative Considerations of Deregulation," *Journal of Social and Political Studies*, 3 (Winter 1978), pp. 363–77.

31.   Steven Kelman, "Regulation and Paternalism," in M. Bruce Johnson and Tibor R. Machan, eds., *Rights and Regulation* (Cambridge, Mass.: Ballinger, 1982), p. 241.

32.   Ibid.

33.   Ibid.

34.	In addition, the moral significance of acts is diminished if not totally obliterated when they are performed under compulsion alone, as in government-regulated conduct. See Douglas Den Uyl, "Freedom and Virtue," in Tibor R. Machan, ed., *The Libertarian Reader.*

35.	John Rawls, *A Theory of Justice* (Cambridge, Mass.: Harvard University Press, 1971).

36.	For more on this see my "Ethics and the Regulation of Professional Ethics," *Philosophia* (forthcoming).

37.	See my "Prima facie versus Natural (human) Rights," *Journal of Value Inquiry*, 10 (Summer 1976), pp. 119–31.

38.	Randall Dipert and Tom Regan were very kind to give me their advice on the development of several of the portions of this essay. I thank them.

SUGGESTIONS FOR FURTHER READING

Further readings are related below to the various section topics covered in this essay.

§1.	A brief survey of regulatory measures may be found in Jesse S. Raphael, *Governmental Regulation of Business* (N.Y.: Free Press, 1966). The American Enterprise Institute's Magazine, *Regulation*, as well as the *National Journal*, contain up-to-date information on government regulation and its recent discussions.

§2.	Louis M. Kohlmeier, Jr., wrote *The Regulators* (N.Y.: Harper & Row, 1969) with a view to giving a clear overview of the major regulatory agencies and their history. Jonathan R. T. Hughes' *The Governmental Habit* (N.Y.: Basic Books, 1977), chronicles the history of governmental intervention in culture on the American continent.

§3.	A very clear discussion of the aims, methods and moral ideals of the welfare state can be found in Nicholas Rescher, *Welfare, the Social Issues in Philosophical Perspective* (Pittsburgh: Pittsburgh University Press, 1972).

§4.	Barry M. Mitnick's *The Political Economy of Regulation* (N.Y.: Columbia University Press, 1980) is the most comprehensive treatment of the topic from the perspective of political science and public policy studies. Eugene Bardach's *The Implementation Game: What Happens after a Bill Becomes Law* (Boston: MIT Press, 1977) is also a political scientist's examination of many facets of governmental regulation, but with some discouraging conclusions as to the workability of the institution.

§5.	Paul W. MacAvoy's *The Crisis of the Regulatory Commissions* (N.Y.: Norton, 1970) is an economist's critical assessment of the economic regulatory bodies. James E. Anderson's edited *Economic Regulatory Policies* (Carbondale, Ill.: Southern Illinois University Press, 1976) presents numerous fairly sympathetic policy studies of government regulation. Robert A. Kaga's *Regulatory Justice* (N.Y.: Russell Sage Foundation, 1978) chronicles the conduct of the wage and price commission set up by President Richard M. Nixon. Robert W. Crandell and Lester B. Lave have edited *The Scientific Basis of Health and Safety Regulation* (Washington, D.C.: Brookings Institute, 1981), in which some rather disturbing conclusions are advanced about the success of the political process in heeding the advice of science when it comes to forging regulatory policies.

§6.	Yair Aharoni's *The Non-Risk Society* (Chatham, N.J.: Chatham House Publishers, 1981) is critical of the increased concern with eliminating risks through public policy. Robert W. Poole, Jr., edited *Instead of Regulation* (Lexington, Mass.: Lexington Books, 1981), in which several of the major regulatory issues are examined with respect to whether a free market could achieve the legitimate aims of government regulation, concluding with an affirmative answer. Michael S. Baram's *Alternatives to Regulation* (Lexington, Mass.: Lexington Books, 1981) examines the various alternatives to regulation concerning matters of rights violation or injury, involving the judicial system, tort law, and so forth.

§10. Ayn Rand's *Capitalism: The Unknown Ideal* (N.Y.: Signet Books, 1967) is a collection of spirited defenses of capitalism by Rand and some of her associates, based on the morality of rational self-interest and natural rights. Tibor R. Machan edited *The Libertarian Alternative* (Chicago: Nelson Hall, 1974) and *The Libertarian Reader* (Totowa, N.J.: Rowman and Littlefield, 1982), the former with numerous essays critical of government regulation, the latter with numerous essays defending the practicality, efficiency, and morality of the free society (as libertarians understand it).

§11. M. Bruce Johnson and Tibor R. Machan edited *Rights and Regulation* (Cambridge, Mass.: Ballinger, 1982), containing numerous essays pro and con concerning various forms of government regulation. This is one of the few volumes where government regulation is examined mainly from the point of view of its moral and political (including economic) propriety.

8

Ethical Issues in Advertising

ALAN GOLDMAN

《》

INTRODUCTION

Ethical issues in advertising can arise at two levels, the first concerning individual advertisers (the micro-level), the second (the macro-level) dealing with the functions and effects of the institution of advertising. The former cannot be understood well without first understanding the latter, and it is for this reason that we will begin our examination at the macro-level. At this level the principal ethical questions are (1) whether the institution of advertising can be defended on ethical grounds, and (2) assuming that it can be defended in this way, what ethical restrictions, if any, ought to be placed on this institution? Both questions can in turn be approached in at least two different ways. One approach asks whether advertising can be justified within a free-market economy, assuming that such an economy is itself ethically justified. This approach (what we shall call "the free-market approach") will be explained and critically assessed in Part I. A second approach (what we shall refer to as "the rights approach") asks whether the institution can be ethically justified by making reference to certain rights that are essential to a democratic society, assuming that there are such rights. This latter approach differs from the free-market approach because the central question it examines is not whether advertising contributes beneficially to the workings of a free market; the central question is, rather, whether there is a right to advertise, assuming that there are more general rights on which this particular right might be based, most notably the right to free speech. This approach will concern us in Part II.

Since the argument of the pages that follow is long and sometimes wanders over difficult terrain, it may be helpful to state the general conclusions it seeks to defend. As an institution, advertising can be ethically justified, whether we take the free-market or the rights approach. The very principles that justify it as an institution, however, also show that a variety of moral restrictions apply to what advertisers are morally permitted to do (for example, they must not willfully deceive the consumer). Moreover, the restrictions that apply to advertising, given the free-market approach, are the same as those that apply given the rights approach. To show that these restrictions coincide, given either approach, is to make the strongest possible case for accepting them as legitimate, since *if* the institution of advertising has a possible ethical justification, it would seem to consist either in showing that it complies with the requirements of the free market (the free-market approach) or that it is authorized by reference to rights (the rights approach). Only after the ethical legitimacy of the institution of advertising has been shown will we turn to the micro-level — the level of individual advertisers. This we will do in Part III, where it is argued that individual advertisers are bound by the same ethical restrictions that limit the behavior of the institution and so should be held accountable for violations of these restrictions.

I. THE FREE-MARKET APPROACH

§1 VIRTUES OF THE FREE MARKET

The justification of advertising as an institution, given the free-market approach, must appeal to its functions in a free-market economy. For the institution to be positively justified, we must weigh its positive and negative effects and show that its valuable functions outweigh whatever harm or inefficiency it causes. In order to do that, we must first briefly outline the virtues of the market economy itself, as these have been extolled since the writings of the father of political economics, Adam Smith (1723–1790).

The first virtue of a market economy is its efficiency in allocating economic resources, capital, and labor to satisfy collective needs and wants for products and services. In theory, maximum efficiency obtains given certain ideal conditions of pure competition. These conditions include: (1) competition within industries among firms each of which is too small to dictate prices to the market; (2) fluidity of labor and capital, so that these resources gravitate toward industries in which maximum profits can be made; (3) perfect knowledge on the part of consumers of prices and features of various products and services; and (4) knowledge on the part of producers of consumer demand for various goods. Given such conditions, the market, through its price mechanisms, guides profit-seeking producers to allocate economic resources in ways that optimize the aggregate satisfaction of demand — that is, the sum total of wants in society. Goods are distributed in turn to those with greatest demand, the degree of demand being measured by willingness to pay. The result approximates to maximization of utility, understood as the greatest sum of the satisfaction of wants over the whole society. Those goods are produced and distributed that yield the greatest surplus of value over economic costs. That is the ideal outcome, given ideal conditions (including also limits upon inequalities of wealth).

The market mechanism theoretically underlying efficiency of resource allocation was first described by Adam Smith himself. When a certain good is undersupplied in relation to the demand for it, its price is bid upward. Consumers are willing to pay more for a product they want when it is in short supply, and producers can improve their profits by selling the limited supply at a higher price. The possibility of higher profits will attract new resources (that is, capital and labor) to the industry, until the supply is increased and the margin of profit falls again to approximate that of other industries. Thus supply adjusts to demand. Conversely, oversupply of a good means that some of it will have to be sold at a loss, driving resources from the industry and adjusting the production downward. The tendency is toward an equilibrium at which the marginal value of all goods is equal and, taken collectively, maximal in relation to the relative social demand for the various goods.

This process is dynamic and progressive. At the same time as optimal efficiency is achieved in allocating resources so as to satisfy particular wants at particular times, competition generates progress through improvement of productive techniques and processes. Each competitor is motivated to modernize production so as to increase volume and cut unit costs of products. The price a producer pays for obsolescence is being undersold by the more efficient competition and thereby driven out of business. Thus the free market is theoretically efficient over time. It guarantees not only the most efficient use of resources in the present, but the production of more and more goods and services in the future.

In addition to efficiency and utility maximization, a further virtue of the competitive market economy, given ideal conditions, is its maximization of individual freedoms. All transactions within this economy are to be voluntary. Individuals are free to choose their occupations, investors to invest where they like, and consumers to buy or refuse what is offered for sale. For a transaction to take place, given the ideal condition of full knowledge of its features and alternatives, it must be perceived as mutually beneficial by the parties involved. Theoretically, these voluntary transactions tend once again to be utility maximizing. Thus we may add to maximum efficiency the maximum opportunity to make free choices within a market economy.

§2 THE CONSISTENCY OF ADVERTISING WITH FREE-MARKET COMPETITION

Even if we accept the model as sketched as an adequate idealization of a morally defensible economic system, it is initially difficult to find a place for the institution of advertising. The ideal requires relevant knowledge on the part of consumers of the existence, quality, and prices of products, and it is unclear that advertising, at least as we know it, accomplishes this goal. Second, the model also assumes that consumer wants or demands are given and judges the efficiency of the market by the extent to which they are satisfied. Any satisfaction of a pre-existing want is counted as a gain in utility or social welfare. Advertising, however, sometimes aims to create desires in the consuming public, and it is unclear whether the satisfaction of these desires should likewise be counted as a gain in utility or social value. These difficulties will be explored more fully below (see §§7–9). An even more fundamental difficulty demands our immediate attention. This concerns the very consistency of advertising in a free market. The difficulty may be explained as follows.

Our ideal model assumes that consumer demand for a product dictates prices to individual firms, which then manufacture goods until the marginal costs equal the price (that is, until no more profit can be made from additional units). But some economists have argued that advertising contributes to conditions in which producers can control prices. It does so, it is alleged, by creating demand to match planned levels of supply at fixed prices and by helping to maintain near-monopolistic control of particular industries. Advertising's creation of *consumer loyalty* for particular products helps in this regard. Such loyalty, it is claimed, makes it more difficult for new competitors to enter the market. Entry is made more expensive, since it requires extensive advertising campaigns to be successful. Brand loyalty may also be inefficient in itself, since it leads consumers to perceive differences among products when there may be no real differences in quality. Such misperception might cause them to forgo savings in price among identical products, for example chemically identical aspirin tablets, thereby diminishing maximum utility.

More recently, however, economists have taken the opposite stand on this issue. Some have argued that advertising actually facilitates entry of new competitors by allowing them to publicize their products and lure customers away from established firms.[1] The purpose of ad campaigns, it is now said, is to create brand *dis*loyalty. Campaigns are typically directed not at those who already are customers, but at potential new customers. In response to the claim that ads lead consumers to make ungrounded and costly product differentiations, it is pointed out that brand recognition and even brand loyalty create benefits for consumers as well. When shoppers can identify products and their manufacturers, the latter are pressured to maintain quality. At the same time comparison shopping is facilitated among retailers, so that they must sell within price limits.

In assessing this debate, it appears that the claims of the opposing sides may all be true, showing only that advertising produces *both* positive *and* negative effects upon competition and prices for consumers. It seems clear, first, that there have been successful advertising campaigns of both sorts, those that reinforce brand loyalty and help to retain a clientele (perhaps by reinforcing a favorable image of the brand in consumers' minds), and those that lure new customers away from established brands. Furthermore, while brand loyalty may raise successful entry costs, advertising may simultaneously ease entry for those with the capital to mount extensive campaigns. Finally, while ads may create the illusion of product differences where none exist and hence prevent choice of cheaper alternatives, brand recognition, achieved through exposure to ads, does facilitate comparison shopping among retailers. In the absence of data weighing these opposing tendencies across many industries, it seems impossible to justify or condemn advertising by its effects on the degree of competition in various product markets. There is no good reason at present, in short, for believing that advertising is inconsistent with the free market's aims of eliminating monopolies and encouraging competition.

§3 ADVERTISING AND WASTE

To defend the institution of advertising against the charge that it fosters monopolistic control of particular industries is only to show that the institution *could* find a place within a free-market economy, not that it *does* so, and there are any number of arguments that have been given against its place in a free market. One criticism claims that advertising is wasteful of economic resources, even when not directly harmful. If advertising does waste resources that could be used to more benefit elsewhere, perhaps the main ethical imperative for advertisers would be to do as little of it as possible or seek other professions. (Of course it may be that corporations, like individuals, have a right to waste their time and energies if they so choose. It may also be that what is wasteful for the economy as a whole is not so for individual corporations seeking to gain competitive advantages.)

I considered above (§2) the charge that advertising is wasteful in creating illusory differences among products that blind consumers to less expensive alternatives. The answer there was that this is the price of brand recognition, which also allows for beneficial comparison shopping among retailers. Of course advertisers might seek to make brands known without claiming distinction or superiority for them, but the latter is the obvious way to achieve the former. There is another answer available here as well. It is that the encouragement of product differentiation, which underlies claims of differences even when none exist, also motivates genuine changes in products and product features. While some of these too may be trivial or meaningless, cumulatively they may add up to real progress in product design. In rewarding innovation, advertising cannot help but bring about some useless changes along with beneficial ones, but the incentive it provides aims in the right economic direction in speeding progress. In allowing innovation to pay off more quickly, it also encourages investment in new techniques and products. This thesis, that advertising encourages change, complements the previous point that it facilitates entry into markets by publicizing the new. It may appear to contradict the idea of brand loyalty, but we have seen that ad campaigns may focus on either retaining old or attracting new customers (and of course established brands often claim to be "new and improved").

A different criticism is that advertising is wasteful in raising the costs and adding to the prices of products without adding value to the products themselves. This charge applies especially to "defensive strategies," in which large firms increase advertising expenditures when their competitors do so, until a standoff in overall effect is achieved. Advertising generally increases prices, one might argue, because the costs of the ad campaigns must be absorbed by consumers. But this point ignores the fact that, as an effective means of marketing or selling, advertising can lower unit costs and prices by increasing volume and speeding turnover in retail outlets. Thus once again we find opposing tendencies in the overall effects under consideration: advertising can raise prices because its costs are added to products and because it creates brand loyalty and hence fosters monopoly-like conditions; it can lower prices as a cost-effective means of marketing that can also ease seasonal fluctuations, and because it facilitates comparison shopping by price. Some recent empirical studies indicate generally lower prices in industries after the introduction of extensive advertising.[2] This is predictable in those markets in which advertising is introduced or permitted for the first time, for products such as eyeglasses or services of professionals, for example. There profits can be made in volume by underselling those charging exorbitant prices. For most products the truth is probably that advertising, like other capital outlays, can cut unit costs by increasing volume up to a certain level of expenditure, and after that will increase costs.

In judging the wastefulness of advertising, it must be compared to other methods of marketing goods, for example direct selling. Again one must keep in mind, too, that there are different forms of advertising in different contexts, some more or less wasteful than others. Defensive ad campaigns by large and well-established brands may involve less efficient use of resources than campaigns to inform consumers of genuinely new products or features. Finally, we should recognize in this context that use of resources that may be inefficient in the context of our economy operating at full capacity may not be so in contexts of less than full employment and use of other resources.

§4 INDIRECT BENEFITS: SUBSIDIZING THE MEDIA

To defend the consistency of advertising with free-market competition or to answer the charge of wastefulness is only to show that the institution could be justified, given the free-market approach, not that it is justified. To show the latter one must show what social benefits derive from having the institution. Now, the claimed benefits of advertising can conveniently be classified into two groups—direct and indirect. Principal among the direct benefits claimed to result from advertising is the benefit of consumers' having relevant knowledge of the existence, quality, and price of products. How well advertising provides this benefit will concern us shortly (§§5–7). First, though, we should attend to an indirect social benefit that advertising's apologists attribute to the institution they defend. Advertising subsidizes the media, both print and broadcast. Commercial radio and television, as well as most newspapers and magazines, could not survive without this subsidy, certainly not in the forms we know them and at the prices we are used to paying. It can be argued, then, that since these media themselves add much to the social environment in the way of information and entertainment, the institution of advertising is indirectly but importantly valuable in making this possible.

Once again, however, one must recognize as well the negative influence of advertising, especially upon the broadcast media. The main problem, of course, is the desire of the stations, pressured by the sponsors, to appeal to the largest possible audience with every show. The result is the reduction of content and style to the lowest common denominator of taste. Commercial television can be held responsible for debasing American taste, certainly for failing to elevate it and contribute culturally and aesthetically as it could. Advertising sponsors are the main culprits. Not only the "highbrow," but also the innovative, daring, or controversial is shunned as possibly offensive, when sponsors exercise effective censorship over programing. This is true not only of cultural and entertainment shows, but perhaps more seriously, sometimes of news and information programs as well.

Apologists can respond that condemnation of television on aesthetic grounds is a matter of purely subjective judgment. It can be argued that the intellectuals have no right in any case to impose their tastes on the majority, and that sponsors and programs only reflect cultural preferences, rather than dictate them. The question of the objectivity of aesthetic judgments is a large philosophical topic beyond the scope of this essay. We shall have occasion again below (§9) to grapple with the broader question of the objectivity and rationality of judgments expressing preferences. Perhaps in the domain of aesthetics one can use the judgments of those who know all the art forms in question well as a criterion, for example to distinguish grand opera from *The Dukes of Hazzard.* Whether or not such informed judgments would agree and whether or not they would constitute an adequate criterion of relative aesthetic value, the following reasons show that the advertiser's reply above is too simple.

First, we now know, having had a sampling of some alternatives in the forms of public and pay (cable) television, that the medium in other formats can be more sensitive to the tastes and preferences of various cultural minorities. Second, subsidizing television and offering it free to the public makes good economic sense only if the benefits of watching exceed the value of the resources used to produce programs, and if direct payments for those benefits are impracticable or involve high transaction costs. Free provision of a good tends to create overconsumption of that good in relation to its true value comparative to other goods. Free television junk is in fact overconsumed in relation to other forms of cultural enrichment and entertainment. Furthermore, the advertiser offers only a package deal to the public: programs together with ads often viewed as an irritating nuisance. The increasing popularity of alternative television funding bears witness that this package is not always of maximum benefit to the consuming public.

Thus once more we find a mixed blessing at best in the social effects of advertising. In contrast to the last subsection, however, here we can begin to draw some morals for advertisers. The service provided by them collectively in the subsidizing of the media seems clearly preferable when they do not act as censor. Once more we may make this judgment independently of the question of objectivity in aesthetic tastes or values. When commercial considerations come first, this priority is clearly detrimental to the aesthetic value of programs. (Again this may be even more clearly true of the informative value of news and information programing.) Very large audiences can be expected to be attracted only to the familiar and aesthetically uninnovative. But the judgment of artistic merit, as well as that of newsworthiness, ought to be made on intrinsic grounds by those with some expertise, rather than on strictly commercial grounds, if the media are to realize their potential for educating and not simply tranquilizing the American public. In order to accomplish this, self-restraint, sometimes at the expense of the short-term self-interest of particular advertisers and their business clients, is required.

§5 INFORMATION AND TRUTH IN ADVERTISING

If advertising is to be ethically justified, given the free-market approach, it is not enough to argue for its consistency in a free-market economy, or that it is not wasteful of economic resources, or even that it provides certain indirect social benefits. The positive justification must include the direct benefit that allegedly accrues from this institution: namely, the provision of relevant information. This is a role for which advertising may seem to be admirably qualified. Our model of an ideal market includes an assumption of full knowledge on the part of consumers of available products, comparative quality, and price. Maximal value can be obtained by consumers only if they know all the alternative ways of satisfying their desires and the costs of doing so. For any beneficial transaction to occur, people must be acquainted with products available. Advertising so informs them, also often providing data on product features, changes, and prices. Such information must be continuously provided because of the arrival of new consumers, new products, and new product features. Advertising then seems justified in a free market as a valuable source of information. Even when it attempts mainly to persuade rather than to inform directly, it will tell of a product's availability and perhaps of its prominent features.

Although, as mentioned above, it is difficult to tell when a market is maximally efficient in its use of resources to provide information and facilitate transactions, advertising does appear to be a relatively efficient means of doing so because of the large number of people it can reach, as opposed to more direct person-to-person methods of selling. In addition, from at least one perspective it appears to be efficient for the seller to provide the information in this form free of direct cost to the consumer. Because of the number of people a single ad can reach, and because the seller has both the resources and motivation to provide this information to the public at large, advertising appears to involve fewer and lower transaction costs than would the provision of information by direct sale to individual consumers.

Certain moral demands appear to follow quite obviously from this justification. If advertisements are to be justified as sources of information for consumers, then they ought to be truthful and avoid deception. Lies and deception defeat the purpose of informing the consumer so that he can make rational choices that will be to his greatest benefit. A lie is like a form of coercion, in that it narrows or eliminates choice among correctly perceived alternatives. A choice is free only if informed. If, in the area of consumer decisions, free choice is most likely to satisfy genuine desires and maximize welfare, and if the purpose of the free-market economy is to perform the latter functions, then lies in the marketplace tend to subvert the entire rationale of its operation. If consumers are misled, they will no longer be free in their choices and will no longer be maximizing utility; the virtues of the free market will be lost.

One might then conclude that the major moral demand upon advertisers is to tell the truth in their role of informing consumers. We might further strengthen this conclusion by noting the broader negative social effect of ads that routinely distort the truth. Constant exposure to the easy and natural lie, especially in the case of children, who perhaps pay more attention to ads and take them more literally than do adults, lowers respect for the truth in general and weakens the habit of honesty. Commercial discourse constitutes a major part of social discourse. Advertising represents a major link of the commercial community to the general public. Disrespect for truth in the practice of business and in the work of advertisers as the spokesmen for business therefore reinforces dishonesty in politics and other areas of social interaction. This fact in turn appears to reinforce the demand to stick to truth in advertising.

But in specifying the moral imperative more precisely, we come to see that it must be both broader and narrower than the command to tell the truth — broader because it must prohibit certain forms of deception beyond explicit lies, and narrower because not all distortions of truth in advertising are morally objectionable. To lie is to say what is false with the intent and expectation of deceiving one's audience. One can deceive, however, without explicitly uttering any lies; and one can exaggerate or distort the truth without intending or expecting to deceive anyone. I can deceive you if I know you will draw a false inference from what I say, even though nothing I say is literally false in itself. For example, if I tell you that the car I'm trying to sell runs like new, this may be true, but deceptive if it ran terribly when new. Such deception may be as immoral as lying to you. On the other hand, certain literal untruths may be harmless and morally permissible. Artists regularly distort, exaggerate, understate, embellish, or transform reality in their works without the intention or expectation of leading others to harmful, false belief. As long as the aesthetic context is recognized as such, the distortion is not a lie, but an expression of artistic license, which may even cause the audience to perceive a new or deeper truth by perceiving reality in a new way.

Let us then apply these distinctions to the case of advertising. Misinforming the consumer with the intent to deceive is clearly inexcusable for an advertiser. But not all distortion or exaggeration, what advertisers call "puffery," is immoral, if it is highly unlikely that anyone could be deceived. No one is going to be misled into believing that Coke really "adds life" or that Schlitz "has gusto" (whatever that is); but the claim that Bufferin relieves pain faster and with fewer cases of stomach upset than plain aspirin, or that Wonder Bread builds strong bodies in seven ways, fall into a different category. The Bufferin claims have been proved false by independent test; and it is now well known that white bread, even enriched, is poor in nutritional value and may have ill effects on the digestive system. The central demand here is that puffery be readily recognizable as such. When factual claims are made, they should be not only truthful, but supportable by reliable test results.

As mentioned above, while some literal untruths may be harmless (whether they irritate or insult the intelligence is another question to be addressed below, in §9), some literal truths nevertheless may be misleading and therefore objectionable. In one ad campaign, for example, it was claimed that a gasoline with a certain additive produced better mileage than the gasoline without that additive. This claim was true and supported by tests shown the viewers. The implication was that one should therefore buy the brand advertised because it always contained the additive in question. The missing premise, never stated but also implied, if the facts presented were to have any bearing on rational choice, was that other gasolines do not contain the additive. This, however, was false. The ad therefore was objectionably misleading, although nothing explicitly stated in it was false. If consumers ought not to be misled, then such ads are as condemnable as those that explicitly lie. Here consumers who made the obvious inference and were concerned with mileage might have been led to forgo possible lower prices for alternative brands of identical chemical composition. The ad was therefore unfair to them as well as to competitor oil companies.

There will remain in this area borderline and difficult cases. One problem relates to information about negative aspects of products. It appears too strong to demand that advertisers provide complete information about the products they advocate, negative as well as positive. There is first of all a problem in defining what constitutes complete information: some consumers may be interested in certain aspects of products that may be irrelevant to the concerns and choices of others. Second, ads, especially in broadcast media, must be brief and therefore cannot contain in themselves all possibly relevant information. A more reasonable demand is that negative information not be omitted when its omission is likely to mislead directly or to expose purchasers to increased risks of serious harm. Omission of negative facts is directly misleading when such facts negate claims explicitly or implicitly made in the ads. That Wonder Bread is relatively poor nutrition would be such a fact, though it may be enriched with seven ingredients that are separately beneficial when found in other foods. As an example of harmful omission, failure to mention that cigarettes cause cancer and greatly increase chances of heart disease would be objectionable for any advertisement attempting to persuade people to smoke them.

Another problem for the issue of deceptiveness concerns the possible victim of deception.[3] Some moron or deranged person might be deceived by the claim that Coke adds life into thinking that Coca Cola is an aphrodisiac or fertility drug, but we would not be led by this possibility to condemn the slogan as inherently misleading. (It may be misleading in other more subtle ways — see §8.) Should we then say that an advertisement is deceptive only if it is likely to mislead a normally intelligent consumer? That too would be too simple, since children, for example, might be misled with serious consequences by ads that would be benign for normally intelligent adults. A child might be misled by an ad that told him only that children's vitamins would help him to grow big and strong, thinking that he could instantly become a he-man by taking the whole bottle. We must then take both variables into account in providing a criterion for deceptiveness objectionable in this respect — first, the audience to whom the advertisement is addressed, and second, the degree of increased risk of serious harm from being misled into use or misuse of the product. If a specific audience is addressed, typical members of that audience ought not to be misled. But as the risk of serious harm increases, the prohibition against deception must become more strict in order to prevent deception of less circumspect consumers.

Even armed with our criteria, there will again remain morally borderline cases. Is an ad that claims that Geritol cures tired blood objectionable, when the product contains iron, a few vitamins and alcohol? Since there is no such condition as tired blood, the claim may seem to resemble the slogan that Coke adds life: neither is false, both are literally meaningless. Then, too, some users might feel better after using the tonic simply from a placebo effect or the power of suggestion. On the other hand, a genuinely ill person might become convinced that he had only tired blood and might postpone seeking medical advice. Given the severity of this risk, the ad appears objectionable. "Coke adds life," by contrast, cannot be condemned as being a misleading factual claim, since the claim it makes, if any, is so unlikely to be believed, and the risk of serious harm in using it is modest. An objection could center only on the suggested association (a topic to be considered in §8), not on the information or misinformation provided.

§6 INDIRECT INFORMATION

We have considered the idea that advertising as an institution can be positively justified as a provider of information, with its suggested moral constraint that ads must not be misleading in their explicit or implicit factual claims if they are to serve this useful function. Some have argued further in defense of the institution that even when advertisements directly present no facts whatsoever, there is useful "indirect information" that can be gleaned from them. We noted above the obvious, that the existence of the product, its prominent function, and some of its features can be learned from any competent advertisement, even one in the form of a jingle. But there are more subtle inferences that can be drawn as well. They derive from the fact that advertising generally produces profits only for products that will be bought repeatedly by customers first convinced by the ads to try them. The fact that a firm widely advertises some product indicates that they predict acceptability for it or that it is already a success. Since it pays more to advertise winners than losers, and since the advertising itself may increase volume and permit lower unit costs, one can infer than the advertised brand is probably of superior quality or a better buy. At least this has been argued by some economists.[4] We know firsthand of some notable exceptions, however, for example generic-name drugs or no-name tissues and other household products, which, though equal in quality to and lower in price than name brands, are outsold by the latter.

Even if advertised brands tend to be superior values, this information is beyond the sophistication of the average consumer. The conclusion that it pays the consumer to buy advertised brands, from the premise that it pays the producer to advertise winners, is neither explicit in ads themselves nor an inference likely to be drawn consciously by consumers. The economist's point here is rather that even when the consumer is led to buy a particular advertised brand for the wrong reason (for example, because he has been persuaded by nonrational methods), he will still *on average* be doing the right thing. But if this is true, it still does not excuse presentation of false information or deception in advertisements. For even if advertised brands on average offer better buys, this will *not* be true on average of brands whose advertisers must resort to lying or deception in order to sell them. Thus the value of such "indirect information" is not so great that it can reasonably cancel the prohibition against false or deceptive advertising.

§7 IDEAL INFORMATION

Advertising, then, does provide information, including "indirect" information, and critics of the institution are barred, therefore, from objecting to it on the grounds that it always lacks content. In the face of this some critics go on to claim, not that advertising fails to provide any information, but that the information provided by advertisers is neither the most desirable nor the most useful to the rational consumer. That information would consist in full and objective appraisals of products, including negative features, by neutral investigators, of the sort one gets in *Consumer Reports*. For example, there are very few industries or product lines where consumers could make intelligent choices among alternatives based on the information provided by advertisers (think of soft-drink or beer commercials). They offer only information that it is in their interest to provide, rather than what is most valuable to consumers.

In theory, truth, or in this case objective information, is supposed to emerge from the continuing clash of competing claims made by advertisers advocating rival products. The potential buyer is protected in the ideal world of the free-market theorist, first, because he need never buy a product again if it is found unsatisfactory on the first try; second, because, as mentioned earlier, it does not pay to advertise one-time products; and third, because he can obtain information on his own, both from other consumers who have tried the product and from his exposure to competing commercials.[5] Whatever may be true in theory, the preceding is glaringly inadequate in practice. Against the first alleged protection, it is sufficient to note that, with some products, to use them once would be to use them once too often. An eyewash that is advertised as safe but turns out to be highly toxic would be an example. Against the second point, it should be noted that whether a product will be a one-time product usually is not known in advance of its actual market success, so there is no guarantee in buying a newly introduced product that one is buying a good one. As for readily available public information (the third point), a product that is occasionally harmful or defective may not be known to be so by the general public. Gas tanks of Pintos were not generally known to explode until many injuries and deaths had occurred. An individual might not want to assume the risk involved, given the choice, but he might not learn of that risk from other consumers. Certainly he will not learn of it from the advertiser of the product. Nor is he likely to learn of it from advertisers of competing products, free-market theory notwithstanding. Competing firms seem to have found it economically counterproductive to publicize specific criticisms of each other's products. For one thing, this invites retaliation. For another, the over-all effect might be to reduce demand for the products of the entire industry. Thus General Motors does not seek to expose safety defects in Ford's cars. Certainly the desirability of the products of a whole industry is never questioned in commercial advertising. One is told to buy a particular soft drink rather than another, but the harmful effect of all soft drinks is not a topic for commercial ads.

We might note in passing (since it will be relevant later as well, in §10) that the realm of politics, in which the value of a free market of competing ideas for generating rational choices was first defended, is different in these respects. Politicians do criticize one another specifically, and often stridently. While the over-all effect might be to lower voter turnout, the consequence is not the same as in the case of public disaffection with an industry's products. We cannot collectively opt for no politics or politicians (no matter how appealing the idea). On the other hand, some politicians, very successful ones recently, do advocate less government involvement in private and commercial life, in contrast with the lack of advocacy of less consumer buying and spending by advertisers. Thus the spectrum of competing views projected from advertising is far more restricted than that from the political arena. The belief that competition among advertisers will increase information and, with this, increase rational, knowledgeable choice is consequently less justified here than is the analogous belief about political competition.

Given the bias of commercials, there are sources of information for consumers far preferable to that provided by advertising. These include private consumer research groups, such as Consumers Union, that sell their information in the form of periodicals and books, as well as government-subsidized studies, such as those sponsored by the Food and Drug Administration. Despite the transaction costs involved, one must ask whether, all things considered, private, independent consumer groups are economically sounder as sources of information than advertisers. Those who want and benefit from the information provided by such groups can pay for it without having others bear costs locked into the prices of products.[6] It is economically more efficient to have people pay directly for benefits they seek. There is nevertheless a free-rider problem here, since individuals can hope to benefit freely from information paid for or acquired by others. This means that the value of the product (here information itself) may not be adequately reflected in economic demand for it. This in turn justifies government subsidies for the provision of neutral consumer information.[7] One may of course doubt the government's efficiency in this area, and more important, its neutrality. The main danger is its corruption by the industries being researched. But the information provided is in any case no worse than that from advertisers, except perhaps for being more readily believed.

The argument of this subsection weakens the positive justification of advertising as a source of information for consumers. But we must qualify this conclusion by noting again the many different forms that advertising takes. Classified ads announcing the availability of particular goods tend to be purely informative and cannot be replaced by other sources of information. The alternative sources we discussed (for example, Consumers Union) are suitable only for research into features of large classes of products. Commercial advertising of the type that comes more readily to mind will undoubtedly continue to exist, despite the preferability of other sources of information. For its main function from the point of view of business is not that of informing, but persuading, to which we now turn. Despite the centrality of this latter function, advertisements will continue to provide some information to consumers as well. And the information provided has social value, but only as long as the moral constraints we have developed are observed. It would be unreasonable to expect advertisers to fulfill the ideal of providing complete information, but it is not unreasonable to require that they not use means inimical to the ideals of the free market.

§8 NON-RATIONAL PERSUASION

A central function of much advertising, we have just said, is to persuade people to buy products, and though it is possible that such ads contain some information, even if only of the "indirect" variety, and thus go some way toward providing consumers with relevant grounds on which to base their product selections, it does not follow that the means used to impart this information are acceptable in all cases. One method of persuading someone to buy something is simply to inform him of its features and availability. This suffices when the object is known to satisfy some pre-existing desire. A slightly more complex method that better fits our usual concept of persuasion consists in showing someone that he *should* desire something because it is a means to achieve something else that he desires. This is still a typical form of rational persuasion — one provides reasons for desiring or obtaining something, reasons that are to be consciously weighed and accepted or rejected by the person addressed. Advertising can take either of these forms. But the more controversial method bypasses reason, and even conscious thought processes, for the most part. It attempts rather to create an association in the consumer's mind between its product and some image that expresses a subconscious wish or desire, or, perhaps more sinister, between the absence or lack of the product and an image expressing some subconscious fear or anxiety. The consumer is then to choose the product as a way of fulfilling his wish or avoiding the object of his anxiety, but without realizing this as his motive.[8]

An example of the former variety of this method is once again found in the "Coke adds life" jingle, as the song is accompanied by pictures of healthy athletes engaging in some strenuous activity. Here the association is suggested with images of health, youth and vitality. It is facilitated by certain features of the product itself — not ingredients genuinely connected to health, but the sparkle in the taste and the caffeine and sugar in the content, the latter of which do add a temporary lift, making one's existence "more lively." The positive image created for the product here is especially apt for counteracting the conscious knowledge that colas are, if anything, detrimental to health (and certainly to teeth). Another similar example is the "Now comes Miller time" commercial. Here the image is that of a reward for a job well done. We are led to associate drinking this beer with having performed well in our careers, tasks, or responsibilities. Since we would all like to think of ourselves as worthy of praise and reward, we are to choose Miller in fulfillment of this wish, without necessarily realizing we are doing so. Advertisers of many such products with functionally identical competitors (for example, beers, cigarettes, automobiles) seek to differentiate them by associating the products with certain personality types to which certain classes of persons aspire. We are all familiar with the Marlboro man, a rugged Western type, or the liberated woman who smokes Virginia Slims, or the tuxedoed owner of a country estate who drives a Cadillac.

An example of the second negative variation on this method is the mouthwash commercial in which the husband and wife awaken and cannot face each other until rinsing away their bad breath. This ad plays upon our fear of rejection, especially by loved ones. We can avoid such dire consequences by buying the product in question (after gargling, the couple smile and kiss). There are many variations for similar products that seek to make us associate not only various body odors, but stained clothing ("ring around the collar"), and so forth, with rejection and failure. Especially objectionable are such ads for products that offer not better hygiene or cleanliness, but possible harmful effects, for example feminine deodorant sprays.

The psychological theory behind typical variations on these methods is eclectic, a mixture of Freudian ideas and behavioral conditioning methods. Notions of subconscious wishes, fears, and sublimations combine with techniques to induce association by conditioning. Methods of advertising that make little sense if we think of them as means of providing information become intelligible under this alternative analysis. The seemingly endless repetition of literally meaningless jingles, like "Coke adds life," cannot inform anyone of anything. Nor do they make much sense as reminders of the existence of products, as some economists claim. We all know of Coca Cola without being constantly reminded, and new purchasers learn of it from those who already know. But as a form of inducing association by conditioning, repetition comes to be perfectly intelligible. These commercials attempt to engrave an image of their products in our subconscious, and this requires a process different from that involved in informing or reminding us of a fact.

This form of advertising becomes the norm in industries in which products are more or less standardized or functionally equivalent, or in which they serve no vital need not served by alternative products. When there is no obvious connection between some product and the satisfaction of a pre-existing specific want for it, advertising can turn a product into a *symbol*, a tangible something that, in various ways, is associated with some less specific need or drive — for status, power, acceptance, and so forth. The recent success of designer jeans, after extensive ad campaigns, bears further witness to the potential of the method. But though economically successful at least some of the time, advertising that rests on persuasion through the creation of images might be condemned on moral grounds. Why?

First, it can be claimed that such ads are manipulative and border on coercion. Persuasion by rational means, by offering a person reasons why he ought to act in some way, treats him as an equal and respects his right of free and informed choice. We have seen (§§5 and 7) that one positive function of advertising can be its contribution to this process in providing information that the consumer can use for a knowledgeable free choice among products. But when the influence is subconscious, the persuader appears to claim an unfair advantage. He does not present his audience with a choice or set of reasons. The persuasion is more like a command of a superior to an inferior, in some ways perhaps more coercive than a command that one can consciously refuse to obey. Here one cannot refuse to be persuaded or influenced, for the target of persuasion is not aware of being so influenced. In this respect subconscious persuasion appears similar to deception. Like deception, it prevents informed choice and obscures alternatives from its victim, here the alternative of refusing to be persuaded or accept advice. The method appears then to violate a central requirement of at least one major moral tradition, the imperative to treat other persons as equals and to respect their rationality and freedom of choice. It also seems to contradict a major justification of the free economic market: that the system permits all economic transactions to be voluntary. A consumer's decision to buy is not voluntary, it can be argued, when he has been unduly influenced in that direction.

The plausibility of this condemnation will depend upon three factors: the depth of influence and attendant success of these advertising methods; the extent to which we believe that individuals normally are rational and free in their choices; and the extent to which the importance or triviality of the choices at stake determine the permissibility of various methods of persuasion. Appeal to our emotions or aesthetic sensibility rather than to conscious reasoning processes cannot in itself always be condemned, if only because of its pervasiveness. When trying to persuade my wife to go to a movie or out to dinner, I am likely to be more successful in appealing to pleasing images than in stating objective reasons why going out is a good idea. Should I be condemned for this appeal? In a less trivial context, much of art and literature appeals to our emotions through symbolic image and metaphor, distorting and transforming reality to influence our perceptions and sometimes our actions. We do not fault the artist or novelist for this.[9] In the context of business, we would not want to demand reduction of all products to purely functional features. The shape of the product, the colors, the package, all affect our aesthetic sensibility, but the world of the consumer would be dull indeed if these were reduced to uniformity. Can we then blame the advertiser for presenting products in pleasing settings and associating them with pleasant images? While desires may be thus induced in us, it is unlikely that we often choose which desires to have in any more rational way.

It seems, then, that if we are to condemn non-rational methods of persuasion, our moral criterion must refer at least in part to the consequences in particular cases. It appears to be the creation by these methods of wants that are irrational or harmful that is objectionable. But there are two other factors that relate more directly to the methods themselves. The first is the degree to which the subject could be expected to resist the persuasion if he believed it against his better interests to follow it — that is, the degree to which his choice remains free even when under its influence.[10] Normal adults are not so captivated by particular advertisements that they can be said to be controlled or coerced by them. To be aware of the nature of the appeal is to be better able to resist it. (The cumulative effects of stereotypical images on social perceptions of roles may run deeper.) Children, on the other hand, are far more vulnerable to manipulation by these means. The morality of non-rational persuasive advertising directed at them stands more open to serious question. Second, the importance of the choices at stake matters. The peddling of political candidates by sophisticated Madison Avenue techniques looms far more ominous, perhaps calling into question the justification of the democratic process itself, than the attempt to influence us to drink Coke instead of Pepsi. (In the political arena it cannot be claimed that *only* the consequences count, that it is only who wins the election that matters; clearly the process has importance in itself.) As the stakes increase, freedom of choice becomes more crucial and advertisers more sinister when they rely on non-rational influence.

The comparison of advertising to art, the suggestion that advertising becomes art when it symbolically transforms reality in appealing to our emotions and sensibilities, invites further criticism on aesthetic grounds. First, even when the aesthetic element in ads represents good or original art (and how often is that the case?), we can object to its subordination to an unworthy end. That an artistic work should serve some further purpose beyond aesthetic enjoyment is not in itself objectionable. Such is the case with all architecture and functional pottery, for example. But the banality of the function, for example to convince us that Coke is better than Pepsi, can cheapen the artistic medium. It is nevertheless difficult to press this objection seriously. If we are going to be subject to advertising, we ought not complain of the aesthetically more pleasing ads even if the art is more worthy than the product it advertises. The contrary, more serious complaint on this score is not that so many commercials simply lack artistic merit, but that they irritate in being garish, repetitious, intrusive, and trite. Advertisers have on occasion admitted to being purposely irritating in their ads in order to attract attention.

While it is true that a commercial cannot serve its function if not noticed, and that being noticed becomes more difficult amidst the increasing din of other ads, this does not give license to pollute the environment with constant noise and irritation. Such repetitious noise is economically dysfunctional as well. When we are constantly bombarded by signals, it becomes more difficult to process information contained in them. While it is also true that not only ads, but many movies, books, and musical compositions are vulgar and trite, this does not render poor taste less objectionable in advertising. Irritation is rather more condemnable where less avoidable; and many ads, for example on billboards, are more difficult to avoid than books or films. When their displays are intrusive and unavoidable as well as irritating, we can derive a further moral demand here upon advertisers to desist or change their format.

§9 CREATED DEMAND

The argument of the previous section challenged a certain kind of advertising (persuasion through the creation of images) because of the method used. It is also possible to challenge the institution because of the ends it achieves. The influential contemporary American economist John Kenneth Galbraith raises an objection of this kind, one that emphasizes the phenomenon of created demand, a phenomenon that, in Galbraith's view, calls into question the traditional justification of the free market. As noted earlier (§1), that justification, at least in part, is given in terms of the efficient satisfaction of existing consumer wants. However, if wants themselves are created by the very process that helps to satisfy them, the traditional justification fails. It applies to a reality where wants are given, not to one where they are continualy being brought into being. The fact that the institution of advertising, especially through its reliance on non-rational means of persuasion, is responsible for the creation of consumer desires, makes that institution's place in a free market especially problematic, in Galbraith's view. It is not just the methods used that are troubling; it is what is produced by the methods used — namely, new desires, especially desires for new products (such as designer jeans) — that is troublesome, both economically and morally.

Galbraith views the phenomenon of created demand as providing an explanation for an otherwise puzzling fact: that the abundance of material goods in our affluent society has not led to reduced desire for them or to the diminishing marginal utility that one would expect as the amount of goods increases.[11] Galbraith's point needs some explaining. A standard traditional economic assumption was that as an individual acquires more of a particular good, he derives less utility or satisfaction from additional units of it and is willing to pay less for them, until the point of satiation is reached and he desires no more even free of cost. For this individual, the utility of possessing more of the product is a thing of the past. What is true of the parts may be expected to be true of the whole in the case of material goods. As consumers as a group collectively amass more and more material goods, possession of such goods should naturally sink into the background of their concerns, much as we cease to be concerned with collecting greater amounts of air and water when both are readily available. If we are to continue not only to desire but to work hard to acquire all the material goods our modern economy can produce, we must come to have desires for them that we previously lacked.

Since the method business uses to create these desires is advertising, advertising, on Galbraith's view, is responsible for the phenomenon of created wants. Moreover, since advertisers tend to promote consumer goods that are privately produced and purchased, as opposed to promoting increases in such public goods as schools, parks, roads, and certain hospitals, demand for the former tends to be artificially inflated while demand for the latter is inadequate. In our society, Galbraith holds, private material goods tend to be overconsumed, and public goods and services underprovided, relative to their total value. Since advertising, by creating consumer desires, is responsible for this imbalance, and since the imbalance is at odds with what should result in a free-market economy, advertising can be faulted when, as it frequently does, it creates new desires for material goods.

Three questions press themselves upon us at this juncture. First, does advertising create desires or wants? Second, if it does, does it follow that the advertising used to create these new demands is to be ruled out, given the free-market approach to assessing the ethics of advertising? And third, assuming that advertising creates desires for privately produced and sold material goods instead of for public goods and services, thereby fostering a materialistic lifestyle, is that reason enough to condemn the creation of such desires, again viewed within the perspective of the free-market approach? We shall consider each of these questions, in the order given.

a. Does Advertising Create Wants?   There is something of a paradox in the fact that many foes of advertising attribute great power and effect to the institution, while its apologists attribute to it a far more minor role. When businessmen are accused of corrupting American morals or endangering health and lives by pollution and dangerous products, they standardly reply that they only give the public what it wants. Their profits, they tell us, derive from catering efficiently to public demand. When advertisers are accused of debasing American values, of creating insecurity, conspicuous consumption, or materialistic status-seeking, their response is similar: they cannot create desires, only tell us how to satisfy those we have. Galbraith, as we have seen, assumes the opposite view. With this as background, we can then specify a whole spectrum of positions on the influence of advertising and on the advertiser-consumer relation. These range from the claim that advertisers brainwash unwilling consumers through subconscious manipulation into wanting what they do not need, to the reply that advertisers merely inform those with set wants of the availability of products to satisfy them.

Economists also dispute the effects of advertising on the distribution of demand itself. A common view used to be that effects are limited to shifting demand within particular industries, that there is little effect among different industries, suggesting little or no effect on over-all demand levels for the economy. Recent studies, however, indicate results in shifting demand among industries as well. One recent study in fact concludes that advertising can be a more important variable than price.[12] Given the principles of a free-market economy, the advertiser seems to be caught in a dilemma on this subject. If he claims not to be effective in stimulating demand, then he can be accused of wasting economic resources without results. But if he admits to creating demand, he is accused of creating unnecessary material wants and causing consumers to waste their money (or their lives working for it). In either case, what advertising does is at odds with what, ideally, we look for in a free-market economy.

There is a way of escaping between the horns of this dilemma, however. It lies in the recognition that *stimulation of demand* for products need not be equivalent to *creation of wants* where none existed before. We have here two distinguishable questions at two distinct levels: "Can advertising create demand for specific products or types of products?" and "Can advertising alter personalities by creating new drives and depth motivations?" A middle position here could provide an affirmative answer to the first question and a negative answer to the second by holding that, for most people, ads can cumulatively specify targets of originally amorphous wants and drives, helping, along with other social environmental influences, to give these wants a more definite shape. Advertising, as one among many factors in the social environment, reinforces certain pre-existing tendencies in personalities and directs certain broad underlying desires or drives into specific wants. For example, we desire mobility and come to want specific automobiles; we desire comfort and come to want air conditioners (when the latter were first introduced into homes, surveys indicated little interest prior to advertising). More controversial, but still undoubtedly successful in some cases, is the specification of wants by association of the product with symbols expressing less conscious but no less real social drives — for status, power, acceptance, sexual allure, virility, or femininity. For instance, a man desires virility and power and comes to want horsepower in his car or a certain brand of cigar. But again the personality trait probably exists beforehand. It may be exploited by advertisers; it is unlikely that it is created by them.

This middle view represents a statistical guess. All depends upon the particular individuals sampled, and their openness to persuasion and suggestion. (Children as a class are without doubt the most vulnerable in this as in other ways. We will need to specify special moral restraints in relation to them. See below, §14.) But the middle position is supported by both the proven effects of advertising upon demand and its spectacular failures. (It is always well to remember the Edsel.) The upshot is that Galbraith seems to be both right and wrong — right in believing that advertising influences demand, but wrong in supposing that advertising is the ultimate cause of any of the wants or desires to which business products, and the means used to advertise them, cater. Original wants and desires, those that exist before and independently of advertising, can be shaped in a variety of ways, and advertising is just one among these influences. The influence of family, peers, and educational and religious institutions are no less real.

b. The Effects of Created Wants Since the question of advertising's role in the creation of consumer demand is controversial, it is worth asking what would follow if it turned out that advertising did in fact create desires where none previously existed. Given the free-market approach to the ethical assessment of the institution of advertising, a central question would be whether the consequences of allowing the creation and satisfaction of these desires would be beneficial. Galbraith, for one, sometimes argues that the satisfaction of created wants *may* not raise levels of utility or well-being and thus *may* not be in accord with the ideals of a free market. At other times he seems to hold a stronger view — namely, that wants that must be created *are* less urgent, different from needs, less worthy of attention, and thus incompatible with the goals of a free-market economy. The stronger thesis is wrong on all counts.

What counts as a need varies with stages of economic development. That a particular desire does not become focused in a particular way until shaped by exposure to advertisements does not prove that it is less urgent once formed. Such wants may come to qualify as needs when the desired goods become widely available, when society adjusts to their availability, and when individuals within that society come to require these products to function optimally. Automobiles in our country and air conditioners in its Southern sections qualify as objects of need, although no one thought to want them until they were produced and publicized. That virtually all offices and most homes in Miami are air conditioned, but most schools are not, strikes me as an injustice perpetrated by selfish adults against their children. Stifling schools represent an unjust denial of need, despite the fact mentioned earlier that demand for air conditioning originally had to be created. Furthermore, even created wants that fail to qualify as needs may be no less worthy of respect or fulfillment. Desires to attend (or for that matter to compose) grand opera must be instilled and learned. They are created by the same musical masters who satisfy them, but this does not render the whole process any the less satisfying. Despite being self-sustaining in Galbraith's sense, such cycles express what is most exalted in human nature.[13] On the other hand, wants that are or become physical needs may not be respectable and may call for elimination, if possible, rather than satisfaction. The need for heroin may be physically urgent but less worthy of respect than the desire for aesthetic enrichment.

Thus, contrary to Galbraith's thesis, wants that are created may come to be needs, may be urgent, and may be worthy of our attention, as witness the need of children for air conditioning. But the falsity of the stronger thesis suggested by Galbraith leaves his weaker position intact: creating a want and then satisfying it does not necessarily leave the user at a higher level of well-being than he was before. The desire for heroin is one example that shows that having one's desires satisfied does not always make one better off. To put the point more generally, merely to show that the market can satisfy those desires it creates is not to provide an adequate criterion for determining which desires the free market *ought* to strive to satisfy.

But now we have a problem. How shall we identify the needed criterion? One possible answer posits some ideal of human nature and permits economic arrangements that satisfy only those wants that are consistent with the favored ideal. We might aim, for example, to create desires for philosophical and aesthetic enrichment, as opposed to more wants for material gadgets. The major problem for views of this kind concerns who has the authority or knowledge to say what the ideal of human perfection or achievement is. Given that different ideals may be championed by different but equally competent individuals, one ought to be highly skeptical of perfectionist criteria for evaluating wants and desires. Such criteria, when actually applied, would assault the great liberal traditions of Western civilization, traditions that insist that each individual be allowed maximum individual freedom to determine what each wants and how to get it.

A second attempt to specify the needed criterion leaves intact the liberal goal of allowing each individual to be sovereign over what to want and how to achieve it. This attempt specifies criteria of rationality that, though they apply to every individual, do not rule out any desire except those that are irrational for particular individuals. A desire for something is irrational and therefore unworthy of fulfillment, according to this view, if (a) the object is desired as a means to something else but is unsuitable for that purpose; or if (b) fulfillment of that desire blocks the satisfaction of other desires that the individual would acknowledge as more important on the individual's own scale of values; or if (c) the costs of fulfilling that desire outweigh the satisfaction to be derived, again for the individual in question.[14]

The application of these criteria to those consumer desires influenced or created by advertising is no easy matter. Certainly it is impossible to condemn all created desires as a class. Less bold, and therefore potentially more credible, is the view that certain *kinds* of desires are irrational and thus unworthy. For example, might we not condemn all desires for products based upon association with unconscious symbols (say, acceptance or sexual allure) rather than upon inherent features of the products themselves? Appealing though this may seem, some apologists of advertising have actually argued that such associations *add genuine value* to products for consumers. The effect, they claim, is similar to placebo effects of doctors' prescriptions. If a patient believes that a pill will cure him, sometimes the belief itself helps. Similarly, it is argued, if a consumer believes that a Mercedes will give him distinction, he can get value and satisfaction from the car beyond the means of transportation.[15] In judging this claim, it is once more impossible to generalize fully. The "added value" thesis wrongly assumes that enough value is *always* created in the momentary satisfaction of any desire to outweigh other considerations. This is false, and we should therefore identify a criterion that avoids this mistake. If the product generally is not a means to fulfill the desire with which it becomes associated, if fulfilling that desire with that product may well block the individual's satisfaction of other desires believed to be more important by the individual, or if the costs to the persons addressed (not merely monetary) would be generally judged too high by these individuals when reason is in control, then the advertisements are morally objectionable.

By way of examples we may begin again with the "Coke adds life" jingle. The purpose here, we have said, is to create an association between the soft drink and images of health and vitality, probably to counteract conscious knowledge that colas are not particularly healthful. But precisely because the ad attempts to establish an association of means to end, of Coke to health and vitality, when the means are entirely unsuitable and even inimical to the end, the ad is objectionable on these grounds. The placebo effect here is probably too weak for serious consideration. Consider another example previously mentioned: "Geritol cures tired blood." Cannot the psychological association established itself help the user to feel better? Perhaps it can, but the problem here lies in the violation of the second part (b) of our criterion. Use of this product may cause the person who is suffering from more than "tired blood" to forgo or delay obtaining needed care or medicine, when what he really desires is long-term cure. Again the ad is objectionable. Also to be condemned is cigarette advertising, especially of the type that seeks to create an association between smoking and virility, sexual allure, feminine liberation, and so forth. Such ads are impermissible according to the first and third parts of our criterion. Cigarette smoking is not a means to virility, and so forth, and the costs to individuals in terms of high risk of cancer and heart disease are too high, according to most rational estimates. As in other contexts, so here too, there are borderline cases. Owning a Mercedes may be a means to stature for some, so that presenting the car in that light in commercials may not obviously mislead. Whether the costs of the status symbol are too high depends upon the wealth of the audience addressed and the actual functional benefits of the automobile in comparison to others.

c. Advertising and Materialistic Values While our criterion here allows for evaluation of particular advertisements, judging the more general claims of Galbraith is more difficult. The plausibility of the claim that advertising induces overproduction of private material goods and underprovision of public services depends again on how deep we take the influence of advertising to be upon American values. It is interesting to note here the recent success of the political movement that claims the opposite—that is, that government is over- rather than underspending. Of course one could again attribute the success of that movement to the persuasive influence of advertising; but one might equally attribute Galbraith's preference to the leftist leanings in his educational experience. At issue here is the source of the materialistic bias in American values and the penchant that Americans seem to have for "conspicuous consumption." We must ask first whether advertising is indeed the source of this phenomenon, and second, if it is, whether this fact alters the amount of utility or satisfaction derived from the two sorts of goods—

material goods and public services. If the long-range utility of material possessions is increased sufficiently, this would appear to remove any objective basis for criticism, as we are driven back to a matter of subjective preferences.

It seems impossible to judge the extent to which advertising is responsible for materialistic values in our society. For one thing, the use of material possessions to indicate class status has been common in earlier and even in primitive cultures. From headdresses to palaces and coaches, the upper classes have long been anxious to surround themselves with signs of their positions. For another thing, the more widespread materialism of our culture can be given several alternative explanations: our having more wealth to spend on such goods; the fuzzy boundaries of our social classes, defined more by wealth and possessions than in earlier more rigid societies; the mobility of people in our society, and the security that certain major possessions can give in a context of rapid change.[16] When more permanent roots are lacking, the class and personal identities of individuals may be more closely connected to their material possessions.

Perhaps Galbraith's thesis need not probe so deeply here, however. We need not blame advertising for basic traits of the typical American personality in order to claim that we spend too much on cars and clothes and too little on schools. The more easily demonstrable effect on demand for various types of products, the middle position advocated above (§9a), might suffice to support the claim that private goods are overconsumed in our society. But again on the other side is the recently expressed belief of many voters that government has been spending too much rather than too little. There is also the problem here of authority to decide our relative priorities. Even under the influence of advertising, it may be that we trust ourselves better to make consumption decisions than we would trust economists or the government. (I shall take up the broader question of regulation in the next section.)

A different criticism claims, not that advertising creates our deepest aspirations and goals, but that it standardizes and stereotypes them,[17] even for those for whom they may be out of reach. Ads constantly present us with their images of the good life. The images do tend to reflect a shallow materialism, exalting the importance of the products they advocate. While we pointed out earlier that advertising tends to encourage diversity or differentiation among products, its broader social effect may be to encourage conformity among lifestyles by bombarding us with its stereotypes of success. These stereotypes may be objectionable in more narrow senses as well, for example the typical pictures of women in subservient roles, either in aprons or low-cut evening gowns. Whether the life of material pursuits typically idealized in advertisements is generally fulfilling is a deeper question, but one which morally minded advertisers ought to ponder. Encouraging the expression of personality tendencies in certain channels may be little different morally from creating them, if the ideal expressed is not one to which its advocates wholeheartedly aspire. What is true in regard to responsibility for individual products advocated in ads holds true also for lifestyles implicitly edorsed and encouraged. If advertisers must accept responsibility for the former, they cannot ignore their broader social effect either.

Thus far I have been assuming, with Galbraith, that advertising shows the way to satisfy those desires it helps create. I have been questioning with him the overall utility of the process even when the desires in question are satisfied by consumption. Equally important to note is that ads stimulate the same desires and create the same insecurities in regard to personal appearance, status, and acceptance among those who may not have the means to alleviate them. From an economic point of view this may not be bad, encouraging these people to work to acquire the means for material acquisition (although it may also encourage crime). But again the effect on personal happiness is far more problematic.

We may summarize the discussion of Galbraith. Whether or not he is correct about the relative values of public and private goods, he is right to distinguish between the economic effects of advertising and its broader social effects. What may be an unqualified plus from the point of view of the traditional economist, the satisfaction of desire as expressed in demand, may be problematic from the broader view of over-all utility in the socio-economic process. In the days when demand expressed mostly basic needs, the equation of economic efficiency with social utility was less questionable. Now, while advertising may be economically useful in stimulating demand and productivity, advertisers should consider also the nature of the desires they nurture. They should avoid creating irrational desires and fostering lifestyles to which they and their consumers would not aspire in their more rational moments.

II. THE RIGHTS APPROACH

To this point the ethical assessment of the institution of advertising has been carried out in terms of the free-market approach. That approach assumes that the free market is itself an ethically justified economic system; what it asks is whether, given this assumption, advertising can find a defensible niche within the system. As was remarked in the introduction to the present essay, however, it is possible to approach the question of the ethical status of the institution of advertising in a quite different way. This second approach (the rights approach) attempts a defense of this institution, not in terms of its conformity with the goals and principles of the free market, but in terms of the right to freedom of expression — the right to free speech.

Whether or not persuasion produces consequences judged beneficial by third parties, the right to attempt to persuade others without coercion, to advocate particular points of view in public forums and media, is central to the democratic process. Whatever the over-all effects, businesses therefore have the right to promote their products and services, and advertisers the right to provide this service for them. Advertising is a form of speech, and as such it seems to require no further justification than appeal to the right of free expression. The latter exists as long as others have no right to silence such speech, which, it seems, they do not.

Viewed from the vantage point of the free market, appeal to the right to advertise is most relevant in those contexts in which it has been unduly curtailed and controlled by monopolistic interests, as in the areas of professional and semi-professional services—lawyers, doctors, opticians, and so forth. Restriction and prohibition of advertising in these areas, under the guise of maintaining professionalism and quality service, actually disserves the clientele and allows exorbitant prices to be maintained. It took the Supreme Court to strike down on constitutional grounds this form of control by self-serving professional associations.

The relevance of a right to advertise, once its boundaries are properly located within those of the broader right of free expression, extends beyond the free-market goal of breaking monopolistic control of various services. The appeal to this right, properly construed, can justify certain advertising practices that seemed problematic within the free-market approach. The correct interpretation of this right can also reinforce those ethical constraints on advertisers developed from the alternative approach in the earlier sections of this essay.

§10 THE QUESTION OF REGULATION

Suppose we grant that there is a right to advertise. There remains a constitutionally supported distinction between commercial and other relevant forms of speech, that is, political and literary. Congress is granted the right to control commerce, but not to abridge other forms of speech. Although recent court decisions have widened the boundaries of protected free speech to include some commercial advertising, this extension still depends upon the content of the advertisement or announcement, in particular whether it contains material of public interest, which, if it does, would place the ad within the political as well as commercial arena.[18] The present legal status of commercial discourse may be unstable and open to question, however. For the government to judge the content of a form of speech in order to decide whether the speech can be regulated by the government itself may seem inimical to the concept of free speech. One prominent contemporary scholar in the areas of law and economics, R. H. Coase, has recently questioned more broadly the entire distinction between political and commercial discourse and the grounds for protecting the former but not the latter from government interference.[19] Economic freedoms, he points out, are as important to us as political liberties. Free speech, he argues, is as essential to the free commercial market as it is to the democratic political process. Why should we trust the government to interfere in the former but not in the latter?

The answer lies in noting genuine moral as well as legal distinctions between commercial and non-commercial discourse. Coase is correct that certain economic freedoms are central—for example, the freedom of individuals to work, invest, and consume as they choose. But even in these areas there are limitations to protect others as well as the agents themselves. One cannot buy dangerous explosives or work on certain jobs without wearing safety equipment; one cannot invest in the heroin trade. In the realm of speech, the right to advertise does not include a right to defraud, or moral license to mislead people into buying harmful products. Legally, the Federal Trade Commission requires that advertisements be truthful and that their factual claims be substantiated. Such requirements, of course, would not be tolerated in other realms of discourse. We would not trust the government to prohibit political speech it judges to be untrue or literary works it holds misleading or even subversive. Lying by politicians or by private citizens generally is not illegal; nor should it be. Yet the regulation of advertising is morally justified. Again, how can we justify this distinction?

As noted in an earlier section (§7), there are differences between politics and advertising that explain why we have greater trust in the clash of political debate to produce rational choices. We may expand upon those distinctions here. Individuals are more easily deceived about the nature of products for sale than about political ideas. Defects in commercial products are more easily verified by expert researchers, even though the defects may be technologically complex and thus hidden from average consumers. It is therefore reasonable to require pre-market tests of products by experts. The position of the government also differs in the two contexts. Whereas the interest of the government in power renders it unreliable in regulating political speech, it can more easily serve as a neutral third party in protecting consumers against abuse. The objective verification of fraud and potential harm in products as opposed to political ideals and literary works, and the greater probability of neutrality on the part of government in the realm of commerce, sufficiently distinguishes the two contexts.[20] Government regulation of political speech inhibits rational choice in the long run; regulations requiring truth in advertising can facilitate it.

Not only deception by politicians, but lying among private citizens must remain generally unregulated and unpunishable by law, again in contrast with commercial contracts and advertisements. Private lies are not always wrong: "white lies" may be required by etiquette or kindness, or to prevent greater evils from occurring. The distinction between private and commercial speech is not to be found here, however, since we have noted (§5) that some literal falsities in advertising amount to "puffery" and so are morally unobjectionable. The main difference in these two contexts relates to the possibility and methods of enforcement. The costs of enforcement in the private sphere, not least in loss of privacy, and the probability of abuse on the part of the enforcers would make the cure worse than the disease. But enforcement of truth in advertising can be reasonable, and the privacy of advertising firms and of their corporate clients is not of major moral concern.[21]

In endorsing regulation of advertising, we must recognize certain negative consequences. First, strict scrutiny of factual claims may lead advertisers to reduce their content, relying instead upon non-rational methods of persuasion. One could argue that the net result is less information to consumers. We can reply that less information is better than false or misleading information. In addition, information that gives good reasons to prefer the product remains valuable for use in ads. The public can still recognize substantiated claims of superiority in product features, and such claims are likely to be more persuasive than meaningless jingles, with less repetition required. Second, it has been argued that regulation makes ads more believable in the eyes of the public, which only makes it easier for the less scrupulous to deceive.[22] But to argue in that way against holding advertisers to the truth suggests more generally that we ought not to encourage honesty, since honesty as a rule makes deception in particular cases easier. The argument is absurd.

We must recognize, second, that not all morally objectionable practices on the part of advertisers can be made illegal or regulated. Fair regulation requires objectively verifiable criteria on which to base enforcement. It must therefore center on fraud and deception in factual claims and upon limiting promotion of obviously harmful products such as cigarettes. Non-rational persuasion that creates false associations or insecurities, or that encourages pretentious and unfulfilling patterns of consumption and lifestyles,[23] cannot be prohibited, since enforcement of the prohibitions could not be fair and noncontroversial. Such practices nevertheless remain morally objectionable. On the question of irritation and aesthetic pollution of the environment, regulators must be limited to restrictions on amounts of advertising permissible in various media, without judging aesthetic merit. It is reasonable, for example, to prohibit the complete obfuscation of our landscape by billboards, but not to prohibit specific ads as too irritating. (I omit discussion of explicit sexual material in ads, since this would take us into the issue of pornography, beyond the scope of this essay.) It nevertheless remains wrong again for advertisers to irritate or harass us in order to gain our attention.

Despite the limitations on regulation, then, it is clear that the right to advertise does not include a moral right to deceive, mislead or harass, or to create or foster insecurities or self-defeating values. The legal right to advertise is narrower than the corresponding right to free noncommercial speech. The moral right to engage in specific advertising practices is narrower still, not including certain activities that cannot be legally sanctioned (because of the costs involved). That there is a right to advertise as part of a broader right of speech and expression means that advertisers need not justify their profession by demonstrating its over-all positive effects, any more than defense of a right to life must turn on the good consequences that flow from recognizing it. Nevertheless advertisers may feel comfortable with the fact that they do provide valuable information to consumers in some ads and of course provide economic

benefits to their business clients. But justification of the institution of advertising, insofar as it appeals either to the contribution advertising
makes to over-all social utility, or to rights, depends upon advertisers'
obeying the moral demands we have identified in the preceding.

III. ETHICS FOR INDIVIDUAL ADVERTISERS

§11 MICRO-LEVEL MORAL DEMANDS FROM MACRO-LEVEL FUNCTIONS AND RIGHTS

In the course of exploring the economic and social functions and effects
of advertising, we have specified several moral principles applicable to
individual advertisers and ad campaigns. These constraints must be observed if advertising is to be justified either by the free-market or the
rights approach. A review of these constraints and their application is
the topic of this final section.

The first positive function we discussed was the subsidizing of print
and broadcast media. The social effect here is optimized when sponsors
exercise restraint in their inclinations to censor program material in
order to appeal to uniformly large audiences and avoid offending them.
Only uncensored media can educate the public taste rather than accom-
modating to its lowest common denominator.[24] Here is the first case of a
moral demand that may run counter to the profit-maximizing motive of
the advertiser and his client. The injunction against censorship is a genuinely moral requirement, since the social effect of commercial censors
seems no less pernicious than that of government censors.

A function more intrinsic to advertisements themselves is the provision of information to consumers enabling them to make more rational
choices among products so as to better satisfy their desires. The performance of this function requires that advertisements be truthful and verifiable in their explicit and implied factual claims. "Puffery" or hyperbole
must be clearly distinguishable from factual claims by the audience addressed. The ads must not deceive members of that audience, this requirement becoming broader and stricter when the product is potentially harmful and the intended audience less worldly wise (for example,
children). While the advertiser is not morally required to aim at providing complete information, material omitted must not negate claims
made or implied, or relate to probable harm from the product.

Moral demands upon advertisers in their role as persuaders or crea-
tors of demand are somewhat more subtle and less subject to legal sanction, but nonetheless real. The basic principle regarding effects of persuasion is that advertisers ought not to create desires whose fulfillment
would be more harmful than beneficial to consumers. More broadly, the
principle we proposed prohibited encouragement of irrational desires.

Desires are irrational, we said, if their targets are falsely believed to be means to ends sought, if their satisfaction blocks that of other more important desires, or if the costs of their satisfaction are too high. Proscribed are desires for specific products known by the advertiser to be harmful, as well as yearnings for a lifestyle out of reach or ultimately low in over-all satisfaction. In regard to the former, the advertiser's ignorance of the harmfulness of the product he advocates is normally no excuse. Since he shares responsibility for the consumer's buying the product, he must share the blame for the harm that results. To avoid such blame he is obligated to find out, within reasonable limits, the nature of the products he sells.

Especially in regard to the rationality of lifestyles idealized in the advertiser's images, questions may arise for our principle concerning the relevant point of view. What is fulfilling for one person may not be for another; hence the rationality of desires can and does vary from individual to individual. The advertiser must rely here upon his own values and his knowledge of the audience he addresses. While he may without impropriety advocate products and even lifestyles he does not find personally appealing, he should not become a spokesman for what he considers harmful or irrational from the point of view of his typical audience. (The excuse that he is only a mouthpiece for his business client, who has a right to such an advocate, will be considered below, in §12.)

Turning to the method of non-rational persuasion itself, important moral considerations included the resistibility of the appeal to the audience, that is, whether their choices under its influence remain free, and the importance of the choices at stake. The former is especially relevant in the case of children, where the advertiser must exercise extreme caution and restraint. The latter is most relevant in the political arena, where the advertiser's influence may be most pernicious. At the same time, however, restrictions on the promotion of political candidates are not only difficult to enforce legally, but also difficult to specify on moral grounds. Persuasion, as we have said, is an essential part of the democratic process, and a right to persuade is included in a right to free speech. Ideally persuasion should consist in rational argument. But the merchandising of political candidates by ad campaigns in the media has become a major part of the persuasive process in our political arena. We have by now grown accustomed to the emphasis upon the personalities, appearances, and speech mannerisms of the candidates. Not only public relations and advertising professionals, but also reporters and media journalists have encouraged this emphasis, minutely analyzing after each television debate whether this candidate smiled at the right time or that one sounded firm enough. Image-building can no longer be realistically prohibited, although political promoters ideally ought to emphasize substantive issues. One hopes that voters will retain rational contol over decisions and the ability to separate political views from images. Perhaps here the clash of competing ad campaigns can cancel out much of the effect from image-building, if limitations are placed upon cost. If, instead, non-rational persuasion continues to increase its influence on election outcomes, we can expect the gap between appearance and substance to continue to widen in our highest office-holders.

Weaker moral demands relate also to the aesthetics of advertising. The advertiser ought not to harass or irritate us intentionally or pollute our natural or aesthetic environments in order to get our attention. Such injunctions become moral (although not major) when the ads are difficult to avoid. When one can choose whether to read or view material, its content is a matter of taste alone, and the only relevant moral principle specifies a right of free expression. But when the material intrudes upon our sensibilities without being sought out, as so much advertising does, we have the right not to be unreasonably offended or harassed, and the advertiser ought to honor that right according to his own sincere aesthetic appraisal.

§12 ADVERTISING ETHICS, BUSINESS ETHICS, AND ETHICS

It was argued earlier (§10) that appeal to the right of free expression only reinforces the moral restraints on advertising developed in terms of its functions within a free-market economy.

This right of advertisers must be limited by other rights of their audiences. These include rights not to be deceived, misled, harassed, or manipulated. These injunctions against deception, manipulation, and harm that we derived first from consideration of the economic functions of advertising can therefore be seen also as specifications of principles in business ethics, and ultimately of the more general principles of common morality. Such fundamental principles and rights apply directly to business contexts and to advertisers as business advocates. This direct application is worth emphasizing because of a dual inclination to deny or overlook it. The inclination arises first in the broader business context. We noted above (§9) a standard excuse for ignoring ordinary moral considerations in marketing decisions, the claim that business managers must cater to public demand and can do so only by aiming at maximal profits. Underlying the claim is the assumption that efficient satisfaction of consumer demand honors public free choice and maximizes utility.[25] We have seen that this assumption lies clearly open to question when we acknowledge the effects of advertising both upon the knowledge of consumers and upon demand itself. The advertiser cannot trust to the public's informed preferences or to the competition to guide the unrestrained pursuit of profit or self-interest toward maximal social benefits. He must rather follow his common moral sense and the more specific constraints we have derived here.

The advertiser's inclination to disavow moral responsibility for the products he promotes and desires he creates or focuses on might arise also from reflection on his position as advocate for his business client. The dilution of responsibility in such relationships, both in business and legal practice, is a common danger. Advocates ascribe responsibility for morally charged decisions to their clients, while in fact they strongly influence or make those decisions and affect outcomes. The right to advertise, defended above (§10), includes a right of business managers and professionals to hire advertisers as their spokesmen. But it does not include, we noted, a right to promote harmful products or to deceive. The advertiser as advocate cannot remain a neutral, morally detached mouthpiece for his client; he shares all responsibility for effects of the product. While in some professions, for example medicine, the central problem in client relations appears to be the unwarranted restriction of client authority, in advertising the problem is often the opposite, a pandering to the business client's interest at the expense of other moral considerations. But the notion of a professional as a "hired gun" is as objectionable in advertising as it is in law, the other major advocacy profession.

In addition to the two standard excuses for ignoring ordinary moral conscience, the first appealing to the public's freedom of choice and the second to the duty of client advocacy, there are two others that may be heard in business contexts. One is the Hobbesian argument (named after the English philosopher Thomas Hobbes, 1588–1679) that failure to serve the client's interest or aim at maximum profits at all social costs will cause defeat by the competition and death to the firm. Hobbes' claim was that there could be no moral obligations in a state of total war, where curbing self-interest by moral restraint means self-destruction. Whatever the merits of the argument in its original context, it certainly loses force when transposed to contexts of lesser competition than war. If generalized beyond its original scope, it could both negate *all* moral demands that counter self-interest and excuse *any* wrongdoing that is widespread. That the unscrupulous may profit (or "nice guys finish last") provides no genuine moral excuse for being unscrupulous in business. The advertiser who refuses to pander to potential clients that produce inferior or harmful products is doing the right thing even if not maximizing his profits.

Finally, one sometimes encounters in business and its allied professions a more pervasive moral myopia, bordering on moral skepticism, the denial that we can know clearly what is right and wrong in the contexts in question. In law this attitude often assumes the form of the claim that determination of moral right awaits legal decision; the businessperson claims that market forces determine right courses of conduct. The general problem of moral skepticism is beyond our scope here[26] (few people are skeptical of claims of wrong or wary of criticizing the law or the market when it comes to harm to themselves or their families). But the question is largely irrelevant to the constraints upon advertising practice that we have identified. For these follow not only from principles of common morality, but also, as we have shown, from the economic justification of the free-market economy. Those committed to that system must observe the rules intrinsic to its proper functioning.

Whether we adopt the economic viewpoint, or the broader moral point of view that includes specification of moral rights, we find the same ethical requirements for advertisers. The convergence of these two approaches makes the strongest case for the validity of these demands.

NOTES

1. For a discussion of this issue, see Jules Backman, *Advertising and Competition* (N.Y.: New York University Press, 1967).

2. See, for example, Robert Steiner, "Does Advertising Lower Consumer Prices?" *Journal of Marketing*, 37 (1973).

3. See Ivan Preston, "Reasonable Consumer or Ignorant Consumer? How the FTC Decides," *Journal of Consumer Affairs*, 8 (1974).

4. For example, Phillip Nelson, "Advertising and Ethics," in R. DeGeorge and J. Pichler, eds., *Ethics, Free Enterprise, and Public Policy* (N.Y.: Oxford University Press, 1978).

5. Compare Harry Johnson, "Apologia for Ad Men," in J. Wright and J. Mertes, ed., *Advertising's Role in Society* (St. Paul: West, 1974), p. 243.

6. Compare Ezra Mishan, "Commercial Advertising: A Skeptical View," in A. Hyman and M. B. Johnson, eds., *Advertising and Free Speech* (Lexington, Mass.: Heath, 1977), p. 64.

7. The point is argued also by Henry Grabowski, "Advertising and Resource Allocation — Critique," in S. F. Divita, ed., *Advertising and the Public Interest* (Chicago: American Marketing Association, 1978), p. 79.

8. The most celebrated discussion of the method is by Vance Packard, *The Hidden Persuaders* (N.Y.: McKay, 1957).

9. Compare Theodore Levitt, "The Morality (?) of Advertising," *Harvard Business Review*, 48 (1970).

10. This criterion is suggested by Stanley Benn, "Freedom and Persuasion," *The Australasian Journal of Philosophy* 45 (1967).

11. John Kenneth Galbraith, *The New Industrial State* (Boston: Houghton Mifflin, 1967), pp. 208–10; see also Galbraith's *The Affluent Society* (Boston: Houghton Mifflin, 1976).

12. William Comanor and Thomas Wilson, "Advertising and the Distribution of Consumer Demand," in S. F. Divita, op. cit.

13. Compare F. A. von Hayek, "The Non Sequitur of the Dependence Effect," in T. Beauchamp and N. Bowie, eds., *Ethical Theory in Business* (Englewood Cliffs, N.J.: Prentice-Hall, 1979).

14. Included under (b) and (c) are those alternatives forgone in the attempt to satisfy the desire in question.

15. The general point is argued by Martin Mayer, *Madison Avenue, U.S.A.* (N.Y.: Harper and Row, 1958), pp. 312–24.

16. The latter factor is emphasized by Andrew Hacker, "A Defense (or At Least an Explanation) of American Materialism," in Wright and Mertes, op. cit.

17. Ernest van den Haag, "What to Do About Advertising," *Commentary*, 31 (May 1962).

18. *Bigelow* v. *Commonwealth of Virginia*, 421 U.S. 809 (1975).

19. R. H. Coase, "Advertising and Free Speech," in Hyman and Johnson, op. cit.

20. See Vern Countryman, "Advertising Is Speech," in Hyman and Johnson, op. cit.
21. The notion of privacy appears to make sense in the corporate context only as a concern to protect trade secrets from competitors.
22. Phillip Nelson, "Advertising and Ethics," op. cit.
23. I refer here to lifestyles that are unfulfilling or ultimately unsatisfying to the agents themselves. No ideal or perfectionist criterion is assumed or suggested (see §9b).
24. Again here I am not presupposing ideal or objective criteria of aesthetic merit. I assume only that commercial interests are irrelevant to aesthetic ones, and that there can be education in aesthetic media.
25. For a full discussion of the argument in the broader business context, see Alan Goldman, *The Moral Foundations of Professional Ethics* (Totowa, N.J.: Rowman and Littlefield, 1980), ch. 5.
26. See Goldman, op. cit., ch. 1.

SUGGESTIONS FOR FURTHER READING

Further readings are listed below under the section numbers of the essay to which they are most relevant.

§1. The operation of the free competitive market is described in any standard economics test. The source of these descriptions is Adam Smith, *The Wealth of Nations*. A useful introductory text that emphasizes the virtues of the free market is Paul Heyne, *The Economic Way of Thinking* (Chicago: Science Research Associates, 1976).

§§2–7. Collections of essays that explore the economic social effects of the institution of advertising include: S. F. Divita, ed., *Advertising and the Public Interest* (Chicago: American Marketing Association, 1974); Otto Kleppner and Irving Settel, eds., *Exploring Advertising* (Englewood Cliffs, N.J.: Prentice-Hall, 1970); and John Wright and John Mertes, eds., *Advertising's Role in Society* (St. Paul: West, 1974). On the specific question of deception in advertising (§5), see the section on advertising in Tom Beauchamp and Norman Bowie, eds., *Ethical Theory in Business* (Englewood Cliffs, N.J.: Prentice-Hall, 1979); also the section on truth-telling in Thomas Donaldson and Patricia Werhane, eds., *Ethical Issues in Business* (Englewood Cliffs, N.J.: Prentice-Hall, 1979,). For a broader discussion of the morality of deception and lying, see Sissela Bok, *Lying* (N.Y.: Pantheon Books, Random House, 1978).

§8. The most sustained criticism of nonrational persuasion as used by advertisers is to be found in Vance Packard, *The Hidden Persuaders* (N.Y.: David McKay, 1957). This book is written in popular style but remains the classic on the subject.

§9. The major source of writings on the topic of created demand is John Kenneth Galbraith. See his *The Affluent Society* (Boston: Houghton Mifflin, 1976); also *The New Industrial State* (Boston: Houghton Mifflin, 1967). A well-known reply to Galbraith is by F. A. von Hayek, "The Non Sequitur of the 'Dependence Effect,'" *Southern Economic Journal* (April 1961).

§10. A collection of essays concerning the right to advertise and the relation of this right to that of free speech is Allen Hyman and M. Bruce Johnson, eds., *Advertising and Free Speech* (Lexington, Mass.: D.C. Heath, 1977). On the question of regulation, see also the section on regulation in S. F. Divita, *Advertising and the Public Interest*, cited above.

§11.   For further discussion of the obligations of individual advertisers, see the section on advertising in Burton M. Leiser, *Liberty, Justice, and Morals* (N.Y.: Macmillan, 1979); also the section on advertising ethics in Richard DeGeorge and Joseph Pichler, eds., *Ethics, Free Enterprise, and Public Policy* (N.Y.: Oxford University Press, 1978).

§12.   Further reading on the location of business ethics within the broader perspective of moral theory can be found in Thomas M. Garrett, *Business Ethics* (Englewood Cliffs, N.J.: Prentice-Hall, 1966); also Alan Goldman, *The Moral Foundations of Professional Ethics* (Totowa, N.J.: Rowman and Littlefield, 1980).

9

Transnational Transgressions

HENRY SHUE

I. INTRODUCTION

§1 THE ADVANTAGE OF BEING IN TWO PLACES AT THE SAME TIME

American students who have traveled abroad and have had sense enough to avoid the "tourist traps," the hotels and restaurants that charge the same prices charged by hotels and restaurants in their wealthier home countries and that therefore have few local customers, soon find countries in which they can either live like kings by spending at the same level they would spend at home or live as well as at home while spending much less. This is of course because of the enormous differences in the cost of living between the wealthiest countries, like the United States, and the poorer countries that make up most of the world – the countries of the so-called "Third World." The thought soon occurs to you, "Wouldn't it be great if my income could continue at United States levels and my expenditures could be at Third World levels? Oh, to live on Bali with even a middle-class United States salary!"

The difficulty is that it is not easy to arrange to receive the salary paid to people in wealthy countries without living in a wealthy country. But then one's expenditures are also at the wealthy country's level. It is not impossible for individual people to arrange to work both sides of the street in this way. United States citizens can, for example, retire to the old country and live there on their Social Security checks, which, if the old country has a sufficiently lower cost of living, will enable them to live much better than they could in the United States. One can also, obviously, simply restrict one's optional expenditures during the year while earning one's income at the higher rate and then live it up abroad

271

during vacation. There is no way, however, during most of life for most people to arrange to receive their income in a wealthier country and to spend it in a poorer one where it will buy more.

This good fortune, unavailable to most individuals and businesses, is standard operating procedure for transnational corporations, corporations that "live" simultaneously in many countries, buying supplies and paying labor wherever on the globe they cost least and selling products wherever on the globe they cost most. You will never find an executive of a transnational who is not enthusiastic about "free trade."

This advantage of operating simultaneously in multiple markets at radically different economic levels is one that not even the most powerful governments in the world can arrange for themselves: Even the government of a superpower like the United States must try to balance its budget while receiving and spending for the most part within a single national economy. To get some sense of the issues at hand, suppose the United States government should fire many of its office workers in Washington and transfer the paperwork to another English-speaking country where salaries are much lower, say, Ireland. Faster than you can say "Erin go bragh," the federal budget of the United States would turn from red toward black. But you can imagine the political rumpus that the sharp increase in unemployment would launch.

Naturally the name of the game is to buy low and sell high, and the underlying rationale for this part of the activity of contemporary transnationals is not fundamentally different from the rationale of the seventeenth-century traders who sailed their tall ships to China to buy silk for next to nothing and then sold it dear to the European aristocracy. Today the margins can be much lower because the number of transactions can be so much higher, thanks to air freight for the silk and computer transfers through international banks for the funds. But the basic pattern is the same; it's just faster now.

But the greatest strength of the transnational does not reside in its global reach, which enables it to buy materials and hire labor in the poorest countries and sell products in the wealthiest; its greatest strength lies in its being the only significant kind of genuinely transnational institution there is, literally *sui generis* — one of a kind. Other international institutions, such as the United Nations, are all multinational rather than transnational. The United Nations, for example, is composed of representatives of many nations, but every official delegate to every UN agency represents a single nation. Many institutions are multilateral or multinational in this sense: they represent or stretch across a number of nations.

A transnational corporation by contrast need have no particular allegiance to any one nation. By "living" in many places at the same time, it "lives" nowhere in particular. It operates in many nations while belonging to none. And a large transnational is effectively outside the control of any national government. Many mechanisms contribute to this immunity from control by government, but one of the clearest is a widely used accounting technique called transfer-pricing. Let us see how it works.

§2 A DELICATE BALANCING ACT

Suppose Global Aircraft and Stormdoor Corporation (GAS), International, mines its bauxite in Zaire, processes the aluminum in Jamaica, and assembles its planes and doors in the United States. How is the tax GAS-Jamaica owes the Jamaican government to be determined? The Jamaican government could in theory set a tariff on the value of the bauxite shipped by GAS-Zaire to GAS-Jamaica. But that bit of theory, many believe, would not further Jamaican interests if applied in practice. Not only would it discourage GAS-International from maintaining its Jamaican subsidiary and doing its processing there; the GAS accountants could maintain that the raw ore was actually of relatively little value and gains significant value only *after* the processing inside Jamaica. Thus the imports by GAS-Jamaica would be of relatively low value, and its exports would be of relatively high value. The Jamaican government, it seems, would do well to try another approach.

Jamaica might think, then, that a fairer and more remunerative tax would be a value-added tax applied to the value added by the processing conducted on Jamaican territory. But this move would whet any GAS accountant's appetite for numerical intrigue. GAS's accountants could now maintain *either* that the pieces exported by GAS-Jamaica were actually not of very much higher value (and that the significant addition of value came from the designs used in the final assembly by GAS-USA), *or* that the ore exported by GAS-Zaire was now worth considerably more than it used to be, *or* both — so that, in any case, the difference in value between GAS-Jamaica's imports and exports would show up in the balance sheets as being worth much less than you might think. A transnational like GAS can put an individual country like Jamaica between an economic rock and a hard place.

In part this is because the prices at the various stages are largely internal (to the transnational), administered prices. GAS-Jamaica is "buying" from GAS-Zaire and "selling" to GAS-USA. The parent transnational, GAS-International, has wide discretion over how these transfers are priced and can to a considerable degree determine thereby its own tax liability. In theory some institution could audit all these transfer-prices — could verify, for example, that the difference between the value upon exit from Zaire and the value upon entrance to Jamaica was attributable to conventional transportation costs. But that auditing body would itself need to be multinational, if not transnational. And there's the rub. There is no transnational auditor. The United States government, for example, can audit GAS-USA, but has no authority to demand records from GAS-Jamaica or GAS-Zaire. In theory, all governments concerned could pool information, but in fact they do not. Nor are they likely to do so if left to their own short-term national interests. Since one government's gain in taxes would to some extent be another government's loss, nationalistic inclinations of this kind are not apt to give rise to intergovernmental cooperation.

This extremely simple example hardly begins to indicate the advantages that any large transnational economic organization brings to its contest with national political organizations. When one adds to a transnational's ability to exploit a particular nation's tax and investment codes (and the differences among them across nations) the additional capacity to benefit from the full array of currency exchanges and other banking transactions available to the sophisticated corps of lawyers and accountants who work for any major transnational and command all the information they need — when one combines all these factors, one gets a glimpse of the staggering array of strategic and tactical options transnationals have in comparison to representatives of national governments with their partial information and limited jurisdiction. In the case of the weaker Third World governments the confrontation is simply no contest.

For these reasons transnationals raise many special questions that other corporations, even very large and powerful ones, do not raise. But to make the present examination of transnationals more manageable, we will limit our inquiry to just one question — the deceptively simple one of how the wages paid in a poor, or Third World, country by a transnational corporation based in a wealthy, or First World, country should be determined.

People everywhere care greatly about how much they are paid for doing work that frequently they do not especially want to do. For wage-earners in the Third World this is often literally a life or death issue — a difference in salary that strikes us as "peanuts" may determine *how many* children will starve, not whether any will. When, therefore, we limit our inquiry to this question about wages, it should not be assumed that we choose either an unimportant or a simple issue. It is clearly no exaggeration to say that lives hang in the balance. And the complexity of the issue will soon emerge.

II. EQUAL PAY FOR EQUAL WORK?

§3 UNIVERSAL AND EVERYWHERE

Nothing is so appealing as a simple solution to a complex problem, and so it is that, having sketched the unique power of transnationals and duly noted the gravity of the question we seek to answer, we are likely to be attracted initially to a very straightforward proposal. Since no principle can be a *moral* principle unless it applies equally to all relevantly similar cases or, to put this same point in different words, unless it is universal, all that we need do, it might be thought, is formulate a principle concerning wages that meets this requirement and our work will be done.

Alas, things are not so simple. Though it is true that any moral principle must apply to all relevantly similar cases — must, that is, be universal — the requirement of universality is a merely *formal* requirement. Universality is also a merely *necessary*, not a sufficient condition, of moral acceptability. By itself, that is, the requirement that a moral principle must apply equally to all relevantly similar cases does not disclose *which* similarities are the relevant ones. Indeed, principles that are highly objectionable in their substance, in what they prescribe or permit, can satisfy the requirement of universality, as the following example illustrates.

During the period when the British Navy had taken control of a number of China's major port cities, the British authorities decided to reserve the most beautiful parks for their compatriots and erected at the entrances to the parks the infamous signs saying: "No Dogs, No Chinese." The principle expressed on these signs was perfectly universal. All dogs without exception and all Chinese without exception were excluded from the parks. There was no discrimination among dogs or among Chinese or — this obviously is why the Chinese have never forgotten the insult — between dogs and Chinese. What the principle "No Dogs, No Chinese" prohibited strikes us as morally repugnant. And yet it meets the requirement of universality. So a principle's meeting that requirement is not enough to establish its moral acceptability. Formal universality is not sufficient for moral acceptability.

It might be thought that a simple adjustment will save the decisiveness of the formal requirement of universality. Of course, it may be said, the requirement of universality was never intended to mean that everyone and everything — sticks and stones, lizards and Lilliputians — were to be treated identically. Of course, it may be said, what was wrong with British policy was precisely that it treated the Chinese like dogs. We are not expected to treat persons and non-persons alike — we are simply expected to treat *all persons* alike.

But this is wrong — and still too formal — in both what it affirms and what it denies. In some respects we may and should treat people and animals alike: If I can eliminate some intense agony at little cost or risk to myself or anyone else, I normally ought to do it irrespective of whether the sufferer is man or beast. More relevantly, it simply is not true that we should or even may *always* treat all persons alike. The special treatment and assistance owed to the blind and the deaf, for example, are not owed to those with normal sight and hearing. Even sex, age, and race can mark a relevant difference in some cases. For example, since the aged are vulnerable to threats that the young can handle for themselves, the aged have rights to protection that the young do not share. So the decisiveness of the requirement of universality cannot be saved by assuming that it requires that we treat all (and only) human beings in the same way. This assumption does not stand up to clear cases.

What the preceding discussion of universality indicates is this. A moral principle must apply across some category, large or small: all human beings, all blind or deaf persons, all women. The categories to which some moral principles apply *include more* than the species *Homo sapiens* (for we *morally* ought not to cause animals to suffer gratuitously), and some principles may non-arbitrarily apply *only to a sub-class* of human beings (for example, those who are aged or blind). It should come as no surprise that very difficult, important questions arise concerning how and when to limit the scope of a moral principle or, alternatively, how and when to limit the category of individuals to which it applies. In the particular case of the question central to this essay — namely, how should the wages paid to Third World employees by transnational corporations be set or established? — what we want to know includes (1) what in general are the morally relevant considerations for determining what people should be paid; (2) whether wages paid by transnational employers to Third World employees are set in ways that respect the appropriate moral principle(s); (3) if not, what, if anything, can be done to remedy these transnational transgressions; and (4) which individuals or institutions have the responsibilities to apply the remedies. These four questions will concern us in the sequel.

§4 "LEAVE IT TO THE MARKET"

One way to answer the first of the above questions is by appeal to what we will call *the free-market principle*, the principle that wages ought to be set by local markets for labor without any assistance or regulation from other parties. The morally relevant consideration for setting wages is assumed to be what the market forces of supply and demand dictate. Wages are to be set by what individual workers are willing to take and employers willing to pay — neither more nor less.

The free-market principle certainly meets the requirement of universality (after all, *all workers* and *all employers* are to be treated similarly) and so cannot be dismissed on purely formal grounds. But few will find this principle's implications morally hospitable. The brutality of the recommendation to "leave it to the market" emerges as soon as one considers that the pool of labor in the Third World is for all practical purposes unlimited. With unemployment rates of fifty percent not uncommon the only floor under wages is set by the amount of income that will buy just enough food to keep the worker from collapsing, and of course individual workers will sometimes take less than that for as long as they last. Where the demand for labor is radically less than the supply, that is, unemployment rates are in the twenties, thirties, and higher, to say that anything the market will bear is acceptable is to say that absolutely anything is acceptable, or in other words, is to have no standard at all and simply to allow workers to be used up like raw material.

Anyone who fails to find this treatment of human beings intuitively objectionable is unlikely to be moved by any additional considerations, but it may be worth noting how unfair the bargaining situation constituted by this "free market" is. Many of the Third World's unemployed have literally no alternative to any job they may be offered by a transnational. The transnational, in contrast, will typically have unlimited alternatives to any given worker or local group of workers, as is obvious from the level of the unemployment rate. There are some qualifications upon this point. Extractive industries, for example, must drill or mine wherever the resource in question is found. They cannot simply threaten to pull up stakes and move elsewhere, although they can, and often do, import workers from outside the locale of a mine if the local workers are not amenable to accepting the firm's terms. But most kinds of firms can be located virtually wherever labor with the requisite level of skill or strength is found, subject only to consideration of such costs as transportation and communication, which are generally unlikely to matter nearly as much as labor costs. So, no, the free-market principle, despite its universality, is not a satisfactory principle that answers our central question about wages.

§5 LITERAL EQUALITY?

Appeal to the *equal-pay principle* would give a very different answer to our question. This principle declares that people ought to receive equal pay for equal work wherever they live, Phoenix or the Philippines. Again we have a principle that easily meets the test of universality, only now we have one that admits of several possible interpretations. On one reading, "equal pay" means "the same pay," so that, on this interpretation, what the equal-pay principle requires is that people who do equal work are to receive the same pay. Interpreted in this way, the equal-pay principle has bizarre implications. To pay a woman assembling microprocessors in one of the poorer Third World countries the equivalent in the local currency of the same number of dollars paid a woman in California's "Silicone Valley" for the same work might mean that the woman in the poor country earned several times more in one week than the majority of the rest of the population of the country earn in a year — and far more in one year than most other people in the country earn in their whole lives.

One could try for a more plausible interpretation of "equal pay for equal work" by suggesting, not equivalent amounts of income, which would give the Third World worker a far higher standard of living than her California counterpart, but equivalent standards of living. But this too would be too much. One cannot ignore the enormity of the current inequalities among nations. The standard of living of a California assembly-line worker would give a worker in many Third World countries the same standard of living as much of — not all — the elite of her own country. While she might well have done more to earn her income than they had, implementing the equal-pay principle in the way prescribed by this interpretation would be unrealistic.

§6 ANALOGICAL EQUALITY?

I do not see much promise in scratching around for additional interpretations of the equal-pay principle that might seem to yield more reasonable implications than those traced so far. Though there are quite a few variants we have not discussed, all face the same insuperable problem: The contexts are *so radically different* (because of the radical inequalities among nations in standards of living) that "equality" of pay between two of the more distant contexts, such as the United States and a poorer member of the Third World, can be given a plausible interpretation only by means of so much tugging and pulling on the meaning of "equality" that the resulting "special" interpretation threatens to lose all resemblance to anything recognizable as genuine equality. To see a third, and final, illustration of the difficulty of retaining much sense in the notion of equal pay for equal work, where the "equality" must stretch between radically unequal contexts, consider one more attempt at a reasonable interpretation of the equal-pay principle. Instead of either of the first two, rejected interpretations—literally equal pay and pay sufficient for an equal standard of living—we might offer the following: The worker employed by the transnational in the Third World should be paid a salary that will enable her to be as well off, relative to the other members of her own society, as the worker employed in the First World is, relative to the other members of her own society. "Equality" is now being given an analogical interpretation: The requirement of equality of pay is now taken to mean a requirement of pay that places a person in an analogous economic position.

This third interpretation certainly does not seem to require too high a salary to be an economically or politically feasible undertaking for a transnational to make. On the contrary, this interpretation of the equal-pay principle is in danger of turning out to be too low. In the poorer Third World countries a small percentage of the people typically have very high incomes, while the vast majority of the population has little — or no (cash)—income. A slight increase in income for the assembly worker in question might well catapult her into the second-highest quintile of the population, or in any case into a percentile much higher than the comparable worker in the Silicone Valley, without providing her with an income adequate to support herself and other members of her immediate family for whom she is responsible. The absolute amount of her income might still be inadequate for her physical needs.

This is the opposite of the problem with the first interpretation that took equal pay literally. To require *absolutely* equal amounts of salary between two contexts with radically unequal standards of living seems intuitively too high a requirement. But to require *relatively* equal amounts of salary (for example, salaries falling respectively into the same percentile of the national income distribution), as on the third (analogical) suggestion, seems intuitively too low a requirement. Neither of these intuitions has to be treated as definitive, but they do indicate further the extreme difficulty of working with the notion of equal pay in radically unequal contexts.

III. EQUAL RIGHTS AND THE SETTING OF WAGES

§7 EQUALITY REVISITED

It still seems that there must be some sense in which workers in the Third World deserve equal treatment with workers in the First World, even if "equal pay for equal work" is a useless slogan for this case. Our underlying conviction is that whether or not it makes economic sense to pay them equally, they still deserve to be treated equally — treated equally as human beings. They deserve, as much as workers anywhere else deserve, to be treated equally and fully as human beings.

But what does it mean to treat people as equally human in such cases? If we acknowledge that people working within different national economies with radically unequal standards of living may be paid unequal salaries, how do we treat them as equally human? Do we just smile and ask about the children as we hand over an obviously inadequate paycheck? Presumably this requirement imposed by shared humanity has a bit more substance than that!

The free-market principle that we considered earlier was a procedural standard in the sense that it approached the determination of the appropriate level of wages only indirectly, by specifying only the process to be used in order to arrive at the appropriate level. The suggestion, which we rejected, was that any actual level that resulted from the market would, in effect, be blessed by the procedure that produced it.

By contrast, each of the three interpretations of equality that we considered were substantive standards. Unlike the free-market principle, each of these three equality principles attempted to spell out directly the appropriate level of wages. Each attempted to say, in effect, here is where the wages should be set. Once we have noticed the distinction between procedural and substantive standards, we can readily see the possibility of formulating a procedural standard that is an expression of the equality principle.

One way to treat people equally is to treat them as being equally entitled to an explanation of why they should go along with any arrangement that is not initially appealing to them. Equal treatment grants that other people have interests, goals, values, and plans of their own and that they therefore are entitled to be shown how and why acting in accord with *my* interests, goals, values, or plans is compatible with *theirs*. Put negatively, treating other people as equal is avoiding manipulation in favor of rational persuasion and negotiation. Rational persuasion and negotiation are acknowledgements that other people also have plans, which may or may not be compatible with my plans for them. If I want other people to cooperate freely with my plans, I must show how mine mesh with theirs. If they do not in fact mesh, I may have to modify mine

somewhat — this is negotiation. In more traditional philosophical terminology, to treat other people as equally human is to treat them as having
a right to be autonomous — as having, as we now say, an agenda of their
own that, if I want to be on, I must ask to be on.

Treating other people as equally human complicates life enormously.
Things go much more smoothly when people can be manipulated, deceived, or evaded — the saving in time, for example, is tremendous, compared to explanations and negotiations. But if we are to respect other
persons, we must allow them to participate in decisions about what is to
be done by allowing them to propose participating only on terms more
acceptable to them than the terms we propose. To do so can lead to genuine negotiation, not the kind that simply reports a position that is not
going to be changed. Providing for this kind of participation is, ultimately, respecting the liberty of the others. It is treating them *as having
a right* to choose not to go along on the basis of accurate and adequate
information about the proposal.

§8 EQUALITY AND WAGES

The procedural standard for setting wage levels between employees in
the Third World and transnationals that treats the workers as equally
human is that wages should be the outcome of discussion and, if need be,
negotiation between the worker and the employer. Otherwise the wage
is simply imposed, in violation of the worker's liberty.

Why would this make the wage imposed? Might we not say that the
worker is at liberty to refuse the job and thereby reject the wage? To say
this would be to misunderstand the idea of liberty. People are at liberty to
refuse jobs only if they are independently wealthy, and thus do not need
to have a job in order to have an income, or if another job on better
terms is available. To have no realistic alternative means of support is
not to be at liberty to refuse what is offered. One might as well say these
workers are "at liberty" to buy a Mercedes. In countries in which one-
quarter, one-third, or even one-half the population are unemployed it
will be rare for realistic alternative means of support to be available. More
often than not, if there is no room for discussion about the terms of the
jobs offered by any one firm, there will be no room for discussion at all.

The fundamental objection we can raise against the conflicting procedure recommended earlier by the free-market principle now comes into
clearer view. The reason permitting the salaries paid to Third World
workers to be as low as allowed by a market with a virtually unlimited
supply of workers is so obviously objectionable is that it treats individual
workers as expendable, replaceable raw materials, not as human beings
with interests, goals, and values of their own, individuals entitled to an
opportunity to participate effectively in those processes the outcomes of
which are likely to make a significant difference to *their* interests, goals,
and values.

§9 PROCEDURAL EQUALITY IN SETTING WAGES

People are being treated as equally human, we have said, only if they have the opportunity to participate effectively in making decisions the results of which are likely to affect them significantly. Since decisions about what wages are to be paid is a matter that in all likelihood will affect workers significantly, they are treated as equally human only if they have the opportunity to participate effectively in the determination of their wages. However, since most workers in the Third World, taken individually, normally have no realistic option other than to accept whatever pay is offered, to "discuss" wages with individual workers, on the pretext of "negotiating" about them, is rhetoric at best, deceit at worst. *Only if* workers are able to join forces and have their shared interests considered together is there any chance that they will be effective parties to the determination of what wages will be paid. Only then, therefore, will they be treated as equally human, given our proposed standard of procedural equality. And thus it is that we may offer a clear and forceful answer to our central question. *When it comes to the setting of wages, people are being treated as equally human only if their wages are the outcome of a process of fair bargaining between the transnational corporation and a freely functioning body that represents the interests of the workers, a body that ordinarily will be a freely functioning trade union.*

In answering our question as we do, then, we attribute to the workers of the Third World a moral right (and this, one of the very few) that is recognized legally in both the International Covenant on Civil and Political Rights (Article 22) and the International Covenant on Economic, Social and Cultural Rights (Article 8). The Civil and Political Covenant says:

> Everyone shall have the right to freedom of association with others, including the right to form and join trade unions for the protection of his interests.

So in requiring that transnationals negotiate not with individual workers but with trade unions, we do not champion some radical transformation of international thought regarding human rights. We endorse a portion of the current consensus. In fact, many will read the call to implement "the right to form and join trade unions" in the Third World as far too conservative.

§10 CAN UNIONS FULFILL RIGHTS?

Except for people who are members of unions (and probably for some of them too) the subject of trade unions seems to strike most people in the United States as a thoroughly dull, and not really very important, matter. And in fact many unions in the United States are themselves thoroughly dull and not very important. United States unions seem to run the usual gamut, from those controlled by the underworld, at one extreme, to those essentially controlled by the management, at the other. Between the extremes are some that are competent and a few that are forceful and significantly effective. But the ordinary United States citizen can be forgiven, I think, for assuming that unions are not of much consequence.

The topic of unions has livened up, sadly, as I am writing this because a military dictatorship has just seized power in Poland in an effort to suppress the independence of the free trade union, "Solidarity," which was "free" in the sense of being controlled not by the party and not by the government, but by workers themselves. The national and international crises produced by the emergence of a largely free union in Poland are the most striking recent evidence that union activities can be a significant and serious matter.

The Polish Army's confrontation with Solidarity has served to remind us that communist states do not tolerate free trade unions. Neither do many other one-party states. In Mexico, for example, the one large confederation of unions has an extremely cozy relationship with the one party that has ruled Mexico without interruption since early in this century. The Republic of South Africa continues to allow the all-white unions, with the full legal rights to bargain and to strike, to exclude blacks, who must form their own unions with only partial rights. And right-wing dictatorships around the globe routinely treat unions as threats to national security, from the Republic of South Korea, where the government in 1981 promulgated laws closing all branches of the Korean labor federation and stripping workers of union membership; to Guatemala, where trade unionists are specially targeted for execution by government-coordinated terror squads; to Turkey, where during the last year the martial-law government has closed not only the main labor federation but other smaller ones as well and allowed several union leaders to die mysteriously while in custody or to undergo torture.

Still, while unions may be somewhat important, especially to the people who are, or would like to be, in one, are they really the stuff of universal human rights? Unions are, after all, merely mechanisms and means for pursuing economic interests. They may not seem, well, sufficiently noble to be the subject of a human right. Unions seem too mundane and ordinary.

This doubt reflects, I think, at least a partial misunderstanding about human rights. The fundamental notion that every person, however modest his or her merits, is entitled to the satisfaction of a few minimum demands is itself a rather lofty ideal, daring in its attempt to impose a basic equality upon the given inequalities among concrete individuals. That the frump and the wimp have the same bedrock entitlements as the beauty and the hero is not only a comfort to the armies of the ordinary but an excitingly counter-intuitive thought. The notion of human rights is grand and even noble in its commitment to see minimal dignity and respect accorded even to the mediocre and the disreputable.

But the content of many human rights — including, I have argued, some of the basic rights — is utterly mundane. No right is more basic (or more universally accepted in principle) than the right not to be tortured, but there is nothing grand about merely not being tortured. No romantic conception of the human body is involved in the justification for the prohibition against torture. There may be, once again, a certain nobility about the extremity to which equality is extended when it is maintained that even torturers themselves retain an equal right not to be tortured. But it is only the form — specifically, the sheer equality — of the right that is grand. Its content — not having your body or your mind messed over against your will — is simple, ordinary, and wonderfully unexciting. And not being tortured is simply a means. No one is imagined to take delight, or even much satisfaction, merely in not being tortured. The absence of agony is merely a precondition for any delights or accomplishments.

Roughly the same is true of other critical rights. If the right to due process, for example, is a basic human right, it is not because very many people take pleasure in the delays, tangles, expenses, and hassles that participation in the judicial process involves even when you are absolutely faultless. The enjoyment of due process is simply a means to the avoidance of a worse fate.

IV. ARE UNIONS IN THE THIRD WORLD PREMATURE?

§11 TRANSNATIONALS AS TRUSTEES OF WORKERS' WELFARE

The right to form and join a trade union is an internationally recognized legal right, which, if the preceding argument is sound, has a firm moral foundation, since, without the right, workers in the Third World would be treated as less than equally human. Still, many object to implementing this right now in the Third World. Although the right to form and join unions is a constitutionally protected right in the United States, for example, it is claimed that the political, social, and economic realities of the Third World make it unrealistic or impossible to implement this right now. Certainly the many Third World governments that ban or harass all forms of associations of workers seem to see some difficulties. The right frequently is conceded in theory but denied in practice.

What good reason could there be for not allowing workers in the Third World to exercise their right to organize in order to protect their own interests? One reason would be the availability of some other organization or institution that would do such a superior job of protecting the workers' interests for them that their right to look out for their own interests could be overridden. One kind of candidate for that role is the transnational corporation, which is in certain obvious respects a superior form of organization.

The transnational wants to do what is efficient over-all. Its rationality is at a global level of organizaton. This is in fact often presented by spokesmen for transnationals as the basis for the uniquely valuable contribution the firms can make—they can utilize resources from around the planet in the mix that is rational at the most comprehensive level, with all things considered. This means, however, that any given national subsidiary of a transnational is not necessarily operated in the manner that would be best for that subsidiary if that subsidiary by itself were the whole corporation. Each subsidiary is operated in the manner that is best for the transnational corporation as a whole. The parts serve the whole. There is a division of labor among all the subsidiaries that serves the best interest of the parent transnational. This division is not necessarily what would be best for each subsidiary if each subsidiary were an end in itself.

For example, suppose the Indonesian subsidiary of a transnational is doing very well and generating considerable profit that could be reinvested in Indonesia in a manner that would increase the rate of profit for the Indonesian subsidiary. The Brazilian subsidiary is not doing so well, but with a large infusion of capital for new technology could have an even higher rate of return than the Indonesian subsidiary would if all the capital generated by the Indonesian subsidiary were reinvested in Indonesia. Clearly the central management might choose, in effect, to reinvest the profits made by the Indonesian subsidiary in Brazil, not in Indonesia. If reinvestment in Brazil will bring a higher rate of return, then this is, other things being equal, what is rational from the global point of view? But it may very well not be best—or, even, good—for the Indonesian subsidiary, which will then do less well than it would have if its profits could have been reinvested in its own operation. What is best for the whole is by no means always best for each part considered separately. The central choice to move capital from Indonesia to Brazil might well affect the wages for the jobs in Indonesia, not to mention the rate of increase in the number of jobs for Indonesians.

Doing with each part what is best for the whole might be called "global logic." The point here is that global logic will sometimes necessitate following a policy with the resources of the subsidiary in one nation that is quite different from the policy that would be generally best for that subsidiary by itself. Now, so far this discussion of global logic has said nothing directly about what is best for the workers in a single national subsidiary. But if the global logic that the management of a transnational can be expected to follow will sometimes sacrifice the general interest of one subsidiary as a whole in order to promote the general interest of another subsidiary, it is perfectly clear that the specific interests of the workers in any one subsidiary can be expected sometimes (at least) to be sacrificed for the benefit of some other subsidiary—not necessarily the benefit of the workers there, of course—and thereby for the benefit of the total operation at the global level. There is no reason to believe, therefore, that decisions made by transnational managers will generally be in the best interests of the workers in any particular country. Indeed, the managers cannot possibly be good trustees of global corporate interests *and* of the interests of workers in every country, because these interests sometimes conflict.

I have said nothing so far about how much the international headquarters of a transnational is likely even to know about the needs of the workers in its Third World subsidiaries. You can probably guess how well accountants and lawyers in Manhattan understand, say, the effects on the traditional family in the tropics of some of their policy choices, such as the policy of using young women instead of men for certain assembly operations (on the official rationale that young women have more "nimble fingers") and thus leaving traditional male breadwinners unemployed, and embittered toward the women who suddenly support them financially. But the main point is that any ignorance and indifference about cultural damage, for example, are for the most part irrelevant because global logic must impel decision-making away from doing even what is best for a given subsidiary when the subsidiary is viewed as a whole, much less doing what is best specifically for the workers in a given subsidiary.

The global logic of the transnationals, which dictates managing each subsidiary to the benefit of the transnational as a whole, makes it extremely unlikely that policies will be set so that the interests of the workers of every subsidiary will be promoted. That would be likely only if there were a miraculous multiple coincidence of interests of the following form: The course of conduct that is best for the transnational as a whole, and the course of conduct that promotes the interests of the workers in country A, and the course of conduct that promotes the interests of the workers in country B, and so forth, are all the same course of conduct. The regular occurrence of so many multiple coincidences strains credulity.

Thus, if the question were simply, Who is more likely to promote effectively the interests of the workers in one national subsidiary of a transnational firm, those workers themselves or the managers who set global priorities for the transnational? the answer seems clearly to be: probably the workers themselves, since they will at least be attempting to promote their own interests, while the transnational's managers will view that as a fortunate side-effect, at best, of the pursuit of other, broader goals. Other things being equal, one is considerably more likely to attain a particular goal if one is actually trying to attain that goal, as, in the case of the goal of the workers' welfare, the workers are and the corporate managers are not.

But the question in the preceding paragraph was not our question. Our question was a much tougher one: Given that workers everywhere have an internationally recognized legal right to union activity, is it clear that workers in the Third World would be so much better off if corporate managers looked after their welfare for them than they would be if they pursued their own welfare themselves through union activity, that their legal right to union activity should be overridden? To this question the answer is very clearly No.

§12 THIRD-WORLD GOVERNMENTS AS TRUSTEES OF THEIR NATIONS

A kind of argument very different from the one in the preceding section might be given for the same conclusion that the legal right of workers to form and join unions should not be honored yet in the Third World. Even a genuine right, like the right to participate in unions, can sometimes be overridden by a great public purpose, when it is impossible to respect the right and still attain the purpose. Naturally, such arguments should be greeted with skepticism, because it is frequently not impossible, but only inconvenient, to attain major national goals while respecting rights. And one of the main purposes of rights is precisely to prevent governments from always simply doing what is most convenient for them. But the national government of a country is normally expected to be promoting broader public interests of the kind that we would ordinarily be willing at least to consider allowing to override some narrower interests, and possibly even some rights.

Perhaps at an early stage of development it is necessary to have economic strategy set by people in a position to adopt a long-range and broadly national view that takes into account not only current wages for this generation of workers but also, for example, the need for reinvestment that will generate more jobs for future generations, the need for policies on the utilization of renewable and non-renewable resources that will benefit the nation as a whole over the long term, and the need for transfers into the country of technology and management skills that will increase the extent of the nation's mastery over its own house. In this case, might it not be better for the national government to set wage levels, or to negotiate them with the transnationals, on the basis of a coherent national plan for development rather than having policy be influenced by individual unions or even national federations of unions merely looking out for the immediate interests of those who happen currently to be employed? Almost certainly, union members will be a minority of the population—in many Third World countries the employed are a minority of the labor force! The government can defend the majority, any threatened non-unionized minorities, future generations, and the natural resources and the other wealth of the nation. The government can, in short, defend an enlightened version of the national interest that takes into account the rights of all affected.

Spokesmen for Third World governments frequently give just such reasons for refusing to implement in domestic law the right to unions established in international law, and the kinds of purposes envisioned for national government activity by such rhetoric are among the purposes for the sake of which "governments are instituted among men." Governments are, however, also—and, many would argue, primarily—instituted to protect moral rights by implementing legal rights. Is it really necessary to suppress the workers' right to participation in the choices that will shape their own lives in order to accomplish all these other worthy purposes?

The trouble with the argument that because the government can and ought to take the broader, longer view, it must not allow unions to press narrower, more immediate views is not that the premises about the nobler purposes of government are not correct — they are correct. The trouble is that the premises do not lead to the conclusion in support of which they are offered. Granted that the national government should defend future generations, the unemployed, the conservation of natural resources, and so forth, what follows is certainly not that unions should not be allowed to function at all but at most that the fulfillment of union demands must be limited at the point at which other legitimate and vital national interests are being threatened. In no way does it follow that unions should be made illegal or harassed by the government.

It follows only that if unions have become so powerful that they are pushing around the transnationals and forcing the transnationals to make decisions, for example, to over-consume non-renewable resources or to pay such high salaries that reinvestment in new technology is dropping to a degree that will severely limit future growth in productivity, the government should step in and defend those more reasonable policies of the transnational. But powerful unions pushing around transnationals who are pursuing the national interest of their host country are hardly the problem in an age in which one is far more likely to find union leaders tortured or executed by terror squads indulged, if not coordinated, by the host government, as, for example, in Guatemala and Turkey in 1981, or simply arrested and put in concentration camps, as, for example, in Poland in 1981.

§13 ARE UNIONS IN THE THIRD WORLD POINTLESS?

Perhaps neither transnational corporations nor national states would be such effective trustees for the interests of Third World workers that those workers could reasonably be expected to give up the exercise of their internationally recognized right to form and join unions. It certainly does not follow that the workers' own unions will be any more effective in protecting their rights, and this creates a final, deep problem. If the unions would not serve effectively either, and we knew that, then to offer the workers unions as the embodiment of the principle that they are to be treated as equally human would be to make an empty gesture. But what reason is there to think that provisions for unions might turn out to be empty gestures?

The source of the difficulty is what we called at the beginning of this essay "the advantage of being in two places at the same time." Transnational corporations are operating in several countries at once. If the workers in any given country attempt through their union to insist upon some demand that the transnational does not want to grant, the transnational can in many cases shift a particular project or even its entire operations out of the country in which the workers are making the demand and into some other country where the workers are more compliant. Clearly the best strategy for dealing with the transnational maneuverability of the firms would be a transnational union. If the union for workers of a particular kind extended across as many nations as the firm for which they worked, the firm might not be able to play off the workers in one country against the workers in other countries. The transnational union might enable all the relevant workers to take the same position against the firm in question.

This strategy, which seems certainly to be the best, faces two critical difficulties. First, the same kind of "global logic" that dominates the reasoning of the transnational firms might well dominate the reasoning of any transnational union. That is, those who make the central decisions for the transnational union are liable to do what is best for the transnational union as a whole, and this may well not be what is best for the workers in any one nation. It may simply be a fact that what is in the interest of the workers of one, two, or a minority of nations is in conflict with what is best for the majority of workers or for workers in the majority of countries. It is impossible to avoid in principle, and very unlikely that one can avoid in practice, conflicts between the welfare of the whole and the welfare of some of the parts in the case of unions any more than one can in the case of firms.

The second difficulty is more fundamental, in the sense that it would have to be overcome before a transnational union could even be created. This is simply the problem of nationalism, which has infected every attempt to form anything like an international or transnational association of workers. The loyalty of people to their own nation is frequently stronger than their loyalty to, or sense of solidarity with, workers who do similar jobs in a different nation. Frequently, a worker will feel, rightly or wrongly, that over-all he or she shares more interests with other people in his or her own country than with workers of the same kind in a different country. One need not either welcome or condemn this kind of allegiance to a person's own community in order to recognize that it is extremely powerful, and it has been the bane of many an abortive international movement.

The two difficulties are of opposite kinds. The latter is rooted in the difficulties of shaping a genuine whole with unified purposes out of parts that in the beginning have different if not conflicting interests. The former grows out of the tendency of a whole, once well-organized, to sacrifice the interests of individual parts to the over-all interest — indeed it is knowledge of the tendencies toward global logic that is one of the inspirations for nationalistic logic.

Now, I am in fact quite pessimistic. It may well be the case that only transnational unions can deal effectively with the power of either transnational corporations or national states. But the fear of the use of global logic within any transnational union, I believe, is almost certain to stimulate a nationalistic reaction that will work against transnational unions' ever coming into being. The one hopeful possibility that I can see is that one interest that is common to the workers of all nations is precisely their interest in defending the right to form and join unions. So it seems possible that associations of workers from various countries might be able to agree at least upon the importance of working together to protect the right to unions. Agreement upon this right, of course, is not the same as agreement upon which interests are to be pursued while exercising this right. But the adequate expression of the principle that all people are to be treated as equally human requires only that workers' rights to form and join unions be protected — it does not require that it should be somehow guaranteed that the right will be used in the strategically wisest manner. The main responsibility for protecting the workers' interests must in practice be left to them.

Does this mean that we consumers in the First World of products made in the Third World bear no responsibility toward Third World workers? Not at all. Everyone shares in duties to avoid depriving others of what they have rights to. This means that we through our government ought at the very least to avoid contributing to the capacity of governments that repress unions — governments like those in Poland, Turkey, Guatemala, and South Africa, for example — to continue their repression of this right. Exactly what is best done will naturally vary from case to case, and this is not the place for detailed case studies.

Generally speaking, however, the foreign policies of the rich and powerful countries like the United States should elevate human rights like the right to form and join unions from their current status as afterthoughts to prime considerations in all foreign policy, including foreign economic policy. Instead of assessing trade and aid policies purely in terms of United States power and United States wealth, we should also assess them on the basis of their effects on people's ability to exercise their rights. No economic activity is morally neutral when it strengthens the hands of barbaric oppressors like the current governments that rule Poland, Turkey, Guatemala, and South Africa.

Transnational banks, for example, like to insist that they should continue to be allowed to make loans to foreign governments on purely financial grounds. International loans, they claim, are just business and, indeed, strictly their own business. These claims are simply not true, however, when such loans sustain hated regimes that might otherwise collapse. Such loans assist in the deprivation of rights, and there is no reason why the rest of us should stand idly by and let them happen. Congress, in particular, should require every bank wishing to operate within United States territory to inform the Senate Committee on Foreign Relations and the House Committee on Foreign Affairs well in advance of the size of any loans planned for governments that are severe violators of rights, such as the right to form and join unions, and to seek permission to grant the loan. When both branches of Congress agree that the loans may extend the rule of repressive regimes, they should deny the bank permission to grant the loan (on pain of loss of authority to operate within United States territory).

To provide capital and technology, not to mention political support and military assistance, to contemporary tyrants is ordinarily to collaborate in their repression of their subjects. Those who claim to have found the extraordinary case in which the tyrant will mellow, or the repressive system will evolve, if only we continue business as usual bear a heavy burden of proof. And those who tell us that cozy relations with rights-violating governments are just business, to which consideration of rights is irrelevant, are just wrong.

SUGGESTIONS FOR FURTHER READING

§§1–2.   For alternative general accounts of transnational corporations, see Richard J. Barnet and Ronald E. Muller, *Global Reach: The Power of the Multinational Corporations*, N.Y.: Simon and Schuster, 1974; C. Fred Bergsten, Thomas Horst, and Theodore H. Moran, *American Multinationals and American Interests*, Washington: The Brookings Institution, 1978; Robert Gilpin, *U.S. Power and the Multinational Corporation: The Political Economy of Foreign Direct Investment*, N.Y.: Basic Books, 1975; and Raymond Vernon, *Storm Over the Multinationals: The Real Issues*, Cambridge, Mass.: Harvard University Press, 1977. For provocative historical insights, see Immanuel Wallerstein, *The Modern World-System: Capitalist Agriculture and the Origins of the European World-Economy in the Sixteenth Century*, Studies in Social Discontinuity, N.Y.: Academic Press, 1976. For a fuller account of transfer-pricing and similar mechanisms, see Constantine V. Vaitsos, *Intercountry Income Distribution and Transnational Enterprises*, Oxford: Clarendon Press, 1974.

§§3–6.   The great historical statements on equality are collected in George L. Abernethy, editor, *The Idea of Equality*, Richmond: John Knox Press, 1959. Major contemporary discussions of equality include Richard B. Brandt, *A Theory of the Good and the Right*, Oxford: Clarendon Press, 1979, pp. 306–326; J. R. Lucas, *On Justice*, Oxford: Clarendon Press, 1980, pp. 171–184; Gregory Vlastos, "Justice and Equality," in *Social Justice*, edited by Richard B. Brandt, Englewood Cliffs, N.J.: Prentice-Hall, 1962, pp. 31–72; and Bernard A. O. Williams, "The Idea of Equality," in *Justice and Equality*, edited by Hugo A. Bedau, Englewood Cliffs, N.J.: Prentice-Hall, 1971, pp. 116–137. For accounts of the activities of transnationals in the Third World, see Thomas J. Biersteker, *Distortion or Development? Contending Perspectives on the Multinational Corporation*, Cambridge, Mass.: MIT Press, 1978 (Nigeria); Thomas J. Biersteker, "The Social and Cultural Impacts of Transnational Corporations in Developing Countries: The Case for the Transnational Corporation," Technical Paper, United Nations, N.Y.: Centre on Transnational Corporations, 1981 (extensive analytic bibliography); Fernando Henrique Cardoso and Enzo Faletto, *Dependency and Development in Latin America*, tr. by M. M. Urquidi, Berkeley: University of California Press, 1979; Richard Newfarmer, ed., *Transnationals, Internation Oligopoly and Uneven Development*, forthcoming; United Nations, Economic and Social Council, Commission on Transnational Corporations, "Aspects of the Social and Political Effects of the Activities of Transnational Corporations," E/C.10/86, 14 July 1981. For provocative case studies, see Gary A. Hawes, "Southeast Asian Agribusiness: The New International Division of Labor," *Bulletin of Concerned Asian Scholars*, Vol. 14, No. 4 (Oct.–Dec., 1982), pp. 20–29; Milton Silverman, Philip R. Lee, and Mia Lydecker, *Prescriptions for Death: The Drugging of the Third World*, Berkeley: University of California Press, 1982.

§§7–10.   On economic rights generally, see Alan Gewirth, "Starvation and Human Rights," in *Human Rights: Essays on Justification and Applications* by Alan Gewirth, Chicago: University of Chicago Press, 1982, pp. 197–217; Louis Henkin, "Economic-Social Rights as 'Rights': A United States Perspective," *Human Rights Law Journal*, Vol. 2, Nos. 3–4 (1981), pp. 223–236; and Henry Shue, "Subsistence Rights: Shall We Secure *These* Rights?" in *How Does the Constitution Secure Rights?*, edited by Robert A. Goldwin and William A. Schambra, Washington: American Enterprise Institute for Public Policy Research, forthcoming. On the rights of workers specifically, see James Avery Joyce, *World Labour Rights and Their Protection*, N.Y.: St. Martin's Press, 1980; and James W. Nickel, "Is There A Human Right to Employment?" *Philosophical Forum*, Vol. 10 (1978–1979), pp. 149–170. On how realistic it is to fulfill rights in poor countries, see Charles R. Beitz, "Economic Rights and Distributive Justice in Developing Societies," *World Politics*, Vol. 33, No. 3 (April 1981), pp. 321–346; Robert E. Goodin, "The Development–Rights Trade-Off: Some Unwarranted Economic and Political Assumptions," *Human Rights Quarterly* (then: *Universal Human Rights*), Vol. 1, No. 2 (April–June 1979), pp. 31–42; and Henry Shue, "Exporting Hazards," in *Boundaries: National Autonomy and Its Limits*, edited by Peter G. Brown and Henry Shue, Maryland Studies in Public Philosophy, Totowa, N.J.: Rowman and Littlefield, 1981, pp. 107–145.

§§11–13.   For further arguments on the prospects for, and alternatives to, workers' protecting themselves, see Charles R. Beitz, "Democracy in Developing Societies," in *Boundaries: National Autonomy and Its Limits*, edited by Peter G. Brown and Henry Shue, Maryland Studies in Public Philosophy, Totowa, N.J.: Rowman and Littlefield, 1981, pp. 177–208; Thomas J. Biersteker, "The Limits of State Power in the Contemporary World Economy," in *Boundaries: National Autonomy and Its Limits*, edited by Peter G. Brown and Henry Shue, Maryland Studies in Public Philosophy, Totowa, N.J.: Rowman and Littlefield, 1981, pp. 147–176; David Hershfield, *The Multinational Union Challenges the Multinational Company*, Report # 658, N.Y.: The Conference Board, 1979; International Labor Organization, *Wages and Working Conditions in Multinational Enterprises*, Geneva: International Labor Organization, 1976; Herbert Northrop and Richard Rowan, *Multinational Collective Bargaining Attempts*, Philadelphia: Industrial Research Unit, The Wharton School, 1979; Paul Trajtenberg and Jean-Paul Sajhau, *Transnational Enterprises and the Cheap Labor Force in Less Developed Countries*, World Employment Programme Working Papers, WP 15, Geneva: International Labor Organization, 1976; and Michael Walzer, "Town Meetings and Workers' Control: A Story for Socialists," in *Radical Principles: Reflections of an Unreconstructed Democrat* by Michael Walzer, N.Y.: Basic Books, 1980, pp. 273–290.

IO

The Concept of Corporate Responsibility

KENNETH E. GOODPASTER

=============================== «‹›» ===============================

I. INTRODUCTION

§1 A CASE IN POINT

The subject of corporate responsibility is both difficult and complex. It
will help in the discussion that follows to have before us a case illustration in order to anchor various general remarks that will be made about
the case in particular and the topic of corporate responsibility in general.
The following story from the *Washington Star* (March 9, 1980) nicely
provides such a case illustration:

INDIANA'S PINTO TRIAL MAY ALTER
CORPORATE RESPONSIBILITY IN U.S.[1]

Legal history could be made this week in the sleepy hamlet of Winamac,
Ind., if the powerful Ford Motor Co., on trial in the tiny Pulaski County
court, is found guilty of reckless homicide.

The landmark trial stems from a 1978 crash in which three girls died
when their Ford Pinto car was rear-ended and exploded. The state
charged Ford with reckless homicide, alleging that the company knowingly manufactured and marketed an explosion-prone car, and accusing
the No. 2 automaker of failing to warn Pinto owners of the dangers.

Although Ford currently faces numerous civil law suits arising from
Pinto explosions, the Indiana prosecution has broken new legal ground
by bringing criminal charges to bear. Never before in U.S. legal history
has a company faced criminal prosecution for homicide.

In a long, complex and bitterly fought court battle, part-time prosecutor Michael Cosentino, aided by a volunteer band of university professors and their students, has sought to prove that Ford, under pressure to

produce a small, fuel-efficient car, recklessly rushed the subcompact onto the U.S. market in 1971, knowing it to be unsafe in rear-end collisions.

Prosecution witnesses claimed during the trial that design faults in early models of the Pinto, including the 1973 Pinto, involved in the Indiana crash, made the gas tank vulnerable in low-speed, rear-end collisions and the car liable to explode as a result.

Witnesses further claimed that Ford engineers knew of the dangers but decided for cost reasons against modifying Pintos on the production line or recalling those already on the roads.

In its defense, Ford has sought to show that no subcompact comparable to the Pinto could have survived the 1973 crash without fuel leakage and risk of explosion.

Ex-Watergate prosecutor James F. Neal, who has led the auto company's defense team throughout the trial, told the court that the Pinto in which Judy, Lynn and Donna Ulrich died in August 1978 had been rammed while stationary by a Chevrolet van travelling at least 50 mph.

Neal asked the court to reject the argument that Ford acted recklessly in failing to construct the Pinto to be capable of withstanding such a high-speed, rear-end collision.

Following closing statements by both sides tomorrow, the jury will decide whether Ford is guilty of the criminal charge. If convicted the auto company will be liable to fines totalling $30,000.

Those who have followed the trial closely since it began nine weeks ago believe that Ford's lawyers have succeded in establishing sufficient "reasonable doubt" for a "not guilty" verdict to be returned. But this trial has been full of surprises and if a guilty verdict is reached, the shock waves will ripple through U.S. industry.

Legal experts claim that a successful prosecution in Winamac will pave the way for similar criminal law proceedings against companies in other states. At present 38 other U.S. states possess statutes that would allow companies to be prosecuted under criminal law for serious offenses. So far they have shied away from using them but a precedent in Indiana could change attitudes dramatically.

If Ford is found guilty, the decision would also have a major impact on the civil, product-liability cases involving the Pinto now pending in courts throughout the country. Punitive damages could be substantial and that could hurt Ford financially at a time when the automaker is hard pressed by rising production costs and plunging profits on the domestic car market.

Other companies are keeping a close eye on the Winamac trial, for the product liability implications of the Pinto case extend well beyond the auto industry. Manufacturers of faulty products in other sectors could find themselves facing criminal charges which, ultimately could be extended to include company officials.

Business claims that the introduction of criminal liability will destroy the so-called "corporate veil" and expose U.S. industry and businessmen to costly and burdensome restrictions. But those in favor of making companies answerable for their actions in the criminal courts are confident that this will reinforce the often inadequate civil law constraints on corporate behavior.

Ultimately, it is argued, the Pinto case is about the rule of law and whether companies and their officials should be above it.

§2 THE POINT OF A CASE

As most readers are aware, Ford Motor Company was found innocent of the charges brought against it in this case. And it is not the purpose of this essay to second-guess the appropriateness of the verdict or the legal complexities involved. But it will be useful to have this case in mind as we try to clarify the concept of corporate responsibility, especially as it might be contrasted with individual responsibility, since it was Ford *as a corporation* that was on trial. It should be added that the choice of a case in which the moral issue is harm to the consumer or the general public is not meant to suggest that there are not other, equally important areas of moral concern, for example, worker safety, affirmative action, environmental protection, truth in advertising, and questionable foreign payments. Corporate responsibility can and should be exercised in any context in which moral values and obligations are relevant, and this usually means any context in which the interests or rights of persons are significantly affected by the corporation. Whether these persons are employees of the firm or "outsiders" would seem to make little difference. The case of the Ford Pinto is simply a convenient port of entry for an inquiry with more general application.

II. DEFINING MORAL RESPONSIBILITY

§3 BUSINESS ETHICS

Analyzing the concept of corporate responsibility is a central part of the larger area of inquiry known as business ethics. Under the more general heading, topics as wide as the ethical legitimacy of capitalism and as narrow as the personal moral dilemmas of business executives in day-to-day decision-making (for example, whether or not to break a promise in order to obtain a contract) are discussed and debated with great enthusiasm. But between the wide and the narrow lie questions that have to do with the management of the modern business corporation as a unit: questions about the policies and competitive strategies adopted by corporations, and questions about how such policies and strategies are to be implemented. In our opening case, Ford Motor Company confronted a long series of difficult policy questions, starting with competitive response to foreign imports and including engineering safety, product liability, and public relations. Issues of corporate responsibility, therefore, are of larger scope than the issues at stake in personal executive choices. Individuals make corporate policy decisions, of course, but these decisions are not merely personal — they are choices made *for and in the name of* the corporation. The notion of corporate responsibility finds its home in this larger context. At the same time, issues of corporate responsibility are of smaller scope than the ethical foundations of capitalism, since they presuppose to a great extent the fundamental legitimacy of capitalism — private property, for example, and free enterprise.

Since business ethics is a part of philosophical ethics generally, we expect and find that its divisions correspond to the divisions most frequently made in philosophical ethics, namely, *descriptive ethics*, *normative ethics*, and *analytical ethics* (sometimes called *meta-ethics*). Each division may be briefly described in the order just given.

It is possible to describe the values and moral obligations that businesspersons or business organizations subscribe to, the values and obligations they accept and seek to foster, as part of a neutral portrait of their shared beliefs and attitudes. The portrait is neutral because it does not itself favor or oppose the moral beliefs and attitudes it describes. It merely states that members of the business community generally, or of a particular company, have these beliefs or attitudes. To offer such a portrait would be to work in the area called descriptive business ethics.

Normative business ethics, in contrast, would involve the articulation and defense of basic principles or frameworks of right and wrong, good and bad, virtue and vice, as they apply in a business setting. Normative business ethics would concern itself not with describing values and obligations as perceived in the business world, but with prescribing (and, presumably, defending) values and obligations, sometimes in very general terms, sometimes in very specific terms. Unlike descriptive business ethics, which neither favors nor opposes the moral beliefs and attitudes it describes, normative business ethics is not morally neutral.

Analytical business ethics, finally, would deal with questions of meaning and justification, that is, questions having to do with the use of moral discourse in the business environment, the appropriateness of applying moral categories to institutional actors (and not simply to individuals), and the problems presented by moral disagreement both within and between different societies. Most of the discussion in this essay will fall under the two headings of normative and analytical business ethics, though near the conclusion we shall give some attention to descriptive issues (see Figure A).

In summary, the analysis of the concept of corporate responsibility involves primarily normative and analytical inquiry into the middle range of questions posed in business ethics, the range of questions dealing with the formulation and implementation of corporate policies, goals, and constraints. This range of questions is distinguished both from questions of personal ethics among business managers and from questions about the legitimacy of business enterprise in the first place. In the next section, we shall take the first step in our inquiry by distinguishing among several senses of the word "responsibility" in order to focus attention on the most important sense for our purposes.

FIGURE A   Wide and Narrow Issues in Business Ethics Related to
Divisions of Ethical Inquiry

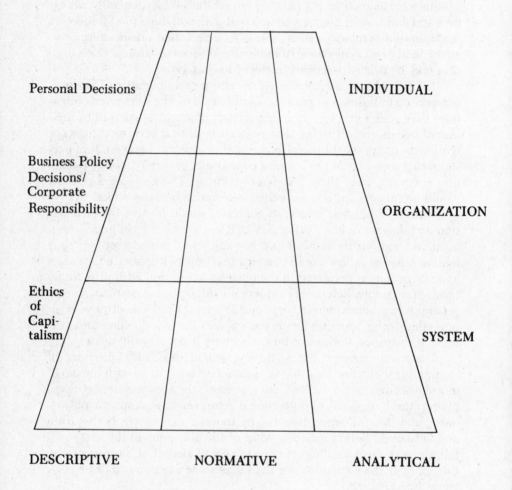

Personal Decisions   INDIVIDUAL

Business Policy
Decisions/
Corporate
Responsibility   ORGANIZATION

Ethics
of
Capi-
talism   SYSTEM

DESCRIPTIVE   NORMATIVE   ANALYTICAL

§4 SENSES OF "MORAL RESPONSIBILITY"

Let us begin by focusing on the semantics of the phrase "moral responsibility" as it is applied to individuals in their daily lives. Once we have ar-

ticulated the shape and substance of the central idea for such "personal" applications, we can then turn to the context of the modern business corporation to see what parallels, if any, obtain. By proceeding in this way, we are taking some sound advice from Christopher D. Stone, law professor at the University of Southern California, who remarks:

> If people are going to adopt the terminology of 'responsibility' (with its allied concepts of corporate conscience) to suggest new, improved ways of dealing with corporations, then they ought to go back and examine in detail what 'being responsible' entails — in the ordinary case of the responsible human being. Only after we have considered what being responsible calls for in general does it make sense to develop the notion of a corporation being responsible.[2]

The justification of the basic strategy behind this way of approaching corporate responsibility will be sketched in §§7–10. For now we shall simply treat it as a useful expository device, rather than as a special principle or method in business ethics.[3]

Three distinctions must be made to sort out the relevant semantic aspects of the concept of moral responsibility as it applies to individuals. First, we must distinguish among three uses of the term "responsible" as it is used without the modifier "moral." I shall refer to those uses of the term as *causal, rule-following,* and *decision-making,* respectively. In the *causal* use of the word, we say of an individual that he or she is responsible if we mean to draw attention to the fact that a certain action or event was brought about by the individual in question, wholly or in part, in contrast to some other individual or to some other explanation of how things happened. Thus, for example, we might ask who was responsible for a broken window, seeking to establish whether praise or, more likely, blame was appropriate and to identify the individual or individuals in question. In the causal sense, we speak of "holding" persons responsible, and we are concerned with determining such matters as intent, free will, and degree of participation, as well as reward or punishment.

We also speak of an individual's "responsibilities" as a parent or as a citizen or in other roles. This use of the term reflects the *rule-following* sense, not the causal sense. Here the focus is not on determining who or what brought about a certain action or event, but on the socially expected behavior associated with certain roles. Parents have responsibilities for their children, doctors for their patients, lawyers for their clients, and citizens for their country. To speak of a person as responsible in such contexts is essentially to commend him or her for following the rules or meeting the expectations of his or her station.

But there is a third use of the word "responsible" that is distinct from both the causal and the rule-following uses. Because it relates to the way in which an individual thinks about and responds to situations, we can call it the *decision-making* sense of the word. When we say of Bill Jones that he is a responsible person, we convey that he is reliable and trustworthy, that he can be depended upon to interpret situations and take

actions that manifest both integrity and concern for those affected by
them. The emphasis is not on Bill Jones as the agent who brought about
a certain result (the causal sense), or on his following rules or role-
expectations (the rule-following sense) but on his independent judgment
and the ingredients that go into that judgment. It is this third sense of
"responsibility" that will be of primary concern in what follows.

The second distinction relates not to the senses or uses of "responsibility" so much as to the function of the modifier "moral." When we speak
of an individual as "morally responsible," our usual intention, when the
phrase is not simply redundant, is to contrast moral responsibility with
other possible interpretations of responsibility. Most frequently, the contrast is with "legal responsibility." We acknowledge a difference in the
causal sense when we distinguish between individuals' being legally responsible ("liable") for an event and their being morally responsible for
it. Similarly, we understand the difference (rule-following sense) between a person's legal responsibilities and his or her moral responsibilities in a certain role. The latter are often said to include but go
"beyond" the former. For example, the legal responsibilities of parents to
their children are part of their moral responsibilities, but their moral
responsibilities do not stop at the boundary of the law. It is not illegal for
a parent to criticize a child to the point where the child loses any sense of
self-worth, but a parent who did this would act in a morally irresponsible manner. In general the modifier "moral" is used to signal a broad
context in which the notion of responsibility is to be situated, a context
that validates attributions of responsibility to individuals according to
criteria distinct from, for example, law, religion, etiquette, and custom.
Sometimes philosophers unify the special criteria at work in this context
as stemming from "the moral point of view," an idea discussed more fully
in §6.

The third distinction has to do with the *force* of attributions like "She
is morally responsible in her decision-making." That is, once we are
clear about which *sense* of "responsible" is at issue (in this case, the
decision-making sense), and once we recognize that it is *moral* responsibility rather than, say, legal responsibility that is meant, the question
arises: In saying that an individual is morally responsible, are we merely
describing certain of his or her cognitive, emotional, or decision-making
characteristics or are we instead (or also) *commending* and *recommending* them? To put this question another way, Is the concept of moral responsibility, as we are pursuing it, a normative concept or a descriptive
concept, or some mixture of the two?

The answer to this question is that it is a mixed concept. That is,
though it *can* be used purely normatively as an expression of praise with
no "content" (perhaps as some people use the word "nice"), and though
it *can* be used purely descriptively with no implication that being morally
responsible is somehow desirable, we usually use the concept of moral
responsibility with *both* a descriptive *and* a normative force. We use it to
say something about individuals that could be said in purely "neutral"

language (for example, he or she sees the world in certain ways), but we also use it to recommend the characteristics referred to as characteristics that individuals *should* have, not simply as characteristics that they might or do have. Tracing some of the elements of descriptive and normative force in the concept of moral responsibility is our next task. Up to this point we have, through three distinctions, clarified the main quarry: decision-making responsibility (versus causal and rule-following); moral responsibility (versus legal and other types); and moral responsibility with a mixed force (versus purely descriptive and purely normative). And it should be noted that we have restricted ourselves only temporarily to the attribution of moral responsibility to individuals. Later we shall train our attention on organizations (corporations) as the key entities for such attributions.

§5 RESPONSIBLE THOUGHT AND ACTION

In the previous section we saw that the concept of moral responsibility, at least as we plan to use it, has both descriptive and normative parts. It is our purpose in this section to elaborate further on those parts, in an effort to discern more clearly what the concept of moral responsibility means in practice. It should be stated at the outset, however, that this effort does not represent a full-dress analysis in the form of necessary and sufficient conditions. The more modest goal of uncovering "elements" of our idea of moral responsibility is all that is sought. What a precise analysis might involve, and indeed whether a precise analysis is possible, are questions we shall leave to one side. Aristotle was perhaps the first, but certainly not the last, to note that in matters of ethics, one must be satisfied with the level of precision that the subject matter allows.[4]

As we move toward a more reflective understanding of the elements of the concept of moral responsibility, two observations should be kept in mind. First, to say of an individual that he or she is morally responsible is to say something directly about the person and only indirectly about the actions or behavior of the person. To say that individuals are morally responsible, in the decision-making sense distinguished earlier, is to say something *about them*, about the cognitive and emotional processes that precede and accompany their actions; it is not to issue a verdict about the rightness and wrongness of their actions in every case. We can imagine attributing moral responsibility to a person in a commendatory way while nevertheless disagreeing with the decision made by that person in a particular case even to the point of believing that the action taken was morally wrong. Some philosophers would characterize this feature of the concept of moral responsibility by saying that it refers to "subjective" rightness (or in the case of irresponsibility, wrongness), while "objective" rightness and wrongness are the central concerns of ethics. But this would be too hasty. For the fact is that though moral responsibility may be a virtue insufficient to insure complete moral rectitude in what one does, it is clearly to be thought of as an essential, even dominant, component. Actions that are taken without it might in some cases be "objectively" right, but more frequently they will not be. And actions that are taken with it might in some cases be "objectively" wrong, but more frequently they will not be. Think of how uneasy most of us would feel about someone who said "I believe in behaving honestly with people, because it really pays off." William K. Frankena, a leading American moral philosopher, has perhaps put the matter as nicely as it can be put:

> Well, then, whom should a moral spectator rank higher, a person who does the right thing from bad motives or one who acts from good motives but does the wrong thing? Which person should he or she regard as morally better? In reply, the . . . thing to say is that the question is wrong.[5]

Frankena goes on to suggest, however, that all things considered, we lean toward virtue and (in our case) responsibility:

> One can [ask] who is better from the point of view of morality, the right-doing or the well-motivated person, to which the answer is probably the latter, because having such people around is likely to result in more right-doing than having people around who only happen to do what is right because it fits with their other ends.[6]

Our first observation, then, is that the concept of moral responsibility is normative with respect to the virtues of individual decision-making more than with respect to the rightness or wrongness of specific actions or behavior. It is what we might call a *process-concept*. This fact underlies a certain restraint in the compliment being paid to an individual in calling him or her "responsible," a restraint rooted in the gap between dispositions and actual behavior. But the restraint is in no way a suspension of normative force altogether. We are approving of the taking of the "moral point of view" in decision-making when we characterize a person as morally responsible, even though we reserve the right to criticize the results of the responsible exercise of that point of view in any particular case.

The second observation to be kept in mind about the concept of responsibility supplements the first. Attributions of moral responsibility are not only process-oriented rather than aimed directly at the content of behavior, they are also *generic*. That is, the cognitive and emotional processes associated with moral responsibility are less specific than those associated with the principles usually discussed in normative ethics. Attributing moral responsibility to an agent is not *in itself* attributing, for example, utilitarian or non-utilitarian reasoning to that agent. Nor is there any other specific moral principle (for example, egoism, contractarianism) *logically* implicit in the generic attribution of moral responsibility to an agent. This fact should not be taken to suggest that the concept of moral responsibility is *empty*. The point is simply that the content possessed by the concept is on a higher level of abstraction than the level of specific normative principles — much as the notion of the "moral point of view" is "above" specific ways of applying it in moral rules and principles.

To attribute the normative-cum-descriptive concept of moral responsibility to an individual, then, is to allude to certain *generic* decision-making traits (cognitive and emotional dispositions) of the individual. It is not to pass judgment directly on the rightness or wrongness of the individual's acts, nor is it to impute a specific normative ethical principle to the individual's reasoning.

§6 ELEMENTS OF MORAL RESPONSIBILITY

What, then, are the characteristic dispositions that give descriptive, albeit generic, meaning to the concept of moral responsibility? What makes the morally responsible decision-maker tick?

One way to answer this question is to look at the main components of the "moral point of view" at it is normally understood, in order to capture the basic spirit of moral responsibility. When we do this, with the help of philosophical literature on the subject, we discover two principal components, which we shall call rationality and respect.[7] Rationality involves the pursuit of one's projects and purposes with careful attention to ends and means, alternatives and consequences, risks and opportunities. Respect involves consideration of the perspectives of other persons in the pursuit of one's rational projects and purposes. In the words of Kant, respect implies treating others, especially affected parties, as *ends* and not *mere means*. It implies a self-imposed constraint on rationality, born of a realization that the worth of our projects and purposes resides in the same humanity shared by those who are likely to be affected by them. Taking the "moral point of view," therefore, has both a self-directed component (rationality) and an other-directed component (respect). These, at least, provide us with an understanding of the spirit that underlies the concept of moral responsibility. But how does this spirit become embodied in the actual decision-making processes of the responsible individual?

There are four main elements that most of us would recognize as essential, elements that correspond to four stages in an individual's movement from thought to action:

1. perception,
2. reasoning,
3. coordination, and
4. implementation.

We shall examine each of these elements as they contribute to morally responsible decision-making.

1. Perception All rational decision-making must begin with an agent's perception of his or her environment. Information-gathering is a necessary first step toward thoughtful action. But perception is not entirely a passive and neutral process. Philosophers and scientists have long recognized that perception has an active dimension and that an agent structures and packages information in accordance with both personal and social concerns and interests. Thus when we inquire about the *moral* aspects of perception, we are inquiring about the way in which and the degree to which an agent structures and categorizes the "moral data" available. And "moral data" is defined with attention to the two components of morality mentioned earlier. A morally responsible person will gather and take seriously as much information as practically possible regarding the impact of his or her decisions, not only on his or her goals and plans (rationality), but also on the goals and plans of others (respect). In the words of one writer, the responsible person's perception is in this way "stamped with moral categories."[8] Someone who ran across a crowded park oblivious to the presence of others, stepping on adults and children as if they were part of the landscape, would clearly exhibit a lack of moral perception. Such a person might "see" those in his or her environment, but would respond to that information in much the same way as to rocks or logs, that is, as potential hazards on a running course, not as human beings.

Moral perception manifests itself, then, largely in the way that an agent structures and defines his or her decision-making environment — whether and how moral issues are *recognized as* moral issues demanding the kind of attention discussed in (2) and (3) below.

2. Reasoning   Once an agent has gathered the relevant information from the environment according to some set of moral (or amoral) categories, that information becomes "input" to the reasoning process. The morally responsible individual not only *perceives* differently from the morally irresponsible individual, he or she also *reasons* differently about matters of right and wrong. Moral reasoning is the process by which one moves formally or informally from premises to conclusions about what one ought to do. A utilitarian, for example, will reason about right and wrong in terms of the social costs and benefits of the courses of action available. The utilitarian seeks to maximize the expectable utility or happiness or pleasure brought about by his or her conduct for all those affected. Non-utilitarians will reason in terms of principles or moral precepts that are not exclusively utility-maximizing in character. A nonutilitarian might, for example, reason that since a certain option available involves lying to people, it should be ruled out as unacceptable.

The important point for our present purposes is that we expect *some* process of moral reasoning from a morally responsible individual, even if the premises of that reasoning are unspecified. And we differentiate moral premises from other kinds because they are rooted in the components of rationality and respect for others mentioned earlier.

3. Coordination   We might have called the reasoning process referred to under (2) "reasoning internal to the moral point of view," in which case what we are here calling "coordination" would be "reasoning external to, but including, the moral point of view." Coordination is the process whereby an individual's moral evaluation of his or her options is integrated with various *nonmoral* (do not read "immoral") imperatives. Deciding on how to respond to racism in one's immediate social environment requires looking at alternatives morally, of course, but also legally, economically, and politically.

Most of us understand the coordination process as a process of establishing some *congruence* between our basic moral obligations and demands that stem from other sources. These other sources, of course, often intersect with morality. Simple prudence or self-interest, employment contracts, legal requirements, and various role-expectations (for example, manager, engineer, senator, physician) all make demands on us that we might classify as "nonmoral"; yet they are demands that we take seriously and that we hope ultimately will not conflict with basic morality.

The process of coordination, then, is a feature of the morally responsible person's character that goes beyond both perception and moral reasoning strictly defined. It takes the individual a step closer to action by integrating moral thought with the larger constellation of needs and interests that make up his or her decision-making "platform." Some philosophers have argued that the coordination process is really unnecessary, since moral reasoning by its very nature takes priority or is "overriding" in relation to other practical concerns. This is a debate that we cannot enter upon here. We can note, however, that even if moral reasoning is or should be somehow authoritative, there may still be more and less effective ways of recognizing that authority in practical affairs. The morally responsible individual presumably looks for the more effective ways, and this is the effort we are calling coordination.

4. Implementation   The final stage in the process of moving from thought to action, and so the final arena in which moral responsibility can be expected to manifest itself, is implementation. Here we assume that perception has given place to reasoning about what should be done, and that the remaining task lies in *how* to make things happen. As the proverb has it, a certain road is "paved with good intentions." Moral responsibility, most of us would agree, includes more than perception, reasoning, and coordination. It includes a measure of seriousness about detail that makes the difference between wishful thinking and actual performance, between "seeing it" and "seeing it through." There are here, as with the other three processes, numerous sub-processes involved. Implementation in the context of moral responsibility calls for an understanding of natural and social forces in the vicinity of one's proposed action as well as perseverance in guiding one's decision toward realization. An individual who *perceived* the dangers of a romp through the crowded park, who *reasoned* that others should not be hurt and who *coordinated* that conclusion with his or her desire to reach the other side as quickly as possible, might still fall short as a responsible agent, if, in implementing the decision to follow the less populated path, he or she ignored the complexities of the chosen route, only to get lost.

We can summarize the foregoing in the following diagram of the elements of moral responsibility, each finding its spirit in rationality and respect, and each providing a stage in the process of embodiment.

FIGURE B   Elements of Moral Responsibility

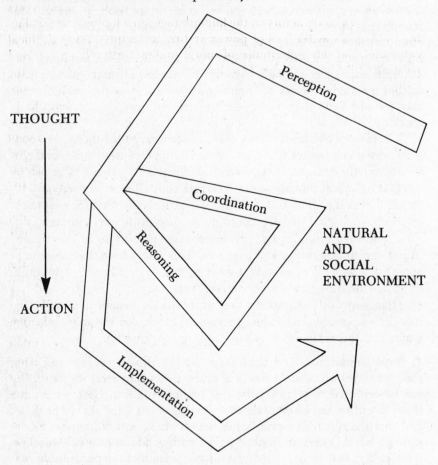

III. THE PRINCIPLE OF MORAL PROJECTION

§7 SHIFTING THE UNIT OF ANALYSIS

Up to this point in our discussion, very little has been said explicitly about business ethics or about corporate responsibility. Our main focus has been the concept of moral responsibility as it applies in our ordinary lives as individuals. We have seen that the underlying spirit of the concept is rationality combined with respect for others, and that this spirit manifests itself in four stages or processes: perception, reasoning, coordination, and implementation.

It is now time to make a very important theoretical shift from the individual as the primary unit of analysis to the organization, specifically the modern business corporation. The motivation for this shift comes from the widely appreciated fact that corporations play a more significant role in the lives and livelihoods of individuals today than ever before in history. Private and public institutions have in many ways become the primary actors on the human stage, enveloping if not replacing individuals as the loci of power and responsibility. Yet our ethical categories and our inheritance of moral understanding have not kept pace with this development. They have focused almost exclusively on the individual person (abstracted from organizational constraints and opportunities) as the subject for moral guidance.

It might be argued, of course, that there is no need to shift to a new unit of analysis (the corporation) in order to do justice to ethical issues in business. Individuals, it might be said, are the proper subjects for moral guidance, whether they be within or outside corporate roles and offices.

Such an argument has merit, but it fails to take seriously enough the fact that organizations are more than simple collectivities or groups of persons without structure, like passengers on a train. The actions and decisions of corporations are not usually a simple function of any single manager's values. Even the chief executive officer of a corporation often must, in his or her leadership role, work indirectly in efforts to guide the large organization toward its goals. Internal factors like management incentives, research and development, labor relations, and production processes combine with external factors like resource availability, government regulation, and competitive pressures to condition, if not determine, the decisions of even the strongest top executives. The point is that having a conscience in the running of a large corporation does not translate automatically into running a conscientious corporation. The latter requires an "institutionalization" of certain values, not simply the possession of those values in one part of the organization (even if that part is at the top of the hierarchy). Similar remarks would apply to other organizational characteristics like competence, intelligence, conservatism, aggressiveness, and innovativeness. The traits of individuals in all of these areas are critical, but managing their *joint force* demands a larger perspective and a larger unit of analysis than is afforded by concentrating exclusively on individual values. Add to this the "personhood" imputed to the corporation by both law and generally accepted accounting principles, as well as the "personality" imputed in recent discussions of corporate "culture," and the case for shifting our unit of analysis (from the individual to the organization) becomes very hard to set aside.

§8 STATMENT OF THE PRINCIPLE

Once the shift to the organizational unit of analysis becomes intelligible, that is, once we acknowledge the sense that can be given to seeing the organization itself as an agent in society, analogous to the individual while made up of individuals, we are then in a position to press two questions: (a) What is it for an organization (like a corporation) to be morally responsible? and (b), Do we really want to encourage corporate moral responsibility once we understand its implications?

We shall have more to say about negative answers to (b) in §§11–12, but for now we can simply use the affirmative answer as a way of defining "the principle of moral projection." The principle of moral projection (MP) may be formulated in this way:

> (MP) It is appropriate not only to *describe* organizations (and their characteristics) by analogy with individuals, it is also appropriate *normatively* to look for and to foster moral attributes in organizations by analogy with those we look for and foster in individuals.

Put in its simplest terms, the principle of moral projection states that we can and should expect no more and no less of our institutions (taken as moral units) than we expect of ourselves (as individuals). In particular, *moral responsibility*, as we have analyzed it earlier in our discussion, is an attribute that we should look for and try to foster in individuals. The principle of moral projection, therefore, invites us to explore the analogues of moral responsibility for organizations. The concept of corporate responsibility could then be seen as the moral projection of the concept of responsibility in its ordinary (individual) sense.[9]

Ford Motor Company, as noted in the case illustration at the beginning of this essay, was brought under indictment as an organic unit. Neither Henry Ford nor Ford's top managers nor other *individuals* were defendants in the Pinto trial. And though it is true that Ford's *legal* responsibility was, by definition, the issue in the eyes of the court, *moral* responsibility was just as surely the wider issue (as it very often is in legal proceedings).

But then what characteristics was the "moral defendant" supposed to have exhibited—*as an organization?* This brings us to question (a) above. In the next section we shall trace (for the corporation) the elements of moral responsibility outlined earlier for the individual.

§9 TRACING THE ELEMENTS

We saw in our earlier discussion (§4 and §5) that the concept of moral responsibility could be understood in terms of two main components, rationality and respect. We also saw that these components become operational in four stages or processes of decision-making: perception, reasoning, coordination, and implementation. If the principle of moral projection (§8) is to provide the conceptual link that we seek, then we must ask ourselves what organizational counterparts there might be to the four stages or processes. Let us now turn to this task.

First, *perception*. Just as individuals faced with the demands of rationality and respect must gather information from their environments about resources, opportunities, risks, and potential impacts of alternative courses of action, so too organizations of individuals must "perceive." Whether the term "perception" is used or not is, of course, unimportant. The fact is that an organization like Ford Motor Company is constantly monitoring its environment, gathering data relevant to marketing, accounting, finance, production, personnel, government regulations, and so forth. These data, once gathered, are processed through various parts of the organization, purified, clarified, simplified, and ultimately either "forgotten" or stored for use in decision-making by line management. And like all forms of perception, organizational perception is inevitably "selective." Not all available data, let alone all potentially relevant data, are gathered. Moreover, even the information that is gathered is frequently lost in processing and transmission within the organization, sometimes happily and sometimes unhappily. "Perceptual selectivity," then, is a characteristic of organizations as it is of individuals, and it lies as often at the root of an organization's competence as it does at the root of an organization's incompetence.

In the moral realm, perception becomes crucial because it is the beginning of responsibility. As we saw in our earlier discussion, it is possible for someone to be perceptive in various non-moral ways but relatively "blind" or "insensitive" when it comes to morality. This can happen because certain data are simply not gathered at all (for example, data about worker safety, health effects of products on consumers, environmental or social impacts), or because even though data are gathered, they are "forgotten" or "lost" in the system. The result is selectivity in moral perception on the part of the organization as a unit. Important information for responsible decision-making by management is simply unavailable.

Thus a central characteristic of a morally responsible organization will be what one writer refers to as its "information net" in those areas of its operation that significantly affect the lives of others (consumers, the general public, future generations, workers, shareholders, managers themselves, and so forth).[10] If an organization's information net is woven so as to capture, store, and eventually use morally important feedback regarding the organization's impact on others, that organization manifests "respect" for others (and so moral responsibility) more than an organization that fails to do this.

In our case example, Ford was charged with "reckless" behavior because, it was alleged, the company had "knowingly manufactured and marketed an explosion-prone car." If this were true, then the organization's *perception* was probably not in question. In order for Ford to have "knowingly" done what was alleged, it would presumably have had to have "perceived" the hazards of the fuel system before the decision to start or continue production. On the other hand, the allegations might

have been aimed at some kind of culpable ignorance on Ford's part —
"perceptual selectivity" regarding test data or test procedures. If so, then
lack of moral perception might well have been the key to the criticism of
irresponsibility.

In sum, the first of the four elements of moral responsibility seems
clearly to apply to organizations as a necessary (not sufficient) condition
just as it applies to individuals. And it applies on two levels: information
gathering and information *processing*. As with individuals, moral
"blindness" can afflict organizations as actors in their environments.

The second element of moral responsibility is moral *reasoning*, the
introduction of moral principles or norms to the relevant data in an effort to arrive at ("derive" may be too strong) a normative conclusion. In
the context of organizational decision-making, the process or activity of
moral reasoning might take place either formally or informally. If informally, it may often be simply a matter of an understood but unwritten
set of values or principles that make up the "culture" of a corporation.[11]
Moral reasoning in its informal aspect would amount to the weighing of
alternatives in decision-making with attention to both potential injustice
and potentially harmful consequences of corporate activity. Such considerations would find their way into corporate strategies and choices
largely through the "private" values of key managers together with
whatever selectivity might be exercised in appointing key managers in
the first place.

Moral reasoning becomes a more formal organizational characteristic when explicit provision is made in the decision-making process for
the introduction of moral premises. This can happen in a number of
ways: corporate ethical codes, along with guidelines for internal compliance; specific incentives for middle management regarding morally
motivated goals like affirmative action, worker health, product safety,
truth and taste in advertising; board committees mandated to oversee
general or specific areas of moral significance; and even top officers and
staff charged with primary responsibility for corporate ethics in both
policy and management development.

The organizational (corporate) analogue to the moral reasoning that
we expect of responsible individuals lies in precisely those areas of
organizational structure and style that contain and moderate key economic decisions. To the extent that the decision-making processes of the
organization in the economic realm are systematic and self-conscious,
we might expect a similar phenomenon in the moral sphere, not as a di-
version from or dilution of corporate purposes, but as an indispensable
safeguard for the humanity of those purposes.

To return to our case example, Ford Motor Company was charged,
implicitly, with not exercising its capacities for moral reasoning. Mechanisms and voices that might have been expected to modify or even prevent the marketing of the Pinto fuel system were alleged not to have
been effective. Ford's reasoning, it was claimed, was purely economic

when it could or should have included greater concern for consumer safety. The corporation's reply was that moral considerations did in fact enter the decision process and did in fact control it. The accidents were not, it was said, the result of either absent or faulty moral reasoning on Ford's part, but of factors in the collision situations for which Ford could not reasonably be held accountable.

The "mind" of the corporation, of course, is at least as inscrutable as the mind of an individual when it comes to moral reasoning, so it should not come as a surprise that such matters are hard to ascertain after the fact. One thing that is clear, however, is that moral reasoning can be enhanced in an organization by efforts of upper management and boards of directors to understand the formal and informal frameworks that do and those that should guide decision-making. If furthering corporate self-interest is the only or the dominant imperative in an organization, or if significant principles like social justice are seen to take a back seat to less important moral considerations, mechanisms could be devised that would correct the imbalance. Like individuals, organizations can evolve and develop to more mature stages of moral reasoning as they become aware of inadequacies.

Turning now to the third element of moral responsibility discussed earlier, *coordination*, we confront a character trait whose organizational analogue is all-too-often sorely lacking. Essentially, coordination consists in creatively managing multiple nonmoral imperatives as they relate to and sometimes press against the conclusions reached by moral reasoning. Instead of interpreting the decision-making environment as a tangle of "trade-offs" and moral compromises, the responsible organization, like the responsible individual, aims at congruence among moral and nonmoral aspirations. By its very nature the modern business corporation seeks economic objectives like return on investment, market share, and growth. It must be responsive to government regulation and competitive pressures. Skillfully orchestrating the joint fulfillment of these objectives and various moral imperatives, both in the short run and in the long run, is no easy task. Yet it is a task that in many ways epitomizes the role of management. It is often easier to talk of inevitable moral compromises in the name of corporate "survival" or the need for jobs than it is to generate options that are simultaneously responsive to both economic and non-economic values. A measure of idealism is often a necessary ingredient in the operating procedures of organizations that take coordination, and thus moral responsibility, seriously.

In our case example the central business challenge for Ford Motor Company seems to have consisted in meeting jointly the imperatives posed by foreign fuel-efficient imports, tough domestic competition, and engineering safety demands. The charge against Ford was that it "traded off" the last of these out of concern for the first two. If this were true (the corporation denied that it was true and won), it would have represented a failure in coordination and thus a failure in moral responsibility. The task of coordination lies in avoiding such "trade-off" situations by devising alternatives that make the multiple objectives involved congruent or jointly achievable. Institutionalizing such coordination is, of course, not simple. It consists of integrating the formal and informal mechanisms of moral reasoning with the wider set of organizational needs and goals. And as with the individual, the happy path on which virtue is rewarded often proves elusive.

The fourth and final element of moral responsibility is what we have called *implementation*. For the individual, implementation consists in the passage from intentions to action through self-monitoring, matching appropriate means to ends, and sustaining motivation and control. For the organization, similar factors come into play. Corporate strategies are no more than words without careful attention to the complexities of their implementation. Corporate management must constantly use its sources of influence to motivate and facilitate effective organizational responses to plans and policies. This is achieved through such things as adjustments in the structure of the organization, the degree of autonomy given to various divisions, incentive (and disincentive) systems for management and labor, and even occasional direct intervention by top management.

Just as we might have doubts about the responsibility of an individual who was morally perceptive and who reasoned carefully about the rights and wrongs of his or her conduct, but who paid no attention to the steps necessary to bring thought into action, so too we would have doubts about the responsibility of an organization that gathered and processed morally relevant information only to let it atrophy in the executive suite.

Recalling Ford's handling of the Pinto, we can imagine circumstances in which the company's perception and reasoning might have been unimpeachable, but in which implementation fell short. Suppose, for example, that the engineering or product-testing branch of the corporation discovered dangerous impact characteristics in the Pinto design and communicated this to upper management (perception). Suppose further that management concluded that the implied risks to consumers were unacceptable and that the fuel system could and should be made safer (moral reasoning and coordination). The implementation of a decision to redesign the fuel system would still require careful attention to such things as:

a. effectively communicating the decision to the production center of the organization, possibly through several layers of management;
b. cost controls and retesting during the redesign process;
c. recall and replacement of any fuel systems already produced; and
d. fostering a general understanding down the line of what was being done and why.

In the absence of such concern for "making things happen," an organization's moral responsibility, like an individual's, would be open to question.

Summarizing the discussion thus far, we can say that the four stages or processes identified as elements of individual moral responsibility have reasonably clear organizational counterparts. This fact, illustrated by means of the Ford Pinto case, provides us with a richer understanding of the concept of corporate responsibility. The responsible corporation is, in general, both rational and respectful of others in the conduct of its business affairs. More concretely, the responsible corporation manifests in its organizational structure, its control systems, its manufacturing and marketing practices, and its management development efforts, the four elements that we have seen to be characteristic of responsibility: moral perception, moral reasoning, coordination, and sensitivity to implementation.

The progressive clarity that such an analysis offers for understanding both the normative and the descriptive aspects of corporate responsibility should be encouraging. And though further analysis and more clarity is possible (and desirable), we can at least begin to appreciate the power of the principle of moral projection in taking us this far.

§10 "CONCEPTUAL THERMODYNAMICS"

We mentioned earlier that the principle of moral projection would be used as a helpful expository device until the main elements of corporate responsibility were traced. Now that we have done this, it behooves us to reflect more carefully on some of the methodological assumptions of the principle and to air some possible objections.

One of the basic physics lessons of the turbulent decade of the seventies was that to do useful work requires *sources* of energy more "concentrated" than the energy thrown off after the work has been done. The second law of thermodynamics tells us that the use of energy (either renewable energy or non-renewable fossil fuels) exacts a price, and that in nature, as in economics, there is "no such thing as a free lunch." If one seeks to power an engine, turn a turbine, or simply pedal a bicycle, there must be more concentrated energy at the input than at the output. Work is done by diverting some of the flow from well-ordered material to less well-ordered material. Entropy (disorder) increases.

This physics lesson, which is now understood by a wider public than ever before, has an interesting analogue in the realm of concepts and theories. If one is pursuing not physical work, but intellectual work — if one seeks to render a phenomenon more intelligible than it was before — then one's resource must have more "intelligibility" to it than whatever it is one would like to explain. In the world of ideas and explanations, the "resources" are *theories* or what are sometimes called "models." Just as we cannot do useful work by trying to get a waterfall to flow upward, so we cannot get useful explanations by using theories or models that are less intelligible than the phenomena they are constructed to illuminate.

Plato understood this principle of "conceptual thermodynamics" very well. He applied it to ethics in the second book of his *Republic* where he was seeking a "model" for explaining justice or virtue in the life of an individual:

> Imagine a rather short-sighted person told to read an inscription in small letters from some way off. He would think it a godsend if someone pointed out that the same inscription was written up elsewhere on a bigger scale, so that he could first read the larger characters and then make out whether the smaller ones were the same.
> . . . We think of justice as a quality that may exist in a whole community as well as in an individual, and the community is the bigger of the two. Possibly, then, we may find justice there in larger proportions, easier to make out. So I suggest that we should begin by inquiring what justice means in a state. Then we can go on to look for its counterpart on a smaller scale in the individual.[12]

In a way, Plato is here using the principle of moral projection in reverse: the macrocosm (the community) is being suggested for use as a model of the microcosm (the individual soul). Our own use of the principle moves from the individual to the macrocosm (the corporation). But as Harvard philosopher Robert Nozick points out, the *direction* of the arrow is relative. He is speaking of justice and the state, as Plato was, but the application to individual and corporate responsibility is natural:

> Since we may have only weak confidence in our intuitions and judgments about the justice of the whole structure of society, we may attempt to aid our judgment by focusing on microsituations that we do have a firm grasp of. . . . Since Plato, at any rate, that has been our tradition; principles may be tried out in the large and in the small. Plato thought that writ large the principles are easier to discern; others may think the reverse.[13]

The point is simply that the work of a model is to make the less intelligible more intelligible. For Plato, the "bigger" inscription was easier to read. For those of us embarking on the twenty-first century, the reverse seems true. Our organizations and institutions seem harder for us to understand than ourselves. Sometimes smaller "inscriptions" are aids to reading bigger ones. Think of the person unable "to see the forest for the trees."

The "conceptual thermodynamics" of our quest for understanding corporate responsibility, and for grounding business ethics in the process, leads us to apply the principle of moral projection from the level of individual thought and action to the level of organizational "thought" and "action." We do this on the basis of two reasonable assumptions: (1) that morally responsible individuals are easier to "read," and (2) that the analogy between persons and organizations of persons will sustain our efforts.

Some might argue that assumption (2) presents problems. Organizations and persons, they might say, are not at all similar. A full response to such doubts would take us beyond the scope of this essay into biology, organization theory, and even that branch of philosophy known as metaphysics. We shall have to be content here with a less than complete discussion of the main issues. First of all, it must be kept in mind that the principle of moral projection does not depend on the claim that organizations are moral persons in a literal sense, even though some might be tempted to argue for such a view. The idea of "analogous predication" has been with us at least since Thomas Aquinas (1224–1274) applied it to our human discourse about God. The principle of moral projection invites us to predicate moral characteristics (virtues, obligations, duties, and so forth) of corporations by *analogy* with their application to human individuals. Obviously, as with any analogy, there will be (indeed, must be) respects in which the items being compared are not similar. Corporations do not, for example, have feelings or passions, while individuals do. Nor do certain *rights* of individuals have clear corporate counterparts (for example, the right to worship, vote, or draw social security) — though some rights do (for example, the rights to property and free speech). These asymmetries and others are to be expected and do not constitute a serious threat to the strategy we have been using.

The issue is not whether there are asymmetries, but whether such asymmetries as there are undermine the analogy to a point where it no longer sustains our quest for understanding. If corporations were as unlike persons as, say *automobiles* are unlike persons, then it would not be clear what the point of the comparison could or would be. The fact that corporations are much more like persons than not only automobiles but even animals is therefore significant. And this fact is doubtless rooted not only in the intelligibility of attributing *intentions, decisions,* and *actions* to organizational bureaucracies, but also in the intelligibility of attributing *rationality* (or lack of it) to those intentions, decisions, and actions. The psychological underpinnings of moral discourse about individuals will have an analogue in the quasi-psychological (organizational) underpinnings of moral discourse about corporations. And though both structural and environmental features of individuals will differ from those of corporations, sufficient similarities remain to suggest that the differences are either differences of degree, or if differences of kind, then differences of the right kind.

A further, and more positive, indication of the appropriateness of assumption (2) should also be mentioned. The similarity between persons and organizations has been remarked historically from Plato through Hobbes to Freud, and it is assumed in contemporary management and organization theory, law, and accounting as a matter of course. The conviction appears to be not only that human organizations have characteristics that are relevantly similar to those of their human architects, but that those human architects have some things to learn about their own inner lives by looking to the dynamics of larger organizations. From all of these considerations we may conclude that doubts about assumption (2), though they deserve our attention, can be met when sufficient care is taken in the interpretation of the central analogy.[14]

With respect to assumption (1), doubts might also arise. We cannot "project" the concept of moral responsibility to corporations if we do not have a clear and agree-upon vision of what we mean when we call *ourselves* (as individuals) morally responsible. Since, it might be claimed, we lack the necessary vision at the individual level, we cannot have it at the corporate level either.

Such a challenging question deserves a strong reply. For it rightly focuses on the core of our earlier argument. If it could be shown, as some philosophers have maintained,[15] that we live in an age of moral incoherence, an age in which it is virtually impossible to define a unified ideal of moral responsibility, then the projection strategy would in fact break down. Without a model of the morally responsible individual, there can be no moral projection. The search for corporate responsibility either would have to find some new strategy or, more likely, would have to be abandoned.

But our earlier analysis gives us the framework for a reply to this kind of skepticism. We have seen that the foundations of moral judgment and action lie in the moral point of view, and that this point of view derives its guiding spirit from rationality and respect. That moral disagreement is possible, even frequent, among those who take or try to take the moral point of view does not show that we lack a coherent moral vision. At most it shows that the demands of our shared vision are profound. As each of us seeks to develop and improve his or her capacities for perception, reasoning, coordination, and implementation, not only our moral *vision*, but even our moral *judgments* should tend to converge. To claim that such convergence is *inevitable* may be too strong, but to wager that moral dialogue must terminate in impasse is to let either cynicism or discouragement overtake reason.

Our method in this essay, therefore, rests on something of a wager: that even if twentieth-century man finds consensus on *specific* ethical principles difficult to attain, a sufficient measure of agreement about the shape and substance of their source, the "moral point of view," can be found. Since we can map the contours of moral responsibility from this source in categories that are intelligible and functional, the criticism raised against (1) can be met.

Let us turn now from methodological questions to questions about the advisability of *recommending* corporate responsibility, however it may be defined. Here we must confront several alternative views regarding the role of ethics in business.

IV. BUT SHOULD CORPORATIONS BE MORALLY RESPONSIBLE?

§11 DISSENT FROM LEFT AND RIGHT

The principle that has been defended in this essay, together with the illustrations of its application, point toward a model for the corporation and its management that might be resisted. The resistance might stem from either of two implications of the model: (i) the implication that corporate responsibility is, like individual responsibility, a matter of self-imposed requirements rather than externally imposed requirements; or (ii) the implication that corporate responsibility, like individual responsibility, requires departures from (or at least extra-legal constraints on) purely economic, profit-oriented decision-making.

Resistance based on (i) tends to come from those who would prefer to see the state provide whatever "conscience" the corporation might need — through the courts, the legislature, and the regulatory process. The thought is that organizations, especially corporations, are essentially amoral entities — engines of profit or bureaucracies contrived for special purposes, driven by special interests — and that the guidance of these entities for moral purposes must be external. Law and the political process, it would be added, are the appropriate sources for this external guidance. "Moralizing" the behavior of the corporation is best achieved not by modeling its decision-making processes on those of the responsible individual, but by using whatever legal sanctions are available to make wrongdoing unprofitable. Government regulation is the key to business ethics, not corporate self-regulation.

The viewpoint (only slightly) caricatured here is fairly widespread and it obviously deserves consideration. In this writer's opinion, however, it cannot be sustained. For one thing, the external moral guidance being proposed is itself institutional: the legislative, judicial, and regulatory arms of the state. Presumably these moral guides are thought of as capable of moral responsibility. Why then, should it be assumed that corporations are somehow inherently amoral while other organizations are not? It is hard to see how the expediency that is assumed to drive the "engines of profit" is any less amenable to moral responsibility than other forms of expediency, for example, those often associated with the engines of politics and government appointments. It is true that the functions of the state in a democratic society include safeguarding certain basic rights and overseeing basic levels of welfare. Thus it is not inappropriate to suggest that government has a moral purpose. But such an observation is far from the claim that the state must be the source of conscience in the private sector, either for individuals or for organizations.

But there is another problem with the viewpoint under discussion. The law is seldom, if ever, an effective substitute for self-regulation in the moral realm. It is slow, primarily reactive rather than proactive in its operation, and (if unsupplemented) it often encourages rule-following to the letter rather than to the spirit of its directives. Few of us would think of the government and its laws as substitutes for individual moral responsibility, even though we might see them as necessary constraints. Why should we think differently in the case of corporate responsibility?

In sum, the view that corporate responsibility rests or should rest in the domain of external political institutions both underestimates the capacities for moral responsibility in the private sector and overestimates the capacities of government for moral guidance.

We mentioned above that resistance might come not only from those who are skeptical about the self-regulatory dimensions of our model, but also from those who are skeptical about a second of its implications: that corporate responsibility requires departures from purely profit-oriented decision-making. Historically, this form of skepticism is rooted in the economic philosophy of Adam Smith (1723–1790), whose reliance on the "invisible hand" to write morally through self-interested competition in the marketplace forms much of the basis of our contemporary business ideology. The basic idea is fairly simple. If markets are kept competitive, for example, if monopolies are prevented, the forces of business competition will generate the most efficient use of economic resources and ultimately the greatest social good. The role of the state, on this view, must be kept to a minimum. The state should serve as umpire of the competition, keeping it fair. It should perhaps also see to certain basic redistributions of wealth through progressive taxation. What it should *not* do is usurp management's role in the economy. The implication for the corporation, then, is that morality is not its business. The concept of corporate responsibility is viewed either as out of place, or, what comes to the same thing, as exhausted by the obligations of market competition. As does the view from the left, the view from the right resists the idea that corporations should model their decision-making on that of the responsible individual.

Again, in this writer's opinion, the resistance cannot be sustained. Like the view that corporate responsibility is sufficiently provided for by the visible hand of government, the view that it is sufficiently provided for by the invisible hand of the market simply does not do justice to reality. Just as the law is a crude instrument for fostering moral character in the citizenry, the market is a crude forum for encouraging attention to non-economic values that most of us consider essential, values like consumer protection, worker health and safety, racial justice, and truth in marketing. To be sure, there are significant economic pressures for corporations to avoid gross improprieties. A company that ignored product safety and quality or that treated its employees with contempt would presumably not survive in a competitive environment. But the pressures on the other side are also significant, pressures for single-minded pursuit of profits and even for relatively short-term gains that run rough-shod over moral convictions. Too often the very structure of market competition tends to foster dilemmas in which participants dare not take the larger view for fear that others will not and that the costs will be impossible to bear. The results of such market "imperfections" are evident around us: environmentally, socially, and on the international front.

There is another, perhaps more subtle reason why the slogan made popular by economist Milton Friedman, "the social responsibility of business is to increase its profits," is inadequate.[16] It has to do with a troublesome asymmetry noted by many observers between the moral demands made of corporate managers as individuals and the decision-making imperatives that a purely market-based ethic imposes on them in their work life. Philosopher John Ladd refers to this phenomenon as "moral schizophrenia" and argues that it is endemic to capitalism.[17] An influential psychoanalyst, Michael Maccoby, less convinced of the inevitability of the phenomenon, nevertheless describes it as a dominant characteristic of corporate culture, a characteristic that takes a high toll on the emotional lives of executives.[18]

If it is plausible to trace the source of this "double standard" to a present lack of functional congruence between our concepts of individual responsibility and corporate responsibility, and if it is desirable to aim at removing the problem, then the principle of moral projection offers the most promising path. The resolution of the tension between the demands of corporate success and the demands of individual moral responsibility lies in reforming our concept of corporate success. If the responsible organization is modeled on the responsible person, we no longer face the intimidating prospect of "serving two masters." Or if we do, we have some confidence that the "masters" are of one mind, born as they are of one moral ideal. It is false to say that capitalism precludes such convergence. The flaw lies not with capitalism, but with the mistaken belief that organizations enjoy moral immunity.

We can conclude, then, that resistance to the model of corporate responsibility sketched earlier in our discussion, whether it be from the left or from the right, is not sufficient to undermine the power of the model and of the principle that underlies it.

§12 WORRIES FROM THE CENTER TOO

Defending the principle of moral projection against resistance from the left and the right — resistance from two alternative schemes for "moralizing" corporate conduct — is an important task. But no less important is defending the principle from the very ground beneath our feet — what we might call the "center." Here the contours of the issue change. The dissent is no longer from political and economic theory. It springs from some of the deepest debates in philosophical ethics, debates that concern themselves with the coherence of the moral point of view itself.

Philosophers have pursued the nature of the "grip" that morality does or does not have on our mental and emotional lives. At issue is a question about our capacities to direct our lives by the moral principles we so often defend. The rationality and respect that lie at the core of the "moral point of view" (§5) are sometimes thought to generate inconsistent demands, either because they are opposed in their own right, or because the principles to which they give rise (promise-keeping, honesty, prudence, and so forth) occasionally come into conflict. The latter type of conflict can be and has been addressed by philosophical systems in which obligations are treated as provisional or "prima facie" duties, to be weighed in actual decision situations according to some faculty of moral perception or conscience. Though the philosophical issues that make their home here are important, the former type of conflict is even more so, since it claims to find an opposition within the faculty of moral perception or conscience itself. The grounds for this claim deserve our critical, even if incomplete, attention.

What is at issue is the nature of rationality. Some insist that what we call rationality is essentially a matter of efficiently organizing and pursuing the satisfaction of whatever constellation of desires, goals, and needs happens to characterize the actor in question. If among those desires, goals, and needs is something like "concern for others," or if the efficient pursuit of them makes concern for others useful, then rational decision-making will tend in the direction of altruism, or at least respect for the well-being of others. But if concern for others is not among the desires (etc.) of an agent, or if its contribution to the efficient pursuit of desires (etc.) is not considered great, then such concern is not something that rationality asks of that agent.

Opponents insist that this is an overly narrow view of rationality, that the recognition of the moral relevance of others' independent desires, goals, and needs is a requirement of reason (that is, part of what it is *to be* a rational person). These two conceptions of rationality (and hence of morality) reflect two perspectives that an agent can take on his or her own conduct: one "interested," and the other "disinterested." In the former case, reason is seen as the final arbiter of each person's individual needs and interests. In the latter, reason is seen as an arbiter *among* a community of needs and interests, one's own and those of others.

This polarity between internal and external perspectives is not, in this writer's opinion, a polarity that can be resolved by either pole achieving some overriding authority for all cases. And in this fact we find the key to turning back the objection. The polarity is itself a feature of the moral life. The morally responsible individual is inevitably, and perhaps not lamentably, caught up in managing the creative tension between internal and external perspectives on his or her conduct.[19] Whether we understand the rationality and respect that we earlier claimed to be the central features of the moral point of view as independent imperatives or simply as two forms of rationality, the result is the same: Each of us lives out his or her life under their joint authority.

These all-too-brief reflections on the tensions that characterize the moral point of view, although they are of interest in their own right, have special bearing on the subject of corporate responsibility because of the method of inquiry we have adopted: the principle of moral projection. It is not hard to see how the tensions we have alluded to will manifest themselves when they are "writ large" in the modern corporation. Once one takes seriously the suggestion that corporations embrace the moral point of view as an integral part of their operating philosophy, one must also take seriously the tensions that such a point of view brings with it. An organization, like an individual, can be and often is caught up between an "interested" and a "disinterested" perspective on its own decisions. Ford Motor Company, in our case example, may well dramatize the policy difficulties that arise when interests in profit and competition run up against an interest in public safety in such a way as to make the situation seem like a "trade-off." Such difficulties, however, are not a signal that moral responsibility is an impossible ideal and that therefore one of the competing perspectives must be abandoned in favor of the other. We certainly are reluctant (and rightly so) to draw such a conclusion in the case of the individual. The point is that corporate moral responsibility, like its analogue in the individual, requires *management*; management of people and resources, but most importantly what we might call self-management. The modern challenge for the professional manager lies not with the growing number of tasks associated with the growing complexity of the role. Though formidable, the quantitative dimensions of the challenge can be met by more sophisticated approaches to control, production, and organizational structure. The most dramatic challenge lies in the *qualitative* domain — the domain in which management must exercise *judgment* and self-understanding. The competitive and strategic rationality that has for so long been the hallmark of managerial competence must be joined to a more "disinterested," community-centered rationality. Gamesmanship must be supplemented with moral leadership.

The signal to be read from whatever tensions there may be within the moral point of view is that responsibility is an extraordinary virtue, combining internal and external perspectives on action. And the primary obstacle to achieving such a virtue is a myopic insistence that either perspective must displace the other.

The burden of the argument in this essay has been that organizations, like individuals, can and should accept the challenge.

§13 SUMMARY AND CONCLUSION

In this essay we have taken only the beginning steps toward a comprehensive account of corporate responsibility. Using the Ford Pinto example, we have attempted to trace the conceptual parallels between the individual and the corporation. In addition, we have examined the assumptions underlying the method used in our inquiry and have taken account of objections or resistance from left, right, and center. Much more remains to be done, and the interested reader will want to carry the task forward. This will require both more detailed analysis of our concept of responsibility (in terms that admit of functional organizational counterparts) and a more thorough, case-by-case look at corporate decision situations.

The first of these two tasks mobilizes the analytical and normative parts of ethics as a philosophical discipline. The second task forces us into what we earlier referred to as descriptive ethics, and the importance of this more empirical side of the inquiry can hardly be overstated. Armchair reflections about business ethics are no longer sufficient (they never were) for those who are serious about the central issues. The complexities of corporate decision-making generate corresponding complexities for *responsible* corporate decision-making. Without the understanding of such complexities that comes from case study research, the quest for moral understanding in modern business life is empty. But without a philosophical framework and a set of norms reflectively reached, the study of cases is blind.

The *implementation* of the vision set out in our discussion, disciplined both conceptually and practically, leads to a social agenda of considerable magnitude:

1. In the educational domain, it calls for a thorough integration of the humanities with the curriculum in business administration. Such an integration must reach beyond courses on ethics to include the moral aspects of functional specialties like marketing, production, finance, control, and human resources management.

2. In the management development programs of corporations themselves, a parallel effort is needed to extend and supplement an integrated academic formation. Encouragement must be provided to sustain internal dialogue about the moral aspects of the firm's performance.

3. Boards of directors, often if not always the custodians of the longer-range values of corporations, must increase both their vigilance and their effect as they participate in governance. They must contribute directly to the legitimation of moral discourse in long-term planning and evaluation.

4. Most important, top corporate managers must mobilize the powerful sources of influence available to them toward the goal of institutionalizing moral responsibility. Such sources of influence include setting goals, modifying organizational structures, and introducing measurement and reinforcement criteria for business subunits and for individuals. Top managers must come to see themselves not only as stewards of large concentrations of material and human resources, but also as architects of responsible institutions. They must understand that their influence extends to the processes of perception, reasoning, coordination, and implementation discussed earlier, whether the issue be product safety, worker health, environmental protection, or truth in advertising.

5. Finally, the posture of government, in its legislative, regulatory, and judicial functions, must be made congruent with the aspirations of our model. Beyond government's obvious and necessary enforcement roles, it must permit enough corporate freedom for the exercise of moral responsibility. This does not mean *laissez-faire*. On the contrary, it implies new forms of partnership between the public and private sectors. What is crucial, however, is that decision-making responsibility (in contrast to what we have called rule-following responsibility) requires a measure of autonomy for corporations as it does for individuals. A regulatory environment that would seek to *replace* corporate decision-making responsibility is also an environment that would suffocate corporate moral initiative.

No claims are made for the completeness of this agenda. The items mentioned need to be developed at length and we should probably add items (for example, items relating to labor relations and the management of transnational enterprises). Our agenda does, however, point us down a path toward *action*. Thus does our *discussion* of corporate responsibility itself mirror the pattern that has been traced for the concept itself, namely a progression from perception, through reasoning and coordination, to implementation.

NOTES

1. Chris Redman, "Indiana's Pinto Trial May Alter Corporate Responsibility in the U.S.," *Washington Star* (March 9, 1980). Copyright 1980 Time Inc. All rights reserved. Reprinted by permission.
2. Christopher D. Stone, *Where the Law Ends: The Social Control of Corporate Behavior* (Harper & Row, 1975), p. 111.
3. Some of the themes developed in §§4, 5, and 10 of this essay are also discussed in "Can a Corporation Have a Conscience?" by Kenneth E. Goodpaster and John B. Matthews, *Harvard Business Review* (January–February 1982).
4. Aristotle, *Nicomachean Ethics*, Book II, 1094b.
5. W. K. Frankena, *Thinking About Morality* (University of Michigan Press, 1980), p. 50.
6. Ibid.
7. Ibid., p. 26.
8. Stone, op. cit., p. 114. Stone's discussion of the elements of moral responsibility is useful, but less systematic than the approach taken here.
9. I first used this methodological principle in research on values in the electric power industry in 1972. See Kenneth Goodpaster and Kenneth Sayre, "An Ethical Analysis of Power Company Decision-Making," in *Values in the Electric Power Industry* (Notre Dame, Ind.: University of Notre Dame Press, 1977), pp. 238–88.
10. Stone, op. cit., pp. 199–216.
11. See "Corporate Culture," *Business Week* (October 27, 1980), pp. 148–60.
12. Plato, *The Republic*, Book II, 368a.

13.   Robert Nozick, *Anarchy, State, and Utopia* (N.Y.: Basic Books, 1974), p. 205.

14.   Thomas Donaldson, in *Corporations and Morality* (Englewood Cliffs, N.J.: Prentice-Hall, 1982), discusses a number of the asymmetries between persons and organizations that are mentioned here (see especially ch. 2 and 6), but none seem to undercut the present strategy. Also relevant are Peter French, "The Corporation as a Moral Person," *American Philosophical Quarterly*, Vol. 16 (July 1979), pp. 207–15, and Cyert and March, *A Behavioral Theory of the Firm* (Englewood Cliffs, N.J.: Prentice-Hall, 1963).

15.   See Alasdair MacIntyre, "Corporate Modernity and Moral Judgment," in Goodpaster and Sayre, *Ethics and Problems of the 21st Century* (Notre Dame, Ind.: Notre Dame Press, 1979), pp. 122–38.

16.   See Milton Friedman, "The Social Responsibility of Business is to Increase its Profits," *New York Times Magazine* (September 13, 1970), pp. 32–33.

17.   See John Ladd, "Morality and the Ideal of Rationality in Formal Organizations," *The Monist*, Vol. 54 (1970), pp. 488–516. This article is reprinted, with a reply by K. Goodpaster, in Donaldson and Werhane, *Ethical Issues in Business: A Philosophical Approach* (Englewood Cliffs, N.J.: Prentice-Hall, 1979).

18.   See Michael Maccoby, *The Gamesman* (N.Y.: Simon and Schuster, 1976).

19.   See Thomas Nagel, "Subjective and Objective," in *Mortal Questions* (Cambridge: Cambridge University Press, 1979), pp. 196–213.

SUGGESTIONS FOR FURTHER READING

For further reading on the issues discussed in this essay, the reader is encouraged to consult the sources cited in the Notes as well as those that follow.

§§1–2.   Two helpful anthologies on business ethics that include case materials as well as more conceptual discussions are *Ethical Theory and Business*, T. Beauchamp and N. Bowie, eds. (Englewood Cliffs, N.J.: Prentice-Hall, 1979), and *Ethical Issues in Business: A Philosophical Approach*, T. Donaldson and P. Werhane, eds. (Englewood Cliffs, N.J.: Prentice-Hall, 1979).

§4.   In addition to Christopher Stone's discussion (note 2), the reader may find it helpful to compare Graham Haydon, "On Being Responsible," *Philosophical Quarterly*, Vol. 28 (1978), pp. 46–57.

§§5–6.   For further reading on the early part of this section, the reference to W. K. Frankena, *Thinking About Morality* (Ann Arbor: University of Michigan Press, 1980) bears repeating. For a discussion of the elements of moral responsibility from a perspective in moral psychology, see James Rest, "A Psychologist Looks at the Teaching of Ethics," *Hastings Center Report*, Vol. 12, no. 1 (February 1982). Rest's categories are parallel, but not identical to the four described here, and they help in the task of relating empirical research (on individuals) with the themes of this essay.

§§7–8.   The principle of moral projection is described further in K. Goodpaster, "Ethics and Business," *Syllabi for the Teaching of Management Ethics*, Society for Values in Higher Education (New Haven, Conn. 1979), pp. 13–56, and in a review article by the same author in *Ethics*, Vol. 91 (April 1981), pp. 525–30. Also see notes 3 and 9.

§9.   For a stimulating reflection on the themes in this section see Kenneth R. Andrews, "Can the Best Corporations Be Made Moral?" *Harvard Business Review* (May–June 1973) pp. 57–64.

§10.   In addition to the references mentioned in note 14, one might also look at Norman Bowie, *Business Ethics* (Englewood Cliffs, N.J.: Prentice-Hall, 1982), especially ch. 2 and 7.

§11.   See Milton Friedman, *Capitalism and Freedom* (Chicago: University of Chicago Press, 1962). Counterpoint is to be found in J. K. Galbraith, *Economics and the Public Purpose* (Boston: Houghton Mifflin, 1973), especially Part 5. Further insight into the issues latent here is afforded by George C. Lodge, *The New American Ideology* (N.Y.: Alfred A. Knopf, 1975).

§12.   For further thoughts on the "polarity" problem, see W. K. Frankena, "Sidgwick and the Dualism of Practical Reason," in K. Goodpaster, *Perspectives on Morality* (Notre Dame, Ind.: University of Notre Dame Press, 1976), pp. 193–207. Also, Thomas Nagel, *The Possibility of Altruism* (N.Y.: Oxford University Press, 1970).

§13.   For further discussion of various aspects of the "agenda" here, see the works cited by Kenneth Andrews and George Lodge, as well as Robert Ackerman, "How Companies Respond to Social Demands," *Harvard Business Review* (July–August 1973), pp. 88–98.

II

Just Environmental Business

HOLMES ROLSTON III

I. INTRODUCTION

Since business began, some ways of making money have been judged morally unacceptable. But only in the last two decades has business been pressed to cope with environmental prohibitions. Consider for instance the following cases, and notice how what may first seem to be routine and non-moral environmental matters, just business, turn out to involve deeper ethical puzzles about what is just in business. Notice too that the justice we are here called upon to think through is not abstract and impractical; it concerns everyday affairs in the business world.

§1 CASE STUDIES

Case 1. Allied Chemical Corporation, operating an eastern Virginia plant, was charged with intentionally violating environmental protection laws by releasing Kepone into local waters. Denying the charges, the firm pleaded no contest, but was fined $13.2 million, the largest fine ever imposed in an environmental case. Judge Robert R. Merhige, Jr., wrote: "I disagree with the defendants' position that all of this was so innocently done, or inadvertently done. I think it was done because of what it considered to be business necessities, and money took the forefront. . . . Allied knew it was polluting the waters."[1]

Case 2. Daniel K. Ludwig, the wealthiest American, has been bulldozing much of 5,800 square miles of Amazon rain forest, replanting it for silviculture and agriculture, producing mostly rice, paper pulp, and newsprint. His Jari project is welcomed by many as a model for the whole Amazon basin. But this rain forest is the richest biological system on Earth, and how many thousands of plant and animal species Mr.

Ludwig and other Amazon developers are destroying cannot be known because the fauna and flora there are very incompletely studied. Hugh H. Iltis, a leading contemporary naturalist, has condemned Ludwig in a presidential address to the National Association of Biology Teachers for his part in "the enormity of this crime," among the biologically most dangerous and destructive events of this century.[2]

Case 3. Cyprus Mines Corporation, owned by Standard Oil of Indiana and Westinghouse, has proposed a uranium mine, the Hansen project, thirty-five miles northwest of Canon City, Colorado. Permitting agencies have been indecisive over disposal of the tailings, above grade or below grade, more or less expensive to handle depending on trenching involved and isolation from the ground water. Though the uranium is removed, daughter radionuclides remain, long-lived radium that steadily emits short-lived but mobile radon gas, decaying into further contaminants. By dust, wind, leaching, runoff, irrigation, wildlife movements, these make their way into air, water, food. Some studies find that revegetated soil cover would slow this, others find that plant uptake moves radon into the air faster than would a rip-rap cover. Radiation and health risks are debated. The project has stalled.[3]

The sorts of issues raised in these three cases will unfold as we proceed, but right at the start we begin to see how environmental questions have recently awakened us from our ecological slumbers. The Environmental Protection Agency and related regulatory agencies have become major federal powers. There are many state and local environmental rules. Environmental regulation is a daily fact of business life. But business leaders ought not to be concerned merely with obeying the law. They will want to be sensitive to the right and wrong that underlie, or should underlie, the law. Debates about new laws or less regulation will turn on what is just. But how can we decide right or wrong in such cases? That is the central question that demands our attention.

§2 TWO KINDS OF ENVIRONMENTAL ETHIC

Two kinds of environmental ethic are possible. The obvious kind is anthropocentric. Right and wrong are determined by human interest. This ethic (let us call it the humanistic ethic) is secondarily an environmental ethic; concern for the environment is entirely subsidiary to a concern for *humans*, who are helped or hurt by the condition of their surroundings. The other type (the naturalistic ethic), held perhaps more intensely by fewer advocates, is directly about *nature*. It holds that some natural objects, such as whooping cranes, are morally considerable in their own right, apart from human interests, or that some ecosystems, perhaps the Great Smokies, have intrinsic values, such as aesthetic beauty, from which we derive a duty to respect these landscapes. Both types have new moral applications to think through, but the naturalistic ethic is more radical. While few deny that humans have duties to other humans, many puzzle how non-human nature can be the object of duty. Nevertheless, a novel happening in current normative ethics is the emergence

of serious thought about the possibility of a non-anthropocentric, naturalistic environmental ethic. Is there moral awakening going on here,
analogous to that of the days when we awoke to the evils of slavery or of
child labor? People in business are by custom bound to consider the anthropocentric ethic, but not the naturalistic one. But those in the world
of business eventually will encounter the principles and implications of
the latter ethic and, as the proverb has it, there is no time like the present
to begin to do some thinking here. This is not only because some of the
most vigorous critics of business have these deeper concerns, but because
even those who operate out of humanistic motives may find that they
sometimes share sympathies with, and find some logic in, what the nat-
uralists recommend.

We will begin with a sketch of some of the main principles or operating rules of a humanistic environmental ethic (§§3–12) and follow
that with a sketch of some main rules in a more naturalistically oriented
environmental ethic (§§13–22). In a third and final part (§§23–32), we
note how the ethical interplay between business and the environment is
an especially complex thing. Owing both to the nature of business in our
industrial society and to the nature of environmental interactions, complications arise that require us to make ethical judgments in less familiar
and more demanding contexts than ethicists sometimes face. Our final
group of guidelines offers some advice for the businessperson in the midst
of the complexities of environmental affairs. A mosaic of ideas — humanistic and naturalistic concerns, individual and corporate responsibility,
obligations to future generations, shared risks, and so forth — has here to
be kept in focus if we are to form a clear picture of "the facts" and "the
values." Stand too close and we see some details but lose the over-all
design. Stand too far away and we see the shape but lose the substance.
The challenge is to command a clear view.

A further word is appropriate about the style of presentation. Our
over-all argument does not run like the links of a chain, for extended formal argument is seldom possible in ethics. Rather, what unfolds is a
series of maxims, or injunctions, together with explanations and illustrations sufficient for the reader to see what is demanded. This invites critical reflection. So far as readers find, on reflection, that these "commandments" make sense, they will tend cumulatively to support an
over-all ethic, as multiple legs support a large table. These maxims will
be what moralists sometimes call middle-level rules, that is, neither very
general nor very specific. We will give each one a name, so that we do
not forget it too easily.

II. BUSINESS AND A HUMANISTIC
ENVIRONMENTAL ETHIC

Environmental ethics connects us with a problematic theme: how to
harmonize the sometimes dissonant claims of private interests and public
goods. An old ambivalence in the Judeo-Christian mind about profit-

making and how this mixes doing unto oneself with doing for others has reappeared in recent discussions about the social responsibility of business. If moral philosophers have nearly agreed to anything, they agree that ethical egoism (I ought *always* do what is in my enlightened self-interest) is both incoherent and immoral. If ethically enlightened executives have nearly agreed to anything, they agree that profit-making cannot be the *sole* business of business, however much it is a necessary one, and however unsettled the extent of their social responsibility. In a narrow sense, the personal ethic most opposed by ethicists seems to be the bottom line of all business. But in a broader sense, much business is possible that simultaneously serves private interests and public goods. It is hard for a large business to stay in operation, whatever its profits, unless the managers and employees bring themselves to believe that the firm is contributing to the public good. Else, negatively, they must regard themselves as trapped or bury themselves in their own anxiety. But, positively, this means they will try to choose a route that at once serves their profit and the public good, more or less. That much agreement, admittedly rough, reconciles business and moral philosophy enough to let us apply this in environmental ethics.

"Environmental and other social problems should get *at least* as much corporate attention as production, sales, and finance. The quality of life in its total meaning is, in the final reckoning, the only justification for any corporate activity."[4] That demand, with its emphasis, comes from the former chairman of the board of the world's largest bank, Louis B. Lundborg. What would it mean to write environmental ethics into company policy? If that ethic is humanistic, the following ten maxims would be first considerations.

§3 THE STAKEHOLDER MAXIM: ASSESS COSTS SUFFERED BY PERSONS NOT PARTY TO YOUR BUSINESS TRANSACTIONS

Social costs do not show up on companies' or customers' books, but someone pays them sooner or later. Dumping pollutants into the air, water, and soil amounts to having free sewage. A business exports pollution, more or less of it depending on how much one can get past current regulations. The EPA classifies over half of the fifty thousand market chemicals as being hazardous if inadequately disposed of, with perhaps only ten percent being safely handled. Divide or multiply their figures by two or three, and the threat is still serious. Someone has to suffer impaired health, a blighted landscape, and reduced property values, and pay clean-up bills or medical costs. The acid rain falls downwind at home or abroad. Governor George Wallace once remarked, as the winds blew east to waft pollution through the Alabama capitol's corridors, that the odor wasn't so bad. In fact, it was "sweet" because it was "the smell of money."[5] He could more accurately have said that it was the smell of money changing pockets from the hapless victims, who must pay for the damages, to those of the business operators who profited the more from their free sewage.

Here a good company will follow the urging of Henry B. Schacht, chairman of the board at Cummins Engine Company, to consider the stakeholders as well as the stockholders.[6] But it is easy to forget this because of the concentrated benefits and widespread costs. The costs are heavy but too thinly dispersed to keep focused against the lesser but concentrated benefits. Lots of persons are hurt, but they may not be hurt very much, or be able to show very easily the origin of their hurt. Individuals may be too scattered to organize themselves well against the offending company. The stakeholder maxim enjoins concern about all this.

The Kepone fine (see Case 1) shows how legal penalties are developing because business has been notoriously slow to police its spillover. The Superfund legislation of 1980 provides large sums to clean up a hundred orphaned sites inherited from (knowingly or unknowingly) irresponsible practices of earlier years. Many chemical and petroleum companies backed this legislation, a bit grudgingly, perhaps hoping thereby to deal with the tip of an iceberg. They will get off cheaper this way than if the full extent of old costs hidden at fifty thousand sites ever becomes evident. One business by itself can only partially (to use an economist's catchword) internalize these externalities, but every business can as a matter of policy work in concert with others here. Almost every reader is carrying in his body some of the burden of this problem, so there ought to be none unwilling to weigh the moral burden here.

§4 THE COUNTRYSIDE MAXIM: DO NOT ASSUME THAT WHAT'S GOOD FOR THE COMPANY IS GOOD FOR THE COUNTRY

The aphorism of Charles E. Wilson, a famous GM executive, that, "What's good for General Motors is good for the country," is half true, even mostly true.[7] But its untruth comes out well in environmental affairs, where we give the word "country" a grassroots twist to include the people in their urban and rural places. The United States automakers have steadily resisted stronger pollution standards and fuel-efficient cars, foot-dragging all the way. This is true even though the cleaner air was good for the city, the countryside, and all inhabitants thereof, and though smaller cars would have been less demanding on petroleum reserves. Their reason has been that compliance took extra work and put a crimp in the industry's profits. Every developer, realtor, purchaser of minerals and fibers, user of energy, and disposer of wastes will find some ways of doing business better, some worse for the countryside, and here one ought to love his country more than his company. Each business, like each person, lives, eats, and breathes in and on a public reservoir. In this sense there is no such thing as a private business. Garrett Hardin has described in a sad phrase, "the tragedy of the commons," how individuals and their companies can each do what is in their own immediate self-interest but all together gradually destroy the public domain, "the commons," including their neighborhood and countryside, its air, water, soil, forests, resources. They end by destroying themselves.[8]

§5 THE SUNSHINE MAXIM: DO NOT KEEP COMPANY SECRETS THAT MAY VITALLY AFFECT THOSE FROM WHOM THE SECRETS ARE KEPT

This permits a healthy outside environmental audit. A company has a limited right to keep trade secrets and to classify its affairs, but there is a lamentable tendency under this guise to conceal information that might prove detrimental to the company. The reluctance to count spillover costs or the trouble distinguishing the good of company and country make it important to get the facts, and lack of them, out for the purpose of open debate. This is especially important if those who may be hurt are to have the chance to defend their own interests. It took the Freedom of Information Act to disclose that (in 1976) eight thousand pounds of plutonium and bomb-grade uranium were unaccounted for in the United States, enough for the construction of hundreds of nuclear weapons. A corporate polluter once claimed that the amount of sulfuric acid his company dumped into the Savannah River was a trade secret; others have claimed that the public had no right to know what was coming out of their smokestacks. The National Science Foundation's Panel to Select Organic Compounds Hazardous to the Environment sent a survey to industries in 1975 and found that only twenty-eight percent of the industries gave replies that were usable as answers in compiling data, owing largely to the tradition of secrecy in the chemical industries.[9] Subpoenaed documents have often shown companies to be telling less than the whole truth.

Love your "enemies" here because they are in the long run your friends, unless you really don't care whether you harm innocents. Company policy should volunteer relevant files cooperatively, even if this may reduce company profits. It forces you to more care, but the threat of potential harm to innocents overrides reduced profits by operators. The sunshine maxim also requires individual employees to reverse, even to violate, policy that maliciously, tacitly, naively, makes truth the first casualty in an environmental contest. It may require whistle-blowing. The secrets here are sometimes about secrets. For example, the administrators of a nuclear reactor may fail to reveal that they do not know the extent, and cannot diagnose the threat, of contaminants released in an accident. It is hard to maintain credibility when ignorance and mistakes are exposed, but still harder to recover it when once it is found that you have lied or mismanaged the news.

§6 THE LEGACY MAXIM: DO NOT DISCLAIM RESPONSIBILITY IN INHERITED PROBLEMS

Many mistakes were made before hazards were understood. When an individual joins a firm, he or she inherits all its problems (often coinciding with its opportunities) proportionately to his or her influence with that company, the degree of which may advance over time. When a firm enters the market, it inherits all its problems (also its opportunities) proportionately to its share of the market. Both individuals and firms will find themselves with problems for which *they* are not responsible. *Other* actors produced the present situation. We have a rationalizing tendency to conclude that we are not responsible *in* the inherited mess if we are not responsible *for* it. The employee may not have been born or the company in business when the now-orphaned wastes were carelessly dumped. But present operators, both one company and all in concert, can do something about reversing these conditions, as the firms backing the Superfund illustrate. Creatively doing what we can is our responsibility. When we wake up to sufficient environmental deterioration to alarm us morally, the problem is well underway. It is not "our" fault, if we restrict the scope of "our" to present employees and firm, but it is still "our" problem. Voluntarily to join a company is voluntarily to assume responsibility for the effects of its past decisions.

§7 THE NO-DISCOUNT MAXIM: DO NOT DISCOUNT THE FUTURE ENVIRONMENTALLY

We now place a moral check on the practice, used wisely enough in limited places in classical economics, of discounting the future. Initially a function of the interest rate, discounting is philosophically defended because future needs are uncertain and resources shift with developing technologies. We excuse our present consumption by saying that what persons desire varies over generations, and that future persons will have to look out after themselves. Nor do we altogether use up natural resources; we partly convert them to capital, which others inherit.

Such justifications make some sense, but fail when we begin to tamper with what have hitherto been the natural certainties. Perhaps we are not obligated to supply future generations with oil or timber, for they may not need these as much as we do. But water, air, soil, genes, even landscapes are not in this class of resources, because they are more timeless and irretrievable. They define everything else, and there are no substitutes. There is a difference between cutting off a person's paycheck and cutting off his air supply, between eating the harvest and eating the seed corn. We have no duty to leave our grandchildren wealthy, but we ought to leave them a world no worse than we found it, like campers who use a campsite.

The issue is deceiving because we only gradually push the troubled skies and poisoned soils over onto the next generation. When the fifty-five-gallon drums storing our wastes rust out, their labels gone, what then? Toxins in ground water are nearly impossible to remove. If the Pharaohs had stored their plutonium wastes in the pyramids, these would still be ninety percent as lethal as when stored. Radiocontaminants from uranium tailings will be mutagenic for generations. Our books may be black, the GNP up, but how much of this is because of what we have charged to future generations? One shouldn't make debts for others to pay, and especially when there is no foreseeable way for them to pay such debts.

But concerns here are not merely those of safety and a decent environment. They are also about freedom to enjoy the natural amenities. What if the executive's grandchildren prefer warblers, eagles, parks, the seasonal rhythms of a countryside, over the aging shopping centers and hydroelectric plants he leaves them? They might complain that he bequeathed them no capital. They are more likely to complain that he took away their options in wildness, and that business and technology can provide no authentic substitutes. Thou shalt not steal the natural basics from tomorrow.

§8 THE UNCONSUMPTION MAXIM: MAXIMIZE NON-CONSUMPTIVE GOODS

Consumption is what business and even life is all about, for we all consume to live. But in another sense consumption is a kind of wasting disease, one of ineffective use. Perhaps permitted levels of consumption can rise gradually over time, as broader resource bases, recycling methods, and energy techniques are discovered. Then the luxuries of the fathers can become the necessities of the children. Nevertheless, at any given decision point, it is better to favor the least consumptive alternative. Some things can be used without being used up, the difference between a cloth and a paper towel. A trophy hunter brings the buck back with him, a wildlife photographer leaves him there for others to enjoy. So, fiscal concerns being equal, an optics manufacturer might prefer telephoto lenses to crosshair scopes. Often, the less consumptive a good is (a day spent hiking the Appalachian Trail), the higher its quality. Amenity use tends to be non-consumptive, while commodity use tends to be consumptive. A realtor who resolves to keep goods as public and permanent as possible will not seek to convert into posted, exclusive cabin plots land suitable for a state park or essential to the Trailway.

One alarm clock may last two years, another twenty. In our lavish yet cheap, throwaway economy, business has hardly urged efficiency upon its customers. The market is full of planned obsolescence, with far more time spent hooking the gullible buyer into consumption than is spent considering alternative, possibly equally profitable ways of making goods more durable. We too often have (adapting a computing term) a gigo economy, garbage *in*, garbage *out*, because the stuff is not only junk when finished, it is junk when sold. There are some goodies too that should hardly have been made at all. It is unlikely that electric carving knives have really benefited one in a hundred of their purchasers. The advice to eliminate consumptive goods is ridiculous, but the effort to maximize consumptive goods is equally so, and unethical as well.

§9 THE RECONSUMPTION MAXIM: MAXIMIZE RECYCLING

Make it so it will last, but then again, make it so it won't. When junked, can it be remanufactured? Of otherwise comparable materials, which one may be more economically reused? General Motors has had a task force looking for ways to improve the recyclability of cars by changing the materials. Ecologically, one material may be biodegradable, another not. The hamburger must be eaten, but does it need to be wrapped in so majestic a petroplastic carton, used for twenty-five seconds to carry it from the counter to the table, then tossed to lie in a trash heap for decades? The hamburger is digested and eliminated, the nutrients recycled; the wrapper, indigestable by man or microbe, outlasts the life of the burger eater. For that matter, does the hamburger even need to be wrapped, if this requires Mr. Ludwig to sacrifice the Amazon rain forest? (See Case 2.) The soda pop consumed on the trail is soon gone, the aluminum tab tossed there lasts nearly a century. It might have been manufactured affixed to the can, and the can packed out and recycled by deposit or buy-back incentives. A single wood-handled carving knife will outlast half a dozen electric ones; it gives its user needed exercise and no expense. If it ever wears thin, the wood can rot and the steel be remelted, while the plastic from the electric gadgetry lies useless at the dump.

An economist needs to be mindful of what an ecologist calls "throughput" in the system, the movement of energy and materials so that the valuable constituents nowhere choke up, but keep being reutilized in the systemic flows. From one viewpoint this is a matter of expediency and efficiency, but from another it is also a moral concern. How do we spend a resource so as to keep it from being spent forever? How do we recycle value? Nature's bounty and invisible hand once took care of these things reasonably well, but no longer. So business has a new duty.

§10 THE PRIORITY MAXIM: THE MORE VITAL AN IRREPLACEABLE RESOURCE, THE MORE WORTHWHILE THE USE TO WHICH IT SHOULD BE PUT

No resources should go through the economy too cheap to meter, but some are dear enough to need metering by more than market supply and demand. Of those non-renewable and difficult to recycle, some are more crucial than others. The more one does business in this type of resource, the less one ought to manufacture transient, trivial goods, the more one ought to lock it into the capital of the economy. Molybdenum is in relatively short supply, its ores are uncommon. An area known as "Oh Be Joyful" near Crested Butte in Colorado high mountain country, desirable for wilderness, for watershed, for ski development, is believed to have high potential for ore. The large Mount Emmons mine is already being planned nearby. Retained as wilderness, the area would be used non-consumptively, or it could be developed for skiing and lightly used with high public turnover. If prospected and later mined, as urged by AMAX, the area has to be destroyed, with drastic social effects as well on the small town.

Now what becomes of the molybdenum? It goes into solar collectors, which help toward energy independence. It goes into ICBMs, but do we have enough already? It goes into sporting rifles, so trophy hunters can shoot up their game, and into electric carving knives, of which we have too many already. As wilderness, the area is in short supply; but the molybdenum is needed, so it might be sacrificed for true but not for false progress. Solar development, though destroying the wilderness, might be more important than skiing, which doesn't. But if the wilderness is to be destroyed, then the vital mineral should not be indifferently used. Unfortunately in our present capitalist economy (as socialists rightly lament), there is no one to ration the use of such a resource. Until this comes, perhaps by selective taxation, the business community needs to develop some conscience about priority uses for our more critical resources. That is admittedly a difficult assignment, and many will shrug their shoulders and say they can do nothing about the demand for and uses of their products. But that is only to acquiesce in an unjust and clumsy market system.

§11 THE TOXIN-IS-TRUMPS MAXIM: AN OUNCE OF PERMANENT TOXICITY IS WORSE THAN A TON OF PASSING GOODS

The Business Roundtable lobby has complained that federal authorities are overly biased in favor of health protection.[10] There is room to discuss what counts as acceptable risk, especially since minute pollutants are the most expensive to remove, but surely one wants a moral bias in favor of health, over the production of extra goods, public or private. Given the recalcitrant sloth of leaky businesses, one wants lots of such bias. They have preferred to pollute until damage was evident, and impossible or expensive to reverse. They have scoffed at risks, later to eat crow while the public eats their contaminants. Especially in view of time lags here, the margin of error ought to favor those who breathe, not those who pollute. Even in small amounts, such long-term toxicity is foisted unwillingly upon millions not party to the business. The aerial spraying of pesticides, which involves nearly two-thirds of their use, mostly on fiber crops, not food, increases the risk of disease of those downwind, who may derive little or no benefit from the spraying, and take the risks involuntarily. This can happen while short-term goods are sought willingly by the customers, and profits by the operators. If you can't survive without polluting at toxic levels, then you should go out of business; society cannot afford your kind of business. Life shortened and life crippled is life taken; and thou shalt not kill.

The Kepone in the James River will gradually flush out, but toxicity levels are unknown, and when eventually ingested the carcinogen has a latency period up to twenty-five years. (See Case 1.) Here, the more permanent the toxin, the more it counters large amounts of immediate goods. The radioiodine in my thyroid kills me and moves on to others afterwards. Plutonium remains lethal for fifty times longer than any civilization has yet survived, five times longer than *Homo sapiens* has survived. Even the brightest engineer must have a dull conscience to say, with Mr. Micawber, "Oh, well, something will turn up to detoxify it. My decade needs the extra energy." So he builds his nuclear plants, risks the pluto- nium use, and ships his noxious freight down the road out of sight. In view of accidents, terrorism, and even "permissible" exposures, are not the chances better that someone will get hurt by it? Over the long haul, some violations in environmental ethics are more dangerous than those in traditional ethics, because of the threat to so many generations. Since a toxin erodes life and health, a little overrides a lot of the pursuit of happiness. In repeated surveys the public prefers environmental protec- tion over lower prices with pollution by about two to one, and a major- ity in all walks of life will say that environmental integrity at critical points must be maintained regardless of cost.

§12 THE STEADY-STATE MAXIM: ACCEPT NO-GROWTH SECTORS OF THE ECONOMY

Some sorts of growth may occur forever, as advancing technology makes new products possible. Our supply of materials is finite (short of space mining); but materials can be recycled and substituted and energy in principle is in generous supply, although in practice difficult to get cheaply. The growth of know-how may be unlimited, given the ingenuity of hand and brain. At the same time, some sorts of growth have limits, and here the ethical economist mixes savvy with conscience to know what growth to stimulate and what to subdue, before limits are thrust upon him. There are sixty-nine dams on the Tennessee and Cumberland river systems, and perhaps there should be no more. The chamber of commerce might better be of a Lesser, not a Greater Seattle. Perhaps there should not be a greater per capita consumption of electricity, not until we can manage this without those toxins. Perhaps there never need be three televisions in every home. Our United States cars should never have been the two-ton, tail-finned dinosaurs they were in the sixties. Think steady, when enough is enough. Think small, when less is more. A sign of the adult state, surpassing juvenile years, is that physical growth is over, and a more sophisticated intellectual and social growth continues. In these years physical growth may be nonfunctional, even cancerous.

III. BUSINESS AND A NATURALISTIC ENVIRONMENTAL ETHIC

A humanistic ethic may be viewed as a matter of fouling or feathering our own nest. It has insisted on considering a public, not merely a com- pany nest. But ethical concern deepens with the claim that we have comprehensive duties to consider the natural community and its diverse sorts of inhabitants. In this community we humans no doubt have our interests, but these interests are, as it were, investments in a bigger corporation. Here we humans are major but not exclusive stockholders. The place of lesser subsidiaries has to be recognized. In a humanistic ethic, we had only to pull environmental concerns under social values already more or less in place. But with a non-anthropocentric, naturalistic ethic we have to pull social values under an inclusive environmental fitness. When human interests are the sole measure of right and wrong, nature is but the stage upon which the human drama is played. When non-anthropocentrism comes to the fore, the plot thickens to include natural history. The humanistic ethic will still be needed, but if exclusive, it will be pronounced shallow. Any business is wrong that asserts self-interest at cost to the whole public welfare. We have already conceded that. Now we move the argument one step up. The whole human business is wrong if, likewise, it asserts its corporate self-interest at the expense of the bio-systemic whole, disregarding the other stakeholders. We need some enriched moral calculus reconciling human and natural systems, economic and ecological ones.

What values would a naturalistic environmental ethic recognize and seek to foster? That is what the next list of maxims attempts to identify. These value judgments will affirm the worth of objective characteristics in nature (for example: life, rarity, complexity) and deny that nature is in the usual economic sense a collection of resources. But adding to our moral puzzlement, we will find that nearly all these maxims have a humanistic rider. Some benefits may come to humans who recognize the natural excellences. This fits the age-old observation that to respect the integrity of another person is often to gain a benefit from this. Nevertheless the benefit is often nebulous and iffy, softer and more intangible, never very impressive before hard, immediate economic pressures. Humanistic motives are here weak and subordinate. They must combine with some appreciation of nature to bring you to endorse a maxim. This leaves us confused about our motives and principles, but it may nevertheless leave us with operational guidelines so that when in business we can do business with ecological satisfaction.

§13 THE REVERSIBILITY MAXIM: AVOID IRREVERSIBLE CHANGE

We do our business in a many-splendored natural system, one where life has so far prospered. It vastly exceeds our mastery, is incompletely understood still, and its mysterious origins and dynamics are perhaps finally unfathomable. All evolution is irreversible but moves very slowly. Here humans want to avoid precipitous irreversible changes, or even minor ones we later regret. This commandment mixes respect and fear. This natural system, though sometimes hostile, is one in which we have been generated and now flourish. We should respect it as our home soil and be reluctant to do anything that might make it worse for ourselves, worse because we have tinkered with what is already a pretty good Earth.

All business alters nature, and any experimental venture runs some risks. But we should not disturb an ecosystem so that we cannot, if we later wish, put it back as it was. "To keep every cog and wheel is the first precaution of intelligent tinkering," warned Aldo Leopold, a forester and one of the first environmentalists, writing a generation back.[11] We should leave room to reconsider; we should avoid radically closing options. Choose that business which allows us to redeem our mistakes. Any change is to some extent irreversible, but recent technology has made some quite irreversible—the extinction of species, the loss of critical habitat, the shrinking of breeding populations, the introduction of exotic pests, toxins and mutagens in soil and waters. The chestnut and the passenger pigeon are gone forever, the starling and the English sparrow are here to stay. What next with our effluents in the salt marshes, with our acid rain over the Adirondacks, with our bulldozers in the Amazon? What links are being cut, what gene pools overshrunk, what eggshells are becoming too thin?

§14 THE DIVERSITY MAXIM: MAXIMIZE NATURAL KINDS

Nature creates lots of niches and then puts evolutionary and genetic tendencies to work filling these with a kaleidoscopic array, as glancing through a butterfly guide will show. It would be a pity needlessly to sacrifice much, if any, of this pageant, especially if we get in return only more good like that of which we already have enough. Variety is a spice in life. That says something about human tastes, but not so as to overlook the natural spices. There are twenty-two recreational lakes on which to water-ski within sixty miles of the Tellico Reservoir. There was but one rare, small snail darter population before it was drowned by the dam and scattered by hectic attempts to transplant it. The darter had no use, but it could have made the place interesting. This is not an axiom to maximize kinds unnaturally, but only to preserve diversity where we find it naturally, so far as we can, and unless we can find overriding reasons why not.

Often more is at stake than tonic and interest. Natural ecosystems are resiliently interwoven, usually so that when one thread breaks the whole fabric does not unravel. They absorb interruptions well, as when the chestnut was replaced by oaks. But with the advent of monocultures (single crops grown over wide areas), we push the whole surrounding rural system toward a fragile simplicity. Factory forests, growing timber species only, and artificially revegetated mine lands are easy to operate, bring high yields, and lower costs. But they have low stability and high vulnerability to insect pests, diseases, droughts, and erosion. Even when diversity adds no evident strength, some of the natural kinds may have uses of which we are unaware. The remarkable medicinal properties of curare were found in 1940, but there are further stories of Amazon basin plants that dissolve gall and kidney stones, heal burns, staunch bleeding, and provide long-lasting contraception. Some of these plants are common, others endangered, and Mr. Ludwig ought not to destroy the Amazon forest before we know whether those stories are true. (See Case 2.)

At least one can maximize diversity in quality, with all sorts of habitats located so that many persons have access to them. Nothing here depreciates business-built environments. We only insist that some wild ones be kept too. We have no business impoverishing the system. Yet industrial expansion has accelerated the natural extinction rate a thousand times, and we have only a fraction of the wilderness we had a century ago, when our population was a fraction of what it is now.

§15 THE NATURAL SELECTION MAXIM: RESPECT AN ECOSYSTEM AS A PROVEN, EFFICIENT ECONOMY

Business and labor use resources resourcefully, and this effort spent transforming nature sometimes leads us, unreflectively, to see raw nature apart from human occupation as a useless wasteland. But an ecosystem is an economy in which the many components have been naturally selected for their efficient fitness in the system. There is little waste of materials and energy. Wherever there is available free energy and biomass, a life form typically evolves to fill that niche and exploit those resources. The economies we invade are durable, they have worked about as they do for tens, even hundreds of thousand of years, and in this sense each is a classic. Nature is a sort of tinkerer, adapting this onto that, seldom starting from scratch, but by trial and error experimenting with odds and ends on hand, pragmatically insisting that a thing keep working, surviving, or tearing it up and making something else. There is relentless pruning back by a sort of cost-efficient editing process, so that only the fittest survive. Detroit engineers do a lot of this sort of tinkering, pressed toward efficiency, defeated if their trials are structurally or functionally unsound. Even business in general operates much like this.

When we step in, we need to be careful with our massive, irreversible, simplifying innovations, because the chances are that our disturbance will have some unintended bad consequences. Even Ph.D.'s in engineering can be like the foolish natives who slash and burn, and wonder why the desert advances and their economies fail. With their forests gone, the Brazilians may soon be asking why their lateritic soils have lost their fertility. (See Case 2.) One analyst even warns, "The survival of man may depend on what can be learned from the study of extensive natural ecosystems."[12] That is perhaps extreme, but it is likely that our economy can be improved by attention to the efficiency of nature's economy. Again, appreciation of what nature objectively is has a spin-off. Those who prefer to say that the effect on human welfare is all that is valuable here may nevertheless endorse this maxim, only giving a more pragmatic twist to the word "respect." Even in modern business we can ponder an aphorism coined long ago at the start of the technological age by the English philosopher Francis Bacon, "Nature is not to be commanded, except by being obeyed."[13]

§16   THE SCARCITY MAXIM: THE RARER AN ENVIRONMENT, THE LIGHTER IT OUGHT TO BE TREATED

Nature's habitats are unevenly distributed. Grasslands are common, gorges infrequent, geothermal basins rare. Human development has increased the rarity of them all; we have only scraps of once-common ones. The Little Tennessee, now feeding a lake at the Tellico Dam, was one of the last really wild rivers in the East. The rarer an environment, the more carefully we ought to do business there. This will impose minimally on business in general, though it will vitally affect the few companies who work in rare environments. Weyerhaeuser, "The Tree Growing Company," with a generally positive environmental record, owns timberland areas collectively as large as Massachusetts. A few holdings are subalpine forests interfingered with alpine meadows; others are cathedral groves of virgin growth. The former were always relatively rare, the later are now. Weyerhaeuser has been clear-cutting both, and their director of environmental affairs, Jack Larsen, maintains that, while there is a public interest in preserving such forests, this is "not the responsibility of a private land owner," but "a function of government."[14] But this is too simple a shifting of responsibility. Proportionately as these forests are rare, they ought to be cut by selection or remain uncut, whether or not the government is alert about this. The managed, regrown forests that may slowly succeed the primeval ones will not be the equal either for wilderness experience or for scientific study of the rare, virgin forests sacrificed for a quick crop.

The rare environments are not likely to be essential to regional ecosystems, and hence we can do without them. But they may serve like relics, fossils, and keepsakes as clues to the past or to alien and twilight worlds. They are planetary heirlooms that hark back to the wonders of nature, to our broader lineage. Their serendipitous benefit is that, as environments under special stress, they are often good indicators of the first negative effects that humans introduce, good laboratories of exotic survival. Given our bent for radical technologies, it is hard to predict just where the next stress points will appear, and what will be the best laboratories in which to study them.

§17   THE AESTHETIC MAXIM: THE MORE BEAUTIFUL AN ENVIRONMENT, THE LIGHTER IT OUGHT TO BE TREATED

Every businessperson has stood at some scenic point and been glad for the pristine, unspoiled beauty. Teddy Roosevelt exclaimed before the Grand Canyon, "Leave it as it is. You cannot improve on it. The ages have been at work on it, and man can only mar it."[15] The really exceptional natural environments do not need any business development at all. Tastes in beauty differ, but a survey of what most people think will usually do for business decisions. In tougher cases, the witness of experts with enriched aesthetic sensitivities can be sought. Some art is priceless, and all art is awkward to price. Here natural art is not really an economic resource, but is better understood in romance. The technological, businesslike relation of humans to nature is not the only one; and sometimes we wish not to show what we can do, but to be let in on nature's show.

Where natural places are not left alone, we ought to work in and on them in deference to their beauty. The philosopher Alfred North Whitehead lamented a half-century ago, "The marvellous beauty of the estuary of the Thames, as it curves through the city, is wantonly defaced by the Charing Cross railway bridge, constructed apart from any reference to aesthetic values." Society suffered the loss of natural beauty here because "in the most advanced industrial countries, art was treated as a frivolity," and "the assumption of the bare valuelessness of mere matter led to a lack of reverence in the treatment of natural or artistic beauty." In any socially progressive business, "the intrinsic worth of the environment . . . must be allowed its weight in any consideration of final ends."[16]

§18 THE CHINA SHOP MAXIM: THE MORE FRAGILE AN ENVIRONMENT, THE LIGHTER IT OUGHT TO BE TREATED

Natural ecosystems have considerable stamina, but not equally so. Industrial society developed in Europe and the eastern United States where (and in part because) the soils were fertile, the climate temperate, the waters abundant. This sort of ecosystem is especially self-healing and those environments took a lot of punishment and offal. Society moved into the arid West; industrial expansion went multinational, seeking raw materials even under the tundra and sea. We have discovered, often sadly, that old ways of doing business will not transplant to fragile soils. The Alaska pipeline crosses eight hundred miles of arctic vegetation. Some gashes will be there long after the oil is burned, even after the men who made them are dead. The oil shale found in the plateaus of western Colorado is proving difficult to extract without mutilating the terrain. The shale has to be heated, and if this is done above ground the spent shale is hard to revegetate, given the low precipitation and chemical changes in the retorting. If it is done underground, the toxins may contaminate the limited water in the aquifers that feed the few creeks and watering holes. Technologies that might work with thirty inches of rain cannot be used with an eight-inch rainfall.

All this is, in the first instance, the prudent preventing of a boom and bust cycle. But it can be a reluctance to go bulldozing in a china shop, lest what is busted be "ruined," perhaps because of its beauty or rarity, perhaps to avoid irreversible change, or to maintain diversity, or to appreciate the extra regimen in an economic system so soon subject to our distressing it. Fragility alone, like rarity, is hardly a value word. But it has a way of figuring in a constellation of natural qualities; and in the whole pattern we may find some respect for the integrity of a natural place. We may resolve to do our civil business with less insult, less savagery. Vandalism is possible on nature, even in a businesslike way.

§19 THE CNS MAXIM: RESPECT LIFE, THE MORE SO THE MORE SENTIENT

The capacity for quality of experienced life parallels the sophistication of the central nervous system (CNS). Pleasure and pain become more intense as we go up the phylogenetic tree. It has seemed self-evident to moral philosophers that pleasure by itself must be a good thing and pain by itself must be bad. But if evil for persons, then why not for sentient animals? It will not do to say: "Because they are not persons." That indeed is inhumane anthropocentric insensitivity! As Jeremy Bentham, an eighteenth-century English philosopher, accurately saw, "The question is not, Can they *reason*? nor, Can they *talk*? but, Can they *suffer*?"[17] Important differences need to be marked out between domestic and wild animals; the former would not even exist without human care; the latter sometimes suffer terribly in their natural ecosystems. Those who build an environmental ethic on animal rights and those who build it on the characteristics of natural ecosystems do not always agree. But we need not consider such problems here in order to conclude that one ought not needlessly increase suffering. Does not the Golden Rule reach at least this far?

Animal suffering might sometimes be justified by sufficient human benefits. Even then, we ought to do business so as to cause the least pain. We should, for instance, choose the least sentient animal that will do for the purposes of our testing and research. Some human goods may not justify the suffering they require. A pharmaceutical firm, Merck Sharp and Dohme, applied for a permit to import chimpanzees as the only known animal in which a vaccine for Hepatitis B can be tested. But chimps are a threatened species and known to be highly intelligent social animals. The capture of a juvenile chimp requires shooting the mother, and caged chimps are much deprived of their natural life. One analyst concluded, "The world has a growing population of 4 billion people and a dwindling population of some 50,000 chimpanzees. Since the vaccine seems unusually innocuous, and since the disease is only rarely fatal, it would perhaps be more just if the larger population could find some way of solving its problem that was not to the detriment of the smaller."[18] The permit was denied, largely for ethical reasons.

Calves are confined in constricted stalls and, except for two daily feedings, kept in darkness for their entire lives, in order to satisfy a gourmet preference for pale veal, neither more tasty nor nutritious than darker veal. In the Draize test, cosmetics are tested by dripping concentrates into the eyes of unanesthetized rabbits until their eyes are swollen or blinded. The gourmet, the restaurateur, and the perfumed lady who know these things might be less callous. Faced with growing public criticism, Revlon, Inc., has funded a $750,000 grant to find a substitute for the Draize test. Ducks feed on spent shot that falls into their ponds, needing grit for their gizzards, and afterwards die slowly from lead poisoning. The manufacturer, the sporting goods retailer who knows this should prefer steel shot instead.

§20 THE LIFE-SPECIFIC MAXIM: RESPECT LIFE, THE SPECIES MORE THAN THE INDIVIDUAL

Three-quarters of adult Americans (the customers and stockholders of business) believe that endangered species must be protected even at the expense of commercial activity. That alone makes it good public relations to do business protecting rare and endangered species. We have already met some of their reasons: Extinction is irreversible, we lose diversity, beauty, a genetic resource, a natural wonder, a souvenir of the past. But more underlies these, really a religious reason. Life is a sacred thing, and we ought not be careless about it. This applies not only to experienced life, but to preservation of the lesser zoological and the botanical species. Species enter and exit the natural theater, but only over geologic time and selected to fit evolving habitats. Individuals have their intrinsic worth, but particular individuals come and go, while that wave of life in which they participate overleaps the single lifespan millions of times. Nature treats individuals with brief lives, but prolongs the type until it is no longer fit. Long-lived survival trends are at work here. Lost individuals can be replaced, but the species is irreplaceable, and the loss of critical habitat and a shrinking breeding population dooms a species.

Between one and three species vanish every day, and within a decade that could be one per hour. If the accelerated extinction rate is unabated, twenty percent of all species on earth could be lost within twenty years. About half these losses result from tropical deforestation, in which Mr. Ludwig is so vigorously taking part (see Case 2), and the second greatest cause is pollution. Such a threat cuts to the quick in our respect for life. The question now is not, Are they sentient? but, Are they rare? "We had to decide which was more important: saving a rare bird, or pumping more oil and gas from an area which is that creature's only known nesting place in North America. I decided in favor of the bird."[19] So reported Walter Hickel, secretary of the interior, in a 1970 decision for the California condor. "For the birds!" The oil tycoon will say that derisively. "For the birds indeed!" The naturalist will say it too, but more respectfully.

§21 THE NATURE, INC., MAXIM: THINK OF NATURE AS A COMMUNITY FIRST, A COMMODITY SECOND

That ecosystems are intricate communities is an established biological fact, a principle of ecology, which those doing business in nature often run into, sometimes to their regret. In the Pacific Northwest, loggers have clear-cut forests to discover, on some sites, that the forest cannot be regenerated. They did not understand the undercover shielding needed for seedling regrowth, provided by the cooperation of multiple species, sometimes weedy ones, or they did not understand the nitrogen economy, failing to recognize that seemingly useless lichens, found primarily on old growth trees, were critical fixers of nitrogen, which fertilized the forest. In Southeastern pine forests mycorrhizal root fungi are similarly crucial. The picture we get is of a community where parts fit together in what is called symbiosis.

Nature operates its economies in a cooperative mode, if also in a competitive mode. This does not mean that the individual members of the community are even aware of this process, much less endorse it, only that natural systems are selected to form a kind of togetherness. The strivings of the parts are overridden to insure cooperative behavior and functioning in a symbiotic whole. After Darwin, some might have said that nature is a jungle, a free-for-all where issues are settled by pulling and hauling. But after ecology, we get a revised picture of checks and balances that pull the conflicts into an interdependent community. This continues but goes beyond seeing natural systems as tight and proven economies, a fact that we recognized in an earlier maxim (§15). We think now of a community, a web of life, of life forms as flourishing only when interlocked in biological pyramids. In terms of the root metaphor of the word "ecology," a root shared also by "economics," we all live in a *household* (Greek: *oikos*).

Does any ethic follow from all this? Those who accept the prevailing, anthropocentric ethic will still treat things like property and resources, only they may become more prudent in extracting resources or eliminating wastes. But there are others, more naturalistically inclined, who can endorse the natural principle of life-in-community not only as a given but as a good. This account runs as follows. Even in humanistic ethics it is always individuality-in-community upon which ethics rests. There can be overly atomistic views that posit only self-interested individuals looking out for themselves, and some may think that business should be like popular conceptions of Darwinian nature, a field of competition where the fittest survive. But surely a more appealing view is one that can generate some sense of the individual welfare as inseparable from the good of the community, recognizing on a moral level in human affairs what we called symbiosis in biology. We have a doubtful ethic where an individual treats all fellow persons like so many commodities, forgetting how his life is in a community.

But when we turn to natural systems, we find the same sort of thing. The competitions take place in a cooperating community, not a moral or conscious one, but a good one, and when we humans come to do our business there, the principle of community membership, known already in human affairs, is to be continued because it fits well with the biological patterns we find: that life is always life-in-community. This may not derive ethics from natural facts, but it at least tries to fit an ethic to natural modes of operation. In nature there are movements of self-interest that are quite properly present, but these are superintended non-deliberately in ecological systems by nature's overriding hand in favor of an interdependent whole. When humans, as moral beings, enter to evaluate this, they continue by endorsing the principle of interdependent life. We have the right to treat nature as a resource, but also the responsibility to respect the community in which all life is sustained. A business needs prudently to recognize the limits imposed by ecological laws. But it is even better for it to be fitted by moral temper for its place in the whole natural community of which it is a part. Nature is really the ultimate corporation, a cooperation, into which we ecologically must and morally ought to fit.

§22 THE PARENTAL EARTH MAXIM: LOVE YOUR NEIGHBORHOOD AS YOU DO YOURSELF

The surrounding countryside is, as Augustine said of God, that in which we live, move, and have our being. We should not be either irreverent or provincial about this. The local neighborhood is our nearest responsibility; there a business's impact for good or ill is likeliest to be felt. But the successes of big business and the revelations of science have shrunk the world so that our neighborhoods are larger and interlocked. The ultimate neighborhood is the parental Earth, seen so hauntingly in pictures from space. This Earth has generated us and continues to be our life support. It should be the object not only of our prudent care but of our love.

This maxim is rather philosophical and general, but there are immediate, practical applications. We give local care to natural items that have become cultural symbols of home (the Shenandoah, the Mississippi, the bald eagle) but also to landforms just because they are the home in which life is set, to life forms just because they are our "neighbors" — in the Biblical sense. For the average American, already well-heeled and comfortable, from here on these natural things are increasingly worth saving, and if a business continues to destroy them, what benefits it provides are not likely to outweigh the harm it does. Even for the average world citizen, who has real physical needs that business ought to meet, the quality of life cannot really be raised if the quality of the environment declines thereby. Sooner or later, ethics and business must attend to the appropriate unit of survival, and that cannot be less than the whole Earth, the womb of all.

IV. ETHICAL COMPLEXITIES IN BUSINESS AND ENVIRONMENTAL CONCERNS

Moral responsibility in environmental affairs is as complex and novel as any responsibility a business executive is likely to face. This demands decisions that weigh technical, fiscal, social, and moral judgments, often made over long hauls and in the face of unknowns, breaking new ground with an amalgam of humanistic and naturalistic interests. We face two kinds of ethical difficulties. One is where we know what ought to be done but not how to get the company to do it. The other is where we do not know what is right. We do not know the facts, or how to weigh the facts, especially statistical ones. We do not know how to attach values to facts, or how to trade this good off against that one. Decisions will not be ideologically pure, but rather messy (see Case 3). But there is some good news with the bad. The business executive will never be replaced by a computer on which these decisions are programed. There will be an increasing need for business heads that can do hard thinking.

Someone may object that the maxims given so far are useless, because too general and imprecise. It is well to recall that ethics is not geometry, and that we should not expect of one what we require of the other. Remember that a principle or warning can have value even though somewhat general. Though we cannot derive from these maxims concrete solutions for every case, nevertheless they provide a background against which we can explore and assess our practical decisions. Those who share some or even most of them may disagree in practice in some cases, but still they have reference points against which to work, a background against which to sketch the shape of their differences. These maxims have to be brought into cross-play between themselves and more traditional injunctions. One rule may collide with or sideswipe another. These are not maxims from which we can compute exact solutions, but neither are they empty. They lay moral constraints on available options. For actual decisions, we have further moral work to do. But these *prima facie* directives clearly preclude some wrong choices. We cannot eliminate but we can reduce ambiguity by maxims such as these.

Notice that whether an act is *expedient* or *moral* needs to be specified with reference to the actor, the affected class, and the time span. All these are complicated in business morality. Here individuals, who are morally responsible, act for the company, which is owned by themselves, by employers, by stockholders. The company itself has some explicit or tacit policy, and serves the community over both short and long terms, a community populated with changing individuals. A particular decision may be immoral but expedient for stockholders this year, its reverse, a decision that is moral though inexpedient now, may prove expedient five years hence, given ensuing public opinion and governmental regulation. Meanwhile the body of stockholders has somewhat changed, and different persons fill some company jobs, "offices." As a rule of thumb, the farther one looks ahead, the broader the group considered within the company, and the more effective social critics are, the more the moral and the prudent will coincide. As a rule, too, the bigger and more long-lived the corporation, the more fuzzy the line between private and public concerns, which increasingly interlock. Thus it tends to become true for such businesses that what is ethical is self-serving, but not in the way that ethical egoists maintain, but because smaller, shorter-range individual concerns fade into bigger, longer-range corporate and social ones. Meanwhile also, no businesses and no persons within them escape immediate short-range pressures that sometimes pull them toward making short-sighted decisions.

Where moral decisions become complex, they often cease to be absolutely and unambiguously right or wrong, and we seek to judge what is the best of competing but mutually incompatible goods or to choose the least of evils. There is some good to be accomplished on either alternative, some profit, which too is a good, but some products delivered and services rendered which fill public needs. We need the power, the pesticide, the plastic, the paper pulp, but then again can we really afford it at this social cost and consequence? Someone is going to get hurt on either alternative. Here it is tempting to deliver the goods, give persons what they want, or seem to want, and let *them* assume the responsibility. But here, even more than in traditional ethics, the good is the enemy of the best. One has to watch for and compensate for what is called "the dwarfing of the soft values,"[20] that is, where values that are quite important, even of the highest kind, but dispersed and soft, get trampled down before values that are not really any more important, but concentrated and hard, easy to get into calculations and marketable. We have to trade off clear scenic vistas against smoggy ones with cheaper power. Sometimes too persons' actions can be well-intended and still, when their actions combine with others, do ill environmentally. Nevertheless, at other times a great deal of environmental carelessness and even crime stems from rationalizing selfishness. Neither a humanistic nor a naturalistic ethic allows the abdication of individual and corporate responsibility, and the following maxims will help one to maintain a sense of responsibility despite the complexities of environmental concerns, in which it is easy (and sometimes convenient) to get lost.

§23 THE BUCK-STOPPING MAXIM: DO NOT USE COMPLEXITY TO DODGE RESPONSIBILITY

Environmental causal links are multiple, incremental, and long term. Their discovery is slow. Any verification is more or less partial, probabilistic, and backtracking. One can steadily deny that the sulfur dioxide from his smokestack had anything to do with the acidity of a pond two hundred miles away. One can point to closer plumes that sometimes blow that way, cite better-buffered watersheds where the fish still flourish, notice that volcanoes emit some SO_2, and for perhaps a decade debunk the evidence. As one is forced toward compliance, lag times for design, delivery, and installation of anti-pollution technology are easy to use for delays and confusions. With compliance mandated, one can build the stacks higher, if this is cheaper than scrubbers, airmail the contaminants further downwind past the local monitors, and claim that this dilutes them to a now-harmless level. Then the dispute has to start over whether this is so.

Add to this the complexity of the corporation, its business links, and its role in society. Various levels of management can deny authority, since this is often partial, and management can claim to be only agents, not principals, to work for stockholders, whose will seems to be known (to optimize profits by recalcitrant compliance) but who are too diffuse a body upon which to fix responsibility. Compliance will require financing, but will the lending agencies attend to the soundness of the projects they finance? Most banks resist the claim that they have any environmental responsibility; these matters are too complex for them to get involved in. The John Hancock Life Insurance Company, the Equitable Life Assurance Society, and Aetna Life and Casualty have, however, paid considerable attention to the environmental impact of projects they have financed, and sometimes voted the stock of companies in which they have holdings with this in view. Of course causal links and corporate responsibilities need to be clearly defined, for there is no single cause or villain, but the complexity ought not be a hiding place used to postpone responsibility or to subvert the law.

§24 THE NO-COSMETICS MAXIM: DO NOT USE PR TO CONFUSE YOURSELF OR OTHERS

Every company lives and dies not only in the market but also by its image. Here it is tempting to opt for symbolic solutions rather than substantive ones, then to advertise this legitimate but minor cleverness, while ignoring—deliberately or tacitly—the major environmental problems that lie still unsolved. The company builds a model new plant, while continuing to run thirty in non-compliance. It can exaggerate the cost of sound solutions, plead foreign competition, the unlikelihood of better technical solutions, feature the jobs lost in a plant closure, its solicitousness for employees, low profits in that subsidiary, and through it all so advertise the good will of the firm as to look better than it actually is, if management were to be honest with themselves. Diversionary PR only fools others about your worthiness; perhaps it even fools you. The ethical person insists on judging the reality behind the image, and, more than that, judges phony image-seeking to be unethical.

Diversionary PR is not only directed outside the company. The deep need of employees to believe that they are contributing to the public good can be a virtue. But it can also be a vice, because, owing to their need to believe this, employees are easily deceived by company pep talks about its environmental awareness, about its progressiveness before obstructionist Luddites, elitist birdwatchers, and canoe freaks. Here the need for personal self-justification coincides with the company's need for a positive image. This gives employees a tendency to rationalize and adds further to the company tendency to contrive token solutions and cover things up with rhetoric. But all this only confounds the problem. At the core of management, those in charge know the intricacies, possibilities, and costs of environmentally sound business better than the agencies who are regulating them, or the environmentalists who are suing them, and if they don't then they *ought* to—an *ought* with elements of both job competence and morality. A nuclear power consortium should focus on these things, rather than publish a promotional pamphlet that exclaims that God must love nuclear reactors because in the stars he made so many of them,[21] which only diverts attention from whether we ought to build this reactor three miles, not ninety-three million miles, from an elementary school.

§25 THE SECOND MILE MAXIM: MORALITY OFTEN EXCEEDS LEGALITY

"There's no law on the books that says we can't." But environmental novelties are still unfolding, they ignore jurisdictions, and one can expect here a lag time between legislation and the developing conscience. Nor will the law at its best ever embody more than the minimum negative public ethic. It forbids the most serious violations, but it cannot command the second mile of good citizenship. Even the conservative Milton Friedman, doubtful of any social responsibility for business, recommends that business "make as much money as possible while conforming to the basic rules of the society, both those embodied in law and those embodied in ethical custom."[22] That recognizes the gap between the legal and the moral, but is too conservative, because in environmental ethics what is already embodied in ethical custom, beyond the law, is likely to be archaic. Unprecedented sorts of damages may be done before the law and public opinion wake up, but the managers of an offending business may be able to sense and correct trouble much sooner. In this ethic, a business leader is called to live on the frontier. The best will be ahead of government, which itself is often subject to delay and malfunction. Law and politics can be quite as flawed as can business, often more so; and the moral businessperson will not take advantage of outdated law or a do-nothing legislature.

That may seem too much challenge, but consider the alternative. If a company announces that it intends to make all the legal profits it can, though it concedes modest attention to ethical customs, this waves a red flag in warning. Everyone knows that such a business has to be watched like a hawk, past good faith in law and custom, so as to push it toward any deepening ethical insight. People will assume that it will become less ethical with increasing market insecurity. It will only increase its morality at the irritation of its critics, and such a firm can expect to do business in an atmosphere of hostility. The courts, public interest groups, and the press rightly conclude that they will have to drag such a firm along by steady legal and social pressures, lest it fling its legal acid into the wind or clear-cut whatever is legal in Oregon or Brazil, always in the rear, always callous in attending to the fragility or beauty of the environment, to rare species and amenities. Is this the reputation business wants? Unless a firm really is out for pure black profit, it is better to move voluntarily toward compliance and even to go the second mile, especially in those cases where you are soon going to be forced to it anyway. Both those within the firm and those without it will feel better about a morality that exceeds legality.

§26 THE BURDEN OF PROOF MAXIM: RECOGNIZE A SHIFTING ASYMMETRY IN ENVIRONMENTAL DECISIONS

From 1941 through 1977 the volume of manufactured synthetic chemicals increased 350 times, with many of these quite toxic to natural systems and to human biology. Even the most resilient local ecosystem cannot absorb our exhausts, pesticides, and herbicides. Even global currents cannot flush out aerosol fluorocarbons and SST exhausts. The more massive the manipulative power, the nearer one approaches the carrying capacity of the commons, the more the unintended, amplifying consequences are likely to be far-reaching. Such chemicals, unlike persons, are not innocent until proven guilty, but suspect until proven innocent. So the burden of proof shifts, and it is now up to the industrialist to dispatch it. This puts one again on the frontier, technologically and morally. Formerly nature's "invisible hand" ruled over these things, but this is no longer so.

One might have hoped that as our competence increased, risks would diminish. But the depth of upset advances even more, and we remain ignorant of our reach. Uranium was mined by the Climax Uranium Company (now AMAX) from 1951 through 1970 on the south edge of Grand Junction, Colorado. The tailings, containing eighty-five percent of the original radioactivity but thought harmless, were widely used as construction materials in thousands of homes, in schools, and in sidewalks. Not until 1970 did physicians notice a marked increase in leukemia, cleft lip and palate, and Down's syndrome. These causal links are still vague, but established enough for federal and state governments to take emergency action. What are the unknowns at the Hansen mine? (See Case 3.) The regulatory authorities could have made better guesses if they had had the latest report of the National Research Council's Advisory Committee on the Biological Effects of Ionizing Radiations (BEIR III), but during their deliberations that had not been published, because of the inability of members of the committee to reach a consensus.

With ever higher technology, it seems that our power to produce changes overshoots increasingly our power to foresee all the results of our changes. The latter takes much more knowledge. It is easier to make Kepone than to predict what it will do in the ecology of the James River estuary, easier to mine uranium and make reactors than to predict where the mutagens in the tailings will end up and what damage will result. In a way, our ignorance outpaces our knowledge. So we are asking for trouble unless we slow down the introduction of potentially more potent novel changes with adequate pretesting. The unforeseen consequences outnumber the foreseen consequences, and the bad unforeseen consequences greatly outnumber the good unforeseen consequences. Serendipity is rare in high technology. Adding to the problem, many persons in business are paid to introduce changes, new products, the quicker the better. But few are employed to foresee adverse consequences and caution against them. So the government regulates to widen by law the margin of safety. But caution is also a moral requirement in these circumstances.

DDT causes cancer in mice, but it is difficult to show that it does or does not in humans, for we cannot experiment much on them, and everyone is already carrying a DDT load from its previous use. So does one conclude that, since there is no hard evidence, we should continue to use it anyway, at least where it is legal, outside the United States? We would, in effect, be experimenting on humans that way too, and making a profit during the experiment! Or does one accept the burden of proof to show that although carcinogenic in mice it does not cause human cancer? This might perhaps be done by experiments on more anthropoid mammals, or by comparative studies with synthetic chemicals that humans regularly contact, but that we have no reason to think are carcinogenic in humans, and yet that do prove to be carcinogenic in mice. It might be done by comparing more refined measurements of cancer rates with existing DDT loads as these fluctuate within diverse populations, or as they flush out across a period of years. The point is that it is moral to err on the safe side, and that business has the responsibility to argue that the risks are minimal, not to presume so, and to chance the damage. Our grandfathers when in doubt could risk a new fertilizer, but we as conscientious grandchildren must increasingly refuse to act until we prove the limits of our effects. This applies to life's necessities, but also to risks of the natural amenities, which have never before been so threatened.

§27 THE FULL-CIRCLE MAXIM: EXTEND MORAL JUDGMENTS THROUGH THE WHOLE EVENT IN WHICH YOUR BUSINESS PLAYS A PART

While the buck should not pass outside of a given company, the scope of judgment should not stop at the boundaries of that business. One should think as far outside one's business as one can. We cannot tell just by looking at the effects of our own actions, considered in isolation, whether we are acting well. Each of us is a link. Parts tied into wholes cannot be judged in themselves, but have to be judged in the resulting pattern that they constitute.[23] Hitherto an entrepreneur could skimp on this principle, because the results of his enterprise were reasonably evident to immediate parties, and any unintended consequences were likely to be neutral.

But we can no longer assume that new technology or more growth is likely to be positive, or even neutral. What might look good in itself, what has always been good in past contexts, may be bad when seen full circle. Even when technology succeeds, the promised sweetness increasingly comes with much that is sour. The workers have jobs, but for miles around all suffer a blighted health and landscape. Almost invariably when high technology fails, the benefits are lost and their opposites arrive with a vengeance. We need to consider what's left economically, if the gamble doesn't pay off. The Kepone was intended for better crops and a stronger economy, but the result is a crippled company and a poisoned James River basin (see Case 1). The failed reactor can no longer deliver its power; worse, the legacy is expensive and even impossible to clean up. Society is not in the black, nor do we go back to zero, we are deep in the red.

Ethical judgment needs to reach for the compound unit. There is no point surviving on a sinking ship, little point prospering in a deteriorating environment. We might formerly have thought that the relevant unit to consider was merely the company and its customers. Now with sophistication and a sense of danger, it needs to be society, the country, the global Earth!

§28 THE GRANDCHILD MAXIM: THINK FOR DECADES

There are strong pressures to see what the charts look like this quarter, even this week. Some say that the successful business eye has to be myopic. But this is never entirely so, and increasingly less so with the size and longevity of the modern corporation, where collective interests overleap even the lives, much less the interests, of individuals who play company roles. The Weyerhaeuser timber cycle is half a century. No big company can afford less than telescopic vision. Nor do stockholders care only about the next dividend. Most are holding their investments for ten or twenty years; the more dynamic the corporation, the more likely they intend to retire on these investments and bequeath them to their children. They want the firm to make it through the year, but in such a way that the long outlook is promising. They will take reduced profits if they believe the company is innovative and that this increases the quality of the environment in which they retire and in which their children, who inherit those investments, will live. Commercial and home loans are for twenty or thirty years. Why should the lending company think their clientele uninterested in the business stability and the quality of the neighborhood during and after the time that these loans are being repaid? Environmental spending, like that for military defense, is immediately a non-productive cost; its benefits are general and longer range.

The corporate and composite character of the big firm can permit exactly the demanded time scale. The company itself needs what is also required by social and naturalistic concerns. Beyond our grandchildren, future generations may not have much moral or biological hold on us, but if one can see as far as grandchildren, that will do operationally in the present case. Meanwhile the company need not age and die at all, it can be revitalized forever. Couple this with the fact that many of its owners and operators are on board for decades, couple that with the tendency of expediency and morality to coincide over time, and a good business head will think for decades.

§29 THE DO-TO-YOURSELF-FIRST MAXIM: IMPOSE ON OTHERS LOWER RISKS THAN YOU YOURSELF ARE TAKING

Some fishermen work both the James River and uncontaminated tributaries, mix both catches for public sale, but carefully take home a batch of the uncontaminated ones. They represent a multitude who own and operate businesses that require a hazardous waste site but who refuse to live near one, who demand power but from faraway reactors and coal-fired plants. They want goods but not risks. But no one should buy goods and not bear risks. In fact, we should do this risk-bearing without consideration of fiscal costs and their distribution. My profit never permits your poisoning—the toxin-is-trumps-maxim (see §11). But set profit aside. How then do we divide the risks that remain? You ought not impose on others risks you are unwilling to take yourself, in view of public benefits. We have to consider not just degrees of risk, but whether these are distributed equitably and voluntarily or involuntarily.

Most persons do not wish to live within one hundred miles of a hazardous waste dump or nuclear plant, and these folk ought not to demand power or goods that require others to do so. A company that sites dumps or plants any closer to a local population will impose upon them, and operators ought not to do so unless they live within this radius. Removing pollutants escalates in cost with the percentage removed and zero risk is impossible. Some risk is unavoidable, more risk profitable, and there will be cost pressures to set tolerances high. So let the maximum permissible concentration be set by researchers, themselves among the susceptible, who are ignorant of the costs and who must long breathe the air whose toxicity they define. Business is now playing with toxins, mutagens, carcinogens. Let all those involved join in the risks proportionately to the public, but never merely private interests. Without consent, one doesn't gamble with somebody else's happiness, not if the odds are one in a hundred. Nor with someone else's life, not if the odds are one in a thousand. A risk imposed on others should be several orders of magnitude below one for which you will volunteer.

§30 THE TOGETHERNESS MAXIM: WORK FOR BENEFITS THAT CAN BE HAD ONLY IN CONCERT

There is not much point in removing the sulfur from one stack if a hundred remain. One developer may drop an area upon finding that the Nature Conservancy is trying to get an option on it, but a dozen others still bid. Not only is the intended effect lost by the non-cooperation of others, the environmentally sensitive firm is disadvantaged in the market. You cannot always do the better thing and survive, while others do wrong cheaply. Competitiveness here becomes a vice because it encourages gain by eating up the commons. But what one firm cannot afford, all together can. Both the environmental and the economic contexts require that businesses act in concert. Moral success depends on the interplay of many wills. Associations of manufacturers, power companies, and realtors often have considerable persuasive force for broad policy-setting.

Still higher, there may be governmental regulation, zoning codes, pollution standards, taxes, quotas. The historical tendency of free enterprise has been to resist these. But surely they are morally required where the alternative is private profit at public loss. The capitalism that cannot incorporate working-for-benefits-in-concert is doomed, sooner or later, to fall before socialism, if not into totalitarianism. If the association of firms proves to be only the self-interest of companies all over again, a lobby rather than conscience in concert, then we can expect again the social antagonism met earlier for announced legal profiteering (see §25). One should work for "mutual coercion, mutually agreed upon."[24] Perhaps no industry can be trusted entirely to police itself, perhaps we need to recognize this for ourselves and our successors as we face unknown pressures ahead. No company is an island; the bell that tolls for one, tolls for all.

§31 THE QUESTION AUTHORITY MAXIM: STAY CRITICAL OF CORPORATE PRESSURES

A corporate structure tends to deaden and fragment moral awareness. This is because of the individual's partial involvement there, because of a firm's limited functions and claims, because of its collective impersonal nature, because our paychecks lie there, and even though a corporation's long-lived semi-public character permits more moral reach than the individual can have. For many, morality goes off when the business suit goes on, when the time card goes in. We may be given, and want, a job description with sharply defined responsibilities. There are some questions we may not be encouraged to ask; you get the message that nobody here can handle them, you are socialized to forget it and get on with the job. The corporate climate may foster more interest in loyalty than in truth. Perhaps we get moral fatigue, our nerve fails, but what we ought to do is to ask all the questions we would as a parent, citizen, or consumer and give them the answers we would if we were not working for the company.

Some say that philosophy makes a person unfit for business, but this is rather only for unfitting sorts of business. Philosophy urges business by "one able to judge" (Greek, *kritikos*), and judgment is a high-class business skill. Like the university, government, or church, the corporation that cannot welcome and include its critics will grow dogmatic and archaic. There can be reformation only by those who question authority, and, if the critics stay noisy, the moral and the expedient tend to coincide over time. Rachel Carson was right about DDT, Ralph Nader was right about automobile exhausts and air pollution. Our cars, towns, and countryside are the better for them. The Alaska pipeline is better built because of its critics. Conservative business operators said, a century back, they could not afford the abolition of slavery and child labor. They say now they cannot afford environmental responsibility. But the more philosophical executives are setting this right. The profit pressures do need moral watching. Whitehead remarked, "A great society is a society in which its men of business think greatly of their functions."[25] That has now come to include "thinking environmentally."

§32 THE GREENING MAXIM: REMEMBER THAT THE BOTTOM LINE OUGHT NOT TO BE BLACK UNLESS IT CAN ALSO BE GREEN

There is no such thing as a healthy economy built on a sick environment, and we can rewrite an earlier, faulty slogan. What's good for the countryside is good for the company. Not for all companies, but we use this to test for the good ones. Running in the black is not enough if this requires our running out of the green, green being here the color of the natural currency. T.V. Learson, former president of IBM, argues for "the greening of American business," and concludes, "in the end, therefore, the whole question of the environment boils down to a value judgment, a priority setting, and the will to do something about it. Most businessmen I know have made that value judgment. They want a cleaner environment as much as anyone else. I believe they will have the *will* to press on for it too, and to help, through business leadership, in stiffening the national will."[26]

This demand for bottom-line green is because the oceans, forests, and grasslands are the lungs of the Earth. But the reasons are more than obviously pragmatic ones. Business relations are only one of our manifold human relations with nature. This one should not preempt the others that go on after business hours, or when we are no longer consuming. These other ways of pursuing happiness are scientific, recreational, aesthetic, appreciative, pastoral, and philosophical. Both in order that business may continue and in order that we may live well after business is done, we need an environment clean enough to be green. *Clean* has two meanings here: clean in the nonpolluted sense, and clean in a noninterrupted sense. Some areas ought to be absolutely and others relatively clean of human management and intervention. Some spaces should remain rural, some wild. There should be mockingbirds and cottontails, bobwhites and pristine sunsets, mountain vistas and canyonlands. There should remain much of that sort of business which went on for the millions of years before we modern humans arrived. In this sense green is the color of life, the most fundamental business of all.

V. BUSINESS AND NATURE

Every organism must "earn its way" consuming its environment, and business activity follows the natural imperative that we must labor for food and shelter. This much of what *is* the case we can also endorse as what *ought* to be. What nature requires (that we work), what is the case (that we must work), we also morally command (one ought to work). Otherwise we cannot flourish and, in extremes, we die. That much of a bread-and-butter "work ethic" properly opposes a romantic naturalism that wants to leave nature untouched. It can celebrate how marvelously labor and management have brought the environment under our control. At the same time, every organism must be a natural fit, integrated into a life-support system. In the wild, misfits cannot flourish and are eventually eliminated. However much human business revises spontaneous nature, primarily by deliberately adapting the environment to humans rather than humans to the environment, we do not escape the fundamental requirement of inclusive fitness to our surroundings.

Thus, though we must and should work, not all our working is equally appropriate. Any business activity that contributes, even incrementally, to the reduced fitting of humans into the natural system does not really contribute to a better standard of living; it may even imperil our survival. An upset of Earth's carrying capacity is a prospect for today and tomorrow that was seldom a fear for business yesterday. Here labor and management must become sober environmentalists. Again we move from what *is* the case (how life is ecologically grounded) to what *ought* to be (how, given a humanistic environmental ethic, business ought to be environmentally alert and sensitive). Both human ecology and human ethics are inescapably environmental affairs. Locally and globally, humans are interlocked with their Earth, with material and energy inputs, throughputs, and outputs, so that here too balanced budgets are required, not less than in accountants' offices. In that sense *economic* activity sooner or later must be and ought to be deeply *ecological* activity, both adjectives having the sense of life prospering in a home place.

Bertrand Russell claimed, "Every living thing is a sort of imperialist, seeking to transform as much as possible of its environment into itself and its seed."[27] But that is an overstatement, which, taken alone, leads to a social Darwinism thrusting atomistic egos and their firms into aggressive competitiveness, with nothing more. Nature has not so equipped or inclined any one form to transform very much of the environment into itself and its seed. Each life form is specialized for a niche, limited to its own sector but woven into a web so that it depends on many other species in a pyramidal, flowing biomass. Recent biology has emphasized not so much aggression and struggle as efficiency and habitat fittedness. Many animal populations limit themselves to suit their resources. If not checked from within, a species' genetic impulses are checked from without by the "natural corporation" that keeps every living thing in community.

All this is premoral, so what are we to say when, at the top of the pyramid, there emerges *Homo sapiens*, so powerful and unspecialized that, culturally evolving to where we now are, we almost can transform the Earth into ourselves and our seed? The answer lies in nature's simultaneously equipping us with a conscience, not given to non-human creatures. Perhaps this conscience can now wisely direct the magnificent, fearful power of the brain and hand. A naturalistic ecological ethic seeks to realize how conscientious human activity, business included, ought to be a form of life that both fits and befits, however much it also extends, what has previously, premorally been the case. Each life form is constrained to flourish within a larger community. The planetary system carries humans most gloriously, but it cannot and ought not carry humans alone. The best of possible worlds is not one entirely consumed by humans, but one that has place for the urban, rural, and wild. Only with moral concern for the whole biological business can we do our work of living well. This ethic defends human life by balanced resource budgets. But more, it defends all life in its ecosystemic integrity.

Whether Earth was made for us is a question we leave to the theologians, who are not likely to say that it was made for us to exploit. We can meanwhile say that we were made for Earth (if not also by it), and this gives us both the power and the duty so to act that we continue to fit this Earth, the substance, the sustainer of life.[28]

NOTES

1. October 5, 1976. U.S. District Court, Eastern Division of Virginia, Richmond. Judge Merhige's statements were made from the bench at the time of sentencing. The fine was technically reduced to five million dollars when Allied placed eight million dollars into a fund to reduce damages.

2. Hugh H. Iltis, "The Biology Teacher and Man's Mad and Final War on Nature," *American Biology Teacher*, 34 (1972), pp. 127–37, 201–21, especially p. 201f. While this article was in press, the Jari project passed into the control of a consortium of Brazilian operators, owing to Mr. Ludwig's age and to financial difficulties. The environmental outlook of the new owners remains to be seen.

3. For details of the Hansen project I am indebted to an unpublished paper by Thomas J. Wolf.

4. Louis B. Lundborg, *Future without Shock* (N.Y.: W. W. Norton, 1974), p. 128f.

5. Compare a report by Marshall Frady in *Harper's Magazine*, Vol. 240, No. 1440 (May 1970), p. 103.

6. Henry B. Schacht and Charles W. Powers, "Business Responsibility and the Public Policy Process," in Thornton Bradshaw and David Vogel, eds., *Corporations and Their Critics* (N.Y.: McGraw-Hill, 1981), pp. 23–32.

7. See *Time*, October 6, 1961, p. 24. More accurately, Wilson once reported, "For years I thought that what was good for our country was good for General Motors, and vice versa."

8. Garrett Hardin, "The Tragedy of the Commons," *Science*, 162 (December 13, 1968), pp. 1243–48.

9. *Final Report of the National Science Foundation Workshop Panel to Select Organic Compounds Hazardous to the Environment* (Washington, D.C.: National Science Foundation, September 1975), p. 8.

10. *Cost of Government Regulation Study for the Business Roundtable* (Chicago: Arthur Andersen and Company, 1979); *The Business Roundtable Air Quality Project* (November 1980).

11. Aldo Leopold, "The Round River," in *A Sand County Almanac* (N.Y.: Sierra Club/Ballantine Book, 1970) p. 190.

12. H. E. Wright, Jr., "Landscape Development, Forest Fires, and Wilderness Management," *Science*, 186 (1974), pp. 487–95, citation on p. 494.

13. Francis Bacon, *Novum Organum, Works* (N.Y.: Garrett Press, 1968) 1:157; cf. 4:47.

14. Quoted in Robert Cahn, *Footprints on the Planet* (N.Y.: Universe Books, 1978), p. 107.

15. Theodore Roosevelt in a speech delivered there, recorded in the *New York Sun*, May 7, 1903.

16. Alfred North Whitehead, *Science and the Modern World* (N.Y.: Mentor Books, New American Library, 1925, 1964), p. 175.

17. Jeremy Bentham, *The Principles of Morals and Legislation* (1789) (N.Y.: Hafner, 1948), ch. 17, sec. 4, p. 311.

18. Nicholas Wade, "New Vaccine May Bring Man and Chimpanzee into Tragic Conflict," *Science*, 200 (1978), pp. 1027–30, citation on p. 1030. See also Paul R. and Anne Ehrlich, *Extinction* (N.Y.: Random House, 1981), pp. 60–61.

19. Walter J. Hickel, *Who Owns America?* (Englewood Cliffs, N.J.: Prentice-Hall, 1971), p. 151. The decision halted further oil and gas leasing in the Sespe Condor Sanctuary, March 9, 1970.

20. After Laurence Tribe, "Trial by Mathematics: Precision and Ritual in the Legal Process," *Harvard Law Review*, 84 (April 1971, No. 6), pp. 1329–93, on p. 1361.

21. William G. Pollard, "A Theological View of Nuclear Energy" in the *Let's Talk About* series interpreting nuclear power to the public, published by the Breeder Reactor Corporation, an association of 753 electric systems, Oak Ridge, Tennessee.

22. Milton Friedman, "The Social Responsibility of Business Is To Increase Its Profits," *New York Times Magazine*, September 13, 1970, pp. 32–33, 122–26, quotation on p. 33.

23. To adapt a more technical ethical distinction, this requires a teleological concern against a deontological naiveté. One cannot judge the rightness of an act in itself, but has to consider the outcomes of it.

24. Hardin, "The Tragedy of the Commons," p. 1247.

25. Alfred North Whitehead, *Adventures of Ideas* (New York: The Free Press, 1967), p. 98.

26. T. V. Learson, "The Greening of American Business," *The Conference Board Record*, 8, no. 7 (July 1971), pp. 21–24, quotation on p. 22.

27. Bertrand Russell, *An Outline of Philosophy* (N.Y.: New American Library, Meridian Books, 1974), p. 30.

28. The author wishes to thank Richard D. Steade of the Colorado State University College of Business for a number of helpful suggestions.

SUGGESTIONS FOR FURTHER READING

Ethical concerns in environmental affairs, as these affect business, are found in many diverse but interrelated areas, among them environmental ethics, environmental economics, environmental law and politics, natural resource conservation, national and international development, geography, technology and civilization, human ecology. The following list will lead deeper into these issues.

Vincent Barry, "Ecology," ch. 9 in *Moral Issues in Business* (Belmont, Calif.: Wadsworth, 1979).

Tom L. Beauchamp, and Norman E. Bowie, "Environmental Responsibility," ch. 8 in *Ethical Theory and Business* (Englewood Cliffs, N.J.: Prentice-Hall, 1979).

Herman E. Daly, ed., *Economics, Ecology, Ethics: Essays Toward a Steady-State Economy* (San Francisco: W. H. Freeman, 1980).

D. J. Davison, *The Environmental Factor: An Approach for Managers* (N.Y.: John Wiley and Sons, Halsted Press, 1978).

Jean Dorst, *Before Nature Dies* (Boston: Houghton Mifflin, 1970).

Nicholas Holmes, ed., *Environmental and the Industrial Society* (London: Hodder and Stoughton Educational Services, 1976).

H. Jeffrey Leonard, J. Clarence Davies III, and Gordon Binder, eds., *Business and Environment: Toward Common Ground* (Washington, D.C.: The Conservation Foundation, 1977).

George F. Rohrlich, *Environmental Management* (Cambridge, Mass.: Ballinger, 1976).

Donald Scherer and Thomas Attig, *Ethics and the Environment* (Englewood Cliffs, N.J.: Prentice-Hall, 1983).

Presson S. Shane, "Business and Environmental Issues," in *Ethical Issues in Business: A Philosophical Approach*, Thomas Donaldson and Patricia H. Werhane, eds., (Englewood Cliffs, N.J.: Prentice-Hall, 1979).

Manuel G. Velasquez, "Ethics and the Environment," ch. 5 in *Business Ethics: Concepts and Cases* (Englewood Cliffs, N.J.: Prentice-Hall, 1982).

§1. There is more detail on the Kepone case in Beauchamp and Bowie (see reference above). See also Marvin H. Zim, "Allied Chemical's $20-Million Ordeal with Kepone," in *Fortune*, 98, no. 5 (September 11, 1978), pp. 82–90, and Frances S. Sterrett and Caroline A. Boss, "Careless Kepone," in *Environment*, 19, no. 2 (March 1977), pp. 30–37, and references there. For a discussion of the Jari project see William M. Denevan, "Development and the Imminent Demise of the Amazon Rain Forest," *The Professional Geographer*, 25 (1973), pp. 130–35; A. Gómez-Pompa, C. Vázquez-Yanes, and S. Guevara, "The Tropical Rain Forest: A Nonrenewable Resource," *Science*, 177 (1972), pp. 762–65; Norman Gall, "Ludwig's Amazon Empire," *Forbes*, 123, no. 10 (May 14, 1979), pp. 127–44; Philip M. Fearnside and Judy M. Rankin, "Jari and Development in the Brazilian Amazon," *Interciencia*, 5 (1980) pp. 146–56. For radiation risks from uranium tailings see D. G. Crawford and R. W. Leggett, "Assessing the Risk of Exposure to Radioactivity," *American Scientist*, 68 (1980), pp. 524–36. See also a suggestion for §26.

§2. For more on stakeholders, see Schacht and Powers, note 6 above. For a survey of environmental concerns in corporate policy see Leonard Lund, *Corporate Organization for Environmental Policymaking* (N.Y.: The Conference Board, 1974), Report No. 618.

§1. Mobile Oil's ad, "The $66 Billion Mistake," in *The New York Times*, February 1, 1973, p. 35, favoring California over federal standards, illustrates corporate foot-dragging. Du Pont's extensive lobbying and advertising against fluorocarbon aerosol bans, despite mounting evidence of their depletion of the ozone layer, is illustrated by an ad in *The New York Times*, June 30, 1975, p. 30. The Reserve Mining Company case discussed in Beauchamp and Bowie (reference above) is another example.

§7. See David Burnham, "The Case of the Missing Uranium," *The Atlantic Monthly*, Vol. 243, no. 4 (April 1979), pp. 78–82. For examples of corporations lodging release of information about waste emissions, including the Savannah River case, see the *Freedom of Information Act Oversight: Hearings before a Subcommittee of the Committee on Government Operations*, House of Representatives, July 14, 15, 16, 1981 (Washington, D.C.: U.S. Government Printing

Office, 1981), testimony of Ralph Nader (p. 330), and James M. Fallows, *The Water Lords* (N.Y.: Grossman, 1971), especially ch. 9. See also *Toxic Substances and Trade Secrecy* (Washington, D.C.: Technical Information Project, 1977), containing the proceedings of a conference supported by the National Science Foundation, especially the article "Toxic Substances and Trade Secrecy: Rights and Responsibilities" by William Blackstone, reprinted in Scherer and Attig, *Ethics and the Environment* (see general references).

§7.   For the pros and cons of discounting, especially with reference to natural amenities, see Anthony C. Fisher and John V. Krutilla, "Resource Conservation, Environmental Preservation, and the Rate of Discount," *Quarterly Journal of Economics*, 89 (1975), pp. 358–70.

§11.   See for instance the dismal record of U.S. Steel, itemized by John R. Quarles, Jr., "American Industry: We Need Your Help," in Leonard et al., *Business and Environment: Toward Common Ground* (reference above). For public opinion on environmental issues and business, see "The Public Speaks Again: A New Environmental Survey," *Resources*, No. 60 (September–November 1978), pp. 1–6. See also suggestions under §20.

§12.   For steady-state economics, see Herman Daly (reference above).

§14.   For estimates of little-known and unknown Amazon plants that may prove medically useful, see Nicole Maxwell, "Medical Secrets of the Amazon," *Americas*, 29, nos. 6–7 (June–July 1977), pp. 2–8. For how little we really know even about the lands North Americans have long inhabited, including New England and the Midwest, see Wright, note 12.

§18.   For the difficulties of heavy technology on fragile land see *An Assessment of Oil Shale Technologies* (Washington, D.C.: U.S. Government Printing Office, 1980), prepared by the Congressional Office of Technology Assessment.

§19.   For the treatment of animals, see Peter Singer, *Animal Liberation* (N.Y.: New York Review Books, 1975), with discussion of the Draize test on p. 50f, and veal calves, pp. 127–35. For lead versus steel shot, see U.S. Fish and Wildlife Service, *Final Environmental Statement: Proposed Use of Steel Shot for Hunting Waterfowl in the United States* (Washington, D.C.: U.S. Government Printing Office, 1976). The report finds no adverse crippling with steel shot.

§20.   Attitudes of Americans toward endangered species are reported in *Public Opinion on Environmental Issues*, Resources for the Future Survey for the Environmental Protection Agency, et. al. (Washington, D.C.: U.S. Government Printing Office, 1980), p. 18. The alarming acceleration of extinction rates is discussed in *Environmental Quality – 1980*, Eleventh Annual Report of the Council on Environmental Quality (Washington, D.C.: U.S. Government Printing Office, 1980). See also *The Global 2000 Report to the President*, Council on Environmental Quality and Department of State (Washington, D.C.: U.S. Government Printing Office, 1980). See also Norman Myers, *The Sinking Ark* (Oxford: Pergamon Press, 1979) and Paul and Anne Ehrlich, *Extinction* (note 18).

§23.   For environmental policies in banking and finance, see Cahn (note 14), pp. 124–40, who reports that only six in thirty of the major commercial banks have environmental policies, none of these very specific, but found also the positive records of John Hancock, Equitable, and Aetna.

§26.   See the *Progress Report on the Grand Junction Uranium Mill Tailings Remedial Action Program*, prepared by the U.S. Department of Energy's Division of Environmental Control Technology, the DOE Grand Junction Office, and the Colorado Department of Health, February 1979, and available from the National Technical Information Service. The report of the Committee on the Biological Effects of Ionizing Radiations, *The Effects on Populations of Exposure to Low Levels of Ionizing Radiation: 1980* (BEIR III), has since been published (Washington, D.C.: National Academy Press, 1980), but the much-troubled report was never released without dissent among committee members. The ozone threat involves uncertain but drastic and far-reaching environmental degradation. Du Pont has persistently claimed that the connection between fluorocarbons and ozone depletion is not yet proved. The details of this case (given in the Velasquez reference above) provide a good discussion of the necessity for a shifting burden of proof.

§29.   Public opinion about living near risk sites is recorded in *Public Opinion on Environmental Issues* (reference under §20 above), p. 31.

§30.   See Kenneth R. Andrews, "Can the Best Corporations Be Made Moral?" *Harvard Business Review*, 51, no. 3 (May–June 1973), pp. 57–64.

INDEX

ABOUT THE AUTHORS

=====⟨⟩=====

KURT BAIER was born in Vienna, Austria, in 1917. He studied law at the University of Vienna and philosophy at the University of Melbourne, Australia, where he received his B.A. (1944) and M.A. (1947), and at Oxford University, where he received his D.Phil. (1952). He held teaching positions at the University of Melbourne, The Australian National University, and is currently Distinguished Service Professor of Philosophy at the University of Pittsburgh. He has written widely in philosophy of mind, in moral, legal, and practical philosophy. He is best known for his book *The Moral Point of View*.

DAVID BRAYBROOKE, born in New Jersey in 1924, studied at Hobart College before serving in the United States Army during World War II. After the war, he finished college at Harvard, majoring in economics; and took graduate degrees in philosophy at Cornell, following studies there and at Oxford. Besides articles and books on a variety of other philosophical topics, he has published a number of articles on decision-making in business and politics; a book on British efforts to cope with the growth of traffic congestion; and a book, co-authored with C. E. Lindblom, on policy evaluation as a social process—*A Strategy of Decision*. Since 1963 he has lived in Nova Scotia, where he is professor of philosophy and politics at Dalhousie University. He is a citizen of Canada and a Fellow of the Royal Society of Canada.

ALAN GOLDMAN was born in New York City in 1945. He received his B.A. from Yale in 1967 and his Ph.D. from Columbia in 1972. He has taught at Columbia, Ohio University, University of Idaho, University of Michigan, and University of Miami, where he is currently Professor of Philosophy. He is the author of two books, *Justice and Reverse Discrimination* and *The Moral Foundations of Professional Ethics*, and of numerous articles in theory of knowledge, philosophy of language, and moral and social philosophy.

KENNETH E. GOODPASTER was born in Chicago, Illinois, in 1944. He received his undergraduate degree in mathematics from the University of Notre Dame in 1967 and his Ph.D. in philosophy from the University of Michigan in 1973. He has taught at the University of Notre Dame in logic, ethical theory, and applied ethics. In 1980, he joined the faculty of Harvard University, Graduate School of Business Administration, where he teaches a course entitled "Ethical Aspects of Corporate Policy." His publications include *Perspectives on Morality: Essays of William K. Frankena* (1976), *Ethics and Problems of the 21st Century* (1979, with K. M. Sayre), and *Regulation, Values, and the Public Interest* (1980, with co-authors). He has also published widely on moral philosophy and applied ethics in such varied places as *The Journal of Philosophy, Ethics, Environmental Ethics, The Harvard Business Review*, and the *Dallas Morning News*.

TIBOR R. MACHAN is associate professor of philosophy at the State University College of New York, Fredonia, New York. He was born in Budapest, Hungary, from where he escaped in 1953 to move to Munich, Germany, until in 1956 he settled in the U.S. Machan earned his B.A. degree at Claremont Men's College, his M.A. degree at New York University, and his Ph.D. at the University of California at Santa Barbara. His works in philosophy have appeared in such journals as *Inquiry, Theory and Decision*, the *Journal of Value Inquiry*, and the *American Philosophical Quarterly*. He has written for law reviews and several collections edited by other scholars, as well as for general magazines, newspapers, and reviews (*The Humanist, The New York Times, The Los Angeles Times, Libertarian Review*). He is senior editor of *Reason* magazine and director of educational programs of the Reason Foundation, Santa Barbara, California. He is married to Marty Zupan and they have one daughter.

TOM REGAN, a native of Pittsburgh, Pennsylvania, received his undergraduate education at Thiel College and was awarded the M.A. and Ph.D. degrees from the University of Virginia. Since 1967 he has taught philosophy at North Carolina State University, where he has twice been elected Outstanding Teacher and, in 1977, was named Alumni Distinguished Professor. He has lectured extensively on a variety of moral issues, was Distinguished Visiting Scholar at the University of Calgary and Visiting Distinguished Professor of Philosophy at Brooklyn College. He has co-edited three books and is the sole editor of *Matters of Life and Death: New Introductory Essays in Moral Philosophy*, and *Earthbound: New Introductory Essays in Environmental Ethics*. His other books include *Understanding Philosophy*, *All That Dwell Therein: Essays on Animal Rights and Environmental Ethics*, and, most recently, *The Case For Animal Rights*.

HOLMES ROLSTON III was born in the Shenandoah Valley of Virginia in 1932. He was educated at Davidson College, and has advanced degrees in philosophy and in theology from the University of Edinburgh, Union Theological Seminary in Virginia, and the University of Pittsburgh. He has transplanted West and is now professor of philosophy at Colorado State University, where he teaches environmental ethics. He is associate editor of the journal *Environmental Ethics*. His chief research interest is concepts of nature — whether scientific, philosophical, or religious. He has written for *Zygon*, *Natural History*, *Environmental Ethics*, *The Journal of Medicine and Philosophy*, *The Scottish Journal of Theology*, *Ethics*, *Inquiry*, and *Philosophy and Phenomenological Research*, among others. He is a backpacker and a bryologist.

ADINA SCHWARTZ was born in Takoma Park, Maryland, in 1951 and was raised in New York City. She received her B.A. from Oberlin College in 1971 and her Ph.D. from The Rockefeller University in 1976. She taught in the Philosophy Department at Yale University from 1975 to 1982 and is currently attending law school. She has published in ethics and social and political philosophy in such places as *The Journal of Philosophy*, *The Philosophical Review*, and *Ethics*.

GEORGE SHER was born in New York City in 1942 and was raised in Nutley, New Jersey. He received his B.A. degree at Brandeis University and his Ph.D. at Columbia University. He has taught at Fairleigh Dickinson University and, since 1974, at the University of Vermont, where he is currently Professor of Philosophy. His essays on action theory, philosophy of mind, ethics, and social philosophy have appeared in numerous philosophical journals.

HENRY SHUE was born in Staunton, Virginia, in 1940. He did his undergraduate work at Davidson College, studied as a Rhodes Scholar at Merton College, Oxford, and received his Ph.D. in 1970 from the Inter-Departmental Program in Political Philosophy at Princeton University. After teaching at the University of North Carolina at Chapel Hill and Wellesley College he was a founding member of the Center for Philosophy and Public Policy of the University of Maryland, College Park. Now the Director of the Center, he is the author of *Basic Rights: Subsistence, Affluence, and U.S. Foreign Policy* and the co-editor of *Food Policy, Boundaries: National Autonomy and Its Limits* and *The Border That Joins: Mexican Migrants and U.S. Responsibility*. He has published philosophical articles and provided Congressional testimony on a wide range of issues about human rights, especially in poorer countries where he has traveled extensively.

PATRICIA H. WERHANE is a native of Idaho. She received her B.A. from Wellesley College and her M.A. and Ph.D. in philosophy from Northwestern University. She has taught at the American College of Switzerland and is currently Associate Professor at Loyola University of Chicago. Her publications include *Art and Nonart*, an introduction to aesthetics, *Philosophy and Art*, an anthology in aesthetics, *Ethical Issues in Business*, an anthology co-edited with Tom Donaldson, and a full-length book on employee rights, *Persons, Rights and Corporations*. She is also one of the organizers and currently chairperson of the Society for Business Ethics.